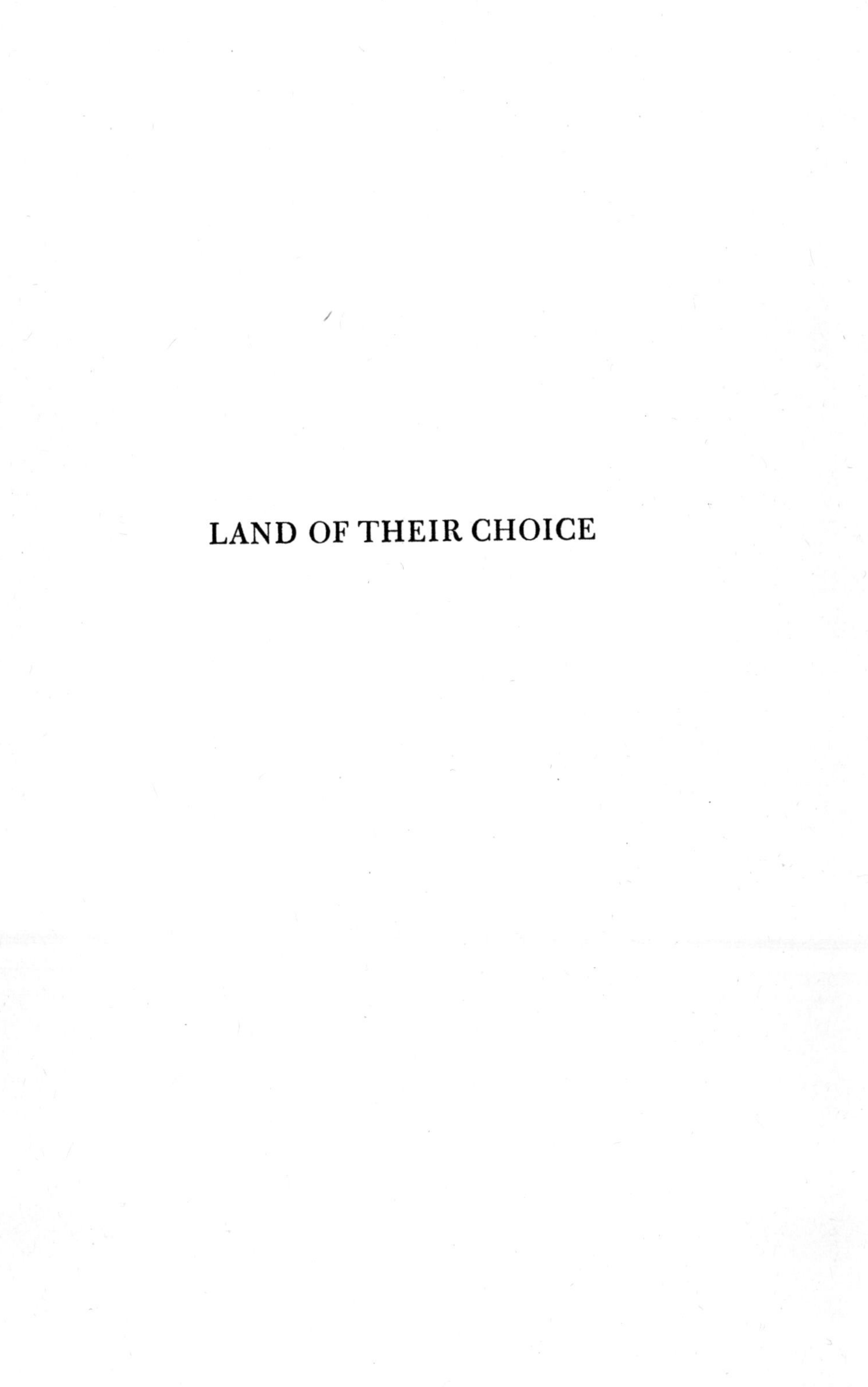

LAND OF THEIR CHOICE

EDITED BY THEODORE C. BLEGEN

Land of Their Choice

THE IMMIGRANTS WRITE HOME

THE UNIVERSITY OF MINNESOTA PRESS

PRINTED AT THE NORTH CENTRAL PUBLISHING COMPANY, ST. PAUL

Library of Congress Catalog Card Number: 55-9368

PUBLISHED IN GREAT BRITAIN, INDIA, AND PAKISTAN BY
GEOFFREY CUMBERLEGE: OXFORD UNIVERSITY PRESS, LONDON, BOMBAY, AND KARACHI

Foreword

THIS book tells at first hand a little-known human story that is a part of the larger saga of America. It is a collection of the letters immigrants wrote home about the land of their choice. The period is that of American westward expansion in the nineteenth century, and the geographic spread of the letters is nationwide.

The documents are drawn from Norwegian migration to the United States, which began in the 1820's with the arrival of the *Restoration* — the "Mayflower" of the modern immigrants from the western half of the Scandinavian peninsula. In its major aspects this migration is vividly revealed in these contemporary records, but the purpose of the volume transcends that story, significant and colorful as it is.

Translated into English, these letters illustrate the value of a very large body of historical material — the millions of letters that immigrants of every nationality wrote to friends and relatives in the lands they had left. They record the experiences, observations, and thoughts of immigrants who made their way in the New World and shared in the building of the nation. The "America letters," as they were commonly called in the Old World, constitute a composite diary of everyday people at the grass roots of American life. Read and studied with care, they afford new insight into the American past while at the same time they reflect the image of America that was projected into the minds of Europeans in an era when millions were crossing the seas and moving west.

My interest in the potentialities of immigrant letters took its rise many years ago when I found and translated into English a little book that was published in Norway in 1838. Written in an Illinois settlement in 1837–1838, the manuscript of this book — Ole Rynning's *True Account of America* — was carried down the Mississippi by an immigrant who then journeyed back to Norway by way of New Orleans and Liverpool and managed to get it published in Christiania. It was in effect a long "America letter," but, in the form in which it reached its readers, it was promptly dubbed the "America book."

The author was a well-educated young man who rose above temporary misfortune in his view of the prospects of the New World. In midwinter he had ventured out from his Illinois settlement on an exploring expedition from which he returned with both his feet frozen and lacerated. In a humble cabin he wrote his account "for the information and help of peasant and commoner," calling his neighbors in to hear and criticize his chapters as he read them aloud. His purpose, he said, was "to answer every question that I myself raised, to make clear every point in regard to which I observed that people were in ignorance, and to refute the false reports that came to my ears, partly before my departure from Norway and partly after my arrival here." His answers were given in chapters crammed with facts and shrewd observation. Discussing the slavery issue twenty-one years before the Civil War, he remarked that "there will in all likelihood come either a separation between the northern and southern states, or else bloody civil disputes." In America, he said, as in Norway, "there are laws, government, and authorities," but here, he added, "everything is designed to maintain the natural freedom and equality of men."

Rynning did not live to see his book in print. Before copies could be brought back to Illinois, he died, a victim of malaria and typhoid fever, and was placed in a hollowed-out log and buried in an unmarked grave. Meanwhile his book reached a wide audience in his home country and influenced the rising stream of emigration. This simple but fascinating book stirred my interest in the whereabouts and contents of the countless letters that must have been sent to Norway and other parts of Europe in the nineteenth century.

The Norse-American Centennial in 1925 added stimulus to this interest in the immigrants and their letters, and three years later, in 1928, I had an opportunity to collect "America letters" on a broad scale. As I traveled about Norway I visited few homes that did not have American connections — and I became acquainted with few families that had not preserved bundles of letters from the United States. At an international historical congress in Oslo that year, I read a paper entitled "The 'America Letters'." The reports of this paper in the press served as a kind of introduction when I went on my collecting errand. Local historians gave me assistance in the many towns and valleys I visited, and plans were developed to have originals preserved in Norwegian collections while I made typewritten or photostatic copies.

Meanwhile my study of the files of nineteenth-century Norwegian newspapers disclosed that through many decades "America letters" had been printed almost as soon as they were received. There had obviously been an immense amount of public interest in the reports, pro and con, which had come from the immigrants, and the letters had contributed in major fashion to a national debate on the merits of emigration. I therefore set in motion a program to copy the "America letters" that had appeared in the newspapers, and at the end of a year, I brought back a large collection of transcripts. From this collection many of the letters translated in the present volume are drawn, and they should be studied as letters read not only by their immediate recipients but by thousands of other people reached through the Norwegian press. So great was public interest that some newspapers gave the "America letters" a most prominent place over a period of some years. In this volume I have purposely drawn heavily upon the newspaper letters, not only for their specific contents, but also because they contributed so widely to the national image that the people of Norway formed of the United States. But I have also included letters, and particularly series of letters, that were copied from original manuscripts. Those familiar with the extent and richness of Norwegian immigrant letters, both published and unpublished, will think of interesting and important letters or groups of letters that I have left untouched and also of regions unrepresented in this collection. Obviously I could have brought together masses of letters for a work of many volumes. It seemed desirable, however, to limit the selections and in many instances to condense lengthy series of letters. I have done this with the belief that the result is representative of the "America letters" and with the hope that the total picture will be filled out by others in numerous publications.

Meanwhile, several scholars have collected immigrant letters. Professor George M. Stephenson searched for such documents in Sweden the year before I went to Norway and has illustrated their value and interest as historical source material in his books and articles, including a memorable essay entitled "When America Was the Land of Canaan."[1] Some

[1] George M. Stephenson, "When America Was the Land of Canaan," in *Minnesota History*, 10:237-260 (September 1929).

steps have been taken toward the systematic collection of immigrant letters in various other countries of the Old World, but much remains to be done. It is my hope that this book may give stimulus to a movement to gather up, preserve, and make available for students of American history letters and diaries of immigrants from all the countries of the Old World.

The timeliness of such a movement is suggested by the emergence of the American Museum of Immigration at the Statue of Liberty, for the announced purpose of telling "the story of how immigrants came from many nations and shared in the building of the Nation." The story can be told and illustrated in various ways. I venture the hope that the Museum will take an interest in the collecting and historical use of "America letters" as contemporary records made by the immigrants themselves as they came and shared in the nation's experience.

Such "America letters" are documents of the past which invite interpretation and use by historians. In a sense, they were the voice of America – certainly "immigrant America" – in an age antedating radio and official State Department programs designed to bring about a better understanding of American life. Broadcast in letters through many decades and from all parts of America, this earlier voice was the unofficial and unheralded, but none the less real, voice of everyday people in America. It is recorded and to a great extent preserved. The letters which make up the record constitute what I have called the "literature of the unlettered." [2] This literature, Professor William Mulder says, is "hidden" – hidden among the grass roots of American life and hidden, too, because much of it is written in languages other than English and difficult to find. But it is hidden for another and more fundamental reason – a failure by historians to grasp its value and implications. An inverted provincialism in American scholarship and letters has too often underestimated the importance of our social, cultural, and economic history at its everyday levels; and many historians have devoted their attention to immigration merely as a problem at a given time. They have taken inadequately into account its influence as a continuing factor in the fashioning of American life and civilization.

If many questions have gone unanswered, the reply is not to be found in the parading of immigrant claims to high distinction, in the spirit of filiopietism. Nor is it to be found in writings by nostalgic or defensive

[2] *Grass Roots History* (Minneapolis, 1947), pp. 14–27.

interpreters of particular immigrant strains in the national total. The answer lies in documents of American history in their full range, critically and objectively studied, and in the validity of a fundamental interpretation of the character of American civilization. Simple forces — and sometimes complex forces — at the bases of American life are fundamental to an understanding of that life. Its surface and spectacular manifestations may be fascinating and even significant, but they are scarcely fundamental. One road to an understanding of America and its past is folk-cultural and grass-roots history, with the use of all the historical sources and special techniques that can contribute to its fullness and richness.

In recent years historians have reappraised the theories of Frederick Jackson Turner, the leading interpreter of the influence of the frontier in American life, but almost no attention has been devoted to his own view of immigration as a factor in that life. As early as 1889 he pointed out that the "story of the peopling of America has not yet been written," and declared, "We do not understand ourselves." He looked beyond the "bone and sinew" and "manual skill" of the immigrants, with understanding that they "brought with them deeply inrooted customs and ideas" and that the American destiny was interwoven with theirs.[3] A little later, pointing to problems in American history that invited careful study, he declared, "We shall not understand the contemporary United States without studying immigration historically."[4] In 1901 he published a series of factual essays dealing with the history of immigration.[5]

Unfortunately Turner never explored that field of history. The rich sources for its cultivation that scholars have newly uncovered were wholly unknown to him, but the significance of immigration continued to seem important to him in his later years. In 1918, reappraising Middle Western pioneer democracy, he moved away from what the late Edwin Mims, Jr., has described as an "emphasis upon cultural homogeneity"[6] and laid stress upon "mutual education," a process of "giving and taking," and the "intermingling parts of a forming society, plastic and absorptive."

[3] "The Significance of History," in *The Early Writings of Frederick Jackson Turner* (Madison, 1938), pp. 63–64.

[4] Turner's address on "Problems in American History," in *Early Writings*, p. 82.

[5] Turner's articles, in the *Chicago Record-Herald*, were on German, Italian, French and Canadian, and Jewish immigration, and a more general review of "The Stream of Immigration into the United States." Unhappily they are of little importance and almost barren of generalization. See *Chicago Record-Herald*, August 28, September 4, 11, 25, and October 16, 1901.

[6] Edwin Mims, Jr., *American History and Immigration* (Bronxville, N. Y., Sarah Lawrence College, n.d.), pp. 44–45.

He wrote about "national cross-fertilization" and saw, as a result of the frontier experience, the "creation of a new type, which was neither the sum of all its elements nor a complete fusion in a melting pot." He envisioned the "possibility of a newer and richer civilization attained, not by preserving unmodified or isolated, the old component elements, but by breaking down the line fences" and "by merging the individual life to the common product." In that product he discerned "the promise of world brotherhood."[7] Turner's thought in 1918 was not so new as Mr. Mims supposed, for it made a junction with his earlier ideas. In any event, Turner's general view of immigration dimly foreshadowed the newer historiography of immigration, which rejects filiopietism on the one hand and, on the other, broadens his own frontier hypothesis into an interpretation that does not leave large areas of American life unexplained.

But the validity of a broader concept of American history does not hinge upon the acceptance or modification of the theories of Turner. He seems to have realized, however vaguely, that immigration and the American transition of people from the Old World had altered the traditional picture of American history, but his own researches did not embrace both frontier influences and the impact of millions of immigrants. His frontier hypothesis was useful in focusing attention upon some of the mainsprings of our national life, but in its major concern, it failed signally to explain the diversity in the customs and attitudes and in the material and spiritual culture of the peoples living within the boundaries of the United States. As scholars have tried to understand the history of the American people in a wider framework, a new emphasis has gradually made itself felt which takes into account the varied backgrounds of the national elements and their part in the peopling and development of the United States.[8]

[7] Frederick Jackson Turner, "Middle Western Pioneer Democracy," in *Minnesota History Bulletin*, 3:393–414 (August 1920).

[8] *Grass Roots History*, pp. 3–13; Edward N. Saveth, *American Historians and European Immigrants* (New York, 1948), pp. 218–219. Among the scholars who have been most influential in forwarding the newer historiography of American immigration, George M. Stephenson occupies a leading place. He was among the first to see and exploit the objective and nonfiliopietistic study of immigration, and his many publications, including the brief but pioneering *History of American Immigration, 1820–1924* (Boston, 1926), his broad-ranging and fundamental work on *The Religious Aspects of Swedish Immigration* (Minneapolis, 1932), his searching article on the backgrounds of Swedish immigration in the *American Historical Review*, 31:708–723 (July 1926), and other essays and documents that he wrote and edited, opened new paths for scholarship. The field was interpreted by A. M. Schlesinger in his essay "The Influence of Immigration in American

For the furthering of this new emphasis the immigrant letters are invaluable source material. The collecting and study of such letters caused Professor George M. Stephenson to suggest that, although we already had monographs and accumulations of statistics on immigration, the field was awaiting a "man with the magic touch" who could convert the records "into a masterpiece of historical synthesis." The story to be told is a human story of everyday people, and their letters are basic. The master, Dr. Stephenson says, must sound "the depths of the human soul and he must analyze the noblest as well as the basest emotions that play on the human heart. He will not concern himself with the people on whom fortune has smiled graciously, nor will he relate the exploits of the battlefield and portray the life of kings and nobles; he will study the documents that betray the spirit, hopes, and aspirations of the humble folk who tilled the soil, felled the forest, and tended the loom — in short, who followed the occupations that fall to the lot of the less favored majority in every land." [9]

When such a master appears, he will make use of the "America letters" as preserved in many languages and in many countries. They will help to clarify, first of all, the image of America in the minds of millions of Europeans who read the simple documents that, decade after decade, were mailed to relatives and friends across the Atlantic. This image was transatlantic and transcontinental. The immigrants described the Atlantic crossing, and their letters ranged across America from New York to California and from Minnesota to Texas. The image was changing and reflected kaleidoscopic scenes through decades when America was moving westward, when frontier succeeded frontier, when economic and political forces were in flux, and through transition from initial immigrant experiences to an established social and economic order.[10] The kaleido-

History," in his *New Viewpoints in American History* (New York, 1922). Marcus Lee Hansen described "The History of American Immigration as a Field for Research" in the *American Historical Review*, 32:500–518 (April 1927), and later enriched the area with his *Atlantic Migration, 1607–1860* (Cambridge, 1940), and his book on *The Immigrant in American History* (Cambridge, 1940), while Carl Wittke, an authority on German immigration, produced a comprehensive work in *We Who Built America* (New York, 1939). For useful listings of writings about the immigrant in American history, see the bibliographies in the works mentioned above, together with Schlesinger, *Paths to the Present* (New York, 1949), pp. 286–289.

[9] "When America Was the Land of Canaan," in *Minnesota History*, 10:237.

[10] An interesting study of "The Immigrant and the American Image in Europe, 1860–1914" by Merle Curti and Kendall Birr appears in the *Mississippi Valley*

scopic quality derives not only from the external events recorded, but also from the changes mirrored in the thoughts and reactions of immigrants as days became months and months years.

The image does not have crystal-clear lines. It is not a neatly posed portrait, fixed in time and place. Nor is it a picture of triumph alone or frustration alone. Its steadiness is strengthened by the character of American opportunity and by the sheer human quality of the story, with all its ups and downs. Human beings, immigrants or native Americans, are human, not lines in a graph. No statistic wrote "America letters" to parent statistics in Europe. Possibly the greatest interest of the "America letters" lies in their utterly human character and flavor. Professor Stephenson, contemplating the power of the letters in fomenting action, speaks of them as "naive accounts of experience written for relatives and friends, who were as simple and naive as the writers themselves." But he goes on to say that it was just this "unconscious" and naive quality "that opens for the historian windows" that afford views into both the cottages of the home country and the log cabins of America.[11]

All the letters in this book were written originally in Norwegian and have been turned into English. The writers were of varied backgrounds and skills. Some of the letters were well written; many show evident effort and awkwardness in handling the language, which is the literary language, not the dialects, of the time. Paragraphs often were long and involved, and not infrequently the expression was overly formal and stilted, bearing the marks of inexperience in writing. Even when using translations made by others, I have felt free, always comparing with the originals, to re-paragraph the letters and to revise the wording where I could make it simple and still retain the meaning of the original. I have not felt it necessary in every instance to give the entire text of a letter or to indicate all omissions by conventional symbols. Where selections

Historical Review, 37:203–230 (September 1950). This study gives much attention to factors other than the immigrant's own letters, such as the official immigration promotion by governmental agencies, the propaganda of railroads and industries, the impact of returned immigrants, and the influence of guidebooks and other printed matter. The authors do not devote much detailed analysis to the "America letters," but they take note of the fact that most immigrants "listened to the voices of friends and neighbors who had emigrated before them." At the end of their review they conclude that "in spite of the limitations, exaggerations, and distortions in the predominant image of America, there was a solid core of reality beneath it."

[11] "When America Was the Land of Canaan," in *Minnesota History*, 10:245.

have been made, I have so signified in notes. The transcripts, photostats, and other documents used are, for the most part, deposited either in the archives of the Norwegian-American Historical Association at Northfield, Minnesota, or in the Minnesota Historical Society in St. Paul. When a given letter or series is available in published form, I have indicated the exact source. The reader, if he so desires, can therefore find the full texts: some in books or articles, others in the form of typewritten or photostated copies, and a few that are available only as original manuscripts.

A few minor explanations should be offered with respect to the editorial methods followed. The salutations in the letters have been omitted, and frequently the closing greetings as well. In hundreds of letters the salutations are similar: "Dear ones at home," "Dear parents (always in my thoughts)," "Most precious parents, sisters, and brothers," and "Dear parents (always loved)." And in the closings of letters greetings often include virtual rosters of entire families and neighborhood circles. The examples quoted are representative of the initial tone of almost all the letters, and it has not seemed essential to record the endearing and occasionally nostalgic terms with which almost invariably they open and close.

Many phrases in the originals nearly defy translation, but wherever precise equivalents do not suggest themselves, approximations are used. Often translatable words have meanings in the originals that are quite different from their English equivalents. The Norwegian mile, for example, is a distance of seven English miles. A *skilling* is not an English or American shilling, but a coin roughly comparable with a cent, and the Norwegian dollar, or specie dollar, was of higher value than the American – Professor Flom equates fifty American dollars with thirty-eight Norwegian specie dollars. A Norwegian *gaard* was a farmstead – a freehold under rules of primogeniture. A *kande* was a can, probably equivalent to a pottle, that is, a half-gallon measure. The rare word *ort* seems to be the equivalent of twenty-four skillings, but is not translatable into English. These items illustrate some of the nice problems confronting the translator of the immigrant letters.

My indebtedness to numerous translators and editors will be apparent throughout this volume. In instances where translations have been previously published, I have indicated the name or names of the translators and the source from which I have drawn my texts in whole or through excerpts. I owe a special obligation to the Norwegian-American Historical Association, for which I have served as editor during three decades. Many "America letters" have been published in its thirty-seven volumes, and where such letters seemed to fit in with the purposes and plans of this book, I have used them freely, often with revisions or through selected excerpts. Many of the translations are my own, but I am particularly indebted to Mr. Borge Madsen, who served as my research assistant in 1953–1954 and gave me invaluable assistance by translating many of the letters. In every instance he and I compared the translation with the original and occasionally made further changes. To all whose translations I have used, and particularly to Mr. Madsen, I express sincere thanks. Dr. Carlton C. Qualey, Professor of History in Carleton College, an authority in this field and the author of *Norwegian Settlement in the United States*, read the entire manuscript, and I am indebted to him for helpful suggestions as well as for the translation of some of the documents, notably a travel narrative included in the chapter called "Journeying toward New Horizons." Zephyra Shepherd, my editorial assistant, has aided me not only in typing the manuscript and making the index, but also in the critical revision of the translations and the historical introductions to the various sections as well as to the entire volume. Without her aid I doubt that I could have completed the book, and I wish to record my deep appreciation to her. I am indebted to the University of Minnesota for a helpful general research grant, and the book in its final form owes much to the interest and competence of the staff of the University of Minnesota Press.

A volume of this kind might have been very extensively annotated, but I have chosen not to do so, partly because my own two-volume work on *Norwegian Migration to America* is in a sense an elaborate footnoting of the letters, which are part of the source materials for that work, and partly because a precise identification of names and the elaboration of details on many other matters seem to me unessential to the understanding and appreciation of the basic content of the letters.

THEODORE C. BLEGEN

University of Minnesota
Minneapolis

Table of Contents

Land of Their Choice

Table of Contents

LAND OF THEIR CHOICE

The Immigrant Image of America

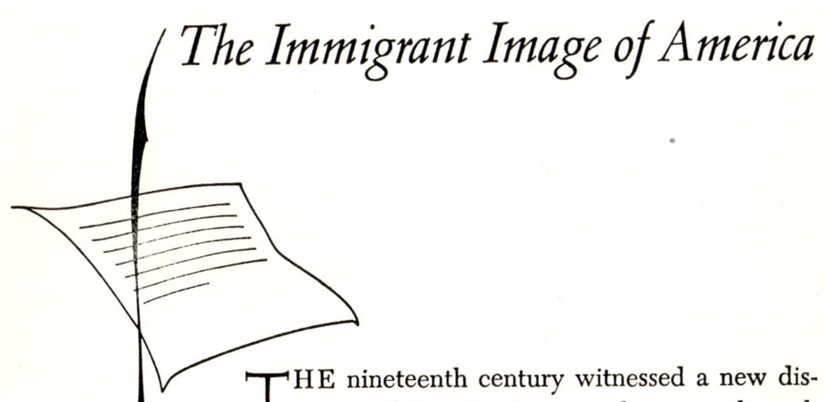

THE nineteenth century witnessed a new discovery of America. It came about, not through the daring of a new Columbus, but as a consequence of letters written by immigrants to the people of the Old World. It was a progressive and widening discovery that played an important role in the migration of millions of Europeans from their home countries to the United States.

Explorers and map makers, ever since the existence and shape of America were first discerned in the fifteenth and sixteenth centuries, had been eager and quick to publish their findings. But the realities of the New World meant little, and indeed were almost unknown, to the everyday people of Europe until they began to read, in their own homes, the firsthand narratives of friends and relatives who had braved the Atlantic and had seen for themselves what America really was like.

Books in earlier times were accessible to only a few, and even in book-reading families precise information about America was uncommon. Not more than a shadowy understanding of the rising giant of the West could be gained from a name, a map, or stray allusions in books and newspapers. There was much curiosity about the western world, but save in circles where it was motivated by self-interest, it did not result in precise knowledge. Once the forces of emigration made themselves felt, the curiosity of all who felt the slightest urge to move and better their lot was as insatiable as it was concrete and practical. People asked questions with a purpose, and they wanted answers. So the letters from across the sea were read with absorbed interest, often passed from one family to another in a widening circle, occasionally made available to newspapers of the neighborhood, and invariably treasured.

Land of Their Choice

In England in the seventeenth century, we are told, a letter from New England was "venerated as a Sacred Script, or as the Writing of some Holy Prophet, 'twas carried many miles where divers came to hear it." * This is a faithful description of the reception of thousands of letters from the New World in the earlier years of the nineteenth century in the Scandinavian North and in other parts of Europe. As emigration broadened and gathered volume from all the countries of the Old World, an interest – and even veneration – like that stirred by seventeenth-century news from the Pilgrims and Puritans, spread until scarcely a home was untouched by it and by the impact of direct communication with the New Canaan. In the Scandinavian countries such letters were called "America letters." The impulse to emigrate was diagnosed as the "America fever." †

The interest in "America letters" had deeper roots than a passing curiosity about the details of travel and of land, prices, work, and hundreds of other items that found their way into homely accounts of personal observation. Underlying it was an awareness that emigration was a choice between two worlds. In the letters immigrants wrote home, they told, from its initial chapters, the story of a decision and its consequences. For most of them there was no going home again, and this they knew. They wrote about the land of their choice. They reported a changed and changing way of life that would shape the lives of their children. Their accounts of travel were accounts of more than travel by water and by land – "for the immigrant crossed more than an ocean and a continent; his traveling was

> . . . across the sprung longitudes of the mind
> And the blood's latitudes." ‡

Breaking his new land, the immigrant also broke with his past, but the latter was a slower process than the former. Yet the process was inevitable, and it had wide reach. As I have written elsewhere, "The immigrant, no matter what country he sailed from, disembarked in a land

* Quoted in S. E. Morison, *Builders of the Bay Colony* (Boston and New York, 1930), p. 342.

† Theodore C. Blegen, *The "America Letters"* (Oslo, 1928), pp. 4–5, and "Early 'America Letters'," in Blegen, *Norwegian Migration to America, 1825–1860* (Northfield, Minn., 1931), pp. 196–213. A companion volume is *Norwegian Migration to America: The American Transition* (Northfield, 1940). Hereafter these works will be cited as *Norwegian Migration*, vols. 1 and 2.

‡ William Mulder, "Through Immigrant Eyes: Utah History at the Grass Roots," in *Utah Historical Quarterly*, January 1954, p. 41.

of different culture. The chests and bundles under which he staggered at the ports of landing were filled with tangible evidences of his own culture: tools, clothing, furniture, food. Just as surely as the farming implements he brought could not be used effectively on American soil or the clothes he wore were not suitable to American temperatures, so too he would find the less material parts of his Old World culture, those packed away in the immigrant chests of thought and tradition, no longer adequate to his needs." *

The "America letters" form a diary on a grand scale, kept by people who were experiencing this change of worlds. Their letters have an unconscious eloquence, sometimes a stylistic simplicity, that makes reading them memorable. I have collected many of them and have found in them "everything from fire and passion to elation and sorrow—the life of 'hamlet, workshop, and meadow,' the reflection of folk characteristics in people undergoing the transition from one mode of life to another." †

The letters are filled with contrasts that spring from idealistic hopes and realistic disappointments. America was indeed the "land of Canaan," and the hopes it inspired are exemplified in millions of letters. But alongside hope is disillusionment. The making of America is a theme that histories, novels, and motion pictures have often apotheosized. The immigrant letters throw light upon some of the cost in human travail and suffering and upon many aspects that are quite without glamor. But no reader, viewing the record across the decades, can escape the impression that the promise and opportunity of America were substantially what the immigrants believed them to be. They were not a myth.

On the other hand, no greater mistake could be made than to suppose that once the immigrants arrived in America, all was sunshine and success for them. They began at the bottom of the ladder. Most of them were poor. They were ignorant of the language of the country to which they had come. They faced disease and unremitting hard work done at a pace to which they were unaccustomed. They felt the pangs of homesickness. Often they were cheated not only by sharp-dealing "Yankees" but also by their own countrymen. They did not always select lands with good judgment. They knew disappointment and tasted failure. But as the decades went by, they got their second wind, won some measure of success, and were joined by thousands of their countrymen. Some

* *Grass Roots History* (Minneapolis, 1947), p. 105.
† *Grass Roots History*, p. 6.

went down, it is true, under the trials they faced, but the majority survived their ordeals and worked their way to "better days." The letters afford pictures of conditions endured and problems faced, but they also supply a needed perspective upon initial troubles.

Reverses could not, in the long run, destroy the implicit immigrant faith in the freedom of the new land. In the 1840's an immigrant correspondence society in Chicago, organized for the specific purpose of writing "America letters," went to the heart of this matter. "Here," said one of the letters, "it is not asked, what or who was your father, but the question is, what are you?" Freedom "seems as essential to every citizen of the United States as the air he breathes. It is part of his life, which cannot be compromised or surrendered, and which is cherished and defended as life itself. It is a national attribute, common to all. Herein lies the secret of the equality everywhere seen. It is an American political creed to be one people. This elevates the lowly and brings down the great."

Eighty immigrant settlers in a Wisconsin community that had suffered tragically from malaria and cholera issued a manifesto in the 1840's that minimized the difficulties of immigrants. It reminded Norway of "the sufferings of those earliest immigrants who opened the way for coming generations by founding the first colony in the United States, the Virginia colony." This manifesto, printed in full in this volume, declares the immigrant faith: "We have no expectation of gaining riches; but we live under a liberal government in a fruitful land, where freedom and equality are the rule in religious as in civil matters, and where each one of us is at liberty to earn his living practically as he chooses. Such opportunities are more to be desired than riches; through these opportunities we have a prospect of preparing for ourselves, by diligence and industry, a carefree old age. We have therefore no reason to regret the decision that brought us to this country." This was more than the voice of four-score immigrant settlers in a midwestern community – it was the voice of nineteenth-century America, a part of that total of opinion and information from the West that "discovered," or revealed, America to the minds of people in Norway and Europe.

An interesting aspect of the letters, from the point of view of the European image of America, is their reflection of a national debate in the home countries on the merits of America compared with the advantages of staying at home. This debate reached into homes, newspapers, books and pamphlets, even songs and ballads. Was the West a mirage? Could the immigrants survive the hardships they would face? Why go to America? Why not stay at home and make the best of opportunities there? Such questions, as they appeared in Norway, for example, in the 1830's, 1840's, and 1850's, were of such major interest that letters of immigrants were snatched up and published in great numbers in newspapers; preachers discoursed on the dangers of emigration; pamphlets were written to discourage prospective emigrants; and the Norwegians who had made their decision and established homes in the New World were glad to join in the discussion. Not a few of the letters in this book are related to and a very part of this debate. Though some immigrants fed the fires of the anti-American writers, most of the new "Americans" defended America and emigration and looked with patient and philosophic eyes at their early woes.

The immigrant's image of America, portrayed with a thousand details in letters, is interesting not only as a record of what was thus transmitted directly to vast numbers of people in Europe in the nineteenth century, but also as a propelling force in emigration itself. There has been all too often an air of impersonality in accounts of American immigration. The coming of thirty millions of people was a movement of such magnitude that, to many, it has seemed futile to try to disengage personalities from the mass. Many writers have forgotten the individual man in the surging complex of international circumstances. World forces pushed people out of their accustomed environment; world forces pulled them westward with magnetic power. But the pivot of human motion is individual life. Migration was a simple individual act – a decision that led to consequences – and the "America letters" were a dynamic factor, perhaps the most effective single factor,* in bringing discontent to a focus and into action. Praise of America pointed to a contrast. The New World, if not a Utopia, nevertheless offered land and opportunity and hope, denied or rigidly limited in the Old. Even if criticism of conditions in the home countries was not explicitly offered, the implication of contrast was always there. And recognition of the contrast turned discontent into resolution.

The effects of the letters were often strengthened by the temporary return home of immigrants – "America travelers," as they were called;

* Carlton C. Qualey describes the letters as "the most potent single factor" (*Norwegian Settlement in the United States*, Northfield, Minn., 1938, p. 60).

and the records tell of many such a returned immigrant who later went back to America as the leader of large numbers of new immigrants.

The "America letters" present these leaders too, not only the rank and file of the immigrant mass. They reveal pathfinders and scouts, men who ventured to frontiers little known, who on their own or as designated agents searched for new Canaans and gave some direction to the course of settlement.* In the letters they appear as pathfinders for the first group migrations, as scouts on the prairies of midwestern states, as investigators of the wooded areas farther north, and as searchers whose travels took them afield from the conventional lines of expansion. The findings of such immigrant chieftains made their way not only into letters but also into newspapers, books, and emigrant guides. Their descriptions fed the flames of controversy on the European side of the Atlantic about the resources and promises of the New World, but they also had a sharp impact upon prospective emigrants. Great forces affected the emigrants – land policy, the particular stage of the westward movement at any given time, the character of transportation by sea and by land, and the changing economic and social conditions in two parts of the world – but it remains true that leadership was a part of the immigrant story.

Some of the "America letters" represented a critical sophistication – those of Ole Munch Ræder, for example. A distinguished jurist in the 1840's, visiting the United States to study the American jury system, Ræder traveled widely among the immigrant settlements and recorded his observations in lively letters that were printed in the press of his own country. His letters are in the tradition of the more searching and valuable European commentaries on American life in the nineteenth century. In the immigrant drama they represent an interlude – a pause for an appraising look-around. Their historical value has been recognized by full publication in book form and the inclusion of passages in such recent anthologies as Henry Steele Commager's *America in Perspective* and Oscar Handlin's *This Was America.*

For the most part the immigrants who wrote home were people of little education, however, and land and work and hardship bulk large in their reports. But it should not be forgotten that life meant more than making a living, more than sheer survival. The immigrants were people.

* Theodore C. Blegen, "Leaders in American Immigration," in *Transactions of the Illinois Historical Society*, 1931, pp. 145–155.

They fell in love, married, and had children. They grappled with the intricate business of learning a new language. They took cognizance of new social and political situations. They became aware of political parties and both national and state issues. They helped to elect officials, and the time came when they ran for office themselves. They had neighbors and friends and became living parts of communities. They concerned themselves with schooling for their children, and for many this seemed the great and open highway to the better days they dreamed of.

Many sought consolation in religion and the church. Not a few of those who come from Norway were pietists, influenced by the teachings of a great lay preacher, Hans Nielsen Hauge, who had stirred a national revolt in his country against the rationalism of the eighteenth century; and their piety was deepened by the psychological turbulence and uncertainty of migration itself. Coming from a country with an established church, they pioneered frontiers where there were no churches of their own faith and tradition among the innumerable sects which flourished in the frontier atmosphere of religious freedom. They felt a need to satisfy in some regular fashion their cravings for the steadiness and comfort that organized worship, as they devoutly believed, would give them.

It is in this context that one must read the expressions of Christian piety that flood the "America letters" and also understand the earnestness with which, from the 1840's on, missionaries from Norway set about establishing what they regarded as religious order out of confusion. The preacher, lay or trained, is an important and influential figure in the immigrant story set forth in the "America letters," but underlying his role was the religious faith that the immigrants held as a shared heritage and as a staff to lean on in times of adversity as well as of success.

Thus the "America letters" are significant for the image of America that they transmitted to the people of the European world, and they were factors in ripening into action the discontents of thousands of people who crowded onto the emigrant ships. They are important, too, for their revelation of immigrants as human beings with names, personalities, and all the attributes of men and women living their lives amid change and struggle. Firmness and foibles, joy and sorrow are coupled, in the writing of immigrants, with dreams of what America might mean not only for their own lives but also for those of their children and children's children.

These aspects of the letters that common people wrote about the land of their choice are of more than passing interest, but, read today, with the aid of a long perspective, they are also of value as contemporary documents of the American scene. This scene was viewed by observers at the grass roots of American society in a period of fabulous change when immigrants, alongside native Americans, occupied successive frontiers in the expansion of the nation.

Such generalizations find illustration in this volume of "America letters." All the letters selected were sent off to Norway in the general period from the 1820's to the 1870's. They represent a geographical spread from the Atlantic to the Pacific. In their entirety, they make up a composite diary that starts, when John Quincy Adams was president, with the "Mayflower" of Norwegian migration and runs until immigrants from the western half of the Scandinavian peninsula had traversed America east to west and north to south.*

The story of emigration is one of mobility. To the immigrant as to others, America, in Archibald MacLeish's phrase, was "west and the winds blowing." Every emigrant had imprinted on his memory the experiences of the Atlantic crossing, and the letters recording them are vivid and memorable. Once arrived at an eastern port, he moved on to the interior, and this odyssey he also wrote about to the people he had left. The crossing of the seas and the way west are essential chapters in the international story of the emigrant who at the end of his voyage became an immigrant.

When the letters begin, in the 1820's, western New York seemed a frontier region. The Erie Canal was opened just before the first pioneers arrived, and the early newcomers used it. Rochester became the center from which they looked out upon the institutions and prospects of the United States. The novelty of the early migrations from western Norway helps to explain the interest and even excitement with which the first returning "America letters" were received, copied, and circulated in wide districts; and there is a firm link between the spread of these letters and the departure in the 1830's of shiploads of emigrants.

Meanwhile, the immigrants had already been infected with the virus of the westward movement. The scenes of their reporting shifted to Illinois and then to Wisconsin. "This is Canaan," exclaimed a writer who

* For general background on the letters in relation to the course of immigration, see my *Norwegian Migration*, vols. 1 and 2.

had sung the praises of America from western New York, but, now in the 1830's, admired the fertile stretches of Illinois. "Norway," he declared, "cannot be compared to America any more than a desert can be compared to a garden in full bloom." But dissident voices came from those who had tasted misfortune, and they were quick to point out that Illinois was far from being a land of milk and honey. So the clash of testimony, soon to resound through the length and breadth of Norway, began; and the testimony became more voluminous and vocal as the emigrant stream turned northward. "Wisconsin is the place," wrote another emigrant in a phrase that echoes through the whole course of emigration with changes in scenes and names of states. But it is often accompanied by qualifications and reservations as illness and other frontier trials dampen earlier enthusiasm.

For many, emigration was not just a single step or venture. It was a series of moves, with the always advancing frontier a beckoning goal. As numbers grew and small beginnings led to compact settlements, "mother colonies" in Illinois and Wisconsin served as centers from which lines radiated to more distant Canaans. And as dispersion proceeded, the letters reflected the story in full range. They told of the ordeals of pioneering; they described humble personal and institutional beginnings; they recorded satisfaction and disappointment; they pictured the isolated farm home gradually becoming part of a community; and they reflected an immigrant community life characteristic of many frontiers across the land. The shadings and gradations of immigrant transition from old to new ways were everywhere apparent, but immigrant roots were striking down into the new soil.

The fresh interest of the "America letters" is strikingly illustrated by the contemporary immigrant narratives of the California gold rush. Few dramatic episodes in American history have attracted more attention than that spectacular treasure hunt, but its story has not yet been fully told. Historians, for all their zeal, have not brought within the compass of a comprehensive and rounded narrative the world-wide, as well as the American, repercussions and aftereffects of the gold discovery. The negligible general use thus far made of the contemporary records of the excitement that swept Norway, once the gold reports reached that northern land, suggests that possibly only fragments of the rich and widespread historical materials in Europe on the gold rush have been found and translated into English. Not one of the California letters here translated from early Norwegian newspapers has so much as been cited in any general work on the forty-niners. With a single exception they are here made available for the first time in English translations.

The immigrant story embraces, in addition to New Canaans of the West and the El Dorado of the forty-niners, the Utopia of the violinist Ole Bull, who in the early 1850's planned a colony in Pennsylvania as a haven for his compatriots. In view of the idealistic hopes of the violinist and the large sums of money he poured into his philanthropic scheme, it is ironical that his colony, named "Oleana" in his honor, is today remembered chiefly because of the satirical ballad "Oleana," which sang its praises in verses that told of salmon hopping from brook to kettle, cakes that rained out of the heavens, and "little roasted piggies" that politely asked one to have some ham. The ballad was what the romantic nationalists in Norway, who branded emigration as national desertion, wanted. The song was chanted to the accompaniment of the folk laughter of a nation. But it was not the ballad that destroyed the hopes of Ole Bull and caused his colonists to go west. It was the inherent defects of the Utopia itself, ill chosen as to lands and weakened by dependence upon the bounty of the paternalistic and impractical Ole Bull. Most of the settlers, after disheartening experiences, pushed out to the Middle West to make their own independent way. Oleana, recalled by a song and recorded in "America letters," is an episode that takes a minor place in the long succession of American Utopias.*

Satire would have neither sting nor enduring humor if its barbs punctured merely false or empty hopes and promises. The laughter at "Oleana" must have been in the end rueful, for no ballad could laugh away the claims of America. Roasted pigs did not roam the streets in search of empty platters and manna did not stream down from the skies, but underlying ironical exaggerations was a firm element of truth, and the "America letters," by their continuing impact, drove it home even to skeptical minds.

The actualities masked by ridicule appear also in the genial exaggerations of a humorist – the brother of the author of "Oleana" – who lived in Lincoln's town in the 1850's and whose letters tell of roads lined with hedges of bacon and tobacco. This writer, Frithjof Meidell, saw the

* See the chapter on "Oleana: A Colonization Project in Pennsylvania," in *Norwegian Migration*, vol. 1, pp. 287–307, and also Blegen and Martin B. Ruud, *Norwegian Emigrant Songs and Ballads* (Minneapolis, 1936), pp. 176–198.

comic aspects of the American West; he penned an amusing and ironical description of frontier town-building; but he also caught the reality of frontier optimism and its foundations.

The highways of immigrant expansion ran west and north, but America was, after all, a gigantic land, and it is not surprising that immigrants came in not only by transportation channels extending from New York and Quebec west, but also through southern doorways. Emigrant ships sailed for the most part along customary routes to the northern seaboard, but they also made their way to New Orleans and to the West Coast—and many immigrants knew steamboat travel both up and down the Mississippi. Texas seems far off the beaten paths of Scandinavian immigrant land-seeking, but Norwegian immigrants were there as early as the 1840's. Their settlements in Texas were islands, not mainlands, of immigrant colonization, but they are interesting in the record of the "America letters," principally through the long-continued writing of a woman who arrived in Texas as early as 1847 and continued her correspondence to the home country for nearly half a century. As her letters and others from the same region illustrate, these immigrant Texans were advocates not only of the glories of Texas, but also for the wider sweep of America—and their voices were widely heard in the home country.

The attractions of the North were greater than those of the Southwest, and Texas never became a focal point for large numbers of Norwegian immigrants. They followed instead the waterways and pathways to the Middle West, to the Great Plains, and to the lands beyond. This book, therefore, closes with northern areas—Wisconsin, Iowa, and Minnesota. From a Wisconsin parish, a frontier minister views the American scene in the 1850's, with an eye to the social transition of his countrymen. A pioneer woman in Iowa, in the 1860's and 1870's, chronicles in a lively personal style the many events and problems of immigrant life, always with thoughts and plans for her children and their education.

At the end are "America letters" from Fredrika Bremer's "glorious new Scandinavia," the North Star State. The beginnings touch the immemorial cycle that swings from humble origins to high future achievement. A farmer writing nearly a century ago from a river valley in Minnesota could not know that one of his grandsons, appointed by the President of the United States, would officially represent in the capital of his own home country the western empire in which he, the immigrant, had cast his humble lot. But still he looked into the future when he wrote simply, "I can say truthfully that I do not regret our coming here."

This sentiment was echoed by many another, including a frontier heroine who faced the terror of Indian war in all its savagery and whose story recalls the comment of Vernon Louis Parrington, "The epic conquest of the continent must be read in the light of women's sufferings as well as in that of men's endurance." * The Minnesota saga also includes the account of a journalist who traveled by oxcart to the north-flowing Red River in the 1860's and penned the praises of its fertile valley, on the rim of the Dakota prairies, with a serene conviction that this, after all, was the real land of Canaan. It would become, he believed, "one of the richest and most beautiful regions in America," and many immigrants took his words as sober prophecy.

The "America letters" as illustrated in this volume have historical breadth and depth. They unfold a panorama not alone of the particular migration they record but of many aspects common to American immi-

gration. Their human interest sustains the view that immigrants are not mere "rows of figures or symbols of trends and inter-relationships." The record is a human one of hopes and heartaches, courage and fear, failure and success, and of ferment and transition to new ideas and habits and ways of living. But the significance of the letters, as has been suggested, goes beyond such considerations, for they delineate, in part at least, the image of America that stirred the people of Europe; and they document important chapters in the social and economic history of the land of their choice, especially on its changing frontiers.

* *Main Currents in American Thought* (New York, single-volume edition, 1930), vol. 3, p. 395.

The "Sloopfolk" Arrive

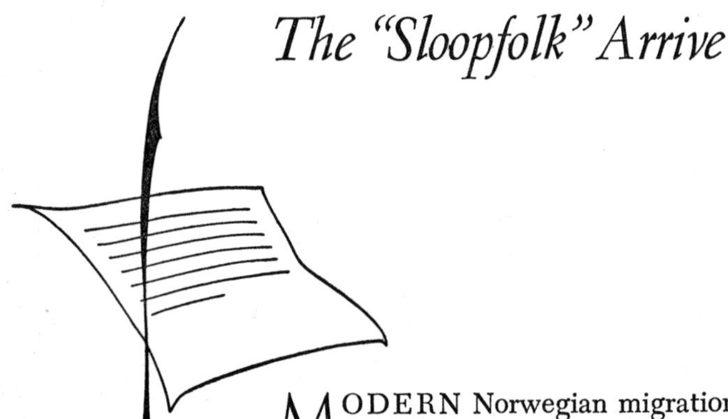

MODERN Norwegian migration to America begins with a "Mayflower" under another name – the *Restoration.* The year is 1825, but across the gulf of time, some parallels and comparisons with the year 1620 suggest themselves. Both vessels were tiny (the Norwegian sloop of 1825 was less than a fourth the size of the historic *Mayflower*); the voyages were long; the people aboard were devout; they were men and women of courage and hope; and their quests set tracks for others to follow across the years.

No newspaper reporter met the Pilgrims at Plymouth Rock, but when the sloop *Restoration,* with fifty-three persons aboard, landed at New York on October 9, 1825, a reporter described it as "A Novel Sight." New Yorkers, reading their *Daily Advertiser* for October 15, came upon this little story:

A vessel has arrived at this port, with emigrants, from Norway. The vessel is very small, measuring as we understand only about 360 Norwegian lasts, or forty-five American tons, and brought forty-six passengers, male and female, all bound to Ontario county, where an agent, who came over some time since, purchased a tract of land. The appearance of such a party of strangers, coming from so distant a country, and in a vessel of a size apparently ill calculated for a voyage across the Atlantic, could not but excite an unusual degree of interest. They have had a voyage of fourteen weeks; and are all in good health.

An enterprise like this argues a good deal of boldness in the master of the vessel, as well as an adventurous spirit in the passengers, most of whom belong to families from the vicinity of a little town at the south-western extremity of Norway, near Cape Stavanger. Those who came from the farms are dressed in coarse cloths of domestic manufacture, of a fashion different from the American; but those who inhabited the town wear calicoes, ginghams, and gay shawls, imported, we presume, from England. The vessel is built on the model common to fishing boats on that coast, with a single mast and topsail, sloop-rigged. She passed through the English Channel, & as far south as Madeira, where she stopped three or four days, & then steered directly for New-York, where she arrived with the addition of one passenger, born on the way.

The reporter's account was fairly circumstantial and compact. True enough, it added some seven tons to the size of the diminutive sloop, it failed to name individuals, it did not note that the "agent" – Cleng Peerson by name – greeted the immigrants as they disembarked, and it did not mention the fact that the vessel was loaded with iron. But it was a kindly and interesting contemporary report of the first act in an emigrant drama that has witnessed the coming of nearly a million people to America from Norway in the nineteenth and twentieth centuries. A later newspaper story told of two agents who had been sent to America in advance of the emigrant party of 1825. A report from one of these led the "little colony" to decide to settle in the United States "to assume the character of American citizens." The second newspaper story concluded with the statement that the folk of the *Restoration* "had sought asylum in this favored land from religious persecution and that they will shortly be succeeded by a much larger body of emigrants."

The story of the "sloopers" has been told and retold in all its details – the Quakers of southwestern Norway whose tribulations were a factor of importance in the genesis of the migration, the sending of agents to America in 1821 to prepare the way, the return to Norway in 1824 of Cleng Peerson, the purchase of a sloop in 1825, and finally the journey itself, which began under the leadership of the Quaker Lars Larsen on July 4 and 5, 1825, and lasted fourteen weeks. In New York the emigrants, unhappily ignorant of American shipping regulations, ran afoul of the federal law that permitted only two passengers to each five tons of a vessel landing at an American port. As a consequence the *Restoration*, to the dismay of the emigrants, was seized, and a fine of $3,150 was imposed upon the owners.*

Three of the sloopers – Lars Larsen, the leader, Johannes Steen, and Lars O. Helland, the master – on October 14 petitioned the United States district judge to intervene with the Secretary of the Treasury to remit both the forfeiture of the vessel and the fine, so that the emigrants

* For full detail on the sloopers, with references to both contemporary records and later accounts, see my *Norwegian Migration*, vol. 1, ch. 2, and *Norwegian Migration*, vol. 2, Appendix.

could proceed, as they explained, to form "a settlement on some of the uncultivated lands" of New York. Ignorant of the laws, they were "without any intent or expectation whatever" to violate them. Their purpose, following the advice of their agent and friend, Cleng Peerson, had been simply to emigrate to the country of which he had given them so favorable a report. Ultimately, on November 15, 1825, President John Quincy Adams, by his own hand, pardoned the sloopers. Meanwhile, most of them had already made their way to Orleans County, New York, to establish the first Norwegian settlement in the United States. "They appear to be quite pleased with what they see in this country," noted the friendly *Patriot* of Albany as they passed through that city, "if we may judge from their good-humored countenances. Success attend their efforts in this asylum of the oppressed." *

Success was their goal, and in time they attained it, but not without difficulties and ordeals, for they began with nothing and only slowly worked their way forward. After about a decade, as the migration from Norway began to increase, many of these pioneer New York settlers made their way to Illinois and the Middle West. The Kendall Settlement, as the little colony established on Lake Ontario, some thirty-five miles northwest of Rochester, has been named, was never very important save as a beginning and as a spot of dispersion. Like the *Restoration,* the place is significant as a prologue. Lines reached out, as the decades passed, from Stavanger to all of Norway, and from the Kendall Settlement to all of the United States; and the success that attended the efforts of hundreds of thousands of immigrants has lent a romantic interest to the initial chapter. In 1825 President Adams pardoned the sloopers – in 1925 President Coolidge told their story in a laudatory centennial address.

The romantic interest is heightened by the character of Cleng Peerson – in Professor Einar Haugen's words, "the mercurial, irrepressible, vagabond-like Daniel Boone of Norwegian migration." For a generation this enigmatic figure gave direction to Norwegian settlement. Pathfinder for the sloopers, he led the pioneers to the Rochester area in the 1820's. A decade later he blazed their trail to the Illinois country. Later he sought out lands in Missouri, Iowa, and Texas, tramping his way

* The news item was copied in the *New York Evening Post,* October 24, 1825, and is reprinted in R. B. Anderson, *First Chapter of Norwegian Immigration* (Madison, Wis., 1904), p. 70. The pardon is described in "John Quincy Adams the Sloop 'Restoration'," in my *Norwegian Migration,* vol. 2, pp. 599–628.

thousands of miles on foot, always restless and curious, singing the praises of America, spinning tales, and encouraging emigrants.*

The first of the immigrant letters in this book comes from the pen of Cleng Peerson. After his first three years in America, he made a trip to Norway in 1824, then hurried back to New York, and on December 20 of that year wrote to the future sloopers, giving them advice, telling them of his plans to buy land for them, and assuring them of a friendly reception when they arrived in the strange New World.

It is difficult to exaggerate the intensity of early Norwegian interest in letters from immigrants in the New World. These "America letters" often were passed from family to family and community to community. Everywhere they spread information about America and stirred interest in the prospects of emigration. Few letters survive the early years of the sloopers, but in the 1830's, when American interest was mounting in Norway, the volume and influence of the letters rapidly increased.

No single early letter writer had more influence than Gjert G. Hovland, an immigrant of 1831 who joined the sloopers in the Kendall Settlement and wrote numerous letters to Norway, beginning in 1835. Hundreds of handwritten copies of his letters were circulated, and some were blazoned forth in newspapers. Their influence had much to do with the broadening of the emigration in 1836. Many Norwegian voices were raised in opposition to emigration and America, and Hovland's letters constituted a vigorous rebuttal. "Nothing," he said, "has made me more happy and contented than that we left Norway and came to this country." In homely detail he spelled out the aspects of American life that seemed to him to justify emigration.

If Hovland did not particularly stress initial difficulties, it should be noted that he wrote after four years of pioneering. Land and liberty and American democracy were undeniable realities to him, but in the many acrid debates that followed in Norway, his letters were contrasted with those of discouraged immigrants who wrote in the first year, when the ordeal of getting started was at its harshest. Essentially the picture Hovland painted was the one accepted by thousands who sought ships to carry them to the New World – and essentially it was true. Portions of two of his letters are presented in translation in the present section,

* See my article "Cleng Peerson and Norwegian Immigration," in *Mississippi Valley Historical Review*, 7:303–331 (March 1921), and a brief sketch in *Dictionary of American Biography* (New York, 1934), vol. 14, p. 390. Professor Haugen's characterization of Peerson is in his essay on "Norwegian Migration to America," in *Norwegian-American Studies and Records* (Northfield, Minn.), 18:9 (1954).

and we shall meet him again after he joins the trek of settlers to Illinois. Though he was a trifle less exuberant in his later praise, he retained his faith in America. In a letter from Illinois, referring to an emigrant who had given up and returned to Norway, he said curtly, "He was not brought up among the class of people able to cope with difficulties."

But difficulties there were, and they began early. Lars Larsen, the leader of the sloopers, was a carpenter who became a shipbuilder in Rochester and whose home is noted in Norwegian-American annals for his incredibly friendly hospitality to hundreds of penniless immigrants who passed through Rochester on their way west. In October 1837 he felt it necessary to address an open letter to the people of Norway, warning them of the difficulties which lack of money and inability to speak the English language entailed. A shipload of ninety emigrants descended upon him at one time in Rochester, seeking shelter and food as well as help in getting jobs. Larsen, in his warning, attempted to stem the tide, as did his wife, the devout Martha Larsen, who faced the massive task of feeding at one time nearly a hundred weary and forlorn immigrants. The country, she thought, was good, but, she sighed, "so many people move in from practically all parts of the world." Most of the immigrants, lacking money, unable to talk English, and without friends, refuse, she wrote, "to bide their time and be patient." The reason for their impatience is perhaps disclosed in another letter of Lars Larsen, written in 1838, when, again reviewing difficulties, he pointed out that the immigrants were "steadily moving west." Rochester was no longer a goal. The America the newcomers were looking for was Illinois and the Mississippi Valley.

Through the great canal, and overland

FROM CLENG PEERSON, IN NEW YORK, TO HIS FAMILY AND FRIENDS *

December 20, 1824

I am letting you know that I have arrived, happy and well, in America. After a journey of six weeks, we reached New York, where I found all

* Both the original text and the complete English translation of this letter were published in my *Norwegian Migration*, vol. 1, pp. 381–385. The original letter is in the Manuscript Division of the Minnesota Historical Society.

my friends in good health, and they received me very affectionately. We stayed there five days and then took the steamboat *William Penn* for Albany, where we arrived in twenty-four hours. This was a distance of 150 miles, or 30 Norwegian miles. The price for each of us was $2 — and we also received free board.

Later we went to Troy and then westward, through the great canal, two hundred miles to Salina Salt Works, working our way. Then we took another boat and went the rest of the way to my friends in Farmington, where I left my comrade. From there I made my way overland to Geneva, where the land commissioner lives, to buy land for myself and for you, as previously agreed. The land commissioner is very friendly and has promised to give us as much help as possible. We came to an agreement on six pieces of land which I have selected, and these will be held for us until next autumn.

I am already building a house, twelve by ten ells, which I hope to finish by New Year's day. We then expect winter to go on for a couple of months, and that will be a good time to haul wood from the forests. When I was in Rochester I bought a stove for $20, fully equipped with pans, pots for meat, a baking oven, and other things — so we shall not need to build a fireplace. I have erected this house on the land I chose for you, whose arrival I am awaiting, but in the spring, if the Lord permits me to live, I shall build on my own land. I have five acres of land ready for sowing and planting in the spring. I have a cow in Farmington which cost me $10, and I have a few sheep. The prices of all things I have reported in Knud Eie's letter.

I am very much concerned in my mind about your coming to America. How I wish the waiting were over when I think of my sister and other friends. How glad I should be to get word that you were coming to New York, so that I might greet you there. I have no doubt that you will be able to journey by way of the canal very comfortably and at a cheap rate. The Friends at Macedon have promised that my sister and the others may stay with them until we get houses built for them.

Many persons are buying land in this vicinity, and there are many cultivated pieces of land that we may work on share. The land around here will soon be filled up, especially that nearest the canal.

I must leave all to Providence. What He wills, you will do. Do not let yourselves be scared away by talk. As long as my faith has kept steadfast, I have received the help of Providence. That is all we can do. I have told you everything orally, and I stand by my promises. If only you will write me in time, then I will do my best.

I have talked with many persons in New York about selling the vessel. You will certainly be able to dispose of a small vessel, but a large one is against the law. Do whatever seems best to you. Young persons can easily get to London and from there to New York for $30. My friends in New York have promised to do all in their power to sell the vessel as advantageously as possible. On the other hand, if you could put your money in iron from Sweden and hire a vessel, that would come to the same thing.

I hope you will write me a letter as soon as you are ready and let me know your intentions. Above all, deal with one another in a brotherly spirit, and in no wise fail to love one another. Let us do that and see ourselves as we really are, wretched and feeble. Then we shall understand that we always need help and salvation from the hand of the Almighty. Then we shall heed His call and admonitions.

Up to the present I have been in good health, as has my comrade Andrias Stangeland. Greet all my friends there – my father, brothers, and sisters, and all other acquaintances.

Room here for all

FROM GJERT G. HOVLAND, AT KENDALL SETTLEMENT, NEW YORK, TO TORJULS A. MÆLAND *

April 22, 1835

I must take this opportunity to let you know that we are in the best of health, and that both my wife and I are exceedingly well satisfied. Our son attends the English school and talks English as well as the native born. Nothing has made me more happy and contented than that we left Norway and came to this country. We have gained more since our arrival here than I did during all the time I lived in Norway, and I have every prospect of earning a living here for myself and my family – even if my family becomes larger – so long as God gives me good health.

Such excellent plans have been developed here that, even though one

* My translation of this letter was first printed as "A Typical 'America Letter'" in the *Mississippi Valley Historical Review*, 9:68–74 (June 1922).

be infirm, no one need go hungry. Competent men are elected to see that no needy persons, either in the cities or in the country, shall have to beg. If a man dies and leaves a widow and children who are unable to support themselves – as often happens – they have the privilege of petitioning these officials. Each one will then receive every year as much clothing and food as he needs, and no discrimination is shown between the native born and those from foreign countries. These things I have learned through daily observation, and I do not believe there can be better laws and arrangements for the benefit and happiness of the common man in the whole world. I have talked with a sensible person who has traveled in many countries, who has lived here twenty-six years, and has full knowledge of the matter; I asked both him and other reliable persons, for I wish to let everyone know the truth.

When assemblies are held to elect officials to serve the country, the vote of the common man carries just as much authority and influence as that of the rich and powerful man. Neither in the matter of clothes nor in manners are distinctions noticeable, whether one be a farmer or a clerk. The one enjoys just as much freedom as the other. So long as he comports himself honestly he meets no interference. Everybody is free to travel about in the country, wherever he wishes, without passports or papers. Everyone is permitted to engage in whatever business he finds most desirable, in trade or commerce, by land or by water. But if anyone is found guilty of crime, he is prosecuted and severely punished.

No duties are levied upon goods that are produced in the country and brought to the city by water or by land. In case of death, no registration is required; the survivor, after paying the debts, is free to dispose of the property for himself and his family just as he pleases. There is no one here who snatches it away, like a beast of prey, wanting only to live by the sweat of others and to make himself heir to the money of others. No, everyone must work for his living here, whether he be of low or high estate. It would greatly please me to learn that all of you who are in need and have little chance of supporting yourselves and your families have decided to leave Norway and come to America; for, even if many more come, there will still be room here for all. Those who are willing to work will not lack employment or business here. It is possible for all to live in comfort and without want.

I do not believe that any who suffer oppression and who must rear their children in poverty could do better than to come to America. But alas, many who want to come lack the means, and many others are so stupid as to believe that it is best to live in the country where they have grown up even if they have nothing but hard bread to satisfy their hunger. It is as if they thought that those who move to a better land, a land of plenty, do wrong. But I cannot find that our Creator has forbidden us to seek our food in an honorable way. I should like to talk to many persons in Norway for a little while, but we do not wish to live in Norway. We lived there altogether too long. Nor have I talked with any immigrant in this country who wished to return.

We left our home in Norway on June 24, 1831. Sailing from Gothenburg on July 30, we landed in America September 18, and by October 4 we had reached this place in the interior where we now live. The day after my arrival I began to work for an American. In December I bought myself fifty acres of land. I put up a house which we moved into in the month of March 1832. I then set to work with the greatest will and pleasure, for the land was covered with trees. In the fall I planted about one barrel of wheat, and in the spring of 1833 we planted about half a bushel of Indian corn and three bushels of potatoes (the latter in May). The next fall we harvested 15 barrels of wheat, 6 barrels of Indian corn, and 14 barrels of potatoes. Wheat, which is grown almost everywhere, is used for daily food. It costs from $3 to $4 a barrel, corn costs from $1.50 to $2.00 a barrel, and potatoes $.50 a barrel. Oats are $1 a barrel, being used not for human food, but for the cattle and horses. We purchased a cow in April of the first year we were here for $18, from which we milked six cans a day and sometimes more. A pound of butter costs, in the towns, from 8 to 12 skillings, salt pork from 4 to 8 skillings a pound, and meat 4 skillings a pound.

Land is measured off here with a pole eight ells and six inches long, this being called a *rod.* An acre measures sixteen rods in length by ten in breadth. One hundred acres, here called a *lot,* is a piece of land of considerable size. I am certain that from fifty acres here, we harvest many times more than from a *gaard* in Norway. I believe that an acre is something more than a *tønde sæd* in Norway; it takes two bushels of wheat to sow an acre.

Six families of the Norwegians who had settled in this place sold their farms last summer and moved farther west in the country to a place called Illinois. We and another Norwegian family have also sold our farms and intend to journey, this May, to that state, where land can be bought at a better price, and where it is easier to get started. There are only enough trees there to meet actual needs. Cattle can be fed there at little cost, for one can cut plenty of hay. The United States owns an untold amount of land which is reserved by law at a set price for the one who first buys it from the government. It is called public land and is sold for $1.25 per acre. Land thus bought and paid for is held in alodial possession for the purchaser and his heirs. Whether native-born or foreign, a man is free to do with it whatever he pleases.

This is a beautiful and fertile country. Prosperity and contentment are almost everywhere. Practically everything needed can be sown or planted here and grows splendidly, producing a yield of many fold without the use of manure.

Law and order exist here, and the country is governed by wise authorities.

I sold my land last summer, in July 1834, and by the transaction got $500 in cash. I have now decided to buy 160 acres, which can be had for $200. The eight Norwegian families still in this neighborhood want to sell their land as soon as they can and move west, for they prefer to live near each other, although many of the natives are people just as good.

In America you associate with good and kindly people. Everyone has the freedom to practice the teaching and religion he prefers. The only tax a man pays here is on the land he owns, and even that tax is not large. Nor are there other useless expenditures for the support of persons — as in many places in Europe — who are of more harm than benefit to the country. For the fifty acres I sold I paid a dollar a year in taxes. On the piece of land we sold there were more trees than I could count of the kind that produces sugar, and these trees were common everywhere. We took no more than we needed for our own use each year. Usually we did this work in March, when the sap begins to rise in the trees. With a small iron we chopped an opening in the bark of the tree, placing under it a piece of hollowed-out wood as a trough. A tree yields from two to three pails of sweet sap a day, and this sap makes sugar, syrup, ale, and vinegar.

There is much more I could write to you about, but I will close for this time, with hearty greetings from me and my wife and son to you, my relatives, and acquaintances. Let us be happy in heart and consecrated in spirit so that when the race has been run, when the pilgrim's staff has been laid down, we may be worthy of hearing the glorious words: "Blessed of my Father, come ye and inherit the kingdom and the righteousness prepared for you." Wherever we may wander in this earthly sphere, let us seek Him who is the true light and life, and follow His voice which calls to our hearts, no matter where we go or stand. Live well in the sight of God: that is my wish as your friend. Greetings to Knud Oppedal and Johannes Hovland and to all who inquire about me.

Here work is better rewarded

FROM GJERT G. HOVLAND, AT ROCHESTER, NEW YORK, TO A FRIEND *

April 28, 1835

I have undertaken nothing so far which has given me more satisfaction than the journey we have made here, though there were many people who described conditions in this country as miserable. I have not yet found them so, nor do I ever expect to. I wish that there were such good arrangements all over the world as there are here: good laws and good order and government by good authorities. The United States are twenty-four in number and have independent governments. Elections are held at certain times of the year to choose a good president for the benefit of the country. He is appointed for four years, and if he is found to be honest, wise in his actions, and useful to the country, he is elected for another four years, but no one may hold the office for more than eight years.

. . . .

We now intend to move farther inland where you can make better bargains in buying fertile land and where it is easier to start. There you can buy land for about $5 an acre for your alodial possession, just as safely as you might go and buy yourself half a pound of tobacco. There are no discriminating laws here. What a man has bought and paid for, he may keep for himself and his family and do with as he

* This letter appeared in *Den Norske Rigstidende,* May 25 and 28, 1837. These issues of the newspaper contain a lengthy discussion of emigration, in which the darker side of the story is underlined.

pleases. Where we plan to move, however, all land is bought from the government, and it is all under a fixed price so that no one who first buys from the government will have to pay too much. I intend to buy initially 160 acres, which can be done for $200. If I could be sure that some of my cousins from Norway were coming here, I should buy more.

If you ever plan to come here, the one thing above all I ask you — as my friend — is that you please call on my cousins in Søndfjord. Let them know that if some of them want to come but can't pay their way, you or some other honest man who wants to come will help them; I shall be very happy to repay you for all your trouble and expense. Whether they are single or married and in poor circumstances, I should like to see them here, for here everyone who wants to work can live well without want. All who are in need and suffer oppression from others or who have to bring up children under straitened circumstances should come; also servants who have to work for small pay and have no prospects of advancement. These things I know from experience. A farmhand who works all the year round gets from $8 to $12 a month, plus board and lodging and free laundry. A girl gets $1 a week or $50 a year, plus board and lodging and free laundry — she only works in the house and has no heavy outdoor work. A farmhand may contract for work on a monthly basis or for six months or a year, as he pleases. A worker on daily wages gets from $.50 to $1 a day, plus board.

. . . .

Thus far things have gone well with us and according to our wish. I have earned more since we came here than during all the time we lived in Norway, and if only God grants us health, I have prospects of a good livelihood for my family and me. I should like very much to talk for a while to many of my acquaintances, but we do not wish to return to Norway to live, not even if I could get one of the best farms at Stangeland free for my alodial possession. You have to work here, as you do everywhere else in the world. Only, here work is better rewarded. . . .

Many large fresh water lakes are located in the interior of the country, hundreds of miles from the coast. On each of them there is much shipping, with steamboats and other large vessels carrying on an extensive trade. These lakes are connected by canals, so that by this means one can travel more than twelve thousand miles inland, and one might travel even farther if the country were inhabited. Of these English miles six hardly make up a Norwegian mile; I should say that eight English miles would be the same as one Norwegian mile.

Sixteen Norwegian families settled close to one another here. Six of them sold their land last summer. Those that remain want to sell theirs as soon as they can and move to the place where we are going. I do not advise anyone either to come or to stay at home, but if any do want to come, they should sell all they have and turn it into money. Besides taking along enough clothes to wear and bedclothes, they should have a supply of food that will not spoil at sea. I paid fifty Spanish dollars for my wife's fare and mine and twelve for our son's.

Best greetings to you, your wife, and children, and God be with you all.

The country is good, but—

FROM LARS LARSEN, AT ROCHESTER, NEW YORK, TO HIS COUNTRYMEN *

October 1837

Spurred by the love I feel for my native country, I hasten to acquaint you with the fortunes of those of our countrymen who have come over here from Norway, and especially of those who came from Stavanger, where I was born. From these I have heard that you are eager to get exact information about conditions in this country. They have also told me that many of you plan to come over here next year, but I should advise these to consider everything carefully before they undertake such a journey.

Consider: (1) that you do not speak the language; (2) whether you have enough money to travel farther inland after your arrival here. This has not always been true of many of my countrymen who have come. What, then, are they to do? They have either to starve or beg in the streets. If the Norwegian and Swedish vice-consul had not been kind enough to help them with money, they would generally have suffered great need and the utmost misery. From the consul they usually come to me in Rochester, and when they arrive here their complaint has usually been that their money once more has given out. Then they ask me for

* This letter appeared in *Stavanger Adresseavis*, December 15, 1837.

help, without which they would undoubtedly be reduced to misery. They ask me for advice about what to do, and I have made all efforts to help them. Since I am their countryman they feel that it is my duty to assist them, which I agree to and am willing to do. But because of the great numbers of those who come to me, it is almost impossible for me to satisfy all of them. The last ship from Stavanger brought about ninety of my countrymen here, most of whom came to my house and stayed there almost three days. I sent about thirty of them on to Illinois, as was their wish. The rest are still in my house, with twelve more who arrived one day after the others; these are housed in one of my boats.

As for the men who run ships for the emigrants or are their contractors and advisers, I should ask them to be cautious and not urge the emigrants to leave without money. If emigrants have no money, they are no better off here than in their own country, in fact scarcely as well off, for there they can speak for themselves but here they have to have a man who can speak for them and manage their affairs. Everybody here as well as in Norway should see to it that he is able to take care of himself. I have looked around day after day to find jobs for my countrymen; but when they have been employed for a day or two, their employers send them back to me and say that they cannot use them because they do not speak the language.

The country is good, but everyone can understand that lack of money here is the same as want anywhere else. The worst handicap is unfamiliarity with the language. Other inconveniences will be added to this, for instance the fact that bills of exchange sent here will invariably arrive later than planned.

Now, my dear countrymen, you have my views concerning those who have already come over, and you may judge the consequences for yourselves. I know that when a person has made a decision, it is difficult to change it; but believe me, I have stated the truth to the best of my ability and can say that very few have been happy on their arrival here. And they cannot go back for lack of money.

I will now leave the matter to your own decision, but I cannot insist strongly enough that you should not leave without enough money to enable you to reach the interior of the country.

Sat sapienti!

I remain your sincerely devoted countryman, always ready to help you.

P.S. Be good enough to insert the above in the newspapers in order that everyone may know the contents. For further proof and corroboration, the Norwegian and Swedish vice-consul is signing his name to testify that this is the truth as fully as we are able to get at it.

ERNST ZACHRISSON

So many people move in

FROM MARTHA LARSEN, AT ROCHESTER, NEW YORK, TO ELIAS TASTAD *

11th of the 10th month, 1837

I cannot let this good opportunity go by without letting you know that we are all well. As Lars is going to New York, I will tell you a little about our conditions, as well as about the other Norwegians here. Twelve Norwegians came here today, and are now sitting at the table eating their supper. About two weeks ago there arrived from ninety to a hundred people. They stayed at our house and my brother's house for about a week, and we furnished meals for nearly all of them. Most of them have now gone to Illinois. Knud Eide with family and Endre Aragebo were the last to leave. There are still five families at our house, of the first emigrants who arrived; among them is Ole Reiersen, who delivered your letter to me. It gave me great pleasure to receive your letter and to hear about all of you. I often think of you, dear friend, and of the other friends at Stavanger. I know that you have to contend with many difficulties both in your own home and otherwise, but, my friend, ask the Lord for strength and patience to deal carefully with the weak. If we walk patiently in the fear of the Lord, and show a good example, then shall we overcome the world.

From Serena's letter I learn the sad news that she has left the Society of Friends. I ask you as a friend that you visit her and speak to her in the greatest humility; then possibly the Lord will still guide her on the way of peace. It is easy to fall, but, when we pray for God's assistance, He will raise us up again. I can scarcely express my feelings toward all of you. Oh, that we may all walk carefully, for we have the same enemy to contend with here as you have, but, if God be with us, then our enemy

* The translations of this letter and the one following were first printed in "Letters from the Sloop-Folk," *American-Scandinavian Review*, 13:361–363 (June 1925).

cannot lead us astray. This has always been my comfort through many trials and tribulations. The dissension among the Friends is the same now as before. Those who have left have shown the world a very poor example. But I shall not say anything more about their time for repentance.

I am glad to say that, as far as I know, my dear Lars no longer associates with them, which is the greatest joy I could desire here on earth. He is greatly interested in church work, is diligent in his work, and we live together with great happiness, for God has blessed us with both temporal and spiritual gifts. We are blessed with six children, five girls and one boy. They are good, healthy, well-behaved children, who give us great joy.

Eilert asked me in a letter last summer to advise him whether he should come here. I can truthfully say that the country is good, O but not so good as it used to be. The country itself is the same, but so many people move in from practically all parts of the world. I will not advise him either for or against coming; he will have to do as he himself sees fit. He asked if he could get land near Rochester. Yes, there is land enough for people who have money enough, but cultivated land costs from $100 to $200 an acre. People who are making a comfortable living in Norway ought to stay where they are, and not come here. When they come to this country, most of them are without money, cannot speak the language, and have no friends. They refuse to bide their time and be patient. Elias, I want to ask you as a friend that you advise no one to come here who cannot help himself, because practically all of them come to us and we cannot help so many. We, of course, do what we can for them all. I have gone around town looking for work for them, and Lars has taken many of them out into the country. We spare no pains to make them satisfied.

They are steadily moving west

FROM LARS LARSEN, AT ROCHESTER, NEW YORK, TO ELIAS TASTAD

9th of the 7th month, 1838

As there is such a good opportunity I wish to inform you that I, as well as my family, live well. As there are so many here who write letters to

Norway, you will understand that each one writes according to the way in which he finds himself satisfied or dissatisfied. However, as I learn to know human nature, I realize that men are continually restless, unless their hearts are where they ought to be. They think of nothing more important than this present life.

However, I want to tell you that we in this country have our troubles, just as well as you do. Personally, I cannot complain, because I have my daily bread and have enough so that I can share with the needy. But many of my countrymen are in a rather bad position, so that, unless charity were shown, I am sure their poverty would shorten their days. Most of them are dissatisfied, and would return to Norway if their money were not gone. Most of them have gone to Illinois or Missouri. They are steadily moving west, and how far they will eventually go, I do not know. I wish to say this much, that those who plan on coming here must be prepared to meet many difficulties that they have never thought of.

Westward to El-a-noy

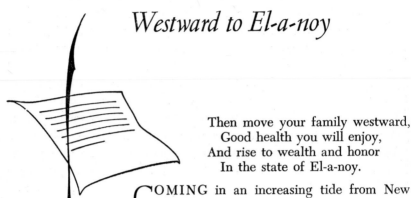

> Then move your family westward,
> Good health you will enjoy,
> And rise to wealth and honor
> In the state of El-a-noy.

COMING in an increasing tide from New York and the Old World, the Norwegian immigrants probably did not sing the ballad of El-a-noy, which pictured Adam visiting the state and imagining it to be the garden he "played in when a boy." * But to them El-a-noy meant land, potential wealth, perhaps honor, too, and, beginning in 1834, they did in fact move their families westward.

Once more Cleng Peerson was their pathfinder. Always restless, he broke away from the New York colony in 1833, traveled to Ohio, across Michigan, and through northern Indiana to Illinois. Some have asserted that he walked north from Chicago to Milwaukee, where he met Solomon Juneau, the founder of that city, who told him that Wisconsin, with its heavy woods, was not suited to settlement. Later, tramping through Illinois, he came to the rich valley of the Fox River. An immigrant who knew Peerson relates the story of this event as it was told to him. "Almost dead of hunger and exhaustion as a result of his long wanderings through the wilderness," Peerson "threw himself upon the grass and thanked God who had permitted him to see this wonderland of nature. Strengthened in soul, he forgot his hunger and sufferings. He thought of Moses when he looked out over the Promised Land from the heights of Nebo, the land that had been promised to his people." †

Peerson trudged back to New York, where his glowing reports re-

* The words and music of this old ballad are printed in Carl Sandburg, *The American Songbag* (New York, 1927), pp. 162–163. See also my "Singing Immigrants," in *Grass Roots History* (Minneapolis, 1947), pp. 31–54.

† The story is told in Knud Langeland, *Nordmændene i Amerika* (Chicago, 1889), pp. 18–19. He seems to have had it at first hand from Peerson, whom he knew well.

sulted in a virtual break-up of the Kendall group the next year. With five families of settlers, the pathfinder migrated in 1834 to Illinois, and the Fox River Settlement, the second of Norwegian colonies in the United States, was established. The news of land in the West was promptly communicated to Norway both by letters and, in 1835, by one of the Fox River settlers, Knud Andersen Slogvig, who, to the people of southwestern Norway, was a veritable Marco Polo returned from an unknown world. "There before them at last," writes Kendric C. Babcock, "was a man who had twice braved all the terrors of thousands of miles of sea and hundreds of miles of far-distant land, who had come straight and safe from that fabulous vast country, with its broad valleys and prairies, with its strange white men, and stranger red men." * Reinforcing his own stories with letters that he carried with him, he did much to spread the "America fever" in the Norwegian valleys, and it is no coincidence that in 1836 two shiploads of emigrants sailed out for America from Norway — and two more the next year. The migration was definitely under way, and the goal was Illinois.

The letters presented in the following pages reflect the excitement of the turbulent 1830's as immigrants viewed the West. The "America fever" ordinarily struck the young, but the first letter is that of a man of nearly seventy years who, though he had barely arrived in Illinois, was already dreaming of pushing on to lands still farther west.

One of the interesting aspects of the immigrant story, as has been noted, was the way the speech of everyday people popularized such terms as "America letters," "America fever," and "America books." The book by Ole Rynning, published in 1838 under the title *True Account of America for the Information and Help of Peasant and Commoner*, was for some years *the* "America book." It was, I have already said, really an extensive "America letter" — a letter to all Norway — that happened to be brought out as a book. An English version of this book is available elsewhere and is therefore not included in the present volume, but it is interesting to find that the unsigned letter dated January 28, 1838, is from Rynning's pen. Its rapid review of the emigration from 1825 to 1838 is almost identical with one of the chapters in the *True Account of America.* Rynning made a deep impression on the settlers who knew him well. One of them thus characterized him, "A great and good idea formed

* *The Scandinavian Element in the United States* (Urbana, Ill., 1914), p. 32.

the central point of all his thinking. He hoped to be able to provide the poor, oppressed Norwegian workman a happier home on this side of the sea, and to realize this wish he shunned no sacrifice, endured the greatest exertions, and was patient through misunderstandings, disappointments, and loss. . . . Nothing could shake his belief that America would become a place of refuge for the masses of people in Europe who toiled under the burdens of poverty." *

Rynning recognized the importance of the "America letters" and particularly of those written by Hovland. Removed to Illinois, Hovland wrote in 1838 to say that the new region was Canaan, but at the same time he uttered a warning that it was no paradise for those who were not ready and willing to work hard.

Cleng Peerson, meanwhile, had already pushed on to a new settlement in Missouri, and the next letter tells of him guiding emigrants from New York to that state – a letter voicing doubt and concern as to the wisdom of emigration. The note of early disillusionment is carried to the extreme in another letter, written in 1839 by one Sjur J. Haaeim to a Norwegian bishop who had published a pastoral letter in Norway adjuring people not to emigrate. Such letters, often reflecting unfortunate local circumstances, quickly met with refutation both in America and in Norway. Another Missouri letter, that of Hans Barlien, while it conveyed to the father of Ole Rynning the unhappy news that his son had died, took a more optimistic view of the American prospects for immigrants. Barlien struck out at land speculators who fleeced the immigrants, but he had high hopes of the society into which he had come.†

The irrepressible Hovland, writing again from Illinois in 1842, turned his attention to the flood of anti-American writings in Norway and wisely suggested that they had been written by "people who have too little experience in this country." Penning his most vigorous refutation of doleful charges against America, he exclaimed, "May the lies be trampled under foot and the truth be made known!"

Inevitably Cleng Peerson, true to his role as an immigrant leader, mixed into the sharp debate that was filling the newspapers of Norway with arguments about America, pro and con. In the spring of 1843 he

* The quotation is from a fellow immigrant of 1837. See my *Norwegian Migration*, vol. 1, p. 93.

† An informing study entitled "A Doctrinaire Idealist: Hans Barlien," by D. G. Ristad, is in *Studies and Records* (Northfield, Minn.: Norwegian-American Historical Asssociation), 3:13–22 (1928).

was again in Norway, and, denying charges that he was there as an "emissary to promote emigration," he nevertheless endorsed Rynning's account of America as "true and reliable," and stated that the bishop's pastoral letter was without "foundation in facts."

Thus the letters mirror the differences of opinion that emigration provoked in Norway and the constantly spreading interest in the New World. Notwithstanding unfavorable reports, emigration continued to mount as people, from one source or another, filled out their information about America.

The land is largely prairie

FROM JOHANNES NORDBOE, AT OTTAWA, LA SALLE COUNTY, ILLINOIS, TO HANS L. RUDI *

April 30, 1837

Your honored letter of August 25, 1835, was received with heartfelt joy on October 28, 1836. A man who returned to Norway from here brought it back with him. Had he returned here at once I should have received the letter sooner, but he delayed until he had assembled about 180 persons, both young and old, most of them from the Stavanger region. The group came in two brigs from Stavanger. The cost of passage for each person amounted to $32. Packed together and with little realization of the importance of good ventilation, almost all suffered from indispositions like diarrhea and seasickness.

A few who took passage from Gothenburg on American ships arrived in good health after a six weeks' voyage. So when Norwegians wish to come here, they should go via Gothenburg, but not too many on each ship. Ships leave Gothenburg all summer, from April to October. For people of eastern Norway it is best to go to Fredrikshald and thence to Svefesund. A little south of there one meets many large open boats that are constantly going southward along the coast to Gothenburg with cargoes of lumber. A man can work his way by helping the two men on one

* The translation of this letter is by Clarence A. Clausen. It was first printed in Arne Odd Johnsen, ed., "Johannes Nordboe and Norwegian Immigration, An America Letter of 1837," *Norwegian-American Studies and Records* (Northfield, Minn.), 8:23–38 (1934).

of these boats hoist sail or row a little when necessary. They speak the Baahus dialect and are easily understood.

On arrival at the customhouse quay of Kloppan at Gothenburg, you should go eastward through the suburb into the city proper and there look for ship broker Ström. Greet him from me, J. Nordboe, and ask his help with the exchange of money and so forth, just as he helped me. Then return to the customhouse. At the far end of the pier is a small house where there are several customs officers who can speak English and who usually have a small boat. For a few skillings one of the officers will take you out to the American ships that lie close by. There they will ask twenty specie dollars for passage, but you can haggle with them and say that you are poor and have too little money. If you can get your board included in the passage, well and good, although it costs more. If not, you will have to supply yourself. If there is no ship to New York, go to a port farther north in America, such as Boston. Many go there, and there are also ships to New Bedford, Newburyport, and other places. When you arrive in America, you take a southwesterly route. People who live in the interior of the country usually travel by land. The emigrants from western Norway do not care to go by land and prefer to travel by boat as they are used to doing. *N.B.* The people of eastern Norway are afraid of the water; those of western Norway fear the land.

Once in New York, go down to the shore where the riggings of ships will be seen and call out: "Svedisker Norveisk Mand." When someone answers, inquire for Bekmann, master rigger; Østerberg, baker; the Norwegian Fr. Wang, merchant, a son of the minister in Waage; and also for Tybring, the son of a minister in Drammen, Johnsen of Laurvig, the Norwegian Williamson, and others. A person from eastern Norway who is not altogether a tenderfoot will be well advised to go inland by road. He should obtain an ax to indicate that he wants work, a couple of shirts for change, two combs to keep himself clean, and a cloth to wrap some food in if he so wishes. This is all a man should carry if he does not have enough money for passage by water. In the evening, when he asks for lodging, he should offer to cut some wood; this is always well received. He will then also get supper and breakfast before he leaves, and for dinner he should do the same. He can travel this way through the entire country – and he will make us happy by coming out here. When he has rested a while with the Norwegians who live here, he may continue his course to Quincy, cross the Mississippi River there, proceed to the town of Franklin, where he may cross the Missouri River to the town of Boonville. There he will find my Danish friend E. Bidstrup, and through him he can locate me.

We intend to move there in a few weeks. We must first sell eighty acres of land we have here, and we will auction off a ten-acre field of wheat, together with our livestock, which includes 7 oxen, 4 cows, and 1 mare. Last summer we were so unfortunate as to lose, by accident, a large and expensive driving ox ($36), a hog, and 4 calves. The 7 oxen, 4 cows, 1 mare, 4 swine, and 20 hens, together with the eighty acres, all of which must be converted into money, should net us $200 and the wheat field $100. With as much as $300 to begin with when we come to the state of Misssouri, we hope with God's help to do well.

This western country is far different from the eastern states. Perhaps you will recall what I said the last time I talked with you – that I would not stop in my travels until I had reached the westernmost part of Missouri. I believe God revealed this to me long before I left Norway. That we have been unable to reach our destination before this is due to our poverty, as well as to the unfortunate sea voyage. Had we arrived without any mishaps, we should have come far enough the first year. But I am glad and thank God for things as they are. If God grants my children life and strength, and if they themselves are willing to work, they will be far more fortunate here than in Norway. *N.B.* It is very easy to raise cattle here and also to till the soil. This year as well as last we have had nothing with which to feed the cattle except what my two sons have cut on the prairie, amounting to about thirty tons (a ton is two thousand pounds). We have had no stable for the cattle this winter, since stables are not used here, which is unfortunate. The winter is very cold, and this second winter has again been long.

The land in the state of Illinois is largely prairie, with little woodland except along the rivers and creeks. The summers are extremely beautiful. Then the whole country, both woodland and prairie, is bedecked with grass and flowers of all colors, which bloom from earliest spring to late autumn. When some fall, others come up. Some big, yellow ones in the autumn have stalks ten feet high. The summer may be compared to an earthly paradise, but the winter, on the contrary, may be likened to a mountain climate.

Here the fields are prepared in the following way: the sod, two and a half inches thick, is turned over by a large plow that cuts strips sixteen, eighteen, twenty, and in some cases twenty-four inches wide. The plow is drawn by five and sometimes six pair of oxen, but most frequently by five. The land broken in the spring is ready by August to be harrowed and sowed with wheat for the next summer, but usually it is allowed to lie until the following spring. It is then plowed with one or two pair of oxen; and corn, wheat, oats, or whatever one pleases is planted. The field is then in fine condition without any need of fertilizer. Cabbages can be planted anywhere, and they grow fast. There are many varieties of pumpkins – I do not know how many kinds. They are usually planted with the corn and grow on long tendrils; they are round or oval in shape and are both large and small, the biggest being about fifteen inches in diameter. Cucumbers belong to the same class and grow equally well here. The same is true of potatoes, which give generous yields wherever planted. Tobacco and pumpkin are native products of this country. Other products are imported and thrive here.

Of Indian corn or maize there are also many varieties. There is much to write about, but space will not permit. Deer are plentiful. They are mostly hunted by Indians, for others do not have time for such things. My son Peder is now away chopping cordwood. As he is not yet full-grown, he cannot earn more than a dollar a day. Wages for labor are very high here. A full-grown man can earn from $150 to $160 in wages in one year. Here a poor young man can soon become a well-to-do farmer if he works hard and uses good sense. He can look forward to becoming rich without usury, a difficult task in Norway.

There are many prairie wolves, but they are small and are not dangerous. However, the sheep must be protected from them. There are also a great many prairie chickens, which somewhat resemble heathcocks in size and are about the same color. The male is larger than the female and similarly colored, but is shaped differently. In the mornings at this time of year their calls resemble those of a male dove. They damage corn and wheat; so do the migratory pigeons, thrushes, squirrels, and other creatures. The wolves damage the sweet pumpkins. We also have bears, but they do no harm. There are not many skunks, but there are some raccoons. There are many varieties of squirrels as well as weasels. Some kill chickens. The wildcats, as large as half-grown dogs, are of a brown-striped color; they are shy and keep to the mountains and caves and thick underbrush. Many kinds of fish are in the streams, but we have little time to catch them. Fishing and hunting are Indian occupations, but most of the Indians have now gone.

Almost all the rivers and creeks have mud turtles, and there are also snakes of many kinds. The rattlesnake is not as dangerous as reported. It is no more poisonous than the one in Norway. It is about the same length but somewhat thicker, brownish-yellow in color with black spots. In its upper jaw are four fangs, two on each side, and at the end of its tail there are some small balls, the size of peas, which are rattled against each other and make as loud a sound as a fly. Since the coming of so many settlers, the rattlesnake has largely disappeared. Some other kinds of snakes are almost worse, especially the so-called copperhead. Last summer we lost a large calf. If it had been at home we could have saved it, but it was in the woods.

The woods are largely oaks, three varieties of walnut, and small hazel bushes. They all bear large quantities of nuts that are good for human beings and of great benefit to swine. These may be sold in town for a dollar a bushel. There are plenty of gooseberries, and they are good. Some cedar trees grow on the dry slopes of sandy hills near rivers. The wild apples are sour, and also the cherries, but some of the plums are sweet and good. There is much sandy rock here, but it is too soft for grindstones except in emergency.

N.B. When we arrived in New York, I was old and poor, with small children. I could not earn much, for they did not wish to employ old people for work. If I had had $20 for a deposit, I could have bought land at $5 to $6 per acre, with interest at 7 per cent. Other Norwegians who secured land made a profit from their labor of $200, others $300 to $400, and so on. Some made $1,500 to $1,600, depending on how poor they had been, and one, who has not yet arrived here, had only $3 when he came, newly married, healthy, and strong, in 1825. When he sells his improved farm, he will have $2,000. Others who came here bought land and are already well established. Those who had already come from Ohio and other states are now wealthy.

It was because of me that the Norwegians came here. I have always been of service to others, but never to myself. When we came here, the land had been surveyed for some time but was not settled, except by a few who are now rich. Then it became known that the land was to be sold at auction. The other Norwegians each bought a piece of land they had claimed at the Congress price of ten skillings – $1.25 – per acre.

It is the low price that has enriched so many. I had to go forty miles northward where there were no human beings except a few Indians.

Even though it was in the wilderness, the piece of land I selected was the best and most desirable I have ever seen. During the winter I returned to the place. With the help of my son and son-in-law, I cut and hauled timber for a house, but since we could not begin to live in it until late in the spring and I became ill in the fall and continued ill through the winter, we had to sell our rights to the large and beautiful farm for $400. This happened last year, and not until then had we begun to get ahead a little.

Within half a year the entire region was fully settled. There is now no more land to be had in the entire state, and therefore we must move southwestward to Missouri. Land can still be bought there at Congress prices. It is not so cold there as here, and the climate is said to be healthful. If I live until we have become settled there, I shall write to you again. I should write a separate letter to Ivar, but I hope that you will read this to him. *N.B.* I owe him for the Løken place that I sold for him. This was the rich man's fault. I do not know how I shall be able to send money to him, nor is he able to come here. I wish very much that both you and he could come. But alas, I do not suppose I shall ever see either of you again. Greet all the people who have known me and all who wish me well. I wish God's blessings upon all of you.

[*P.S.*] The soil consists of gray clay mixed with marl, which, when turned to the air, becomes a fertile, dark loam. Through the ages it has become pulverized and is called prairie soil. Its depth varies from one, two, to two and a half, yes, three feet. It contains a little fine sand and perhaps a little rosin and turpentine. When the tops are broken off certain kinds of tall grass, a clear juice is exuded which smells and tastes like turpentine. Later it dries and becomes a pleasant-smelling, gummy substance somewhat resembling mastic or incense. Almost all the grasses seem to contain some of this substance. Consequently the prairie grass burns more readily than other grass. It is burned off every autumn and spring because it is troublesome and burning improves the hay and pasturage. To mow where dead grass remains is impossible. It is also as sharp as scouring grass and quickly wears out shoes and stockings, and walking through the grass where there is no path is difficult.

The Indians have always burned the forests for amusement, and this has hindered the growth of woods.

If I am lucky enough to find good, satisfactory land where we are now going, I shall take four claims, each of 160 acres, which is a farm large enough for one family. *N.B.* One for me, one for each of my three sons, perhaps, one for my brother, if possible. If not, he might have one of the four if he could come here. If only you and he with your families could be here now, even though you had no one else with you but your wife and youngest daughter! It would be better, however, to have as many as possible along, even though it took more money for the trip. It is best not to take too much baggage, although I should like to get some spruce seeds. Our daughter will remain here. They have done well, have 130 acres, have worked on it for two and a half years, and paid $150 for the farm. If he sold his farm now, he could get $1,400 to $1,500. They have 2 pair of oxen, 3 cows, 6 sheep, many swine, 4 geese, and a great many chickens. Last year a son was born to them, a sound and healthy one.

I am afraid that this is scarcely readable, for I see so poorly and have no suitable spectacles. I hope you will excuse me. I am now 69 years old, my wife 36, my daughter 22, my oldest son 17, the second 15, and the third 12 years of age.

Speculators had already taken up the land

[FROM OLE RYNNING, AT BEAVER CREEK, ILLINOIS, TO HIS COUNTRYMEN *]

January 28, 1838

The first ship that carried Norwegian emigrants to America was a sloop of four hundred *tuns* † which in the summer of 1825 sailed from Stavanger with fifty-two passengers. The ship with its cargo of iron was owned by the passengers themselves. After a voyage of fourteen weeks, it landed in New York, where it faced confiscation, with its cargo, since it was carrying more passengers than the law permitted. But justice was

* Though unsigned, this letter was certainly written by Ole Rynning. It appeared in *Det udflyttede Norge* (Christiania: Folkeskriftselskabet, 1884), pp. 6–8.

† About thirty-eight American tons.

tempered with mercy when it was discovered that the infringement of the law was due to a misunderstanding, for the Norwegians had believed that tons were the same thing as *tuns*.

The passengers suffered a great loss in the sale of the ship and cargo, however. In Norway the ship alone had cost about 1,800 specie dollars, and here they got no more than $400 for everything. The skipper and the mate settled down in New York. Aided by the contributions of some Quakers, the others were enabled to travel farther into the interior, where they bought land in Orleans County, Murray Township, on Lake Ontario, five Norwegian miles northwest of Rochester. Here they had to pay a land speculator who was the agent of an English company $5 an acre. But since none of them had any money, the payment was to be made in installments over a period of ten years. All the land was wooded, and it could only be cleared by hard work. When one considers the meager means of these people and their unfamiliarity with the language, it is very understandable that during the first years they many times wished themselves back in Norway and bore a grudge against the man whose accounts of America had led them to emigrate.

This man was a person named Cleng Peerson, who first came over to America in 1821. His endeavor was then, and is still, to unite all Norwegians into one community owning all its property in common. Since these first emigrants often suffered want in the beginning, Cleng Peerson took it upon himself to travel around among wealthy Americans asking aid for all the Norwegians. This did not meet with everybody's approval, partly because on his excursion he had spoken on behalf of all the Norwegians without asking their permission, partly because he had shown some favoritism in his distribution of the means. None of the Norwegians then had more than fifty acres, and no one could meet the conditions of the purchase. Surrounded by primeval forest and rough ground, they could not find sufficient fodder for their cattle on their own farms but had to mow hay for others in return for a third of it; and then they had to bring home the gains of this backbreaking labor from far away and through thick woods and swamps. Not till the fourth or fifth year did they begin to feel more contented. But they were still in debt for their land and could not see their way to paying anything on the principal or the interest in accordance with their contract of purchase — reason enough to dampen their happiness at the sight of the fertility and richness of the soil.

Westward to El-a-noy

In the meantime Cleng Peerson was always busy. Heavy work was never to his liking, but on the other hand he never aimed at personal profit. He worked for everybody and benefited everybody, but often in such an indirect way that few people or no one gave him any thanks for it.

He was the first Norwegian to come to Illinois – in 1833 – to examine the land out here. Influenced by his reports, most of the Norwegians sold their land in Murray and moved to Illinois in July 1834.

From 1825 to 1836 a few Norwegian families and single persons emigrated now and then; but when one of the first Norwegians here, Knud Slogvig, in 1835 returned to Norway and told about conditions in America, and others – particularly Gjert Gregoriussen Hovland – had written home to their families and friends, the desire to emigrate was awakened in some people. Two ships left for New York carrying about two hundred passengers from Stavanger. One of these ships was at sea for seven weeks and three days, and five of the passengers died on board. The other one was at sea for nine weeks, but all the passengers on this ship arrived safe and sound. Several of those who arrived last year remained in New York, since they did not have enough money to travel any farther. Among the rest, some could not pay their way farther than Rochester, while others managed to make it to Illinois.

The first Norwegians who arrived in Illinois settled down in La Salle County, about one and a half Norwegian miles north of Ottawa, a new town that has been founded where the Rock and Illinois rivers meet. Among the Norwegians who arrived here last year, only a few got land near their countrymen; for all land here either had already been taken up by speculators or was unsuitable for settlers since it lacked woods. Last spring, therefore, a group moved farther west, to Missouri, again under the leadership of Cleng Peerson. Several of them have written to their relatives and friends here and are full of enthusiasm over their new-found glories.

Recently I met two men from Drammen who have lived in America for thirteen years. Their names are Peder B. Smith and Hans E. Hjorth. Together they own about eleven acres of land two and a half miles north of Monticello, White County, Indiana, and besides they possess a sawmill through the operation of which they make a lot of money. Smith told me that he had come to America with no more than $18 in his pocket.

This is Canaan

FROM GJERT G. HOVLAND, AT MIDDLE POINT, ILLINOIS, TO A FRIEND *

July 6, 1838

I cannot neglect my duty to write, reminded as I am of my old native country Norway and my friends there. Since my childhood, I have been very deficient in education, but as I hope that this letter will reach you safely, I take occasion to write with the hope that those who have more intelligence than I will take my humble contribution in good part. More particularly, this is addressed to you whom I came to know as a faithful friend. I know that this year reports on America are not lacking in Norway, as far as they get through; but they differ according to everybody's understanding and insight.

I suppose that people are emigrating in great numbers from Norway now, and every emigrant has a different attitude. Many have arrived here who knew Norway under straitened circumstances, and looking back, they see only the burdens they have cast off and feel happy in their emigration, especially for their children. But those, on the other hand, who grew up in the nurture of pious parents and who always enjoyed earthly happiness, will find sorrow and regret if they expect God to supply them a paradise here without the necessity of working. Everyone who leaves Norway with this fond hope is deceiving himself thoroughly. Anyone who wants to make good here has to work, just as in all other places in the world. But here everything is better rewarded. This fact repels many people, though anyone with common sense ought to know that in time life rewards each as he deserves. Therefore, it seems to me all who take a notion to visit this country had better consider the matter carefully before they leave their homes, nor should they enter upon the venture frivolously or intoxicated by greed for material things. This applies especially to people who vacillate and lack firmness.

Since the length of the journey makes the trip here rather expensive, those who want to manage on their own without contracting any debts must be prepared to pay from seventy to eighty specie dollars for every adult and half that amount for children, besides the price of provisions. When they arrive here, they find that no land is available in Illinois,

* This letter appeared in *Den Bergenske Merkur*, November 30, 1838.

though there is some farther west; but it requires money and patience to get there. The land around here that has enough woodland has been bought up and is inhabited. We have an unbelievable amount of vast grass plains (savannas) that extend for many miles with the most marvelous grazing for the animals imaginable. As much hay as anyone could desire may be mowed with little trouble. Surely no sensible man could wish for a better place. But even so, many people are dissatisfied with everything, especially those who are full of ambition. They bother others with their regrets and pine for the ceremonies and compliments of the fine world. We set little store by that sort of thing here. We who are accustomed to work since childhood feel that this is Canaan when we consider the fertile soil that without manuring brings forth such rich crops of everything. Norway cannot be compared to America any more than a desert can be compared to a garden in full bloom.

I advise ——— to come here before he takes it upon himself to write more books about this country. Thus only can he learn to write the truth. I am convinced that he is greatly mistaken in many things. He does not have to worry about the school system and about churches in this country. Ministers here will travel hundreds of miles to preach the gospel, especially to places where there are no churches, without receiving pay for their services. People here have just as good opportunities to worship God as in Norway. Moreover, let me not forget to give due thanks to your pastor for the splendid truth. . . . *

I am glad that I came here, though things have not always gone according to my wish since I left New York, where I settled at first. That is a distance of 1,500 miles from here as the crow flies, but by the way you travel, it is 2,000 miles. I have bought 160 acres of land which lies in the shape of a quadrangle and is two miles in circumference. The land here is beautiful, but the winter is long with a piercing kind of cold that I have never known the like of before. Moreover, the heat is so intense that sometimes it is difficult to bear long spells of it during our seasons of hard work. Therefore, I do not advise anyone in Norway who is making a good living there to leave it, particularly not older people, for they will not be able to get along. Since they cannot learn the language and are ill suited for hard work, everything will displease them

* The newspaper omits some lines here but says they describe a man who incurred Hovland's displeasure by trying to dissuade him from emigrating.

here. But unattached persons will be able to better themselves. If I live long enough, I plan to visit you some time.

The Almighty Lord will be with you all in your several undertakings. I hope you are well – I am myself well, God be praised.

Cleng Peerson advised us to go to Missouri

[FROM A SETTLER IN MISSOURI TO A FRIEND *]

October 15, 1838

We finally arrived in New York after having been at sea for eight weeks, less two days. There were about seventy passengers on the ship, all Germans, except my fellow travelers from Norway and me. Our accommodation on board the ship was insufficient, and as a result the air was very close and unhealthful. But nobody died, though there was some illness.

We stayed six days in New York until we got our money problems and other affairs settled. Here we met several Norwegians and Danes, among whom was a Norwegian named Cleng Peerson, who has lived in America for about twenty years and knows the country very well, as he has traveled about in almost all of the United States and speaks English fairly well. He advised us to go to Missouri, where he and several Norwegians from the district of Stavanger have made their homes. As he was on his way home, he accompanied us on the long trip across this country, which was quite unknown to us, and this was a great help to us in many respects. In Rochester our group was increased by the family of Ole Reiersen and several other Norwegians.

The trip was very long and difficult, owing to the fact that, because of the unusual drought, the water in the rivers, especially in Ohio, had become so low that the ship ran aground every day or stuck in the sand banks. Then it would take much time and work to get loose again. After much trouble and expense, on October 4 we finally arrived at this place, an area almost entirely uninhabited. A couple of miles farther west the land is completely desolate, until you get to where the Indians live,

* This letter appeared, without a signature, in the *Stavanger Adresseavis*, February 1, 1839.

about a hundred miles from here. We are staying with the nine or ten Norwegians who have made their homes here. None of them has bought the land he has claimed, and most of them do not have any money to redeem it with, so that very soon the land will come up for public sale.

On the whole I had formed a much more favorable idea about the fertility of this land than I actually found to be true. All the way from New York to the banks of the Mississippi, I did not see black mold anywhere but only a soil of a whitish sand, which it is true yielded good crops of wheat and Indian corn, although not without manuring. But the fields of oats and barley looked the way they do in a year of bad harvest in Norway. These grains are said to fail here too, but according to some people, and that is also my own impression, Missouri has the most fertile land of all the states I traveled through. Close to the Mississippi the mold is about three yards deep and under that there is a base of clay, which I could see particularly well at the banks of the river all through the state of Missouri, for the water had carved the soil out in many places and the banks were almost vertical. At the place where we are staying, fifty miles from the river, the mold is only one or two feet deep with a firm base of clay.

Here are large grass-covered plains with bigger or smaller patches of woods in between, so that one may select a piece that has both. It is true that the land here is good, but for a Norwegian or any other foreigner to come this far into the country involves a great many difficulties and privations, even for several years after he has arrived here – privations that can never be completely removed, though they can be lessened somewhat. All the Norwegians I have talked to agree with this. If they had known beforehand what they would have to go through, they would not have undertaken the journey. They have sent many letters to Norway describing the glories of the country, but they never mention a word about the hardships they find here and the difficulties of the journey, about which they now have much to say in conversation.

I, too, have acquired some experience. I shall not go into detail about it, but I think it is my duty to say something. The change in climate causes much illness. During the daytime there is heat here to which we are not accustomed, and the nights are very cool, often with heavy fogs that cause many colds and attacks of ague. Often there is a sudden change from hot to very cold air. To these tribulations must be added the open log cabins, which have chimneys of wood and clay. Only the immediate vicinity of the fire gets warmed up, since there is a draught through the whole house, or rather hut. And yet you have to be thankful if you have such a hut to seek shelter in, in a land that is almost uninhabited. You might think that we would not have to live in such poor houses or travel this far into the country. But only those who have enough money can avoid this, for all land, even in Illinois, has been bought up and can only be had at second hand at prices ranging from $5 to $20 an acre. And as far as building is concerned, it would be very expensive to hire workers. Everybody builds his own log cabin as well as he can, simply with an ax, and for the most part the cabins are without windows. Because of all this, and other matters, I consider it precarious for everyone to go to America. I am thinking especially of N. N. and hope that he has not sold his property; I wish he would wait until I, God willing, have given him more detailed information about this country.

The shortest and cheapest way to get here is via New Orleans and up the Mississippi. From New Orleans it is about 1,800 miles to this place, and this distance is covered on steamboats in ten or fourteen days. But from New York we had a distance of about 2,500 miles, which it took us almost eight weeks to travel, mainly because the route was so difficult. It is a great advantage to bring all kinds of iron tools if you come here. A carpenter's ax, for instance, costs from $3 to $5, and everything else in proportion to this. The transportation is not expensive, since usually you can get your baggage shipped free of charge on the steamboats.

Not a land of milk and honey

FROM SJUR J. HAAEIM, AT MIDDLE POINT, ILLINOIS, TO BISHOP JACOB NEUMANN *

April 22, 1839

Since I now have such a good opportunity to get a letter mailed to my dear native country Norway (the carrier of this letter is Endre Aragebo from Stavanger who is making ready to go back to Norway), I take the liberty of sending you this brief letter, Reverend Sir. My main reason for writing to you is that last summer Johannes Larsen Ulsager from

* This letter appeared in *Bergens Stiftstidende*, March 5, 1840.

Hardanger, in the diocese of Bergen, arrived here, and he had with him a small book entitled *A Word of Admonition to the Peasants in the Diocese of Bergen Who Desire to Emigrate: A Pastoral Letter from the Bishop of the Diocese.* * I picked up this little book at once and asked his permission to read it, which he gave me right away. I sat down and read it through aloud. A great many of the Norwegians living in this vicinity had assembled in the house where we were to hear news from their native country. After I had read from the book for a little while, the women began to cry violently. But some of the men, who were among the first Norwegians who immigrated to America, began to scold me and asked me if I still felt like reading that sort of thing. After that I, too, started to cry and answered them that if they wanted to know the real truth they ought to read this book. But they only continued disagreeing with me. Then I told them frankly that if God the Almighty would help me to save up enough capital to pay my way back to Norway, I should be happier than I could say; and many of those who had arrived there with me said the same. But, unfortunately, we can probably never do this, the way things have turned out for me and many others who would like to go back but who cannot manage to do so because we lack the means.

Now I promise to relate the truth about everything and call God in heaven to witness that I will not say one word that is not true. Most of us left Norway in 1836 and had no better information than some letters written by Gjert Gregoriussen Hovland, who praised both the country and everything in it so that we all imagined that this country must be Canaan, a land of milk and honey, and thought that we should find our countrymen here in very good circumstances. But—unfortunately—when we came to what they called their homes, we saw some huts that looked more like the barricades in Bergen than like anything else, and we could look right through their walls. Another sight caught our eyes: a flock of half-naked children and their parents dressed in rags. In spite

* This book is translated in full by Gunnar J. Malmin in "Bishop Jacob Neumann's Word of Admonition to the Peasants," in *Studies and Records* (Minneapolis: Norwegian-American Historical Association), 1:95–109 (1926). The bishop took as his text Psalms, 37:3: "So shalt thou dwell in the land, and verily thou shalt be fed." An immigrant, taking the bishop to task, amusingly suggested that he had failed to take into account the Biblical injunction, "Multiply and replenish the earth." The immigrants therefore "decided to disobey the bishop's advice and go to the new Canaan, where flowed milk and honey." (Knud Langeland, *Nordmændene i Amerika*, pp. 20–23, and Blegen, *Norwegian Migration*, vol. 1, p. 82.)

of all this, however, we were happy to visit with them, mainly because to them we could speak our own language.

Here, then, we had to start putting up other houses of the kind I have described, and after that every man had to get out and make a living for himself and his family. This was true whether he had owned one of the best farms in Norway or had owned no farm at all. Here we worked the first winter and made a little money. After that some of us wanted to go farther into the country to a state called Missouri, where twelve of us traveled on for another 560 miles and, as we had expected, found land that was not occupied. Here each of us started cultivating a piece of land, and we built houses of the same poor quality I described earlier. We had with us one of the first Norwegian immigrants, who spoke the English language well. The land had been surveyed there and was to be sold, but everybody assured us that it would not be sold for six years. When we had worked it for about three years, however, the land came up for sale, and only three of us were able to buy a small piece. All the rest of us had to give up our land and leave, with no compensation for all our work. Our land was bought by strangers, and we and our families had to go back to the state of Illinois. All this happened last summer.

Shortly after this, illness broke out among the Norwegians, and it was quite pitiful to hear the reports of all this misery. A great many were called away from this earthly existence by the good Lord, and those who survived have not yet regained their health. I was among those who suffered this hard fate. I was laid up last fall, on September 1, and am still not able to earn enough to buy myself a meal.

From my knowledge of them, I shall say a little about the Norwegians who live here. Some of them left Norway because of hatred of the clergy and other officials, others because of hatred of their neighbors, still others because of other vices. When all these come together in one neighborhood, one can imagine what kind of life they lead in these American forests.

Furthermore, there is not a church for a distance of a hundred miles, and we are almost in the worst conceivable state of heathendom in the whole world. Some single persons had decided to go back to Norway, but they died last fall. If these persons had returned home safely, I believe that not so many would have come to America after that.

I could tell a great deal about the Norwegians here, but I do not have enough space. I therefore request that you, Reverend Sir, instruct all my fellow brothers in Christ never to plan on coming over here. I assure them that they will regret it, unless they are among those people who are completely indifferent to everything. I and many others are now in poor circumstances, mainly because of illness. If I dared be so bold as to ask the inhabitants of Bergen if they, out of a loving Christian heart, would be so kind as to give me a little help to enable me to return to Norway with my wife and two children, nothing in this life would make me happier.

It is true enough that the land here is better than in Norway and may be had at a fairly reasonable price, when you can get it at the price settled by Congress. But now all usable land around here is inhabited; now you have to buy it first of those who live on it. This land is called a claim, and later when it comes up for sale, it is bought of the government. And it is true enough that some may manage to do this. But when they are going to settle here, they get to see how it is to live in America. A horse costs $100, a working cart from $80 to $100, a pair of oxen, used for plowing here, from $80 to $100, a cow from $25 to $30. If you leave your home and go on a trip and have to buy food, a meal is three English shillings, that is, one *ort* and twelve skillings in Norwegian money, and a bed for the night is two English shillings, or one *ort*. Thus everything rightly considered, you may well believe that there is not much left of the daily wages, even though they seem to be high.

I thank you most cordially and kindly for your charitable admonition. You are like a true shepherd who takes care of his sheep that go astray. And I assure every Norwegian man that however truthfully I try to write about everything here, I still am not able to depict the truth so well as this little book gave me to understand it.

In Norway I lived on the farm Haaeim in the clerical district of Gravens, Uldvig parish in Hardanger, and I am well known by the minister there, Mr. Røtting, in case you should like to know something about my character from him. E. Aragebo, whom I mentioned earlier, will return to this place. If people in Norway wanted to give me some little aid, it might be sent to me through him, and I should certainly accept it with the greatest happiness and gratitude.

Men of all nations live here like brothers

FROM HANS BARLIEN, AT ST. FRANCISVILLE ON THE DES MOINES RIVER, MISSOURI, TO THE REVEREND JENS RYNNING *

April 23, 1839

I assume that no one who knows the facts has wished to inform you about your son's fate, or has been in a position to do so. Since you probably should know the truth, I shall try to report it to you as well as I can.

Your son himself probably notified you that he had bought land and was living not very far from the city of Ottawa on the Fox River in the state of Illinois, 11.5° west of Washington and 41.5° latitude north, a swampy and unhealthful place which last autumn deprived him and most of the Norwegians there of their lives. The last to arrive there, a group of twenty who had been lured to the place by a Swede, likewise lost their lives along with the Swede.

This news was brought to us by a man who visited that part of the country last year. But neither he nor anyone else knew anything about Rynning's birthplace and parents.

I stayed in St. Louis for sixteen months to find out where the Norwegians were living and also to learn where land is available for those who want to come to America. I have found that all immigrants have let themselves be taken in by the land speculators who have bought up the land, and so settlers have been scattered over almost all of the states. But I have also found land in abundance that is fertile, healthful, and profitable in every respect. On my arrival I approached Congress and the Senate with a recommendation from the American minister in Copenhagen; I therefore expect to get from them a guarantee of the necessary land, so that no land speculator will bother the Norwegians who want to settle here. This land is to the northeast of the Des Moines River and west of the Mississippi, that is, at 41° latitude north and 16° longitude west of Washington. You can claim the necessary land without buying it; and when in ten, twenty, or thirty years it comes up for sale, you can keep what you have claimed at $1.25 an acre, which will be very easy to do then even though you have to start out with nothing.

The most convenient way to get here is to leave from Bergen, that is, when the group that wants to come over here is big enough either to

* This letter appeared in *Morgenbladet* (Christiania), October 10, 1839.

charter or buy a ship and sail north of Scotland direct to New Orleans, and from there take the big steamboats up the Mississippi 1,400 miles (234 Norwegian miles); then you land at Churchville opposite Warsaw at the mouth of the Des Moines River, from where it is 10 miles (1½ Norwegian miles) to this place. A man who is able to buy a cow and some tools may claim land at once and start on his own; but a man who has nothing can get a job at good daily wages, so that soon he will be able to claim his own land.

As the free land I have mentioned is part of the territory of Wisconsin and belongs, so to speak, to no one, it is the freest and is particularly suitable for the founding of a colony.

Our correspondence was interrupted by intervening circumstances, and my earlier letters, together with other papers and books of mine, are now in the hands of my son in Christiania. As a result, the matters mentioned above have not come to the attention of the public in the Old World.

All kinds of people from all nations of the world live together here like brothers and sisters; and in spite of the fact that there are no garrisons of soldiers, police, and the like, you never hear anything about theft, begging, or any noticeable ill will between neighbors. To me everybody is good, kind, and accommodating. Nobody here can take anything away from you by force; but he can do this by cunning, power of money, and forestallment. This I hope to prevent on our claims by the help of Congress and so, in time, to succeed in uniting the Norwegians who are still here.

Speculators who have bought up vast stretches of land have usually got hold of some that is too swampy to be healthful. But since such land is generally very fertile, it is easy for them to lure on to it ignorant people whose way to the grave is thereby considerably shortened.

Since Missouri is a slave state, there are a great many Negroes here. They are held in ignorance and have a superstitious kind of religion, for which they have their own ministers. If a theft is committed, people are sure that a colored person did it, much as a monkey would, so that it is not very difficult to get the stolen goods back; and the thief is given a number of lashes on his bare back, according to the circumstances.

The population of St. Louis is about twenty thousand. My smithy was in a basement facing the street and without a door; yet I never lost any tools, materials, or anything else in my shop, in spite of the fact that in the same house lived eight slaves who were often visited by other colored people passing my basement door. But then they bore me no malice as I was just as pleasant and accommodating to them as to other people.

Since I now live 1,500 miles (about 250 Norwegian miles) from the coast, I know of no better way to get this letter delivered than to send it to New York, to one Miss Laumann from Christian County, requesting her to mail it to Norway.

Give my greetings to all those who are eager for information and tell them that I am as happy here as any person can be, and that those who want to come here may, with a little effort, live just as happily. The cheapest way of getting here is to go from Europe direct to New Orleans and from there take a steamboat up the Mississippi to Warsaw and land on the left bank at Churchville, 10 miles (about 1½ Norwegian miles) from here.

In the hope of remaining in your kind remembrance, I am, reverend sir, your servant.

May the lies be trampled under foot!

FROM GJERT G. HOVLAND, AT MIDDLE POINT,
LA SALLE COUNTY, ILLINOIS,
TO PEDER J. SÆTTEN *

July 9, 1842

I received your good letter of 1836 with great eagerness and was happy to read it. I send you my heartiest thanks for everything it contained. No other letter I have received from Norway surpasses it in content. Now I write for the second time to show my appreciation and in this small way to preserve always the memory of the *brotherly* friendship and association we shared in Norway.

With tender feelings I recall your great desire to come here; and when I consider the straitened circumstances that prevent you from coming, I pity you and especially your children, who certainly would

* Peder J. Sætten had been a teacher in Kobbervig's School, Stavanger. This letter and the one following appeared in *Christianssandsposten*, February 23, 1843. The second letter, which has no separate date or salutation, appears to be a supplement to the first, and was probably also to Peder J. Sætten.

have had a happier future here than in Norway. But perhaps, unknown to me, your fortunes may have changed for the better lately; I should certainly be happy to know that this were so. Word has reached me that you are living in Stavanger, but in what condition I do not know. Several times I have wished that you had come over here at the same time as I did. Then I believe that you would be making a good living now.

Here nobody has to be poor, for I am sure that the man who is willing to take any kind of job he can get and whose wife is a good manager may live far better here on his daily wages, if only they have a simple house to live in. He may even live far better than the farm owners in many places in Norway who eat all their meals from well-laden tables, as compared with the frugal meals the enslaved laborer has to content himself with day in and day out as he and his family go without the necessities of life. Hardly a day passes without my reflecting on how richly God blesses this country every year; and then my heart is moved to pity when my thoughts go back to Norway and I recall the poor people in cities and in the country who had to beg for the bare necessities of life with tears in their eyes. How happy the poor and the landless would consider themselves if they were here, especially those who are honest in purpose and cheerful.

But those who imagine that their every wish will be met without any work are greatly mistaken and will soon be discouraged, like a man from the district of Stavanger who made the trip here a few years ago. Things turned out very differently from what he had imagined; and since he had not been brought up among the class able to cope with difficulties, he returned with his purpose defeated and wholly ignorant about the conditions of the country. The nature of the journey is all that such persons are able to describe — and even that they do inadequately as we see from the sort of books and discourses they concoct to frighten people away from America. Such an attitude is more befitting children than people who call themselves grown up and are supposed to have benefited by higher education.

There is in Norway a book called "The Dawn of Norway" * — I know of no name more suitable for these books on America put out both in Bergen and Stavanger. Everything in them seems misleading, for the truth is replaced by falsehood. We have all been told that "everybody

* A notable satirical poem by J. S. Welhaven.

should speak the truth to his neighbor." Our duty is to guide our neighbor to what is useful for both his soul and body. And we should place the light where it will shine for everybody in the house and not hide it under a bushel and so put it out.

I do not write to persuade anyone either to come here or to stay at home. Everybody, trusting in God, must decide that for himself. The happiness of one person cannot replace that of another, but conscience compels me to reveal the truth to everyone. Some day the omniscient Judge will bring to light everything that is now hidden in darkness and will make known the secrets of the hearts. When I read the productions of Bishop Neumann and others, designed to frighten emigrants away from this country, I am amazed that the word "Christian" can be misused to cover such vain deceit. May the lies be trampled under foot and the truth be made known!

My friend, let me give you a little advice. If you still intend, or plan in the future, to come here and if your means are sufficient to get you across the ocean but not enough to enable you to pay your way any farther without going into debt, then look around for a job and work your way to this place in a little while. But I think it might be best for you to stop in a city called Chicago, sixty-three miles from here, where there are several Norwegians who are doing well. There we shall always have occasion to meet, for in the summer we market our wheat in that city. I would not force my advice on you. Follow God's plan first – and then your own. He who earns a good living in Norway and is getting old had better stay where he is. When we have enough for food and clothes, we should be content. But he who has no steady work and is young will certainly make an advantageous change by coming to this country. Neither I nor the others who have come here and who know the actualities of life in Norway ever miss that country.

Most of all I miss my son, who died three years ago after two months' illness. I shall never be able to forget him. The Lord gave, the Lord took away, blessed be the name of the Lord. I pray that by the grace of God I may spend my earthly life in such a way that we shall meet again in life everlasting before God. Both I and all other Norwegians here are in good health, as far as I know.

I am the owner of 160 acres of beautiful land, a cart, three horses, and as many other animals as I need. Here you can raise as many cattle as you please. The land everywhere is as good as anyone could wish, for everything sowed or planted yields very rich crops without any manuring.

People use much more sense and intelligence here, and they work together for the benefit of the country and the good of the common man. Everything is done in a better way. I read in these false and misleading books or "romances" terrible descriptions of our houses. Here a man builds so that he can actually occupy the house when it is finished – and the better off he is, the more suitably he builds. Many persons in Norway, on the contrary, build so extravagantly that before the house is finished they have lost the ownership of it. I and most of my Norwegian neighbors now own just as good cabins as we had in Norway. If I were known to you and others in Norway as an untruthful man, no one would have to believe my statements; but I swear that every word is true both in this letter and in my earlier ones.

The crops look very rich, both the fall-sown and the spring-sown grains, and will be ready for harvesting soon. If you were here now, you would provide yourself with food for the winter in just a few weeks.

The mail must get off now, so I have little time left though I had much to write about. But this time I shall end my letter to you and your family with my best regards and the sincere wish that the spirit of truth may be in your hearts and aid you in all your worthy endeavors. This is the wish of your far-away friend.

The great in Norway have the upper hand

I have one more thing at heart. Since I have got to know you as a faithful and sincere friend, I am sure that no one could carry out the following request in a better way than you (if it please God, we shall meet again some day and then I will repay you for all your trouble). Would you please, in my birthplace, the clerical district of Askevold in Søndfjord, try to find two of my closest relatives, cousins of mine who were unmarried when I left Norway? They are Hans Hansen, Nordre Gaarden, in common speech called Hauen but written Nordre Folkestad, in Welnæs parish, and the girl Marie Johannesdatter Sannæs in Skiefjorden, Ous parish, in the same clerical district. These two have many brothers and sisters, but I am particularly interested in learning about their personal circumstances. Do they want to come here and are their means sufficient to pay for the journey? I could send them traveling money from here, that is, for their personal expenses. I do not know if they have families, which might be the case.

I wish that all those of my relatives who do not have a secure living were over here, but I do not talk anyone into or out of coming. Everyone must do as he pleases. Personally, I am glad that I got away, and most people here say the same, once they have become familiar with conditions in this country. Even if I had lived in Norway twice as long as I did, I should never have achieved such a fine prospect for making a living in the future as I have now. It is true that I have worked for it, but then everything is rewarded better here. I could get along easily on less than half of what I own. I do not even have to cultivate as much as a third of my land. I own 160 acres, but less than 20 acres, yes half of that, would provide us with food in abundance.

I see from some of these terrible stories circulated about America that food here is very expensive, but we who live here do not know anything about that. A man who is accustomed to work at any kind of job that comes his way will get at least two bushels of wheat in daily wages, sometimes more. If a man here works for one week, he and his family can live well and without worry for two weeks, I am sure of that; but it was not my impression that a simple laborer in Norway could do that, not at the time I was there.

Bacon is bought and sold here in small and large quantities as it is needed, at three Norwegian skillings a pound; meat the same way; butter from four to six skillings a pound. All kinds of tools may be bought here much more cheaply than in Norway, and the quality is good.

These pamphlets on America which are circulated in Norway are to a certain extent written by people who have too little experience of this country. For instance, I read in a book that none of the immigrants is able to build a proper dwelling house for himself. I find many statements like that which are without any foundation in fact and completely false. It makes no difference to us who emigrated. We know everything better here. We know what is true and what is false. But unfortunately many persons in Norway will get the wrong impression, and it may ruin their whole future, especially the future of the needy. The great ones in the country will always have the upper hand; that is why they can issue these misleading descriptions of America.

My friend: Please do not forget what I asked you; if you can, find out everything about my cousins, especially about Hans and Marie. Tell them that I am doing well and that I have no heirs here. I have heard that there are supposed to be two of my wife's sister's children here, but they will not get anything from me. You must not try to put any pressure on Hans and Marie, however, but find out what they really think and let me know. Since they know nothing either about me or about this country, please tell them also that when they come I will give up half of my land for one or both of them. Please write me in detail about yourself and them and send it to me the first chance you get. I shall do the same for you. Two persons are now leaving here who want to return to Norway next spring; they are Cleng Peerson and Elias Svendsen Torvestad from Tysvær parish. When you write, address the envelope this way by writing at the top "Mr." and then "Gjert Hovland."

Best regards to Niels Jondal and his family, but above all my warmest greeting to you from your friend.

I am no emissary to promote emigration

FROM CLENG PEERSON, IN BERGEN, TO THE BERGENS STIFTSTIDENDE *

April 28, 1843

In the *Stiftstidende* for Thursday, April 22 of this year, a correspondent called upon me to "state publicly the real purpose of my present stay in Norway." This request apparently results from the fact that the correspondent regards me as an emissary or recruiting officer for emigrants to North America. Because of this, I consider it my duty to state here, on my honor and conscience, that the sole purpose of my coming to Norway was to visit relatives and friends, from whom I had not heard for three years, and especially to visit my old father, of whose death a couple of years ago I only learned on my arrival.

I traveled from America to London and by way of Hull to Christianssand, thence in four days overland, because of bad weather, to Stavanger, where I have stayed since with friends and relatives. I have

* This letter appeared in *Bergens Stiftstidende*, April 30, 1843.

never set foot in Voss and Hardanger, nor did I ever exchange a word with any of those who now want to emigrate. I did not even bring with me letters from America to these districts, and my own correspondence with my home has been limited to one letter after my first emigration twenty-two years ago. From this everyone will be able to see that I am no appointed emissary to promote emigration, nor a self-established one. I freely admit, however, that to everybody who has asked me about conditions I have spoken unreservedly in praise of North America, on the basis of my experience and conviction of many years, and that on the same basis I have also declared Rynning's book on America to be true and reliable. But Bishop Neumann's pastoral made an unpleasant impression on me and on many others, though we have not, because of this, expressed any hostility toward the Bishop, whose pastoral we naturally realize had no foundation in facts.

I came from Stavanger to Bergen with the steamship *Constitution* and intend to return to North America with Captain Bendixen shortly. I hope that this statement of mine will suffice to establish the utter falsehood of the correspondent's article. Moreover, on further investigation the truth of my statement will readily be corroborated by testimony from other sources.

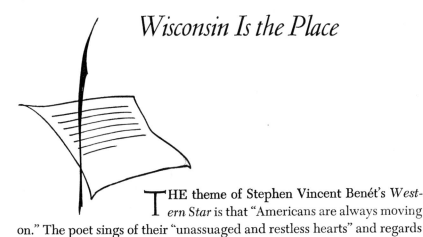

Wisconsin Is the Place

THE theme of Stephen Vincent Benét's *Western Star* is that "Americans are always moving on." The poet sings of their "unassuaged and restless hearts" and regards their mobility as "an old Spanish custom gone astray" or a "sort of English fever." These are poetic guesses that miss the obvious — the vast spaces of America, the waves of young people from the East and from Europe who sought their fortunes in these spaces, and the succession of frontiers that marked the conquest of a continent. Frederick Jackson Turner goes to the heart of the matter when he says that "perennial rebirth," the "fluidity of American life," and the westward expansion of our people have furnished the "forces dominating American character." * Like the Americans generally, the immigrants "moved on" and contributed to the fluidity that Turner noted. The Norwegian was no exception. Sharing in the westward expansion, he pushed northward from Illinois to the rich lands lying to the west of Lake Michigan. He joined Yankee and Teuton in pioneering Wisconsin, entering that future state only seven years after the Indian chief Black Hawk made his last pitiful stand and only three years after Wisconsin emerged as an American Territory, with Madison as its chosen capital.

As a large movement like immigration expands from small beginnings, individuals tend to be lost in a conglomerate, though the letters establish identities and offset the aridity of purely statistical approaches. A half-hundred immigrants from Norway had landed in New York in 1825 — by 1860 in Wisconsin alone there were nearly thirty thousand Norwegians. Mother colonies — among them Muskego, Jefferson Prairie,

* The phrases are from the famous essay on "The Significance of the Frontier in American History," in *The Early Writings of Frederick Jackson Turner*, p. 187.

Rock Prairie, and Koshkonong – had been formed, and from them, on the eve of the Civil War, settlement lines were running throughout the entire Middle West.

As these and other colonies took root, immigrant social and institutional organization began to take shape. Churches, whose spires have multiplied a thousandfold, were started. An immigrant press that ultimately was to witness nearly five hundred separate newspapers was launched. Confronting the initial ordeals of language, illness, and the unfamiliar life of the American frontier, the Norwegian immigrants sought, after the immemorial fashion of human beings, to find poles of stability to cling to. They began gradually to explore and steady their relationships to the larger society, education, and politics of the state and country to which they had so recently come.

The Wisconsin stage of the immigrant saga was marked by exploration and experiment. The newcomers had a boundless curiosity about the land and its resources and people. They were immediately infected by the restlessness of the American frontier. One settlement was no more than begun before it became a jumping-off place for another. There was a drive westward and northward – and there was a turbulent jostling of emigrants newly arrived with those already experienced in New York, Illinois, and elsewhere. But, amid the fluidity, one sees unmistakable signs of the emergence of a more ordered society.

The letters of the time and place take color from given localities. They record episodes and afford casual glimpses. But one reads them with an increasing awareness of drama advanced beyond purely introductory scenes, even though later acts remain to be played by thousands of human beings. Ties with the mother country are intimate and memories fresh, as indeed they are for Americans who today settle in far places of the earth, but, save for a few of the very disconsolate, there is no turning back. And gradually home becomes the American home. By their very ordeals, the immigrants associate themselves with American traditions that reach behind their own *Restoration* to Jamestown and Plymouth Rock.

Returned "American travelers" were treated almost like heroes come back from distant wars. Two brothers, Ansten and Ole Nattestad, pioneering emigrants from the valley of Numedal, had gone to America in 1837, joined Ole Rynning, and settled with him at the ill-fated Beaver Creek colony south of Chicago. In the spring of 1838 Ansten returned to

Norway, carrying with him the manuscripts of Rynning's *True Account of America* and his brother Ole's diary of emigrations, as well as "letters from nearly all the earlier Norwegian emigrants." He made his way down the Mississippi to New Orleans and then to his homeland by way of Liverpool. He managed to get both Rynning's account and his brother's diary published in Norway. The first of the letters that follow is a simple document – a request to the old country for the services of a minister. But behind it is an interesting and even dramatic story. "The report of my return spread like wildfire through the land," said Nattestad later, "and an incredible number of people came to hear news from America. Many traveled as far as twenty Norwegian miles to talk with me. It was impossible to answer all the letters which came to me containing questions in regard to conditions on the other side of the ocean." By 1839 more than a hundred people joined him as he made his way back to the United States.*

When Ansten again reached Illinois, he found that his brother Ole had left the Fox River Settlement the preceding summer and had taken a claim in Rock County, Wisconsin, thus founding the Jefferson Prairie Settlement. Ansten and others promptly joined him, and his letter, published in Norway, was written from that settlement in the autumn of 1839. When Ansten's party, aboard the *Emilie*, was about to sail from Drammen, a young university graduate in theology had delivered a farewell sermon to the emigrants, who hoped that the church department of Norway would ordain this minister for service with them in America. It was to this man, Peter Valeur, that Ansten wrote from Jefferson Prairie voicing the hope that he might decide to come out to the pioneer region, though a formal "call" seemed inadvisable in view of the dispersion and poverty of the emigrants. Valeur failed to understand and grasp the historic opportunity thus afforded him, but the episode is of interest as the first move looking toward Lutheran church organization among Norwegian immigrants in the West.

Meanwhile, the advance of settlers into Wisconsin opened up a different route from that chosen by the Nattestads. One group of Norwegians, arriving at Boston in the summer of 1839, made their way to Milwaukee and there gave up their plan to go on to the Fox River colony in Illinois. A later report recounts that as the Norwegians were prepar-

* For the story of Nattestad and his return to Norway, see my *Norwegian Migration*, vol. 1, ch. 4.

ing to depart for Illinois an American boarded their vessel with a couple of companions, one robust, the other decrepit. The immigrants were at liberty to do as they pleased in a free country, but the American asked them to observe his companions. "Look!" he said, "the robust man is from Wisconsin, where there is a healthful climate and food in abundance. The sick man is from Illinois, where people are destroyed by the burning summer heat and die like flies from the malarial fever." The group gave up the Illinois plan and instead went south of Milwaukee and initiated one of the most famous of all Norwegian settlements, the Muskego colony of Wisconsin.

The time was clearly at hand for some genuine exploration of Wisconsin, and two immigrants of 1839, Johannes Johansen and Søren Bache, assumed this task. In a letter published the next spring in their home town of Drammen, they reported the discoveries they made on a wagon journey from Illinois. Devout Haugeans like so many of the early immigrants, these young men had means far beyond those of the average immigrant, and they were in some sense emissaries from their home district. Their reports were awaited with interest and confidence by many who were dreaming about emigration. Having accomplished their journey, they wrote at great length, taking into account both the drawbacks of life in the West and its potential advantages. They had intended to visit the newly established Muskego Settlement, which in fact they joined the next year and in which they became outstanding leaders, but on this early trip they struck northward to the Jefferson Prairie Settlement and then to lands lying north of that community—the Rock River and Koshkonong regions, where important settlements were to be built later.

Three other immigrants of 1839 struck farther west in Wisconsin, to the lead-mining region, but only after varied and hard experiences while working on the Illinois canal, sailing on a Great Lakes schooner, and fighting the diseases that took so heavy a toll of the early immigrants. Despite their difficulties, they wrote to Norway in 1840 recommending Wisconsin as the best place for immigrants to settle. They could offer no guaranty that "everybody would be happy" in America, but they asserted that, with a single exception, they had heard "no one say that he wished he were back."

Dr. Hans Christian Brandt seems to have been the first trained Norwegian physician to appear among the Norwegian immigrants, and his letter of June 22, 1841, records his first observations of the American scene. He was both critical and caustic. He crossed the ocean with Germans whose extravagant ideas he described as "castles in the air." He looked at the Muskego Settlement in 1840 and then trudged to the Fox River colony, where for some months he practiced medicine. He offered a dark and dismal picture of conditions among the settlers, but his letter must be read with the realization that he saw his countrymen in the very early stages of their difficult struggles to get a foothold in America. Despite disillusionment, he himself remained in the country and ultimately became a highly successful physician in Missouri.

Very different is the contemporary picture drawn by Hans Gasmann, an emigrant of wealth and high standing, formerly a member of the Norwegian parliament, who in 1843 sailed for America. After reaching the interior, he journeyed north rather than south of Milwaukee, settling in the famous Swedish colony of Pine Lake. In addition to taking a claim to 160 acres, he was able to buy a thousand acres outright, and he promptly divided much of his land among four of his sons. His letter, crowded with circumstantial detail, voices satisfaction over the prospects of life in the West.

Norwegians of many different creeds

FROM ANSTEN NATTESTAD, AT JEFFERSON PRAIRIE, WISCONSIN TERRITORY, TO PETER VALEUR *

November 6, 1839

I want to let you know that in the company of several others I reached here, safe and sound, at the end of September. On my arrival in Chicago, I learned that my brother had settled in this place, about ninety miles northwest of Chicago, and was waiting for me. With the others I therefore departed immediately; but when we arrived here, we found that so much land had already been taken that no real settlement of Norwegians could be established here. Most of us consequently will have to move elsewhere to find the kind of place we want. Though there is enough good land to be had here, it will be some time before everybody

* This letter appeared in *Den Norske Rigstidende,* March 1, 1840.

decides where to settle down, for each one usually tries to find the most suitable place to live in. It is difficult to find such places in large enough areas for many families to be able to live together in a community. Here there probably will be only my brother and I.

As far as I can see, it is unlikely that in any one place there will be enough Norwegians to justify calling a minister. It is true that quite a few Norwegian families live in a settlement on the Fox River in Illinois, about sixty miles southwest of Chicago and ninety miles southeast of here; but these are, as far as I can learn, of so many different creeds that a Lutheran minister could not be appointed there. As a result of this and for lack of enough signatures, I regret to notify you that I am unable to complete the application – which it was intended to address to the Norwegian government – to have you ordained as minister for the Norwegians here. If you should decide to come here anyway, which I assume from what you have said, you would be able to function as a minister just the same without being ordained, if the need should arise. The smith Knud Knudsen from Drammen and Clement Stabek have settled about thirty miles west of here. Otherwise no one I know has yet made up his mind where he wants to live, and most of us are staying around here temporarily. At present it is cheap to live here if food is bought at first hand; a barrel of wheat costs only three specie dollars, down in Illinois only two dollars, and fresh bacon six cents a pound.

Best greeting from me and the others.

Many claim better health than in Norway

FROM JOHANNES JOHANSEN AND SØREN BACHE,
AT FOX RIVER, ILLINOIS, TO RELATIVES,
FRIENDS, AND ACQUAINTANCES *

December 31, 1839

We are certain that everybody will be interested in hearing something about our trip, and so we send you the following brief report: On July 15 we left Gothenburg on the ship *Skogsmand*, Captain Rundberg,

* Originally this letter appeared in *Tiden* (Drammen), March 3, 1840. This translation, which is by the Verdandi Study Club of Minneapolis, appeared as "An Immigrant Exploration of the Middle West in 1839" in *Norwegian-American Studies and Records* (Northfield, Minn.), 14:41–53 (1944).

and arrived without incident at Newport Harbor on the second of September. We left on the same day by steamer for New York, reaching there the next morning. Here we stopped only until the evening of the fourth, going by steamer to Albany, where we arrived on the evening of the fifth. We left there the next morning by train for Schenectady. On the evening of the same day we took a canalboat for Buffalo, which we reached on the morning of the fourteenth. We stayed here only three or four hours and then traveled by steamer over Lakes Erie, Huron, and Michigan, to Chicago, where we landed on Sunday, September 22. From New York to this point we had traveled 1,522 English miles.

Here we once more caught up with most of Ansten Nattestad's company. Ansten with a few of his party had that very morning set off for Jefferson Prairie in Wisconsin Territory, about ninety English miles to the Northwest, where his brother Ole had settled last summer. The rest of this group took the same road a few days later. We, on the other hand, set out after a stay of two days for Fox River in Illinois, about seventy English miles to the southwest of Chicago, where most of the first emigrants from Norway now live.

Arriving at this place, we found it a rather discouraging destination for our journey because of all the sickness here – ague and diarrhea – which Ole Rynning reported to be so common among recent emigrants. Here there was not a single house where someone wasn't lying sick. In most houses there were several, and many had died this summer and last, among them Rynning himself. The news of his death was most unpleasant for us, for we had expected to get helpful information from him about many things. He and his company had been very unfortunate in the choice of the land where they settled. It was by a little brook called Beaver Creek, where the ground was so flat and low that after heavy rains it was completely flooded. In the opinion of people with experience, this makes people unhealthy. It is the main cause of the sickness we have referred to. Their attention was called to this situation, but they paid little heed until nearly half of those living there had died. After this the survivors finally left and sought temporary refuge with the Norwegians here. Rynning died last fall, about the end of September, and everyone who knew him testified to his noble character. Many thought that if only he had been fortunate enough to find a more suitable place to settle, he might still be alive.

During the last two summers sickness has been more prevalent than usual. The reason for this is thought to be the unusually great drought and heat, which made the rivers shrink and the swamps dry up. This evaporation is considered harmful to the health. We believe the sickness here must be attributed to the climate's sudden alternation of cold and heat. This is very noticeable here as compared with our climate at home. When we arrived here about the end of September, the cold was so severe one week that it partially froze at night, whereas a part of October was as hot as the dog days are at home in the warmest summer. These changes are said to happen often so suddenly that a person dripping with sweat from the heat scarcely has time to pull his jacket on before he feels the harmful effects of the surprisingly sudden cold. We certainly admit that the sickness is largely the result of such conditions and consequently will afflict to some extent nearly everyone who has not become hardened to them. But we can't help saying – and several people agree with us – that the wretched houses these folks live in contribute to the sickness.

An ordinary living house is built here in one day – at least up to the roof. Its walls are so open that in many places there are three or four inches between logs, and in the winter these openings must be filled in with wood splinters and clay to make the house reasonably tight. Some of this chinking falls out and leaves holes so large that a cat could almost pass freely in and out. People seldom have more than one room, which must serve as kitchen, dining room, and bedroom. There is a loft overhead which is far from being as tight as an ordinary hayloft in Norway, and this must serve as a bedroom when there are more people in the house than there is room for downstairs. It is highly probable that such accommodations, which are so exposed to draft and drifting snow that sometimes the beds are almost covered in the morning with a foot of heavy snow, must have harmful results on the health of those who are used to snug, warm houses. Sometimes the cold here is at least as severe as what they were accustomed to. In fact, one feels the cold even more here on the flat prairies, where there is no protection against the sharp, penetrating north wind.

We do not know, and can only guess, the reason for this poor method of building, but we think that it comes from the American's bent and necessity to move from one place to another. When a person has got a piece of land cultivated enough so that he can earn a little from it, he sells it and begins on a new piece. It sometimes happens that for one reason or another he is obliged to move yet again, without the slightest compensation for his house or the cultivation of his land. Fear of loss has in this way made it necessary for him to build simply. Some of the Norwegians, however, have now begun to put up better houses.

Coming from Chicago to this place we had our first opportunity to see something of the country, which was chiefly prairie, with small wooded sections of oak here and there at intervals of several Norwegian miles. Everywhere the ground was covered with luxuriant grass and with beautiful flowers that still were in full blossom. That the soil here is extremely fertile we could see from the large amount of wheat, corn, and oats that already had been harvested and stood in stacks on the cultivated fields.

The extent of what is under cultivation is most insignificant compared with what is wilderness. It is probable, moreover, that the largest part will always remain wilderness because of lack of woods for building material and fuel for settlers. As far as the quality of the soil is concerned, we assume that what Rynning and others have reported is absolutely correct: that without cultivation it will yield the most luxuriant growth of all sorts, even to the finest kitchen vegetables, and with much less effort than at home.

This year has been unusually productive. As a result, provisions can be had at very low prices. A barrel of wheat (240 pounds, English weight) costs $2; a barrel of corn $1; a barrel of oats $1; a pound of salt pork 5 Norwegian skillings; a pound of meat 3 skillings; and so forth. Wages, on the other hand, are very high by comparison — a half-dollar and board a day for a day laborer in the winter, and $1 to $1.50 a week for a servant girl. She receives as much as $2 if she understands the language. It is easy for girls to find work at any time, whereas it is sometimes hard for men to find work in the wintertime, since the farmers themselves have little to do then. Wages in the summer are usually a dollar a day plus board, however, and one can therefore earn enough to live on the surplus in the winter — and still save money.

This is true if a person keeps his health, but unfortunately many have lost their health during the past two summers. Some have been sick from twelve to sixteen weeks, and many have died. This has been particularly true of the latest arrivals. Of one party, most of whom came from Voss, fourteen or fifteen died. They arrived in Chicago in the severest heat of last summer. Most of them were poor people who had put more than they owned into the expenses of their journey and were forced to get work at once in order to live. Many of them took to canal digging as the steadiest and most profitable – but also the most strenuous and unhealthful – work here during the summer. Most of them came down at once with sickness and were brought to the hospital in Chicago, where only a few escaped death.

Our intention was not to look for land here at Fox River, as we had been informed previously that nothing was available at government prices. Even if there had been, we did not consider it wisest to settle here where the climate, more than in many other places, was so likely to bring on illness. But we did find it advisable to stop here to seek guidance and to consider in which direction we ought to go to find the best accommodations.

The report we had about Missouri did not encourage us to go there, since it lacked good water as well as other necessities. Before coming we had heard Wisconsin Territory mentioned as the place which at the moment was the most popular objective for immigrants. Several persons from Tind, who had arrived before us, had taken that route and settled in the neighborhood of a town called Milwaukee, situated on Lake Michigan. Since this district lies north from here, we assume that the climate there is more healthful and more like the climate Norwegians are used to. So we decided to make a trip there to see it. In addition, plenty of forest and land is said to be available there at government prices.

After a stay of about a month here, we rented a horse and a small wagon, and on October 31 three of us set out. We crossed Fox River about eight English miles above here and took the road to Jefferson Prairie situated about ninety miles away, in Wisconsin Territory, only two English miles from the Illinois border. Here we met Ole and Ansten Nattestad, with most of those who had come with Ansten last summer. Ole had put up a house and plowed as much ground as necessary to raise enough for his own needs, and this year he had his first harvest, which was excellent.

We assumed that the country here was healthful, since there had been no sickness, yet none of those who had arrived last summer seemed to want to settle here because the most and best of the forests had been bought up already. They intended, as we did, to have a look at the country farther north, where, we were informed, there was more and better forest land. But they wanted first to hear the results of our trip. They were all well and seemed to be satisfied, since they were earning good wages by working for the neighboring farmers. But because of the unusual scarcity of money, they were forced to take their earnings in provisions and received a fourth of a barrel of wheat and board per day.

After spending two days here, we continued our journey as first planned, in the direction where the above-mentioned Norwegians had settled in the vicinity of Milwaukee, located about seventy English miles from here. We had covered a distance of about twenty miles on this road when we met a man who seemed to have some knowledge of the surrounding country. He was of the opinion that it would be better to take the opposite route, which went west from here to a place called Fort Atkinson on Rock River, on the other side of which there was said to be more suitable land with sufficient forest. It was already late in the fall, and we considered it doubtful, if we followed our original plan, whether we should be able to reach our objective before snowfall. We therefore took his advice, and after a little more than a day's journey we arrived at the place mentioned above.

Here we had to ferry across the river, and as there were no special roads in the direction we were to travel, the ferryman advised us to leave our wagon with him and borrow a saddle that we might take turns in using. He seemed to be intelligent and to know the lay of the land in the vicinity very well, and we accepted the necessary directions that he kindly gave us and started off, continuing west. We were just under 43° north latitude and about seventy miles farther north than when we started the trip.

The land nearest the river was very low and flat and thinly covered with large and small oak trees. When we had gone about three English miles farther, we came to hills with small valleys that were something new to us. Now the land began to rise, and when we had ascended what we considered the highest elevation, we climbed a knoll to get a view of the surroundings. To our way of thinking, it was the finest view on our whole trip. In all directions little valleys and elevations ran quite regularly from north to south and from west to east, all well covered with large oaks except at the foot of the hills. From our vantage point, the land sloped away gradually so that we could see rather far, and we sighted a pretty little lake in the distance, right in the direction we were headed. After a gratifying look, we journeyed on. To make a more satisfactory inspection we planned to put up for the night and arrived at the appointed place at eight o'clock in the evening.

We found lodging with a Mr. Snele, who had located here this summer and was the only inhabitant in the seven miles we had covered. Beyond him there was no one. He had built his house on the shore of the little lake we had seen, and he had a very fine place. The next morning our host was kind enough to accompany us to look over the land farther west. The prairie recommenced about three miles from his home. Within about a mile of our destination we had to cross a little stream called the Koshkonong Creek. Here land had been bought up and a town laid out, but building had not yet begun. In this stream there was water enough at all seasons for a mill, but there was little current. Even so, it seemed possible that a dam could be made. The land was low on the side of the creek from which we came, whereas on the other side it was higher and steeper. We had quite a distance to climb before we reached the top and could see the prairie.

When we gained the summit, there unfolded before our eyes a grassland which in appearance and luxuriance resembled the finest and most cultivated fields in Norway. Unfortunately the lack of trees made it unsuitable for settlement. Time prevented our going farther as there was no place ahead where we could find shelter. Reluctantly we had to return with our host and spend another night with him.

During the past summer a band of Indians had wandered about in this vicinity. As none had been seen for the past six weeks, it was assumed that they had withdrawn to the western woods where they generally stayed during the winter. Our host regarded them as a peaceful people who roamed about to hunt and fish.

Of all we had seen on our trip, we liked best the stretch of country between Rock River and our host's place, if such were obtainable at government prices. As some had been sold and no one could show us what was still available, we had to let everything else wait until we could get the necessary information at the Milwaukee Land Office. It was not convenient to do so on this trip, however.

The next morning we left our friendly host and hostess, hoping we should meet again. We retraced our steps until we crossed the river. From there we took another way, which first followed the stream, and we happened upon several pretty, new towns. The whole country was very attractive and, where there were trees, it was bought up and settled. Otherwise our journey lay over immense prairies where the grass had for the most part been burned down. One of the prairies we crossed is supposed to be about three hundred miles long. After an absence of about three weeks, we returned to the settlement, where we intended to rest until open roads next spring should allow us to investigate further.

We were gratified to learn that health conditions in Wisconsin were usually good. Where people lived close to the streams, only a few cases of the diseases mentioned had appeared during the summer. In the past fourteen or fifteen years, even these had been new to the region.

Realizing that many of you would like to have our opinion about the advantages one can with certainty expect by coming to America, we can state that anyone who is steady and has the desire and the ability to work will, as far as we have hitherto experienced, always find a good subsistence here.

If you lack the necessities of life for your family and believe the future holds no promise for the better, then you should try America.

To be sure, during the past two years, sickness and death have been prevalent. It can be said of many, "He sought a living but unfortunately found death." This has not always been true, however. In only a few places have diseases been as common and dangerous as here, and many cases have been the result of personal carelessness. Many people have lived here for years without sickness and claim better health than in Norway.

Anyone who has decided to come and has the means to assist others must guard against spending so much that he will lack money with which to buy land on his arrival. Many have become financially embarrassed because of the dishonesty or the death of their debtors. A person who has the opportunity would be smart to inquire of friends who are there as to the best opportunities for the purchase of land.

On account of the high wages and low prices there is little advantage at the moment in working more land than necessary for home use. It would be worth while to bring a good supply of work clothes and bedding. When freight is figured, it is just as cheap to buy heavy articles here. It does not pay to bring guns to sell.

Concerning business, we believe that thorough experience and understanding of the people and their financial system are necessary for hope of success in such a venture.

The laws grant everyone freedom from liability for debts when he moves out of the state. Many take advantage of this fact and become swindlers even though they could pay. Each state has its own bank as well as many branch banks, of which some are always insolvent. All have their own paper money, and, besides, there is always much counterfeit money in circulation. Finally, gold and silver coins of all kinds are valuable as a medium of exchange when they are made of pure, precious metals. It is useless to bring Danish marks and smaller coins of impure silver. On the other hand, larger Norwegian and Danish silver coins and new Norwegian marks are exchangeable for full value. Outside of American money, English sovereigns and five-franc pieces are used here mostly. The first is worth $4.84 and the latter $.94.

As I have said before, tilling the soil under present conditions is not important, but cattle-raising would be profitable under good management. On the large prairies, which offer food for millions of livestock, there is opportunity to feed as many animals as one is able to gather sufficient winter food for. In the fall these prairies are burnt over, a practice doing more harm than good. In spite of the abundance of feed, stock prices are high – a cow brings from $16 to $30, and a pound of butter $.25 in the winter but only half this in the summer. The reason for this difference is that few animals are kept in the winter because they freeze for lack of good barns.

Low-lying, swampy places breed fevers

FROM ANDERS WIIG, BRYNNILD LEQVE, AND JOHANNES WIIG, IN IOWA COUNTY, WISCONSIN TERRITORY, TO FRIENDS *

January 11, 1841

We weighed anchor in Gothenburg on May 27, 1839, and landed at Fall River on August 2. From there to New York the distance is 140 miles. To get there we had to change steamboats once, but since we joined an excursion that was on its return trip, this passage only cost a dollar a person. On our arrival in New York, a Norwegian named Roger William at a transportation office helped to arrange passage for

* This letter appeared in *Bergens Stiftstidende*, July 29, 1841.

us from New York to Chicago on these terms: Every passenger had to pay $14.00 and was allowed to take along free fifty pounds of baggage on the canalboat and a hundred pounds on the steamboat, but for every additional hundred pounds we had to pay $1.50. Lars's children went along free. From New York to Buffalo is a distance of 504 miles, which we covered from the tenth to the eighteenth. In Buffalo we boarded a steamboat on the nineteenth and arrived in Chicago on the twenty-fifth and had thus put 1,585 miles behind us. On this trip the steamboat touched at many towns, especially to take on firewood since coal is not used here.

On our arrival, we were extremely dissatisfied, both because it seemed difficult to find employment and because of the climatic diseases raging here. These are fever ache [malaria], bilious fever, and scarlet fever, each of which appears under many forms. Fever ache, the most common and also the longest lasting, seldom kills if it does not develop complications—and this often happens. It is also called the "shakes," because it regularly, depending on its severity, daily or every second or third day, causes a violent shaking both when it abates earlier or resumes later in the day. It weakens the nervous system to such an extent that anyone who has suffered one attack is in danger of another the following year unless he exercises great caution. After five or seven years, according to report, however, patients are quite recovered.

Many die of bilious fever, from which we have all suffered, though in different ways. This ailment upsets the stomach and disturbs the circulation of the blood, and you cannot get well by letting the illness take its course. If you see a competent doctor at once, however, he will usually be able to cure you in a short time. Scarlet fever, from which few people suffer except children, is said to be contagious. It swells and blocks up the throat and, if a doctor is not available, will kill the sufferer in a few days. These diseases are found in Illinois, Indiana, Michigan, Missouri, and Wisconsin, but in varying degrees according to the locations of the several districts, some being almost completely free of them. Areas around rivers are unhealthful everywhere, as are places where canals have been or are being constructed, and, in short, spots where there is stagnant water or that are low-lying and swampy. Besides, you have to remember to take good care of yourself. It is dangerous to work hard in severe heat, to walk around with wet feet, or to get drenched by rain.

As to employment and wages, everything is now very different here from what it was when Rynning wrote, and this is also true of prices of victuals and clothes, which vary from place to place. As far as we know, monthly wages at the present time are these: in the northern part of Illinois for farm hands $10 to $15; for a sailor $16 to $20; for a captain, who does not have to be a navigator, from $40 to $50; for canal laborers from $12 to $20. These wages only vary with the seasons; otherwise they are the same for everybody, for a man that knows the language and for a man that doesn't. But in the southern part of Illinois wages are lower and in Indiana and Missouri still lower, except where Missouri borders on the Mississippi. In the western part of Michigan and the northern part of Illinois wages are the same.

It must be noted that it is not always easy to get work in the places I have mentioned, except on the canal-building project where some work is done all through the winter, although not so much as during the summer. But though some Norwegians have worked there, I do not advise anyone to go there – partly because of lack of other employment and partly because of unfamiliarity with the language. Apart from the fact that the work there is almost unbearably hard to an immigrant, diseases are more prevalent there than in any other place, and daily reductions in wages of a quarter, a half, and so on are made when work is stopped by storms or for other reasons. Natural phenomena like snow and ice often make it necessary to interrupt the work, and shipping on the lakes is discontinued for four or five months. What I have said thus far about working conditions applies to men. Women, especially young girls, will be able to do relatively better. Even in Chicago, through which so many emigrants pour, Norwegian girls are in great demand. Until they have learned a little English, they get only a dollar a week, but later from $1.50 to $2.00, and because of the high regard in which women are held in this country, they are exempt from all kinds of outdoor work and so are far less exposed to disease.

The prices of victuals in Illinois and in most districts of Wisconsin are as follows: flour, grade A, from 2 to 2½ cents for a half-pound, grade B 1 to 1½ cents; smoked bacon 8, salted bacon 8, fresh bacon 3½ to 4 cents; meat 4 to 5 cents; butter 10 to 25 cents; potatoes 18 to 25 cents a bushel; sugar 12 cents, and coffee 18. Clothes and everything else have gone down, and wages therefore remain proportionately high.

Now to get back to ourselves – when we arrived in Chicago we met Gunder Tvedte. He was out of money, and his son was so ill that it was believed he would die, as actually happened a few days later. Together with him, Niels Wambheim, Lars Spilten, and Ole Svelgen, we went up to the canal, but we left after a few days, discouraged both by the hard work and especially by the diseases raging there. We returned to Chicago, where all three of us, for $18 a month, shipped on board a schooner whose skipper was a sailor from Trondhjem. When we had been on board for ten days, Anders fell ill, and he and Johannes had to go ashore. He received daily calls from a doctor, and Johannes had to stay with him all the time, as the fever was so severe that there was hardly any hope that he would live. After three weeks the fever left him, but he was then so emaciated and weak that another two months went by before he was able to work.

On the same day, all those of our countrymen that I have mentioned were brought from the canal into the poorhouse of the city, where the incompetent doctor in charge tried to alleviate their diseases, already far advanced. All the men died first, later the wives, with the exception of Niels's wife. This created such a stir, however, that the other doctors intervened and severely reprimanded the doctor in question in the newspapers. The children of Ole and Lars were placed with good people. Immediately afterward Johannes fell ill, but his fever was not severe and, as he had a good doctor, he did not suffer too much.

A visit from a doctor costs a dollar here, but since we were regarded as poor we only paid half a dollar. On one occasion, we asked a lawyer if a person who has not been examined is able to practice medicine here. He answered that in the old states he had seen doctors present a large white certificate or *Testimonium Academicum*, but here it was sufficient to fill your shelves with books, then you could start practicing; and, he said, when you call in a doctor, you attach more importance to his having practiced successfully than to his *Testimonium Academicum*. Doctors are not appointed to any one district but settle down where they see the best chances of making a living.

During this time Brynnild was well and in the fall had very good wages; but later, work became so scarce that we did not make more than we spent, as we had to pay $2 a week for board and lodging. At the end of March, Johannes and Johannes Sevareid from Karmsund shipped on board the schooner mentioned earlier, which is now owned by the man from Trondhjem, and they get $16 a month. B. and A. got jobs on the canal project for $16 a month. They worked in a place where the canal, which is 82 feet wide and 18 feet deep, is laid for a stretch of fifteen miles through a whole mountain. For every cubic yard dug out of the mountain the government of the state pays $1.50, and by way of financial support, it has been given every sixth section of land in Illinois by the government of the United States. The canal is to connect Lake Michigan with the Mississippi.

In June B. fell ill, and so they returned to Chicago, where he was soon cured by a good doctor. After that he bought horses and a cart and drove to Wisconsin. On their arrival here, they got a job cutting firewood for a smelting hut at six skillings a cord. A cord is 8 feet long and 4 feet high [and 4 feet wide]. Usually each man cuts two cords a day, sometimes a half more and sometimes a half less. At the end of September Johannes arrived here; both he and the rest of us are well, and the last couple of months we have had a raise in pay of $2. We now manage on our own, work together, make good money, and are very satisfied. The neighborhood here (about two or three counties) is called Lead Mines because there is a lot of lead here. Besides, the farming land is good. It is a little uneven and hilly and everywhere richly supplied with water, which is lacking in Illinois.

A considerable amount of government land is still available here, but in Illinois it is now almost impossible to get good land without buying it from speculators. If anyone finds minerals in the land he has bought, he may keep these as his property; but in places where they have already been found, he cannot yet buy under the present arrangement. In a few places known to contain minerals a down payment of a fifth is demanded. Because of the higher and more northerly location of this state, it is far more healthful here than in the other states I have mentioned. Last summer we heard practically nothing about illness; and everybody agrees that Wisconsin, or the Wisconsin Territory as it is sometimes called, since it has not yet been admitted to the Union, is the most healthful in the United States. No one will catch climatic diseases here unless he undermines his constitution by riotous living. In short, this state is definitely the one we recommend to immigrants.

But although we do not think that anyone who wants to come here should allow himself to be discouraged by fear of illness, and although it is our conviction that every industrious and able-bodied person will make a better living here than in Norway, yet our purpose is not to persuade anyone to come out here. Rather we would dissuade those who are already making a good living. For people's tastes and ways of thinking are so different that it is impossible to say with certainty that everybody would be happy here. But we do affirm that we have heard no one say that he wished he were back, except Sjur Jørgensen who, against the wish of his wife, set his mind on this — a most peculiar decision in the opinion of all Norwegians here.

Well-to-do people should not come here

FROM DR. HANS CHRISTIAN BRANDT, IN WISCONSIN, TO FRIENDS *

June 22, 1841

On May 18, 1840, I embarked in Hamburg to go to New York, where I arrived after a voyage of sixty-seven days. The crossing was difficult and unpleasant. The excessive gaiety of my fellow passengers — some thirty Germans — was not calculated to put me in a good mood, for I was constantly musing on what the future might bring. The conceptions my fellow travelers had formed about America surprised me not a little, as they revealed a great deal of ignorance of the states to which they were going. It seemed to them that America had been discovered very recently: Columbus was still on St. Salvador, Cortes in Mexico, and so on. The object of their journey was to get gold and silver, and they were always talking about this. They seemed to be under the impression that New York's roofs, streets, and alleys were covered with these precious and rare metals and that they were even easily accessible in the rivers. The thing was simply to reach America: with bags full of pure gold they would then return and in the Old World spend what the New World had so generously given them. They were artisans and mechanics and had just enough money to pay their passage across the ocean. But soon, of course, they were disillusioned. Shortly after their arrival in New York, they met some of their countrymen whose truthful accounts completely destroyed their beautiful castles in the air. Hardly one of them got a job as a skilled worker in his occupation, and most of them had to get work at canal-digging, the coal mines, the railroad, and so on.

Everything is here as it is in Europe, only with somewhat greater ac-

* This letter appeared in *Morgenbladet*, September 18, 1841.

tivity. In New York there are a great many foreigners, and many an educated youth of considerable promise there associates with drunkards and good-for-nothings. The prospects seemed somewhat dubious to me, but I was encouraged by an acquaintance I had made during the voyage. I had become the friend of Baron Mattilz, who had left his native country because of his republican views. I spent twenty-five days with him in New York, and it was only chance that I did not make my home in this wonderful city. Mattilz had offered me a loan sufficient to establish a dispensary, which is almost a requisite for the practice of medicine. But first I had to learn the English language, and the time that was required for this I was to spend with Mattilz. In the meantime, Anchersen arrived with some Norwegian emigrants, among whom were farmer Heg and his brother-in-law from Lier. They asked me to go with them, for I might be of use to them as I knew German, and the area they were to travel through was full of Germans.

I accepted their offer, and we went up the Hudson River, through a canal three hundred miles long, and via Lakes Ontario, Huron, and Michigan to Milwaukee, a city of 1,800 inhabitants in Wisconsin Territory. On this trip I was lawyer, doctor, minister, mediator, everything. A child that was born on the Atlantic was overlain, and I had to function at the burial ceremony. Some of our travelers spent a great many "two-skillings" and other Norwegian coins as current money; they were arrested by the police, and I had to be mediator, interpreter, and lawyer and was successful in my pleading on their behalf. A woman fell ill in Milwaukee and gave birth to a child in a cool night out in the open, and here too I had to function as doctor, police officer, and clergyman, this last at the baptizing of the child.

Twenty miles from Milwaukee there is a Norwegian colony consisting of about twelve families from Numedal, Telemark, and Stavanger. They arrived in the autumn of 1839, bought land at once, and built good Norwegian timber houses. In the same place Bache, Johansen, and Heg have settled and bought a considerable amount of land. It is all wooded, high, and with very good soil. The colonists that have settled here are satisfied and live a quiet, happy life in good understanding with one another. Farther up in Wisconsin there is another colony of emigrants from the autumn of 1839. I did not go there, but it is said that they do not get along too well.

After a stay of a day and a half among these Norwegian farmers, I took a small traveling bag on my back and set out on foot toward the Norwegian colony in Illinois, 150 miles away. On this trip I had to walk through uncleared forests and prairies at first, at times for seven or eight hours without seeing a single human being or a house. Finally I found the main road and then everything was fine. I had seen little illness in Wisconsin, but as soon as I entered Illinois it was common; in almost every house people were suffering from the ague.

The Norwegian colony in Illinois, which consists of some thirty or forty families, is located 150 miles southwest of Chicago between the cities of Ottawa and Charleston, fourteen miles from the Illinois River. A vast prairie here is crossed by the main roads from St. Louis and other cities, and there are Norwegians living on all the various roads. The settlers include earlier as well as more recent immigrants. They all have a good deal of land, some two or three hundred acres with horses, cows, and so on. They live well. For the most part they are ignorant, as unfamiliar with the institutions of their native country as with those of the United States, indifferent to the common good, and sometimes quarrelsome among themselves. Religion means nothing to them whatsoever; they have abandoned its principles completely, and they even leave their children unbaptized and bring them up in deep ignorance. To make a living here as a clergyman would be out of the question. A couple of so-called "holy men" from Stavanger preach and interpret the Bible, but they do not have much of a following, for people know that they are undependable. For four months I practiced as a doctor among these people, but I should have starved to death if I had stayed there, since they would not even pay for the medicine.

At Beaver Creek there is not one Norwegian left. Ole Rynning was practically the last one. He made many sacrifices for the Norwegians, paid the passages of several of them and helped them in everything, and when he himself became destitute he worked with all his might to get on his feet again. One month he worked at the canal, digging, which contributed considerably to the undermining of his health. In the middle of the winter he once walked over a prairie almost barefooted. He was close to his home but could not reach it without help. He was almost frozen to death, when people found him and brought him home. He was then attacked by the ague and later by typhoid fever, which ended his life. Those who owed him money denied it after his death, and his belongings were sold at a ridiculously low price. This is the way the

Norwegian farmers honor the memory of the man to whom they owe so much, the man who made so many sacrifices for them! The little book he published was based on the accounts of others rather than on his own experiences, and if he had lived, he would have changed many things in a new edition.

In Missouri there was a Norwegian colony which has now moved to Iowa Territory. Here live the emigrants Hans Barlien and Hans Agger, who has married and is a competent quacksalver. I have seen an application from Hans Barlien to the Norwegian king for 100,000 specie dollars as compensation for his ill usage by Norwegian officials. He stayed a long time in St. Louis to devise an improvement in steam engines by which water, gas, and fuel might be saved. But poor Barlien! the engine would not run.

[*Morgenbladet* summarizes the next portion of Brandt's letter: Brandt declares that his expectations have not been fulfilled. He complains of dishonesty in public administration, lust for money in many Americans, and especially of the many swindlers who profess to be practicing medicine. He believes that Americans have little interest in scientific research, but finds general education good in states like Massachusetts, Pennsylvania, Indiana, Ohio, but neglected in other states. Brandt then goes on to discuss the advisability of Norwegians' emigrating to America.]

I advise the student, whether of law, theology, or medicine, against going to America. I know that Danish, German, and even Norwegian students have had a hard time making a living, and even competent graduates have had to take undignified jobs as bartenders. Offices are crowded, and clerks are found in abundance. There are also many artisans, but perhaps tanners, shoemakers, tailors, or carpenters might find it easier to make a living here than in Norway, especially in the western states. The seaport towns and the larger cities are everywhere so crowded that workers and artisans are often unemployed for periods of six months or more.

The only one I advise to come here is the farmer, although not the one who is wealthy and making a good living in his native country, for he will have too great difficulties and wish that he were back home again. Everything goes against him: language difficulties bother him, he gets into wild forests or vast prairies where he often has three to seven miles to his nearest neighbor. There is no church, no divine service, no friends or acquaintances; in short, everything is unfamiliar. To hire laborers to work on the farm is very expensive, and because of this and the low prices on grain, it is often difficult to make a profit on the large farms. Besides, the well-to-do foreigner is in grave danger of being exploited in some way. I know many people who have come over here with capital and have suffered considerable losses, while those who had nothing have learned to work ahead to success through adversity and tribulations. This is true of the Norwegian farmers; several of those who had capital have suffered setbacks – others, on the other hand, who had nothing, now own homesteads. Thus I advise only those to come here who have the funds necessary to pay for their passage and to buy forty acres of land, though twelve acres may be enough for a family, as the land is fertile. I advise people to select places that are elevated, half prairie and half forest. I prefer Wisconsin to Illinois; it is higher, has fewer swamps, is more healthful and on the whole more fertile. Besides the water is bad in Illinois but good in Wisconsin, and the best areas in Illinois have been brought up by speculators.

Employees are not treated here as servants

FROM HANS GASMANN, AT PINE LAKE, NEAR MILWAUKEE, TO HIS BROTHERS-IN-LAW AND SON-IN-LAW *

October 18, 1843

I know that you, my dear friends, and many others expect to see some lines from me, and I ought to have written to you long ago. I have not done so sooner because I promised several persons in Norway to tell them about America, and I thought that the longer I postponed writing, the more nearly complete I could make the report. Now I know that my stay here has not been long enough to enable me to give a satisfactory account. I imagine it would not help much even if I postponed writing yet longer, as greater experience and knowledge are needed before one can make a fairly complete report that might serve as a useful guide to my dear countrymen.

On August 3 we landed at the city of Milwaukee, where I found accommodation for my family while I traveled up the country to look for

* This letter appeared in *Christianssandsposten*, December 22, 1843.

land. After I had looked around a little I came to the place where Ellev Bjørnsen Tungen lives, about twenty-six miles northwest of Milwaukee by a lake called Pine Lake. Here I found the land very beautiful, neither flat nor very hilly, but pleasantly sloping. The woods are not dense here but have attractive openings. That is, the trees are scattered so that you can plow between them, and when you see this land, it looks like a garden full of large fruit trees. I know of no better comparison to anything in Norway than to Mr. H. Møller's fields at Porsgrund. The beauty of the land is increased by the great number of lakes and rivers. These lakes are full of fish, and in the rivers are many water mills. I like the land here extremely well. A drawback is that the government has decided that a canal is to be dug from Milwaukee to this area, and a company received a contract to do this. The work was begun, then stopped, and the government has brought a suit against the company. Until this suit is settled, the land – five miles on either bank of the projected canal – cannot be sold; for no one knows what the price will be. If the canal is finished, the price of the land will be $2.50 an acre; but if the canal comes to nothing, the price will be half of this, that is, the same as for other land. In the meantime, anybody who likes may claim this land ("to claim" is to take possession of a piece of land and work it without paying for it right away). Generally land that is claimed has to be paid for within one year, but this canal land cannot be paid for until the suit is settled, which may not be for four or five years.

Many of my countrymen who came here with me have taken out claims. They are Tollef Wase, David Førre, Aslak Møe, Torkild Listuel, Daniel Ballestad, Peder Maueraasen, Ole Bougerød, Tosten Dagsrød, and Svennung Lien of Bøe. I took out a claim to a quarter section, that is 160 acres, to live on until I had looked around more and bought land, for it is cheaper to live in the country here than in the city. I have now been building and live in a very beautiful place by a small lake and surrounded by oak trees almost as in a garden. But you may well believe that the buildings are not large or elegant. In America people are very frugal in this respect; first you cultivate your land, and later, when you have earned enough to make a living, you build. Besides, the boards you would need for roofs and the like are very expensive here, not for lack of forest or of sawmills – for here are many sawmills and everybody is surrounded by forest – but since all wages are high, lumber, because of the sawing, becomes expensive. My house, therefore, consists merely of a living room, kitchen, pantry, with two small upper rooms and a little clothes closet – that is all. In addition to this, although it is usually not done here, I have built a stable and barn for my livestock. I have two very beautiful brown driving horses, four driving oxen, four milch cows, and two big calves that came along with the cows. A shed for the hogs is not used here; the hogs go out all the time, feed themselves on acorns, and in the fall grow so fat that it is impossible to get them any fatter. Thus you can have as many hogs as you like here without the least expense.

Our neighbors are pleasant, and our social life very genial. Quite a few Swedish families, of whom some belong to the nobility, are living here, as is also a very interesting Dane who arrived here last summer.

When I had built a house so that I could bring my family up here, I looked around for more land. Nothing I found pleased me more than the land about five to six miles northwest of where I am living at present. Here I have bought a thousand acres of land. I had planned to buy more; but since taxes here (although they are most insignificant), would increase the more land I bought, as they are computed according to one's visible property, I would not buy more right away. Taxes on other property are based on your own statement, and usually they do not amount to much. Probably many people in other countries are surprised that the American government can function with such a small income in taxes; but the Americans have learned to apply the old saying "to live within one's income." Doubtless much is saved because the military and officials are fewer in number than in many other countries, and the salaries and pensions of officials are not nearly so high as in Europe. The military is, as I have said, small, but it is well paid, and though small, it is adequate – probably because it is not used so extensively here for guards and parades – for a line of protection against the Indians, so that you feel quite safe from them.

The land I have bought is very beautiful; it is square in form, and through it flows a charming little stream – a river as it is called here. It consists partly of openings, partly of denser good woodland of oak, elm, walnut, maple, and other species. Besides, it has some little prairies where I have mowed all my hay for the winter. I plan as soon as possible to put up a grain and sawmill in the river. Since there is always a great demand for boards and I have enough wood, I imagine I shall make quite a profit on this venture.

I wish I lived closer to the city; but since all land between here and the nearest city has been taken, to buy some would be very expensive. For when land has been cultivated and houses built on it, the price asked for half of 160 acres is usually $3,000 to $4,000. Besides, as the land becomes inhabited the cities will soon spring up. About ten or twelve miles from here a new town called Prairieville * has already arisen; it is developing rapidly and offers many opportunities for work.

As I have said, my dear friends, I dare not yet hope to give you a complete and entirely reliable account of this country and conditions here. But I can safely say that the country is beautiful and very fertile and that I do not think the reports you have read in Norway have praised it excessively. In many ways, it has exceeded my expectations, so that I am happy about my decision to come here and hope, God willing, that I shall never regret it. By this I do not mean to say, however, that it might be a good thing for everyone to come here; for they who come here without money and with families who are unable to work and without previous acquaintances here often experience great hardship at first, especially before they are able to move into the interior of the country. I have not seen any beggars, however, since I set foot on American soil, and thefts, likewise, are extremely rare. The reason for this is probably that victuals here are very cheap when you buy them at the right time, that is, in the fall. For instance, a bushel of wheat . . . costs half a dollar; a pound of meat two or three cents (about two to three Norwegian skillings); a pound of bacon two cents, and so on. Sugar you make yourself from the sugar maple tree, and coffee and rice can be bought very cheaply. And when you add to this the fact that wages are high – they have fallen somewhat here, however, as a simple laborer now only gets from $6 to $10 a month plus good food – then it is obvious that no one suffers great want. That workers are forced to take old clothes and other goods at high prices in payment for their work, as has been said in Norway, is not true. Work here is mostly paid for in cash, usually in gold and silver, which are the most common kinds of currency. Paper money is scarcer. If a worker is paid in provisions, he gets them at the usual, current prices. The American treats his employees well; he does not treat them as servants but as his helpers. He expects good work, it is true, but then wages, food, and treatment are as fine as you can wish for.

* Now Waukesha, Wisconsin.

I have proof that it must be good to live here: it is only five years ago that people began to cultivate the land, and now there are some who sell many hundreds of barrels of wheat, potatoes, and corn and have already become wealthy. But then the farmer here does not have many burdens which might curtail his property; for apart from the fact that taxes are a trifle, he is exempt from many other expenses that one has in Europe — there are relatively few officials here. The greatest public expense you have is that of building and paying for your own churches and schools. The ministers are paid from the American missionary fund with no expense to the citizens. Now we Norwegians and Swedes have also decided to build a church and have chosen a man who lives here and who is a graduate in divinity for our minister. But first he has to take the usual examinations. When he has passed these, he will be appointed minister by the bishop and be paid in the same manner as the other ministers. So you see we are not nearly so heathen as people in Norway believe. On the contrary, Americans are extremely devout and observe the Sabbath religiously.

Although, my dear friends, I am happy here, I do not advise everybody without exception to come. Single, unattached persons who can work, families whose members are able-bodied and have a little money to live on at first, and carpenters — all these, I believe, may safely come here. But those who plan to buy land and who are not able to earn anything by their work must have enough money to live on the first year as well as something for the next; for they cannot expect any harvest from the land until one year has passed, and not enough until the end of the second year. Large families that are unable to work or that have little money should not come. Several such families who arrived last year have suffered many tribulations. I do not think that any craftsmen except carpenters would be very successful here, for the factories turn out too many products in their line of work; but I do not know conditions in the cities well enough to be able to say anything about them with certainty. It is safest of all for those people to come who can buy the necessary land — and sufficient land for an ordinary family to live on would here be forty to fifty acres — who are able to work or who have able-bodied people and enough money to live on until their first harvest. They must also have a little money for a house and draft animals. Such persons can look forward to an old age free from care. I believe that you, my dear brothers-in-law, are in a position to come here without any misgivings; and if you do come, be assured that we will do everything we can for you. On the other hand, I know that you, my dear son-in-law, do not wish to leave your native country. If in time you change your mind, you and yours will be heartily welcome at our place.

Now be good enough to give our best greeting to all my friends. Give my love to my brother-in-law, *Lehnsmand* Pedersen, and his family; best greetings to all my former people, tell them that we are well except that the children have had a little ague, which is common here but not dangerous. Also greetings to Mr. Bagger; please ask him not to forget the newspapers next summer.

If anyone wants to write me, my address is: Mr. Hans Gasmann, c/o Mr. Shepardson and Farwell, Milwaukee, via New York, in America.

P.S. If you show this letter to Mr. Bagger, you might ask him if he will have it printed in the Skien newspaper so that others who have asked me to write may see it.

The Atlantic Crossing

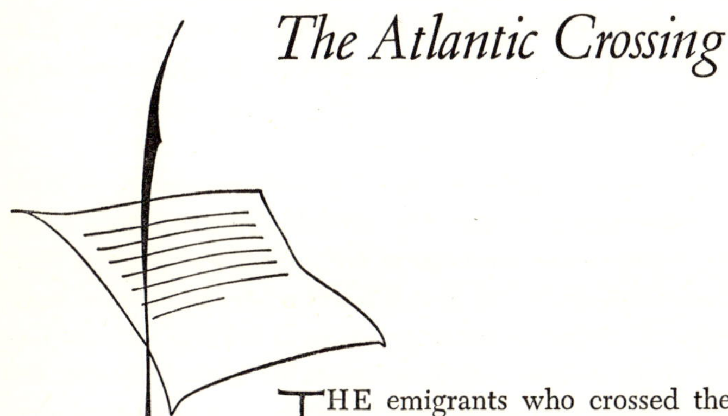

THE emigrants who crossed the Atlantic in sailing vessels were quick and eager to tell their friends at home about the difficulties, as well as the pleasant experiences, on their long voyage. When Rynning's *True Account of America* was published in 1838, prospective Norwegian emigrants found in its pages advice distilled from experience.* Only the preceding year Rynning had made the Atlantic crossing in the bark *Aegir*, one of eighty-four emigrants who spent more than two months at sea before they landed at New York harbor. His book was a printed immigrant letter addressed to everybody. He spoke with authority and was listened to with respect.

When Rynning wrote, he could not know or visualize the horrors that were to mark the Atlantic crossing for thousands of European emigrants. "Many regard the trip across the ocean as so terribly dangerous that this one apprehension alone is enough to confine them forever to their native country," he said. "Of course, solid ground is safer than the sea; but people commonly imagine the dangers to be greater than they really are." He lacked first-hand information about the shamefully crowded vessels that were scourged by cholera, typhus, typhoid fever, dysentery, and measles. His experience was too limited to reveal the conditions which, in historical perspective, would one day cause an American historian, Carl Wittke, to compare the sufferings of immigrants on the Atlantic with those of chained Negroes in "the middle passage during the African slave trade." Nor did he envisage the deaths of the Atlantic

* My translation of Rynning's *True Account of America* was first published in the *Minnesota History Bulletin*, 2:221–269 (November 1917) and was brought out in book form, with the original text and a somewhat fuller historical introduction, by the Norwegian-American Historical Association in 1926.

crossing — a mortality that led Friedrich Kapp, decades later, to say, "If crosses and tomb stones could be erected on the water as on the western deserts, where they indicate the resting-places of white men killed by savages or by the elements, the routes of the emigrant vessels from Europe to America would long since have assumed the appearance of crowded cemeteries." *

But Rynning had good advice to offer. He asked emigrants to leave Norway early in the spring so that, after arrival in America, they could plant potatoes, turnips, and buckwheat with the hope of crops that would help them to weather their first difficult winter in the new land. Such advantages coincided with the break-up of winter, with its forbidding rigors on the Atlantic, and as decade succeeded decade, the chosen season for emigration was always the spring — March, April, and May, with full tide in April.

How could the emigrants guard against the hazards of the journey? Rynning met this question with a wealth of specific information. They must carry with them, he said, provisions enough to meet their needs for twelve weeks. He pointed out the importance of foods that would not readily spoil, and he mentioned a long list (some items of which would not last as long as others). This list included dried and salted meats, dried and smoked herring, beer, flour, peas, cereals, potatoes, rye rusks, coffee, tea, sugar, cheeses, even butter. Because of the danger of sickness, he also advised supplies of brandy, vinegar, wine, raisins and prunes, a cathartic, sulphur powder and ointment, spirits of camphor, and "Hoffman's drops." Cleanliness was important, and he suggested that the emigrants have sufficient "linen for change," salt-water-soap, and "good fine combs."

Rynning also advised the emigrants to make careful contracts with their captains, especially as to water and wood. The water must be kept in good casks, with enough to give each emigrant three quarts a day during the voyage. If some of it spoiled, the good water should be used before the bad, and the captain should drink from the same casks that supplied the emigrants. These were but a few of the many items that Rynning discussed. He also mentioned bedclothes, spinning

* Carl Wittke, *We Who Built America* (New York, 1939), p. 113. After quoting Kapp, Wittke adds, "Many did not survive the ordeal; others survived it only to fall victims in American ports to disease or to some of the worst exploiters of helpless humanity that any generation has ever seen; and many no doubt cursed the day they ever left their native firesides."

wheels, pipes, fishing tackle, books, tools, pans, kettles, and other needed articles.*

Apart from the initial expenses and the wrench of leaving familiar scenes, the problem of emigration was formidable. Emigrant reminiscences tell of long winters busy with preparations for the following spring – the making of clothing, the building of chests to be crammed with supplies, the slaughter of cattle and preparation of meats, the baking of flat bread and the fashioning of wooden barrels in which to stow it, the planning of auctions to sell things that could not be carried away, and the last-minute preparations for the journey to the seaport where the emigrant ship was waiting for its load. Perhaps novelists will have to join hands with historians in picturing and interpreting what the uprooting of people meant through the long months of planning and work that preceded the severance with ancestral ties – ties often rooted in the Middle Ages. The pictures are of more than externals – they are of thoughts and imaginings, for emigration was a transfer not alone of bodies but of minds and traditions and human ambition and hope. "All through the winter darkness," wrote a Norwegian-American woman many years after the event, "I helped my mother with the preparations. In the evening darkness my brother and I often sat and built air castles, dreaming of what we should do when we got to America." †

Ultimately the day came when the emigrant families set out for the port of departure. Not a few made their way to Sweden, Germany, France, or England to catch emigrant packets for America, but emigration helped to bring into being the Norwegian merchant marine, and large numbers of the emigrants in the earlier decades sailed on Norwegian ships. The backbone of transatlantic commerce for Norway, a noted historian has said, was the emigrant traffic.‡ As the emigrant tide rose, a veritable fleet of vessels was built to combine the emigrant traffic with trade in passage to the United States and Canada. The shift from New York to Quebec in the early 1850's came as a direct result of the modification of English navigation laws, with the profits in the lumber trade from Quebec a second magnet. By 1861 Quebec in a

* Rynning's *True Account of America*, pp. 94–100.

† See chapter entitled "From Old World to New," in *Norwegian Migration*, vol. 2, pp. 3–36. Vivid accounts of the Atlantic crossing are given by Ingrid Semmingsen in her two-volume work *Veien mot Vest* (Oslo, 1941–1950).

‡ Jacob S. Worm-Müller, quoted in *Norwegian Migration*, vol. 2, p. 10.

single season saw 130 Norwegian sailing vessels carrying emigrants to Canada and goods out of Canada.

Thousands of immigrant letters take up the story at this point. They tell of the scenes of departure; the farewell sermon; the mingling of sadness and the joys of anticipation; the primitive accommodations; the bunks for sleeping; the arrangements for cooking; the problems of water and supplies, sickness and storm, birth and death, patient suffering, fading (or rising) hopes, strength and persistence; games and joys that relieved the anxieties and fears, and perhaps the sufferings, of many; captains who were like fathers to emigrant groups; and dreadful voyages on which men and women were treated like animals, especially on English and American packets. It was fortunate that the emigrants, for the most part, were young and strong, just as it was – and is – fortunate that human beings are resilient, able usually to survive conditions and experiences that seem, when recorded later, to have been beyond human endurance.

The Atlantic crossing was remembered by the thousands who survived it, and its memories have been gathered up as lore passed on, generation after generation, to the present. Even with its pleasant interludes, such as fishing on the Newfoundland Banks, the voyage was sheer ordeal. Not a few perished – theirs are the unmarked graves in the Atlantic – but the great majority got to the Promised Land. What they went through is an epic that has not yet been pictured with the insight and imaginative power it merits.

Most immigrants, soon after they landed, found occasion to write to their friends and relatives across the waters. The voyage was fresh in their minds, and they naturally gave attention to its details. Not a few of the letters elsewhere in this book, centering upon other aspects of the immigrant story, inevitably touch upon the Atlantic crossing, and in the present section only a few, in which the crossing is of major concern, have been selected. They do not give the full picture of the journey from Old World to New, but they catch up typical aspects of it.

An immigrant of 1837 reports the arrival of a group of parched immigrants who found themselves plunged into financial difficulties as soon as they came to the New York quarantine station. A letter from 1842 sketches the beginnings of an Atlantic crossing, and a later letter chronicles the arrival of the vessel, the *Washington*, in New York, with a lively picture of an emigrant wedding at the quarantine station. There is heartfelt praise in a letter of 1843 for a captain and a mate who were humane and considerate of their passengers.

But often there was little to praise and much to condemn. "Away! away!" wrote the Norwegian poet Wergeland in the 1840's of the emigrants. "Draw up the gangway! We'll pack you bumpkins like herring in a barrel, 'tis only an interlude between barrel and palace." * The palace or its equivalent—not quite so fantastic as the ironical song implied—was at any rate far in the future, whereas the packed barrel was immediate and all too actual.

In the 1840's the Norwegian government was stirred by dire reports from America, which told of one vessel of 140 tons that carried 210 passengers and another on which thirty emigrants died during the voyage. An attempt was made to pass a regulatory law, with strict control of the physical conditions of the emigrants on board the transatlantic vessels and with precautions in the interest of cleanliness and decent sanitary conditions. But this proposed law was defeated by a slow-moving and unsympathetic Norwegian parliament, and eighteen years went by before a somewhat similar act became law. Meanwhile the New York authorities and the United States government made efforts to improve the situation, Castle Garden was established, and more stringent laws were passed to reduce overcrowding and to improve conditions on board the emigrant vessels. Both the laws and their enforcement were defective, as Wittke points out, since there was "no coordinated American immigration policy," but what was done amounted to recognition of "the eventual responsibility of the Federal Congress for the immigrant traffic." †

It is against this background that a letter written late in 1843 by the captain of the emigrant ship *Salvator* should be read. This captain, Johan Gasmann, was admired by those fortunate enough to make the Atlantic crossing under his care. His letter went to a brother who was a member of the governmental commission that investigated the conditions of emigration and proposed a regulatory law. Wise and humane

* Wergeland's play "The Mountain Hut," written by the poet on his deathbed in 1845, seems to have had as its original title "Emigrants to America." The phrase quoted is from one of its songs (Theodore C. Blegen and Martin B. Ruud, *Norwegian Emigrant Songs and Ballads*, Minneapolis, 1936, p. 91).

† In both volumes of *Norwegian Migration* I have dealt with the governmental attitude toward regulation of the immigrant traffic, and the subject is also discussed at many points by Professor Wittke in his *We Who Built America.*

in its suggestions, the captain's report is a vivid and valuable document of immigration in the days of the sailing vessels.

An immigrant of 1844 complains bitterly about the lack of drinking water during the crossing. His letter, only parts of which are translated, has a note of tragedy in it, for his journey ended at Chicago with the deaths of his wife and daughter. Fifty-three emigrants sign, in 1849, a letter of appreciation to a Norwegian captain who carried a group from Norway to America in forty-two days in his brig, the *Favorite.* "The crossing was terrible," writes an immigrant of 1853, describing a nauseating voyage from Liverpool, and in the same year a dozen artisans who had taken passage on an English packet wrote a joint letter picturing such conditions as remind the historian of the infamous "middle passage." Of interest is a letter from 1854 which describes in some detail the unaffected joy, for Norwegian emigrants, of fishing at the Newfoundland banks; and in the same year an emigrant named Stammerud tells of the Atlantic crossing,with fishing at the banks, but with the dread cholera joining the party on its dismal way to the American interior.

A letter-diary kept by a young bride, Gro Svendsen, gives a spirited account of an emigrant voyage in 1862. In a later chapter the story of this woman, who pioneered on the Iowa frontier, will be followed through the 1860's and 1870's.

The section appropriately closes with a brief account, from a letter of 1866, describing the beginnings of yet another emigrant voyage. Whatever the hardships of the Atlantic crossing, beginnings are at the heart of the story – beginnings and the promise of America as goal.

Some suffered greatly from thirst

FROM A STAVANGER EMIGRANT, AT ROCHESTER, NEW YORK, TO FRIENDS *

October 2, 1837

I owe it to all my friends whom I can never forget to let you know that after seventy-four days' voyage, I and my dear family and all the others on the same ship have safely arrived in America, and thus far

* This extract from an emigrant letter appeared in *Stavanger Adresseavis*, December 15, 1837.

everybody has been in good health. Besides I must tell you what happened to us after the voyage, and how the passengers were treated.

When we left Stavanger each person was promised two quarts of water a day, but we did not get more than a quart and a half. Thus, those who had not brought much beer for the trip suffered greatly from thirst. When finally we arrived at the quarantine station, we encountered many difficulties. Captain Pedersen ordered everybody to be on deck at four o'clock in the morning, and during the commotion that followed he told us that each person had to pay four specie dollars in landing money, instead of the two and a half specie dollars that our charter stipulated. But as we refused to pay more than the two and a half specie dollars that had been agreed upon, we had to take our baggage below, and he said that we were to remain there until we paid what he asked for, four specie dollars. So most of us were forced to pay.

When we finally got ashore in New York City, we addressed ourselves to the Norwegian-Swedish consul. He ordered the captain to pay back the money which the passengers had paid in excess of the amount agreed on and also the bill of exchange which Consul Krog had made out for a sum of 1,750 specie dollars. But the result was that we got nothing and the passengers were delayed in New York for five days and were unable to travel on.* Then the consul lent them enough to get to Rochester. When they arrived there, they were in the same situation. Two Norwegians, Lars Larsen and Ole Eie, took care of them and for several days provided them with food and shelter, and even lent them money to enable them to reach Illinois, where I hope someone will help them. . . .

A happy voyage to us!

SUMMARY OF A DIARY WRITTEN ABOARD SHIP †

June 3 to 9, 1842

On June 3 in the morning the ship weighed anchor in Laurvig Bay, passed with a fresh northern breeze through Fredriksværn harbor, sa-

* From *Handelstidenden*, No. 1273, it may be seen that later the emigrants got back about two thirds of this sum.

† This selection appeared in *Skiensposten*, July 22, 1842.

luted the fortress with four shots and the steamship *Prince Carl* with three hurrahs, with the salutes being returned from both parties, and entered the open sea with all well on board.

In the evening the wind dropped, and because of the rolling of the ship seasickness spread among the passengers, who were forced to go to bed. The next morning the *Washington* was rolling a great deal, but the weather was beautiful and almost calm, with the wind from the north. The wives of Halvor Jørusdal and Lars Folseland, who suffered most from seasickness, complained moaningly of dizziness. Toward evening the wind freshened, the rolling diminished, and we had our last glimpse of land. The captain asked if departing from their native country meant very much to the emigrants and urged them to take their leave of it now, since they probably would never see it again. But they were all happy and elated and only asked if the headland they saw was Lindesnæs, and then burst out laughing, with the words: "A happy voyage to us!"

The next morning it was eight o'clock before anyone appeared on deck, but as soon as the first one got up, the others followed like ants out of an anthill. The sea was calm, and the ship moved forward as smoothly as if it were on a lake. The seasickness seemed to be gone completely. It was Sunday, and they all deserve praise for starting at once to get washed and putting on their Sunday best, after which they joined in prayer with much devotion. During prayer some of Mynster's "Considerations concerning God's Omnipotence and Omnipresence" were read aloud, and before and after the reading a hymn was sung to the accompaniment of a flute and violin. In the evening there was much gaiety on board, with a great deal of music and dancing. Four members of the crew and four of the passengers played the violin and one of the crew played the flute. The merrymaking, the captain observes, was conducted in a very respectable and orderly fashion, and on the whole he admires the politeness and good manners of these farmers from Telemark.

On June 6, 7, and 8 the weather was still good, and the women occupied themselves by knitting and sewing, the old people by reading and singing hymns, while the men would stand almost continuously with their hands in their pockets, gazing out to sea. Some grampuses appeared and followed the ship for a while, attracting much attention. The passengers thought they must be sea horses, for they seemed to move ahead at a gallop. On the ninth we had, still with the best possible weather, advanced so far into the Channel that the captain hoped, God willing, to be on the Atlantic next morning. All the passengers were in good health, and all was well on board.

At the quarantine station, a wedding

FROM A TELEMARK EMIGRANT, IN NEW YORK, TO FRIENDS *

August 10, 1842

On Saturday, July 30, the *Washington* arrived in New York with all well on board and all of its Telemark passengers in the best of health.

From the time they left the English Channel until they approached the banks of Newfoundland they had had a fine crossing, but here the fogs, so common along the North American coast, set in, and with them came illness which soon gave cause for serious alarm. The symptoms pointed to cholera, and at one time twenty-five or thirty of the passengers were very sick. But the captain soon checked the disease by putting the patients on a very strict diet, by observing great cleanliness and fumigating the ship with chlorine and vinegar, and by applying the medicine and tonics he had at hand. On the arrival at the quarantine station, the last trace of the illness had disappeared.

On the second day after the arrival of the *Washington* at the quarantine station a wedding was held on board. The groom was Anders Larsen Folseland and the bride Olloug Olsdatter. The wedding ceremony was conducted in English, and the captain stood beside the minister and translated his words as he read them aloud. On the right side of the groom stood the collector, the cashier at the customs office, and on the left of the bride was the doctor of the quarantine station; both of these men were held in very high regard there. The bride wore a simple but pretty dress of dark cloth and on her head she had a crown of flowers which had been obtained ashore. The groom wore a black coat and pantaloons. All the passengers and the whole crew were dressed in their best clothes. Everything was conducted in a very orderly fashion and

* The letter from which this is an excerpt appeared in *Skiensposten* on September 5, 1842.

with true solemnity. After the wedding the doctor gave the spouses all the rules of hygiene which they should follow to remain strong and healthy – then all sails were set, and a few hours later the vessel dropped anchor in the harbor of New York. In the evening there was dancing on board till midnight, and everybody had spent a very pleasant day, in a seemly and becoming manner.

A captain who does not swindle passengers

FROM THE SATISFIED PASSENGERS ABOARD THE BRIG HERCULES, TO READERS BACK HOME *

July 5, 1843

Concerning our emigration to North America in 1843, we should like, to the best of our ability, to make the following statement, which may be of interest to several readers:

On May 12 at one-thirty in the morning, ninety passengers from Drammen in Norway went on board the brig *Hercules* commanded by Captain Overvien, and after a successful and rapid crossing we anchored in the harbor of New York on July 4, the day which solemnly marks this country's independence. It is not necessary to describe here what happened on the voyage, but everything went very well. Thus we received very special attention from our captain and his mate Hans Friis, as no day went by while we were at sea without their coming down and asking us if we lacked anything and promising, if this were the case, that they would do everything in their power to provide us with what we needed. Each evening they held a devotional hour with prayer and singing, and every holiday something was read from the Bible, and all of this was conducted in the proper spirit of devotion. On the whole, they behaved very kindly toward us in all possible ways, for which we thank them from the bottom of our hearts, and we recommend everyone who plans to go to North America to the care of this sensible captain.

Concerning the rumors about his having swindled passengers, we are

* This statement, signed by Hellik O. Holtan, Gulbrand G. Holtan, Knud Belteslia of Flesberg, Halvor A. Aasen, Halvor K. Laugen and Gunder K. Laugen of Rollaug, Even Foslia, Petter Skarbraaten of Sigdal, Anders Gundersen, Jens Guttormsen, and Ole O. Aasen, was printed in *Den Norske Rigstidende*, November 22, 1843.

convinced that these must have arisen by misunderstanding or else be completely false. We also thank the rest of the crew for their kind and good behavior toward us.

This we have drawn up briefly and simply and to the best conviction of our consciences, in the sincere wish that it may be brought to the attention of the public.

Some arrived in New York virtually destitute

FROM CAPTAIN J. G. GASMANN, ON THE SHIP SALVATOR, TO HIS BROTHER CONSUL J. GASMANN *

December 18, 1843

As I have learned that a committee has been appointed to report on safety measures with regard to possible future emigration to North America and that you are one of its members, I wish to make a few statements concerning this matter and hereby offer the following information:

1. Since the safety of many people is involved in these expeditions one must first of all be sure to use only good and well-equipped ships — in my opinion none under seventy or eighty lasts capacity. It is true that smaller vessels may be just as safe, but they are more liable to be washed by waves, which forces the passengers to remain below with all the hatches closed, as soon as the strong winds and the heavy seas so characteristic of the Atlantic set in. In such close quarters the air is quickly contaminated, and soon diseases will break out. It is also impossible to keep a small ship as dry to leeward as a larger vessel, and it has been proved that excessive moisture is the cause of much illness on board a ship during long voyages. Moreover, and very important, a smaller ship provides too little space on deck for the passengers to take the necessary exercise.

2. Every ship that carries a full load of passengers (see the Act of

* Consul J. Gasmann had been appointed by the Finance Department of the Norwegian government to serve on a special commission to draft a law regulating emigration and the conditions on emigrant vessels. The original of this letter is in the archives of Norway's Social Department, Lovkontor: Utv., Kong. Prop. 1845 Oslo. A transcript which I secured in Norway is in the archives of the Norwegian-American Historical Association, Northfield, Minn.

Congress of 1819) should measure at least 5¼ to 5½ feet between decks. No more than three bunks in a row and two in height should be allowed, and the space between the bunks should be left clear so that it may be cleaned easily.

3. No ship that carries passengers should be loaded, with iron or other goods, to more than two thirds of its full capacity. In case it carries a full load of passengers it should carry no cargo between decks where the passengers have to stay; it should have enough space on the lowest deck for kindling wood, provisions, and baggage, leaving the area between decks unobstructed.

4. The ship should carry at least three quarts of water a day for each passenger for twelve weeks and enough provisions for the same period.

5. For the sick there should be on board wine vinegar, wine, and sugar. If no doctor is on board, there should be a "ship's dispensary" with instructions for its use.

6. Every ship that carries a fairly large number of passengers should post instructions for them on how to behave during the voyage.

Let me describe here the arrangements I myself made during my last trip. Every morning the decks were swept clean and every third day they were washed and scrubbed, and if the weather permitted, bedclothes and other baggage were brought up on deck for airing. When the middle deck was scrubbed the passengers had to stay above until things got dry below; if the air was bad below we fumigated with vinegar. Ventilation was obtained by keeping all three hatches open all day, and as the ship was completely waterproof we poured a lot of ocean water down through the pumps and then pumped it out again to clean the air in the lower sections. In humid, foggy weather it is a good idea to place some heating pans with coal between the decks to dry and clean the air.

The passengers should be encouraged to exercise on deck as much as possible. Light or fire should not be permitted during the evening or night except in case of emergency and then only in a lantern. From time to time the crew which is on watch during the night should inspect both the middle deck and the lower rooms to avoid the danger of fire.

When the passengers embark, their food should be examined to make sure that it is of sufficient quantity and good quality. Water keeps best in containers made of spruce wood.

Since many of our countrymen do not know the facts and may have set out on the journey to America without knowing how much money they need to reach the interior of the United States (Wisconsin, Illinois, and so on) I here list the costs as they are at present:

Fare for an adult from Norway to New York, 20 specie dollars	
Commutation, hospital, customs office	$ 1.75
Transportation from New York to the interior	9.00
Provisions for 12 or 14 days under way	5.00
	15.75
Plus Norwegian specie dollars	20.00
All told	$35.75

For children under twelve the fare from Norway to New York is half the adult fare, that is, 10 specie dollars and 4½ dollars to the interior, while the tax of $1.75 is the same for children and adults.

I do not know for certain how much money you would need to travel via Havre de Grace, but I assume that it will be at least 50 specie dollars, as you may often have to wait three or four weeks in Havre for a ship to New York. That was the case this year when some had to return to Norway, and many arrived in New York in the most pitiful condition, without a skilling to pay for their maintenance and further transportation. Some of these even told me that they had been maltreated on board the American ship by which they arrived. And as they lacked food, they had to buy provisions on board, at very high rates. They arrived in New York virtually destitute.

In New York there are not a few officious countrymen of ours. As soon as a ship arrives, they force themselves upon the passengers and suggest to them all kinds of projects. They promise to provide transportation for the newcomers at much more favorable conditions than the captain or his agent or commissioner can get for them, which is certainly false. But it is true that these men will get the emigrants off at half a dollar below the fare designated by the established Emigrant Transportation Company, and even so they pocket half a dollar per passenger. But the truth of the matter is that the transportation they get for the emigrants is not safe and often takes eight to fourteen days longer than is ordinarily the case. So many passengers are loaded into boats that illness and death have often resulted from this treatment. And it has even happened that emigrants have been put ashore still halfway from their destination.

I think that emigrants should be warned about this, and I do not believe that any Norwegian captain who has been entrusted with command of a ship in these waters would be so mean as to take advantage of his poor countrymen's ignorance. Besides, everybody will be able to learn the prices and fares of the Company, and he will also be able to tell the exact time of arrival at his destination. The vessels of the Company provide very good accommodations.

As far as I have heard, the Wisconsin Territory – where most of the Norwegian emigrants go – is a beautiful, fertile, and healthful country; but as I have not seen it myself, I shall let Brother Hans describe it more fully.

Like so many pigs stowed together

FROM GUTTORM R. THISTEL, IN CHICAGO, TO FRIENDS *

January 3, 1844

First I want to warn all those of you who are planning to undertake the journey to America to make contracts with the skipper with whom you are emigrating. You must insist that you be given at least three quarts of water a day. We got no more than one pint and almost died of thirst. It was not very good water either, for it tasted and smelled so bad that we had to throw it up.

On your departure from Bergen, you will lose nothing by changing your money into five-franc pieces, piasters, doubloons, Norwegian silver specie dollars, but avoid small change. When you get to New York, you must be very cautious about changing your money into gold pieces, for many of these are false, made of both tin and glass. Again, when you come to New York you must be sure to draw up a clear, specific contract with the skipper who offers to take you up through the canal. Many will present themselves, but you must be careful. Do not go by freighter but by steamboat instead, and you will arrive two weeks earlier. It only costs two dollars more. I and the people with me went by freighter and were under way for more than a month, and we suf-

* The leter excerpted here appeared in *Tiden* (Drammen), May 29, 1844. The omitted portions concern living conditions, farming customs, and matters which are taken up elsewhere in this book.

fered great misery. We neither had room to sit down nor stand up. We felt like so many pigs stowed together. On our trip up the canal on the canalboat we had such fine weather that we could walk on the banks of the canal alongside the boat; we gathered much fruit, especially apples, and brought it on board the boat in big sacks. You must be careful not to eat too much of this fruit, for it caused severe illness among us. . . .

I shall have to conclude this letter soon, but I must tell you which of our group died. The last night we were in Buffalo, September 22, my wife fell ill, and yet we had to travel on for about five hundred miles. When we reached Chicago on September 29, she died at four o'clock in the morning and was buried at seven the same morning. Then my little daughter Thorbjør was taken severely ill. Grief and exhaustion overwhelmed me. Eight days later my daughter died! I brought her with me to my destination, where she now lies buried. Anna Guldteigen also died during the journey. On October 9 we arrived at the place in Chicago where we wanted to settle, then Erik and Undi Guldteigen from Wiig fell ill; they were both buried on the same day that their brother, who had lived in America for two years, came to meet them. Ole Guldteigen likewise died. Hans Dalen fell ill, too, and around All Saints' Day had to be transported up through the country in a wagon. The cold was so severe for nine days that one could hardly keep warm by walking. A couple of days before they reached their destination, Hans also died.

The crossing was very fast, forty-two days

A TESTIMONIAL TO CAPTAIN WESTERGAARD, FROM EMIGRANTS SAFELY ARRIVED IN NEW YORK *

1849

As is well known, we left Stavanger on May 16 and continued our voyage with alternately good and bad weather until June 20, when we

* This testimonial, which was signed by H. A. Asbjørnsen, P. Magnus, and fifty-one other passengers, was printed in *Stavanger Amtstidende og Adresseavis*, August 10, 1849. Subjoined to it is the editor's comment that he has had a letter from Captain Westergaard stating that Westergaard accompanied his passengers to Troy, New York.

took pilot on board fifty miles from New York. The crossing took forty-two days, which under the circumstances must be considered very fast and is due solely to the excellent sailing of the brig. Better accommodations than those enjoyed by all the passengers on board the brig *Favorite* can probably not be found on any other vessel in Stavanger. When we the undersigned recommend this ship as one of the best on which such a voyage can be undertaken, we do this also because of the care which the master, Captain Westergaard, showed all his passengers. For not only was he very kind and pleasant to us during the whole journey — especially after our arrival in New York, where we, as foreigners unfamiliar with the language, badly needed the advice and help of an honest man — but on the whole we appreciate the time and attention which Captain Westergaard so unhesitatingly gave to all of his passengers.

We are now in New York and we have not had to worry much about the problems of our transportation into the interior of the country, for Captain Westergaard himself has ordered a steamboat for us at a low rate and arranged for our embarkation, and he has also promised to accompany us to Troy, a distance of 180 miles. Thus we now leave the vessel on which we had such a pleasant passage, and it will be sad when we have to take leave of our good Captain Westergaard, who with the greatest care, kindness, and obligingness has gone with us on this long journey. We consider it a dear duty, as a token of our gratitude, to give him this letter, and we request that it may be published in *Stavanger Amtstidende* for the information of those of our countrymen who might decide to follow us to America.

The only law that prevailed was club law

FROM AN EMIGRANT WHO CROSSED ON AN ENGLISH SHIP, TO HIS MOTHER *

[1853?]

The crossing from Liverpool was a bad one. We went on board our ship on October 13 and left on the morning of the fourteenth, but we did not get any farther than to an anchorage about half a Norwegian

* This letter appeared in *Christiania-Posten*, February 12, 1854.

mile from Liverpool, where we were forced to stay until the eighteenth because cholera had been raging on a few ships that left about the same time as we did. On one of the ships which had left a couple of days earlier 125 persons had died, but on board my ship only twelve persons died during the voyage, and a child was born three days before we reached the shore of America.

The crossing was terrible. Three days after we had left land, we had a frightful storm, and during the night we lost the mainmast and the foremast, so that later we had to get along by means of jury-rigged masts and sails. Many of the berths on the lower deck collapsed, and water poured down through the hatchways so that coffers, trunks, sacks, and all kinds of loose objects floated around in the water and were in great part broken against the sides of the ship because of the terribly heavy sea. That many provisions were spoilt and clothes and the like damaged by the water is easy to understand. This storm lasted two days and two nights, and during this time we had to go both hungry and thirsty, since we could not manage to prepare anything in the galley where everybody was supposed to cook his own food. We could not get any fresh water either.

In the galley there was a large stove; but as there were always a lot of people who wanted to cook, the only law that prevailed here was club law. The strongest and most aggressive could always, although with difficulty, get something cooked, while the weaker and more timid got nothing or had to content themselves with being the last in line, at the risk of having their pots, with half-cooked food, thrown off the fire when the stronger were pleased to come back.

Fights and quarrels were daily occurrences, and the company had done nothing to make sure that everybody was treated justly and the promises that had been made were kept. In Christiania we were promised all sorts of things—for instance, that the food would be excellent. With regard to this, let me give you just one small illustration of the way these promises were kept. Every Saturday we got our provisions; they consisted of six or seven biscuits, about three eighths of a pound of brown sugar, a little wheat flour, some rice and groats, and ten pounds of beef; the meat was to last for the whole passage, but most of it was bone. What kind of food do you think one could prepare with this, especially since we got so little water for cooking that we might very well have used up all of it at once?

At our departure we were promised a sufficient amount of fresh water, but we got so little that we had to be satisfied with making a small cup of tea in the morning and cooking a little porridge later in the day. As for getting water to quench our thirst, that was out of the question. We could not make any broth with the meat we had been given but had to cut it into small pieces and cook it with the porridge. I used the wheat flour I had been given for baking a small cake on Sunday; and being fairly strong and aggressive I shoved back at people and succeeded in getting this holiday treat for myself. Otherwise, our daily fare was the small cup of tea I have mentioned and a biscuit in the morning and porridge for dinner. For supper we had nothing, and I can truthfully say that never in my life have I suffered more, nor do I believe that people can suffer more than do the emigrants on the overpraised ships of Morris and Company.

From the knowledge I have of America now, I think I shall never suffer such want anywhere as I did on board the ship, where we were so starved and thirsty that I thought I should never set foot on land again. God be praised, during the crossing I did not suffer from any other illness than hunger and thirst. From what I have already said, you may imagine how my life has been during this time, for I went on board on October 13 and did not get ashore till November 28. What I had to live on during the crossing, besides the provisions I have mentioned, was a piece of bacon I had bought in Liverpool for one English shilling (about one *ort* and eight Norwegian skillings), but it was not bigger than what you, Mother, usually sell at home for two skillings.

As far as I am concerned, I advise everybody, friend or enemy, *not* to come here on the advertised ships of Morris and Company, and I believe that very soon similar warnings will be received in Norway from several persons who have taken this passage trusting in promises. He who wants to travel to America should go with Norwegian skippers and Norwegian ships. They are always the best. You cannot trust the many emigrant Irishmen and Germans or have any faith in the magnificent promises of the English shipowners. Your life and health are rarely safe on board these ships, and at the very least you must be prepared at any time of day to have a sack of coal or some other heavy object dumped down into your berth or on the table where you had planned to partake of your more than frugal fare. Personally, I got off with a cut in the arm from a big iron hook. It was dressed by the ship's doctor, but it grew worse and immediately we landed I sought another doctor, with good results. As the wound had become full of proud flesh, he cauterized it with silver nitrate for eight days. After that I got a small box with plasters by means of which the very dangerous wound was healed.

Some were beaten badly about the head

FROM A GROUP OF PASSENGERS ON AN ENGLISH PACKET, ARRIVED IN NEW YORK, TO THEIR COUNTRYMEN *

November 30, 1853

All of us have suffered so much hardship and seen and heard so much evil during our passage from Liverpool to America on the English packets this year that we feel it is our duty, without delay, to inform you of all this. In particular, we wish to notify those of you who may already in good faith have heeded the shameless lies and frauds of the agents of this company. Least of all is the fact that *none* of the obligations of the company toward us was kept: we did not, for one thing, receive the supply of food and drink that we were entitled to by our contracts. But far worse than this, the crew treated the poor passengers in such an inhuman way that one cannot listen to these descriptions (which are all alike) without shuddering. Several of us addressed ourselves to the Norwegian-Swedish consul here about this, but an indifferent shrug of the shoulder and something that sounded like "a private affair" and "go to a lawyer" were all the satisfaction that we were able to obtain from him. And this despite the fact that when we arrived here, several of us had to be taken to the hospital. Some had been beaten so badly about the head that there was reason to fear for their lives. Even if they should recover, they will show the scars of this treatment for the rest of their lives. Still others had had one or several ribs broken. One

* This open letter (some lines at the beginning of which are omitted in the translation) appeared in *Morgenbladet*, January 14, 1854. It was signed by H. Stabel, Shoemaker; L. Arneberg, Tailor; A. P. Haugaard, Tailor; P. H. Thoresen, Carpenter; C. Svensen, Tailor; O. H. Dorff, Carpenter; O. P. Christensen, Carpenter; L. Christensen, Carpenter; H. Qvam, Tailor; P. L. Løkke Ihlsing, Carpenter; C. Sørensen, Carpenter; and J. Gjermundsen Brandvold, Carpenter.

passenger had had three or four teeth knocked out. Another had had his breastbone broken by an inhuman English mate who kicked him in the chest with his heavy sea boots because the passenger did not understand how to comply with the orders of this monster.

Furthermore, we suffered so much from lack of water and from the fact that we received only about a third of the provisions to which we were entitled that we became starved and weak and could hardly walk. Our contracts stipulated that our food would be well prepared; instead of this we ourselves had to cook (and pay for the privilege at that) the provisions that were thrown to us as if we were so many dogs. Besides, very few had brought any cooking utensils, for why should they have brought a lot of these when our contracts provided for prepared food? It was a daily occurrence to see starving women and children fight for the food which was brought to the dog and the pigs that were kept on the deck of the ship. This may give you a fairly accurate idea of the kind of crossing we had.

Although we are all well satisfied with our passage across the North Sea on the steamship *Courier* and with the trip from Hull to Liverpool and our stay in that city, we emphatically urge you not to follow that route, for your things will be stolen and in return you will acquire a lot of lice and other vermin.

We have met several times to decide which way would be the best to notify our countrymen of the monstrous treatment all of us have received – part of which is of such a nature that it cannot be printed – and we agreed that publication was the only means at our disposal. Therefore, then, we warn all those of our dear countrymen who want to go to America, that if you do *not* wish to expose your daughters, your sisters, and wives to the most disgraceful and dishonorable treatment, then do not go to Liverpool. And to those who want to preserve their lives, their health, and their limbs we say likewise, do not go to Liverpool. And to those who do not want to be treated like mad dogs or beaten with the rattan as soon as they show themselves on deck, we say the same. And those who after much maltreatment have no wish to be put in iron chains for the amusement of a ship's crew lower than beasts should not go by that route either.

If we were to describe all the bloody incidents we have witnessed, a more skillful hand than the one that wrote these lines would have enough material to fill several volumes. But this should be enough to give you an idea of conditions on all of these Liverpool packets without exception. We feel better now that we have fulfilled this duty toward humanity, and our only wish is that these lines may be made known as widely as possible. Then it will be up to you whether you want to pay attention to them or not. All the undersigned hereby testify that the above description is truthful and honest.

At Newfoundland we caught seventy cod

FROM OLE OLSON ØSTERUD, IN RACINE COUNTY, WISCONSIN, TO HIS BROTHER *

June 21, 1854

Since we have had the good fortune to arrive at our destination, I must write you as I promised and tell you about our journey.

We boarded the ship on April 10. Pastor Bruun came and gave us a farewell sermon. At five o'clock in the morning of the eleventh we lifted anchor. The wind was favorable so that we passed Farder Lighthouse at five in the afternoon. We reached Arendal at four in the afternoon. Then we sailed northward toward Bergen, and on the afternoon of the fifteenth caught our last glimpse of Norway. The last we saw of Norway was high, snow-capped mountains.

On the sixteenth a storm arose from the southeast which lasted until the afternoon of the seventeenth, when we came within shelter of the Shetland Islands, which we passed on the north. We saw Feiril Lighthouse, and at six o'clock in the morning we entered the Atlantic Ocean. After that we had a good wind until the twenty-third so that we usually sailed eleven miles [Norwegian] in a watch (a watch is four hours). We had clear weather until the twenty-second and then a little rain and later head wind until April 30. On May 1 we had the most severe storm of the whole trip. It came from the northwest and later from the west, lasting until the fifth; then it was calm until evening, when a southwest wind arose, so that we made eleven miles in the watch. During the night before May 6 we crossed the outermost Newfoundland Bank. The fol-

* This letter, translated and edited by Henrietta Larson, was published in *Studies and Records* (Northfield, Minn.: Norwegian-American Historical Society), 3:59–64 1928).

lowing night we almost ran into a floating iceberg, which was much higher than the ship's masts, and on the seventh we saw three large icebergs, which you can believe was a remarkable sight.

We reached the Grand Bank of Newfoundland on May 8, and there we fished on the eighth, ninth, and eleventh. We caught seventy cod. Our fishing lines were forty fathoms long, so they reached the bottom, and the hooks were large and strong. Those who fished pulled and pulled and jerked the lines until they felt they had caught something, and some found the hook caught in the belly of the fish, the tail, the back, or wherever it might happen. It mattered not whether one had bait, for few had bait on the hook. So the *torsk* was really a *tosk.** There must have been an abundance of cod on the bottom. They weighed about one Bismer pound [thirteen and a fifth pounds], some more, some less. So we all had fish to eat a couple of times, and it was very good.

After that we had head winds until the fifteenth, when we had a favorable wind. About half past seven in the morning our captain sighted America, but later the fog closed in and we could not see land even though we sailed terrifically until noon, when we ran into a lot of floating ice and could go no farther. Some thirty-six ships were cruising about here and there, unable to advance, and here we also lay to because of ice and fog and could go no farther till the twenty-fourth. At ten o'clock of the forenoon of that day we saw America. On the twenty-fifth we sailed past St. Paul, a lighthouse on a small island in the center of the mouth of the St. Lawrence River. . . . On either side we saw land, with forests and mountains as in Norway. There was still considerable snow on the right, but flatter land, quite uninhabited, on the left. We did not see land again before the morning of the twenty-seventh. At nine in the morning of thirtieth we took a pilot on board ten miles from Quebec. Here again we saw land on both sides, with smoke rising everywhere on the left where settlers were clearing and burning. A little farther on, the country was built up on the left; and still farther, on the right, also. In the afternoon of June 1 we reached an island where a doctor lived. We anchored at this point, and at nine in the morning of the second the doctor came on board. Fifteen minutes after eleven that evening we anchored in Quebec Harbor.

No one was allowed to land before a doctor had come on board and

* A *torsk* is a cod; a *tosk* is a fool. The pun, untranslatable into English, is an old favorite in Norway.

examined us. He came at nine in the morning of the third. We were then allowed to land, and at twelve o'clock on June 3 we stepped onto American soil for the first time.

They were attacked by cholera

FROM J. STAMMERUD, IN LA CROSSE COUNTY, WISCONSIN, TO A FRIEND *

August 16, 1854

During our stop at the Banks the crew fished a great many codfish and a couple of flounders which weighed more than twelve pounds. The fish was distributed among the passengers, and this was a welcome change in our diet. On July 10 we caught sight of the American continent, but there still remained all of the St. Lawrence River, and during this part of the voyage we were slowed down by constant head winds. On July 17 we took an American pilot on board, and on the morning of July 22 we dropped anchor at Quebec. We left the ship on July 25, but we did not try to see the city as cholera was raging both there and in all the other cities along the way. We registered with a railroad and steamboat line which was known by Stangeland. He joined us on our ship in Quebec, and though the journey up through the country was long and strenuous, we managed fairly well, as Stangeland had got us an honest man as interpreter. Without a good interpreter the trip would be far too difficult and expensive. We stayed the second night in Buffalo, and here one of our group who was from Toten died of cholera. From Buffalo we went by steamboat to Monroe, and from there by railroad to Chicago, where we arrived on August 1 and where another two members of the group had to stay as they were attacked by cholera.

During the passage from Norway two children died on board our ship, and in Quebec a woman from Valders fell ill with cholera, so that she and her family had to stay behind there. On the train, on our way to Rock Island, some Irishmen entered one of the cars at a stop and started a quarrel in order to get money, but as some of the railroad personnel appeared, we managed to avoid these people. It is said, how-

* This excerpt from Stammerud's letter appeared in *Christiania-Posten*, October 19, 1854.

ever, that two Swedes who got off the train there with some other persons were found killed in a well the next day.

Although the journey has been long and difficult, neither my wife nor I have regretted it thus far, thank God. But then we have, up till now, enjoyed good health both during the passage and the travel in this country. I have seen much fertile land but also much that was barren, and I dare not as yet make any definite statement about America, as I am still far too unfamiliar with the country. I am negotiating about the buying of land, but there is not much government land available here, because speculators have bought up most of it. You have to be cautious, since otherwise you may easily be cheated. . . .

To see land once again!

FROM GRO SVENDSEN, ABOARD SHIP, TO HER PARENTS*

April 20 to June 21, 1862

April 20, 1862, Easter Sunday. Many of us left the boat to attend festival services in Børre Church. The well-known Pastor Dietrichson preached the sermon. He is an excellent speaker. There were many people in church, some of them odd-looking characters. However, who am I, little Gro, to find fault or make sport of anyone?

On the way home we met a young man, a real chatterbox. I enjoyed talking with him, and on parting he said he would like to come on board that afternoon to continue the visit. Well, he actually did come, a tall, handsome young man, with curly hair and kind eyes. But enough of this!

That evening there was a dance on deck. We were urged to join in the merriment, but since we don't waltz and have no interest in learning, we shall have to manage to live without waltzing. These are not times for dancing.

* A large collection of manuscript letters written by Gro Svendsen has been preserved at her original home in Hallingdal, Norway. Some years ago a Norwegian scholar, Dr. Arne Odd Johnsen, supervised the preparation of typewritten transcripts of these letters for the Minnesota Historical Society. These were translated and edited by Pauline Farseth and Theodore C. Blegen in a volume entitled *Frontier Mother: The Letters of Gro Svendsen* (Northfield, 1950). The complete text of the diary-letter from which the present extracts are taken will be found on pp. 12–26 of that volume.

April 21. We were scheduled to sail, but a dead calm prevailed. That same day the captain's father and several other people came on board. I paid no attention to them, however, as I preferred to be alone. I had too much to think about.

On that day Fredrick Larson, the young man I met Easter Sunday, came on board again; in fact, he came several times. I didn't talk too much with him because some of the mischief-makers frightened him away. One of the boys warned him that he had better watch out for a very jealous man who was secretly waiting for a chance to beat him for talking to me. The poor boy became so frightened that he jumped over the railing into his boat and rowed speedily to land to escape the terrible men of Hallingdal. It was a pity to frighten him so badly. They were only having fun. I would have the men of Askerstrand know that the men of Hallingdal are not as wild as they appear to be.

April 22. This morning we finally sailed down the fjord. We could see the Farder Lighthouse, which is a distance of about twenty-five miles from Askerstrand. On that day a young woman from Eker died, leaving three small children, the youngest a little over a year old, the oldest seven years. She had been ill only a few days. So the sloop was forced to turn back to Askerstrand in order that the dead might be buried in consecrated ground. The body was brought to land the twenty-fourth, and the good people there took charge of the burial.

Once again we sailed down the fjord, but not for long. Again a dead calm, followed by a heavy sea and head wind.

April 25. The sea was very rough. The boat rocked so violently that we could hardly walk. Many of the passengers were sick. I was sick, too, and threw up a little. I was not very ill, but stayed in bed the better part of the twenty-sixth. Again a very heavy sea. The boat is rolling far and heavily to windward. We are still safe, but no one knows what ill fortune may befall us before we reach this far distant land. May the Almighty God keep us. . . . Every evening the captain reads a passage from Skriver's *The Soul's Treasure.* It is a great comfort.

April 26. This morning about five o'clock a little girl, only eight weeks old, of the Ness family from Hadeland, died. They buried her in the early afternoon. The ship's carpenter made the little coffin and filled it half full of sand. Then the baby was placed in the coffin. We sang *Who Knows When My Last Hour Cometh.* Next followed a prayer and the committal by the captain, and another song. Then the sailors lowered the little coffin. It was all strangely quiet and solemn. The waves hurried to cover the little coffin.

And now the last glimpse of Norway. It may be somewhere near Arendal, but it's far in the distance like a blue mist; nothing more. I am heavy-hearted.

April 27, First Sunday after Easter. The captain led the worship. My heart was still heavy. My thoughts were with you, my dear ones, and of the services at home. . . . Today my last glimpse of Norway. I shall never again see my beloved homeland. O God of Mercy, my fatherland!

April 30. Storm and a heavy sea. The sloop is speeding on but rolling heavily, and half of the passengers are ill. I, too, have been lying down all day, so I was not able to see the coast of Scotland as we sailed by between three and four this afternoon.

May 1. Today a little bird came flying up to the deck. It had ventured too far out to sea and just wanted to rest its weary wings. But the captain's dog snatched it and tore it to pieces. Poor little creature that sought haven with us, only to be ruthlessly killed!

May 3. Head wind and a heavy sea. The cold waves break against the decks, and the timbers creak in the sloop. The furniture moves about as if possessed. Late in the night the sailors came and battened everything down, and then we finally fell asleep.

May 4. A storm in earnest. The waves are churning white foam and spraying the decks. I can hardly walk the deck. I look out to sea. Nothing but sky and water. I try hard to stifle a feeling of utter loneliness.

May 6. Rain followed by sunshine. Today I called on the captain. He gave me a drink of strong liquor to bolster me up. I borrowed a medical book and took a look at his maps. I also looked over his library.

May 11, Third Sunday after Easter. Day dawned fair and I felt a little stronger. However, the night was stormy as usual. Our barrels of ale and milk had rolled and knocked about in the hold until the fluid spilled out on the sandy floor. So the precious contents are gone for good. A great loss.

May 16. This is . . . our day of prayer. Rain and dismal weather. During the singing and the reading of the prayers, I sat thinking of my dear ones at home, and the dull pain of loneliness came over me again. . . .

Today I saw a flight of sea gulls. It seemed good to see so many living creatures on our lonely journey. I watched their flight until a rainbow appeared in the sky. It had come to me in silent reproof, but also with radiant hope.

May 29, Ascension Day. I am up again. Today I saw a large iceberg which we almost sailed into because of the fog. Somehow the captain had a feeling that we ought to change our course, and so we escaped this disaster. Within the hour we should have crashed.

June 2. There is a shortage of water. We are allowed only two quarts to a person, one quart for each child. Many are short of food. No one can or will help except the Hallingdal folk. When all is said, they are certainly the best in this respect.

June 3. This morning my mother-in-law suddenly was seized with severe labor pains. About nine o'clock she gave birth to a son. I could never be able to describe to you all the excitement when we realized that her time had come. I trembled like an aspen. My help was less than nothing. I was completely helpless. But God—and one of our good friends—did not forsake us. The little one is quiet, and the mother is as well as can be expected.

June 6. This evening the captain wanted to try his luck at fishing. He pulled a large fish up to the side of the boat. He and his men were just striking a hook in the belly of the flounder when the line suddenly broke. The hook tore a deep gash, and the wounded flounder fell promptly back into the water. The men were both disappointed and disgusted.

June 11. This morning my Ole and I were up on deck very early to see the beacon lights from St. Paul's Lighthouse. At four o'clock we saw land. We were the very first of all the passengers to see it. I shall never be able to convey to you my thoughts and my feelings. To see land once again! With hopes of landing soon! Thankfulness to God overwhelmed me.

June 13. At four o'clock we counted eighteen sailboats, and at six o'clock we saw the mainland. That day we also saw a village and a church.

June 19. We passed the island where the doctor boarded the ship. He checked and inspected all of us. We were all well, so he didn't earn any money here.

Just two days ago an emigrant boat from Norway had been here. I think the boat came from Tønsberg. I didn't manage to get the name of the boat or of the captain. We were told that there was an epidemic on board and that eighty of the three hundred passengers had been taken off the boat and lodged on the island. When we went by, we heard that forty of them had died.

We arrived at Quebec at nine o'clock in the evening. The city is built along the slopes of a majestic cliff, and in the darkness the lights were like myriads of twinkling stars.

June 20. I heard a cock crow in the early dawn. I also heard six church bells ringing. The steeples are covered with bluish white zinc, and they shine like silver in the morning sun. It is a beautiful sight.

Today many of the passengers went ashore, and I tasted American food for the first time. It was white bread and fresh milk that I have yearned for so long.

June 21. A steamboat took us up the river through Three Rivers, and we were indeed happy to get away. Just five days ago, we were told, an English skipper had been stabbed to death by the rough and ready men of Quebec. Some of the captain's sailors suffered the same fate.

Many conflicting feelings stir my soul

FROM OLE NIELSEN, AT BERGEN,
NORWAY, TO HIS FAMILY *

April 22, 1866

He who rules over everything has wisely ordained that after some tribulations on the way we have finally embarked on the vessel *Serius,* which is to take us across the ocean. We went on board Friday night and some were already then rather seasick, but thus far my family has been in the best of health, against our expectation.

Although the ship is not very large, as far as I can see it is one of the best and is probably safer for passage than *Norden,* which is also taking passengers on board in the harbor at present. The *Abraham Lincoln,* which has not yet arrived at Bergen, will carry all the people from Hallingdal and some from Valders, 182 persons all told. Those who have not yet reached here will arrive tonight from Lærdalsøren on the same steamboat that we came on, a large boat of the Holland type.

* "Big Ole" Nielsen was a brother of Gro Svendsen. A transcript of the original of this letter is in the Manuscript Division of the Minnesota Historical Society, St. Paul.

Today as I write these lines on the roof of the captain's cabin, the sexton in the town is calling the congregation to church, and in the commotion under and around me many conflicting feelings stir my soul. At the memory of you, my home, friends, and relatives, I shed many bitter tears, but He who inflicts these wounds will surely also heal them. So I leave this place trusting that the Lord will protect us, confident that everything will work out for the best to those who truly love God. Besides I know that you, my dear parents, will pray for me to the Almighty; thus I can lie down to sleep, trusting that the Lord will watch over me at sea as He has done on land.

My father-in-law is with us now, but he will go back to Lærsdalsøren tomorrow on a steamboat. He is bringing you a little something, dear Mother, as a token of remembrance from me – if God will grant us life, we shall give more some other time. Ask the people at Myhrene to greet Lars's mother from him and give her his portrait, also many greetings to the others there. Everybody at Helleng is greeted from us. Anne sends her portrait with many greetings; she hopes that you may receive the picture before we leave Bergen. Little Niels in particular sends his love to Anna; he wants her to know that he has met many little girls here that he calls Anna. He has been a good boy all the time, and all who have come into contact with him have taken fresh courage. I suppost that the news of the accident that happened to Torger will reach home before these lines. Besides I do not feel much like discussing this subject. We see from this incident what heavy punishment the Lord inflicts on those who are slow to seek His grace. I do not know of any other important happenings during the trip.

Scouting the Promised Land

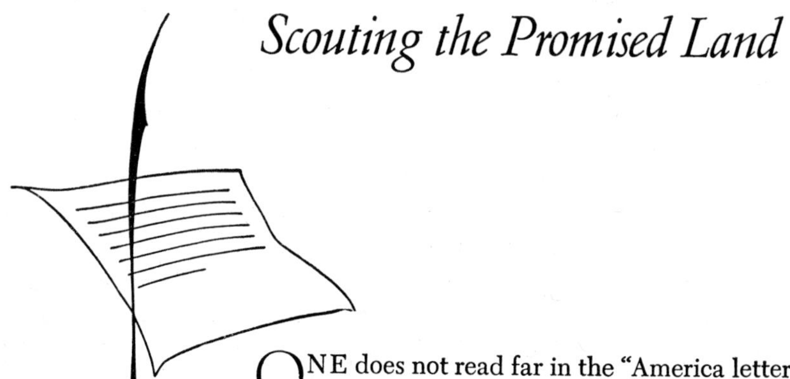

ONE does not read far in the "America letters" before discovering that there were scouts who spied out the land, advance agents of organized emigration parties, men with an urge to see, investigate, and report. Some of these leaders emerged also as colonizers who guided emigrants to the sites they selected.

One of the pathfinders and colonizers in the saga of Scandinavian immigration was Johan R. Reiersen. A liberal newspaper editor in Norway, he had crowded his columns with glowing discussions and reports of America while belligerently urging reforms in his homeland. His writings stirred wide controversy, and he himself became the most prominent of the Norwegian defenders of America and of emigration in the early 1840's.

In 1843 Reiersen journeyed to America, not as an emigrant, but as the emissary of a group of prospective emigrants. His purpose was to see the lands of the New World, prepare a book for the guidance of his countrymen, and if possible select an ideal site for colonization. He did not precisely underestimate the influence he anticipated from his leadership. "Caravans will follow in my wake," he wrote in a private letter before departing for America. The man was indefatigable in performing his western errand. Journeying by way of Havre and New Orleans, he traveled up the Mississippi Valley, saw St. Louis, surveyed settlements in Illinois, Wisconsin, and Iowa, made his way to Texas, and returned to Norway by way of Ohio and New York. He was a good observer, and he read widely in works about America by Lewis and Clark, Schoolcraft, Flint, Long, Peck, James Hall, and others. The book that he published promptly on his return to Norway, *Pathfinder for Norwegian Emigrants* *to the United North American States and Texas* (Christiania, 1844), ranks as one of the comprehensive and informing works about the New World written in the Scandinavian countries up to that time.* Meanwhile, he had written long and interesting letters that appeared in the newspaper of which he had been the editor. In the spring of 1845 Reiersen led a party of emigrants from Norway to Texas, whose advantages he believed outweighed those of the North, and he lived in Texas until his death in 1864. It was characteristic of the man's energy and enthusiasm that before he left Norway for Texas, he established a little magazine called *Norway and America* which he continued to edit from far-off Texas, filling its pages with reports from the Southwest. In the letters given herewith, one written at Iowa City in January 1844, and the other at Cincinnati in March of the same year, Reiersen presents a faithful account of his travels and his findings.

Stopping in his travels at Independence, the jumping-off place for the Far West, he very nearly headed for California. He decided against that far journey, but did not fail to record vividly the scenes surrounding a caravan about to start on its long and hazardous trip four years before the gold rush.

This land's overwhelming advantages

FROM J. R. REIERSEN, AT IOWA CITY,
TO FRIENDS †

January 24, 1844

For a long time I have wanted to write my friends more fully about my journey. Different circumstances connected with my roving life, however, have prevented me. To my friends especially, and to the Norwegian public in general, I wish to give as detailed a presentation of

* I have translated and edited one chapter of Reiersen's book in "Norwegians in the West in 1844: A Contemporary Account," in *Studies and Records* (Minneapolis: Norwegian-American Historical Association), 1:110–125 (1926). For additional information about this immigrant leader, see my article about him in the *Dictionary of American Biography* (New York, 1935), vol. 15, pp. 487–488, and *Norwegian Migration*, vol. 1, chap. 8.

† The translations of this letter and the one following are by Carl O. Paulson and the Verdandi Study Club. They were published under the title "Behind the Scenes of Emigration: A Series of Letters from the 1840's" in *Norwegian-American Studies and Records* (Northfield, Minn.), 14:78–116 (1944).

conditions here as possible, particularly regarding the earlier settlements in America. I also want to emphasize in this report the main results of my observations. At the same time, I wish to give these remarks a stamp of reliability and truth that the combined hue and cry of my enemies will not be able to shake.

After talking with Gasmann and Unonius, as well as with several other intelligent Norsemen who had been here for some time, I found that their opinions coincided with mine on all important points. I decided, therefore, to get their judgment of my comments, which I wrote in a letter to Gasmann, dated Galena, December 12, 1843. This letter was to be submitted also to Unonius, and the opinions of these gentlemen were to be returned to me. Guided by their remarks I planned to present them to my friends in Norway. Uncertain of the place where a letter could surely reach me, I had to ask Mr. Gasmann to send it to my address in New Orleans, where it would await my arrival.

Meanwhile, because it is taking such a long time and I know that my countrymen are so eagerly awaiting my report, I have decided to write my commissioner in New Orleans to ask him to forward immediately, to your address, the letter I mentioned, together with the present one. He will send it by mail to New York. From there it will go by steam packet to Europe. Thus, you will get, I hope, this letter as well as the more complete presentation, without my having seen the comments of Mr. Gasmann and Mr. Unonius.

It is my wish that everything, including this letter, should be published as soon as possible in *Christianssandsposten*, if my sponsors agree with me on this point. I feel that I must apologize for the fact that my style is not so faultless as I should like it to be. A public inn, however, where a person never can get a private room, but must use a table in the main parlor, where one is constantly disturbed by people coming and going, is not, and never can be, the place for creating a stylistic masterpiece.

In my last letter from St. Louis, Missouri, I informed you that I had been in Ohio and was on my way to Wisconsin. I came by steamer to Galena, a town in northern Illinois, the center of the lead-mining district. I left there by stagecoach for Mineral Point in Wisconsin, a new town with about 1,000 inhabitants. I stayed here for several days to secure the necessary information from the land office and then continued my journey to Madison. I stopped to talk with the governor of the territory,

General Doty, who showed me all possible courtesy. With the greatest considerateness, he gave me all the information I wanted.

From Madison I traveled about twenty-five miles west and stopped at Koshkonong Prairie to visit the Norwegian settlements on this and the surrounding prairies within a radius of ten miles. Most of the settlers here arrived last fall. Only a few had been here two or three years and had put up good buildings for themselves. I met a man named Ole Knudsen, a former sexton from Laurdal's parish, who had been in America for four years. He had arrived penniless but had now earned enough money to buy 160 acres of land and stock for his farm. He is a man of more than ordinary education, and he gave me several valuable bits of information.

After a week's stay I traveled on farther by stage through several small new towns to Prairie Village. Here I learned that Gasmann lived about eighteen miles to the northwest. Accompanied by a young Norwegian farmer boy I set out on foot to visit him. On the way I learned that Unonius and several Swedes, as well as a Dane, also lived at that place. I was surprised to learn that the Dane was Judge Fribert, who was very friendly and invited me in to have a cup of coffee.

Mr. Gasmann's house was about a mile away. My nervousness about entering it was fully as great as my surprise had been at meeting Judge Fribert. Rumor at home had reported that Mr. Gasmann, even before his departure, had secretly regretted his decision, and that his wife and children were inconsolable over leaving Norway. Hence I was prepared to find disappointment and despondency within his new home, but I was at once reassured. Mr. Gasmann, as well as his wife and the whole family, were in the best of spirits. Far from regretting their decision, they felt satisfied and were happy at having changed countries. He told me in detail his reasons for leaving Norway. These reasons completely agreed with those that had been expressed so often in *Christianssands-posten* as the opinion of the majority of Norwegian emigrants in similar circumstances.

Mr. Gasmann had put up a temporary log house, a stable, and a barn, as well as a smithy and carpenter shop. He had bought about 1,200 acres of land — timber or forest — also cattle and oxen. He had also bought a beautiful span of horses and a wagon, in which he and his family had that very day attended the dedication of a church in the neighborhood. Everything here breathed life and industry. He has almost all kinds of craftsmen in his own family – smith, carpenter, builder, wheelmaker, saddlemaker, tanner, miller, and sawyer. Consequently everything accomplished here was the family's own work. Next spring he plans to put up a sawmill on his property, which is like a little kingdom.

Gasmann himself had been in good health, and his wife, who had been ailing for a long time, had not felt so spry for many years as she had since coming to America. A similar remark was also made to me later in Muskego by Mrs. Hansen, the wife of the teacher of gymnastics.

I spent a week with Gasmann's hospitable family, who treated me with the greatest consideration. During this time I paid several visits to the Norwegians in the neighborhood, who were all contented and happy.

Chance has brought together here several educated and wealthy men – Unonius, Gasmann, Fribert, St. Cyr, and several other Swedes and Norwegians. They have organized a kind of Scandinavian union, and, remarkably enough, the Swedes have settled on the east side of a little lake – Pine Lake – while the Norwegians live on the west shore. The *Constitution* and the *Union* are small boats in which the neighbors visit each other. Fribert lives among the Norwegians, and many of these poor immigrants are indebted to him for work and good pay.*

The colony has organized itself into a congregation and has elected as its minister Unonius, who is a theological candidate and is to be installed by the bishop of the Episcopal church. Unonius is a cultured and very intelligent man with whom I spent many pleasant hours.

I then went to Milwaukee, a town which in seven years has grown to a population of 6,700. I remained there several days in order to visit the land office to get information concerning the purpose of my mission. From there I made a trip on foot down to a place called Muskego, from a near-by lake of that name, located twenty miles south of Milwaukee. This settlement, of about 2,000 people, is the largest Norwegian one in America. Space forbids my giving a more detailed account at this time of this or the other Norwegian settlements. At a later date, however, I intend to do this.

* On Unonius, the Swedish colony, and the several persons mentioned by Reiersen, see *A Pioneer in Northwest America 1841–1858: The Memoirs of Gustaf Unonius*, vol. 1 (Minneapolis, 1950). This work, translated by J. O. Backlund and edited by Nils W. Olsson, with an introduction by George M. Stephenson, represents a wealth of information about the Pine Lake colony, with identifications of its leaders. Readers will also find much of interest in a collection of *Letters Relating to Gustaf Unonius and the Early Swedish Settlers in Wisconsin*, translated and edited by George M. Stephenson (Rock Island, 1937).

The first thing I did was to hunt up Hansen, the gymnastics teacher. He was right in his element, busy with hunting and fishing whenever he could spare the time from his farming. He also considered himself lucky in his change of fatherland, and happy over the independence that he thought he had gained here.

During the week I spent there I visited Bache, Johansen, Even Heg, and Helgesen from Drammen, as well as several others of the most practical farmers. A seminary student named Clausen had been elected minister and had been installed by a German minister from a neighboring colony.

Elling Eielsen lives here and has also married here. He has been acting as minister and in that capacity has traveled around to most of the Norwegian settlements. Because of certain objectionable actions he has lost the confidence of most of the people. His faction is now quite unimportant and is losing ground daily.*

On my return to Milwaukee I received information that made it seem necessary to visit the northern part of the territory. I went to Port Washington, 30 miles north on Lake Michigan. From there I made several excursions on foot within a radius of 15 or 20 miles. I then continued my journey to Fond du Lac (40 miles) on Lake Winnebago. From there I made several shorter trips into the country. Then I proceeded to Winnebago (50 miles), and then farther down the Wisconsin River to a little town called He (57 miles). Continuing to Mineral Point and through the towns of Belmont and Platteville to Galena, I stopped en route in several places to inspect the land.

It was now my intention, after a fairly thorough investigation of the natural conditions of Wisconsin, to cross the Mississippi to Iowa and to travel through that state to Burlington. I wished, if possible, to go from there by steamer to St. Louis. Drift ice prevented any crossing, and I had to content myself with staying in Galena, either until the ice became strong or the floes disappeared. I used this enforced stay to draft my letter to Gasmann. Since the Mississippi continued unnavigable I thought the best way to use my time was to visit some of my country-

* Few immigrant settlements have been the subject of so much study and writing as the Muskego Settlement in Wisconsin. See the chapter on "Pioneering Wisconsin" in Carlton C. Qualey, *Norwegian Settlement in the United States*, and *A Chronicle of Old Muskego: The Diary of Søren Bache, 1839–1847*, translated and edited by Clarence A. Clausen and Andreas Elviken (Northfield, 1951). An interesting popular survey is N. N. Rønning, *The Saga of Old Muskego* (Waterford, Wis., 1943).

men who lived in Wista or Hamilton Settlement, 30 miles northeast of Galena.

I spent Christmas at the home of a blacksmith named Knudtsen, from Drammen. He has established himself here and has built up an independent fortune. I visited the Norwegians living here, most of whom were busy with lead-mining and smelting, and all of whom without exception earned good money. I traveled with Knudtsen to several other Norwegian settlements – Rock Ground, Rock Prairie, and Jefferson Prairie, 30 to 40 miles east on the border of Illinois and Wisconsin. The most important agricultural improvements that I have seen in any Norwegian settlement had been made here.

I now returned to Galena, where I found letters from home forwarded by my commissioner in New Orleans according to my written instructions. Upon the receipt of these letters I continued my interrupted journey over the Mississippi, which now could be crossed with horses, to Dubuque in Iowa, where the main land office is located. I had a conversation with the governor, General Lucas, and was introduced by him to several members of the legislature, which had just convened. All of these men, with the greatest readiness and eagerness, gave me information and friendly advice.

I stayed here two days, then traveled north to Turkey River (24 miles), and up that river to the so-called "Neutral Ground" (42 miles) and returned the same way. The road ran southward along the Mississippi through several small towns to Davenport, directly opposite Rock Island. I continued west into the country, following 41° 30′ to Iowa City, in Johnson County (52 miles), where I am writing this letter. Here you have the account of my wanderings in "the glorious West," way out to the farthest limits of civilization. In a few days I shall have crossed even this boundary and shall be in the nearest Indian territory.

It is an easy matter to map out a travel route when sitting at home in one's parlor. In figuring on a map, distances seem so trifling and are so deceptive, that even though one figures accurately by degrees, yet it seems that one could easily travel the designated number of miles in a short time. If a person could only travel in a straight line without turning off to the right or left, he might actually cover that distance quickly. But traveling with the purpose that I had, little benefit could be derived from such a hasty trip.

To be able to make any choice, or to give advice or benefit to others, one must see and examine the interior of the country. Furthermore, it would require years to become fully and intimately acquainted with the tremendous stretches of land in this wonderfully beautiful region. In spite of the pains I have taken, I must admit that my knowledge is incomplete and will remain so. My purpose was to get a full and complete idea of the main characteristics of the entire region – its advantages and disadvantages with respect to agriculture and commerce. I hope to be able to accomplish my purpose to my own and my sponsors' satisfaction.

Regarding the choice of the states to which emigration from Norway should be directed, I think I am right in saying that it must lie between Wisconsin, Iowa, and Missouri. For that reason I felt justified in turning my main attention to these territories.

In my last letter, if I remember correctly, I expressed my firm conviction of the inexpediency of any emigration to California as long as such tremendous difficulties of transportation exist. It is necessary either to cross the Mexican Peninsula with its extremely high mountains or to go up the Missouri River and across the western prairie wilderness and the Rocky Mountains. This I have learned by talking with people who have made the trip.

All that I have heard has greatly strengthened my original belief in this land's overwhelming advantages in productiveness and favorable climate. Therefore, instead of visiting California as I had intended, I have decided, as soon as I have traveled through Iowa and a part of Missouri, to go down the Mississippi to the Red River, up this river to Natchitoches on the border of Texas, to inspect the northern part of that state.

In this connection I have been furnished with letters of introduction from Mr. Bryan, the consul from Texas in New Orleans, to several Texas planters of his acquaintance. Although Texas and Louisiana are in the same degree of latitude, the climate of Texas is far more temperate and healthful because of the higher altitude of the section near the mountains in New Mexico. Since I am offered free land for several thousand families, if as many can be brought here, I have felt it to be my first duty to make all investigations within my power in order to advise for or against the emigration of my countrymen to this land. Letters from home have told me of a report by a fellow Norwegian concerning the region near the Gulf of Mexico. Both written and oral reports have it that the southern tracts of land which lie within one and a half to two degrees from the Gulf of Mexico are without exception more or less subject to the occurrence of yellow fever. Health should be the first consideration in the choice of a new fatherland. Healthfulness, productiveness, and a market are the three main points that, to my mind, must determine such a choice.

I have begun writing a description of the West, to be as complete as possible, especially concerning Wisconsin, Iowa, and Missouri. This work will include a presentation of the natural conditions, the soil, climate, products, agriculture, commerce, industry, mineral wealth, opportunities for hunting and fishing, legislation, social conditions, and prospects for the future. It will be bound as one complete unit. Persons desiring to emigrate in the future may be able to judge from this work the wisdom or folly of leaving their own country.

I shall add to this a description of the present condition of the Norwegian settlers, the hardships that they suffer, and ways in which these may be lessened or avoided by future emigrants. In addition there will be an accurate account, based on fact, of the progressive work of a farm and an estimate of its increase in value, as well as useful information about many details which cannot be included under the main points already given.

This little work, which I hope to offer my countrymen, must be considered a small gift on the altar of my country. Since I myself was driven away by jealousy and envy from the valleys to which I had decided to dedicate my future feeble efforts, this is an atonement for the errors which in human weakness I have committed. If it is true that the seeds of virtue lie in our mistakes themselves, then I maintain the confident hope that this seed may grow to a tree whose fruit will give refreshment to thousands who now in slavish dependence gather the crumbs that fall from the aristocrat's rich table.

I have begun a correspondence with one of the largest ship companies in New York, Messrs. E. D. Hurlbut and Company. A merchant named Putram in Milwaukee has given me a letter of introduction to them. I hope an arrangement can be made to allow this company's ships to call at Norway to take on emigrants on the return trip from Havre, Liverpool, Bremen, or Gothenburg. I hope we may be able to charter an entire ship if we can happen on a cargo of the same tonnage. This would make the crossing to America remarkably cheap.

For the benefit of my sponsors, I have decided to prepare a plan for a colony at one or another of those places whose location and natural advantages seem most suitable for a Norwegian settlement. I trust that my mission will not be regarded by them as useless or unsuccessful. If that happens, the blame cannot be put upon my eager efforts to carry out, in full measure, the purpose of my mission.

I am in good health and have been so during my entire trip, which has not been interrupted by a single day's indisposition. If all goes as expected, I hope to be in Norway the last of April. There I think I shall have enough to do for several months.

There are countless things to consider

FROM J. R. REIERSEN, AT CINCINNATI, OHIO, TO FRIENDS

March 19, 1844

Arriving in New Orleans from Galveston, Texas, the twelfth of this month, I immediately called upon my commissioner, Mr. Philippi, and was disappointed to learn that he had not sent my letters to Norway via New York as I had requested. The reason he had not done so was that Mr. Gasmann had enclosed several other letters with my observations on immigration conditions which he wanted me to take back home. Besides there were two or three letters from my own acquaintances. Mr. Philippi, not understanding the language, was afraid he might misdirect them, so let the whole package await my arrival. Since a whole fleet of ships had just recently sailed for European ports, and it would be two or three weeks before another ship would sail for Havre or Liverpool, I decided it would be expedient for me to leave for New York immediately. At the same time, I had not received any answer from Hurlbut and Company in New York regarding my inquiry about freightage. Traveling by steamer to Cincinnati and Pittsburgh and then by rail and canal via Philadelphia, I could reach New York, where packets leave daily for Europe. I can make this trip in thirteen or fourteen days and, because of the fast sailings from New York, gain about a month. At the same time I hope to make some arrangement, if possible, with this freight concern.

For the past month I have been indisposed because of an earache and a swelling behind my left ear. This necessitated my seeing a doctor before proceeding. I consulted an especially competent physician, Dr. Strader, who advised me to go to a newly built hospital, Hotel for Invalids. After an examination, he soon operated. Almost immediately after the release of blood and matter, the swelling and pain left me, but a buzzing in my ear remained. Upon further examination this morning, the doctor found a small polyp in the ear. Even though he says it does not mean anything and is not at all serious, he thinks it advisable to remove it, but cannot be certain how long it will be before I can safely leave. So here I am unexpectedly detained when with all my heart and soul I long to hasten home.

The state of my finances will change drastically. I must admit I am a little worried, although I hope to see my way clear. In the meantime, I can understand perfectly what painful uncertainty the delay of my letters has caused all those interested in me back home. It is now just about the time I had figured that they should reach their destination. I am using the first quiet moment I have found to send you also a short account of the last part of my trip to Wisconsin and Texas.

My last letter was dated Iowa City. From there I took a hurried trip over the border to the most important Indian villages and had a truly interesting conversation with two chiefs who both spoke English. I returned through Jones, Louisa, and Des Moines counties to Burlington (75)* where I became acquainted with a young merchant from St. Louis, Mr. Dixon, who was traveling with his own horses and buggy. He suggested that I accompany him straight through the northern part of Missouri to Weston on the Missouri River. As this was the very part of Missouri – Platte and Osage counties – that I had intended to visit, I accepted his kind offer. After four days of strenuous driving through the most populated part of Missouri, we reached Weston, a young and prosperous little town in the southern part of Platte County. Two years ago it was added to Missouri. From there, I took a trip fifty miles north through Buchanan and Holt counties and returned the same way. Then I took a steamboat down the Missouri to Independence in Osage County on the south side of the river.

This is the town where caravans to Oregon and California or to Santa Fe in New Mexico annually assemble and make arrangements for the long journey across the immense western prairies. In spite of the early

* Presumably this means 75 miles.

season (it was February 4), two parties had already started preparations to leave. One party was composed exclusively of merchants, chiefly from St. Louis, on their way to Santa Fe with merchandise. The other was made up of emigrants from all parts of the United States and a few Germans bound for Oregon. You can easily understand that I seized the opportunity to get all the details of this journey. I introduced myself to a Major Adams, who was to lead the expedition and who already had been in Oregon twice. He readily gave me all the information I desired, showed me maps and plans of the districts through which they were to travel. Had my purse contained one hundred dollars more, I think he could have persuaded me to go along to Fort Hall on the west side of the Rocky Mountains. From there, he said, he would guarantee passage to San Francisco or Monterey in California. In brief, here are the most essential points concerning the route and means of travel.

The way lies entirely over rolling prairies, at first along the Kansas River and then over the flats of the Platte. It is so level and firm that one can use wagons, and carry along everything one wishes. During the last two years a new south pass through the Rockies has been discovered which is so low in elevation one can scarcely notice any ascent. The only perceptible slope was similar to a hill near Weston, he said, and that was hardly as steep as some of the highest hills between Lillesand and Laurvig. The stations, if I may call them such, are Fort Laramie, 700 miles from Independence, and Fort Hall, 500 miles farther on. Here the route forks, one branch leading to California and the other to Oregon. From Fort Hall, he estimated the distance to San Francisco Bay to be not more than 550 miles, and to the mouth of the Columbia, 700 miles. He himself had not been farther than Walla Walla, 450 miles from Fort Hall, to which place he was to guide the present caravan of 80 persons. He took me to an acquaintance of his, a Mr. Burnett, who had been to California. The latter gave me the most glowing description of that country's heavenly climate and fertility. He confirmed everything I had ever read or heard. He assured me, however, that it was very difficult to travel across the Mexican Peninsula and thence by sea, and it would be extremely expensive.

The present caravan had provided itself with light four-wheeled wagons pulled by two mules or oxen. Several emigrants intended to use cows instead of oxen, and Major Adams claimed that this was an advantage in many respects. No wagon was to be loaded with more than

1,500 to 2,000 pounds. The provisions each person should take consisted of the following: 150 pounds of wheat flour, 40 pounds of smoked meat, 10 pounds of salt, 20 pounds of coffee, 20 pounds of sugar, tea, rice, dried fruit, and the like. Every person was obliged to take at least one good rifle, 6 pounds of powder, and 12 pounds of shot. Other articles included were tin kitchen utensils, axes, spades, plows, saws, saddlers' and lumbermen's tools, screws, nails, hoops, and so forth, besides extra shoes for the horses and mules. Loose cattle should follow the procession. They stand the trip well. Loose horses were to be used only in chasing buffaloes, which one would meet 300 to 400 miles from the farthest settlements. A day's journey being twenty to thirty miles, it would take about seventy to eighty days for the whole trip. In Oregon land can be obtained for nothing, but the amount is uncertain. That is to be decided by the present Congress, and it may be assumed it will be 320 acres. In California one can get almost as much land as one wants and can defend. Do my friends have the courage and the desire for this little pleasure trip? But back to my interrupted journey.

From Independence, I took the stagecoach south to Harrisburg, then to Warsaw on the Osage River, from which this region derives the name of the Osage country (altogether about 65 miles). From there again east to Jefferson City on the Missouri (50 miles), where I boarded a steamer for St. Louis. I remained here only a day and sailed down the Mississippi to Natchez in the state of Mississippi and sent my trunk on to New Orleans. With only a light knapsack, I boarded another boat which went up the Red River to Natchitoches, Louisiana, on the border of Texas. From this town there was a diligence, or stage, to Nacogdoches and San Augustine [Texas]. I had a letter of introduction from the Texas consul in New Orleans to a Dr. Hald in San Augustine. He showed me every courtesy, gave me all the desired information, and took me around the vicinity. As there were no post stages established to the south, I had to hire a saddle horse to Austin, the new capital of Texas, located on the Colorado River, 80 miles west of San Augustine.

Congress had just assembled, and I easily gained admittance to the president of the republic, General Houston, who was intensely interested in having immigrants choose Texas as their new fatherland. He assured me that Congress would give a colony of Norwegians all the encouragement that could reasonably be expected. He believed that peace and quiet were as good as ensured since the President of the United States, in his last message, had emphatically declared that a continuation of warlike invasions and forays from Mexico would not be tolerated. He doubted that Texas would be admitted to the Union in the near future. In his opinion, one could consider the Comanche Indian hostilities at an end after their last defeat, and after Texas had established permanent forts along the northwest course of the Brazos and Colorado rivers. Now it seemed that nothing could hinder the rapid progress of the republic in prosperity and wealth, with an industrious and virtuous people occupying the vast stretches of fertile land.

After staying two days in Austin, I took the stage through Bastrop and Rutersville to Washington on the Brazos River (Rio Brazos de Dios), crossed that, and reached Houston, the former capital, after a five-day trip. On March 7 I arrived in Galveston on Galveston Bay, the most important trading center in Texas, of almost 4,000 inhabitants. The steamer *Harry of the West* (as Henry Clay is called by his party) was being loaded for New Orleans. Consequently I went on board. We left the evening of the ninth and reached our destination the morning of the twelfth.

Here you have the barest outline of my two months' journey. Space forbids me giving even the merest description of the regions through which I traveled, the experiences I have had, and the conclusions to which these have led me in choosing a site for a Norwegian colony. The worst of it is that in spite of the investigations, I cannot come to any final decision in the matter. Even after conscientiously weighing the advantages and the disadvantages of the different places, I am still painfully uncertain as to what locality I can recommend as the best selection for our countrymen. Every region offers its advantages, which in turn are counterbalanced by definite hazards. There are countless things to consider. It really would require a whole year to be able to determine where the greatest number of favorable conditions are found. One can certainly not rely upon another's judgment in that respect. Inhabitants of the different states and territories always recommend the region where they reside as the place that should unreservedly be chosen by new settlers. For some, this must be written off as self-interest, but on the whole I really believe it is sincere. Most of the regions combine so many advantages that one overlooks and underestimates the deficiencies and the evils. This is particularly true if one has had no special or personal experience elsewhere. The traveling observer is also influenced by this tendency to be most vividly impressed by the present scene, so that he changes his mind as often as he traverses and examines new regions. At last he develops such a lack of confidence in his own judgment that he is caught in a web of doubt and uncertainty.

While I was in Wisconsin, I was almost sure that was the territory to select. My trip through Iowa considerably modified that opinion. Then my sojourn in western Missouri brought me to a totally new decision, which was again considerably shaken by the trip through Texas. With this uncertainty of choosing rightly, I can do nothing but give a careful and conscientious presentation of the facts and data of each region in respect to everything that may influence one's selection of a future place of residence. Then I can leave the decision to each individual's own choice. I have decided to use my involuntary and unexpected stay here, which the doctor today predicts will last three weeks, in preparing such a description from the notes and experiences I have gathered. Then upon my arrival in Norway soon, I can present it to my sponsors and to the public. Here is a very brief summary:

Wisconsin combines a wholesome climate and an especially good market, but lacks in most places enough trees to meet the needs of a long and severe winter. The cold can be compared to that of southern Norway and necessitates the harvesting of considerable fodder for the animals. The chief product is wheat, which seems to thrive best where the snow covers the ground for several months.

Iowa is better provided with trees for her prairies and has perhaps, on the whole, a more fertile soil, but not so good a market. Ague and bilious fever are very prevalent in those regions that border the Mississippi, while the interior is as healthful as Wisconsin. Wheat in the north and corn or maize in the south are the staples. Both territories are well provided with river and spring water, and both have an inexhaustible supply of lead. Winter in the northern part resembles that of Wisconsin. In the south it is milder, but hardly agreeable on account of the sleet and cold rain instead of snow.

Missouri (the Platte and Osage country) is prairie land, with few trees, mild and short winters, a fairly healthful climate, especially along the Missouri, and exceptionally rich soil. Staple products are grain, corn, tobacco, and hemp, and the country is very well suited to the breeding of cattle and sheep. Not so well watered as Iowa.

Texas (the northern and interior parts) has a healthful climate and no winter. It is prairie land poorly provided with trees, but quite well watered. Its chief products are cotton and corn, harvested two or three times, and it is excellent land for breeding cattle and sheep. Also, the southern part is well suited to vineyards and tobacco, as well as sugar. War with Mexico and with the Indians has hitherto hindered the progress of the country.

It is with a very strange feeling that one may pass in this country through the changing climates of the different seasons in a short time – just a few days – and plunge suddenly from winter into spring and summer. The winter this year was unusually mild in Wisconsin. It wasn't until New Year's that the cold set in in earnest. When I left Galena in the middle of January, it had frozen hard several days in succession. In company with nine other sleighs, I rode the Father of Waters the entire twenty-four miles up to Dubuque. In heavy traveling clothes, over which I had a huge buffalo robe, and with overshoes of buffalo hide, as well as buffalo mittens, I traveled from that point over the prairies. In spite of all those clothes, I just barely kept warm the first two days and nights in an enclosed sleigh. On the third day, sleighing was over. The sun burned sharper, and the air was considerably milder. When I arrived at Iowa City, it was just like spring at home. Through Missouri the air was wonderfully mild and springlike except that the sun burned sharper than at home. Down along the Mississippi the trees were beginning to leaf, and near Natchez, the cherry trees were in the loveliest full bloom. Coming into Texas, I found the prairie fresh and green. In Austin, I ate green peas brought into the market. It struck me as the pleasantest summer, not excessively hot. In New Orleans the mosquitoes and flies had already appeared in swarms.

On my trip through Texas I met immigrants almost every day who were seeking land in different places. Some had whole families in their wagons, which served as substitutes for houses or tents. Not far from Bastrop, I met a driver with a four-spanned wagon and a load of 2,500 pounds bound for Austin. He had been in Texas twelve months, and even though he was a native Virginian, he had resided a long time in southern Missouri. He considered Texas far superior to Missouri for all kinds of agriculture. He enjoyed better health there, he said, and was not plagued to death by mosquitoes. He lived on a high prairie, and when I asked if he did not find the sun unbearable on a clear summer day, he declared that he did not find the heat so oppressive here as in

Missouri and Virginia, for the wind that blew steadily all day made the open prairie quite pleasant.

This must be enough for this time, probably until my homecoming. You have the privilege of using this letter at your discretion. As I am anxious to get this sent with the early morning post and will have no time to write another letter to my family, I beg you kindly to acquaint them with my condition. I am otherwise quite well and am sure this incident will have no other injurious effect than to delay my return. I could ask about and wish to know many, many things, but to no avail. I shall close my last letter from America for the present with friendly greetings.

Spreading the Gospel

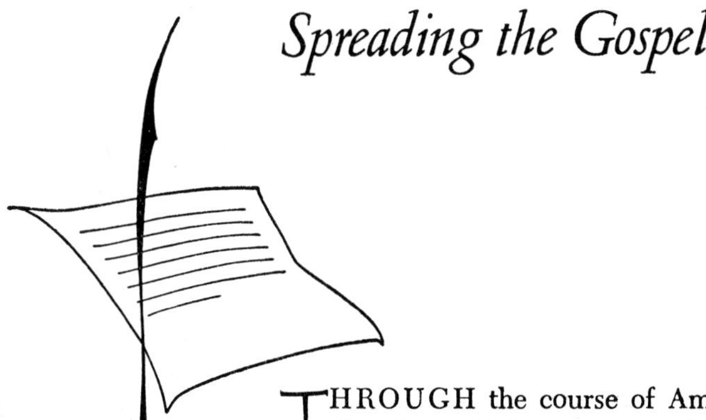

THROUGH the course of American history churches and their ministers have been identified with the country's changing frontiers. Often missionaries to the Indians have preceded the settlers, and ministers have seldom been far behind the pioneers. In many European countries the church, Catholic or Protestant, took an active interest in the spiritual welfare of its emigrated sons and daughters cut loose from established religious ties.

The state church of Norway, it is true, at first showed little concern about its former adherents who had left for America, but at an early date individual ministers threw in their lot with the emigrants, and none was more zealous than the Reverend J. W. C. Dietrichson. He went out from Norway in 1844 to the wild western regions of his emigrated countrymen with the set purpose of bringing religious order out of disorder, organizing congregations on the basis of state-church ritual, and establishing a firm and regular Norwegian-American Lutheranism.

Dietrichson was a young and well-educated minister with high-church leanings. He came of "a military family whose traditions, it is said, included a sharp temper, severity, and lordliness" — and his brief American career unquestionably strengthened these traditions. What he wanted to bring about was, in effect, "an ecclesiastical transfer from the valleys of Norway to the woods and prairies of the West. He intended to assure 'to those who valued the Church of Norway, its ritual and history, an unbroken continuity of this Church upon American soil.'" *

* Blegen, *Norwegian Migration*, vol. 2, pp. 142–143. See also, on Dietrichson and the conditions under which he did his work, Gunnar J. Malmin, ed., *America in the Forties: The Letters of Munch Ræder* (Minneapolis, 1929), chaps. 6–7, and Clarence A. Clausen and Andreas Elviken, *A Chronicle of Old Muskego: The Diary of Søren Bache* (Northfield, 1951).

Arrived in Wisconsin, this energetic minister set about his work with determination, traveled extensively in the settlements, organized congregations, and reproved those who in his judgment were leading the immigrants astray. He scrutinized very critically the credentials of those who had emerged as religious leaders. As he viewed the difficult conditions in which he found the emigrants he was so appalled that he raised his voice in opposition to the entire movement of emigration. He returned to his native country in 1845 and published a book about his travels and observations.* He went back to America the next year with a subsidy from the Norwegian government given him on the virtual condition that he should use his pen to counteract "the disturbing and frivolous emigration desire," wrote letter after letter to Norway for newspaper publication, interested himself in enlisting other trained clergymen to come to the West, and ultimately, after leaving a trail of religious organization as well as of animosities, returned to Norway for good in 1850.

The name and character of Dietrichson are woven into the pioneer story of the Norwegian immigrants, at Muskego, Koshkonong, and elsewhere. In his stormy New World career he had much influence in establishing the immigrant Lutheran church in mid-America as well as in furthering a tradition of religious controversy among the immigrants. The man was sincere and able, but he lacked imagination. He was unable to appraise the price of pioneering in terms of its long-time values; and his appeals to his countrymen to stay at home fell, in the main, on deaf ears among everyday people whose insight was greater than his.

Dietrichson's letters, published in Norwegian newspapers, would make a large volume if brought together in their entirety. Here are presented portions of the letters in the period from 1844 to 1848, translated for the first time into English. Taken as a whole they give a somewhat more genial and less severe picture of this high-purposed missionary than one ordinarily finds in the church histories that recount his career. It is interesting to note that he himself understood some of his limitations, and in one of his letters he cheerfully admitted that he was "better suited for breaking the ice, for plowing and hoeing and rough-planing"

* Dietrichson, *Reise blandt de norske emigranter i "de forenede Nordamerikanske Fristater"* (Stavanger, 1846). This interesting narrative ("Travels among the Norwegian Emigrants in the United North American Free States") has not yet been translated into English.

than he was for "harrowing and filing, for guiding and maintaining." His letters contain vivid descriptions of conditions as he saw them, and he voices his convictions with forthrightness and vigor, particularly in all matters pertaining to emigration itself, which he regarded as a calamity for the home country and an evil for the emigrants themselves.

America, he believed, was neither the "paradise nor the Canaan that people dream about," and his vision was not capable of encompassing the generation ahead save as he worked for the creation of a church that almost certainly would be projected into a long future. Praised and criticized both by his contemporaries and in later times, Dietrichson stood without compromise for what he regarded as right and proper in respect to the immigrant church. The high ceremonial that he established unquestionably added "an element of beauty and dignity and of the consoling security inherent in traditional forms to the lives of frontier men and women." *

A beer glass served as our chalice

WRITTEN AT MUSKEGO, WISCONSIN †

September 25, 1844

On Thursday evening, July 25, I left New York on board one of the largest of the American steamboats, which have so often been described and praised for their elegance. We sailed up the beautiful, swift-flowing Hudson River; but as night came on quickly and we reached our destination, Albany, at seven o'clock the following morning, we did not see much of the beautiful scenery which is said to be found along the banks of this river. At sunrise I was out of my berth to catch a glimpse of some of the beautiful sights. The morning was cool and misty, but gradually the weather improved so that I really discovered many fine views. It is true that I could have taken one of the boats that make this trip in the daytime, but since the fare is then twice as high, it would have made too great inroads on my funds. And as these funds had been supplied me by the Christian sacrifices of others, I preferred here as always to go with-

* Blegen, *Norwegian Migration,* vol. 2, p. 145.

† *Morgenbladet* printed this letter in two installments, December 8 and 9, 1844.

out and save, rather than cut too large a thong out of another man's leather. . . .

The first week I visited several places in the settlement [Muskego] and found that my fear was only too well grounded that the emigrants here have not had very good luck. It is true that they have acquired land: forty, eighty, one hundred and sixty, and some even two or three hundred acres, but many of them owe money on the land and no one has succeeded in cultivating very much. Practically all live in small, miserable log houses consisting of one single room in which everything is crowded together. So far only a few have outhouses. When they have acquired a couple of cows and a yoke of oxen they are considered to be pretty well off here, since only a few have horses. Last autumn there was much disease and misery, but this year things have been better. I have made my home with Clausen's agreeable family and have made my excursions from there. The first Sunday after my arrival, the tenth Sunday after Trinity, I preached to a fairly large congregation in one of the most spacious houses here. A small table with a white cloth was our communion table, and a beer glass and a crockery plate served as our chalice and paten at the administration of the Eucharist.

I preached my sermon deeply moved at seeing so many of my dear countrymen in this distant foreign country, and there was general emotion among the people, who were probably even more vividly reminded of the beautiful services of their native country by hearing the Norwegian language again and seeing the complete Norwegian clerical robes. The next morning, August 12, Clausen and I set out on a journey to Chicago in Illinois to conduct a service for the Norwegians there.

During our conversation about the bishopric we also touched on the question of ordination, and Mr. Unonius then declared that he could in no way accept Clausen as a properly ordained minister because he had not been ordained by a bishop, while he was willing to accept me. He is now trying to give others the same opinion of Clausen, and therefore it is important, also for this reason, that we get a statement from a competent authority in Norway concerning Clausen's ordination. Thus, if it had come about that our old venerable bishop in Oslo had fallen ill when I was about to be ordained and a minister had officiated at my ordination, Unonius would have had to say the same thing about me. Many of the Norwegians do not realize that this attitude is contrary to the teachings of the Lutheran church.

To preserve the ritual of their fathers

WRITTEN AT KOSHKONONG PRAIRIE, WISCONSIN*

December 28, 1844

The conditions I have drawn up for belonging to the Norwegian Lutheran congregation in Koshkonong are the following:

In October 1844, a Norwegian Lutheran congregation was founded among the Norwegians living at Koshkonong Prairie in Dane and Jefferson counties, Wisconsin Territory in North America. The conditions are as follows:

1. Do you wish to belong to the Norwegian Lutheran congregation here?
2. Will you then submit to the ecclesiastical laws which our Norwegian church ritual stipulates?
3. Will you promise that in the future you will not accept or recognize anyone as your pastor and spiritual guide but a person who can prove and clearly show that he has been rightly called and properly ordained by the Norwegian Lutheran church ritual—and will you promise to obey the clergyman, whom you as a part of the congregation choose for your pastor, as your spiritual authority in what he demands of you in accordance with your native country's (Norway's) church ritual?
4. Will you by signing your name here, or having it signed for you, acknowledge that you enter the congregation on the said conditions?

After I had read these conditions aloud, I reminded the people that here they were in the country of liberty, and that everyone was free to join any congregation he pleased, without any person's being able to hurt a hair of his head because of it. I only asked them to consider what they did, if they wanted to separate themselves from the true church of which they had become members by baptism, and urged all who wanted to register as members of the congregation that they must not do this for any other reason than that they wanted to preserve the pure teachings and edifying ritual of their fathers. And thus on this occasion about forty family fathers with their wives and children were registered as members, besides some unmarried persons. Both men and women and confirmed children answered each for himself, while the parents answered for the unconfirmed children. This is the way it happened in

* This letter appeared in *Stavanger Amtstidende og Adresseavis*, March 30, April 3, 7, 10, 1845.

the eastern (the older) part of the settlement—and a few days later I proceeded in the same manner in the western colony, where likewise quite a few people joined the congregation.

The congregation's decision as to its permanent pastor may be made in one of two ways: either it may call Pastor Clausen or me, or it may leave it up to certain men in Norway, whom it will have appointed for this, to call a minister from the native country. If it now should choose me and the conditions it makes are such that I, remembering my holy duties toward my future wife and child, should find them acceptable, what then is there for me to do but to see in this call from the congregation a call from the Lord which I must heed if I want to be true to Him and which I dare in no way decline, in case there should be no Christian theologian in the native country who wanted to take my place and continue the work we have started here? It is certain, however, that if I could follow my bent, I would rather accept the most miserable calling in one of the most desolate places in Norway than a position in any other country for which I was offered many thousands of dollars a year, for my love of my native country has always been fervent and always will be.

As far as I know myself, it is also very likely that I am better suited for breaking the ice, for plowing and hoeing and rough-planing than for harrowing and filing, for guiding and maintaining. I say this both because of my temperament and because of the special talents the Lord has given me (for each of us has his peculiar gifts granted him by the grace of God). Others have excellent talents, and the ability which is required for the guiding and maintaining of a congregation is much finer than the qualities I possess. But may God's will be done and in the course of time bring about the best for us all! The Lord will place me and use me where He chooses. If there is no other solution I shall have to persuade Pastor Clausen to visit the congregation for me during my absence.

The first Norwegian colony I then visited [on a trip to some border settlements between Wisconsin and Illinois] is located at Jefferson Prairie partly in Rock County, Wisconsin, and partly in Boone County, Illinois. It is here that Elling Eielsen Sunve has most of his staunch followers (besides some others in Muskego) among whom he officiates as pastor both by preaching and administration of the sacraments.* As a

* On Eielsen, as he is more commonly known, see my *Norwegian Migration*, vol. 2, pp. 131–137, and the references there given.

proof of the way in which Elling and his followers distort and misrepresent everything that is not to their liking let me cite the following incident:

The last time I visited this settlement and conducted divine service there (in September), some of Elling's most zealous followers were present to watch my words and extract poison from them later to be used against me. That day I took, from Revelation 3:11, the following words for my text: "Behold I come quickly; hold that fast which thou hast, that no man take thy crown." From this I explained how we as Christians and true members of the church must preserve that which we have in the church, lest we lose our crown when the Lord comes. In my sermon I reminded the people that besides the supreme blessings of the church, the pure word, and the holy sacraments, we ought also for our edification to preserve the beautiful ritual we hold from our fathers. This was now interpreted by the Ellingians to the effect that I had taught the people to embrace sin and corruption. Soon after my departure, Elling arrived and received this interpretation from his followers. He took the same text and preached a sermon on the impious ministers who came from Norway, stating that the one most recently arrived had explicitly taught the people to embrace sin and corruption, while he himself taught them something very different, and so on. Such is the way, as I have written before, in which this person is pleased to treat God's word and the sacred sacraments of the Lord! May God have mercy on him!

Peasants will rue the day they emigrated

WRITTEN AT KOSHKONONG PRAIRIE, WISCONSIN*

May 10, 1845

I wish to God it were not true, as it is related here, that so many emigrants have decided to come over from Norway this year! America is certainly neither the paradise nor the Canaan that people dream about. What I wrote about the emigration in my letter of January is true. I know very well that in Norway, as also here, there are only too many

* This letter appeared in *Stavanger Amtstidende og Adresseavis*, July 21, 1845

people who have a personal interest in the matter and they want to make out that what I say is false. Here too many persons are displeased with what I have related, partly because they see their emigration in the wrong light, partly because they are ashamed to admit that they have not gained by it, and partly because they want more people to come after them. It is becoming increasingly evident, that peasants, in particular, who are in fairly easy circumstances in Norway and leave there will certainly some day rue the day they emigrated from Norway. But it is probably no use to speak against something which, according to the personal confessions of some of these people, has become like a disease in those who desire to emigrate: once they have taken it into their heads that they want to emigrate, they cannot be talked out of it. If only my dear countrymen, as proof of my truthfulness, would consider that naturally I am without any personal interest in this matter whatsoever and therefore more able than the emigrants themselves and the publicists at home to see it in a more correct light – what possible reason could I have for lying?

As I have promised to take letters home with me from the emigrants to their relatives and friends, the other day a man of my congregation, Knud Amundsen Jamsgaard from Vinje clerical district, brought me a letter to his brother in Norway. He asked me to read the letter to him, since somebody else at his request had written it for him. I did so and refuted many things in the letter which had been put in a brilliant light in order to induce his brother to join him in America. He then admitted in the presence of witnesses that there was indeed a little something in the letter which was not true, but when I asked his permission to add a few words to the letter concerning this, he would not let me. I then told him that in my next letter to Norway I would mention this example as one of the many illustrations of the way in which letters are written from here to Norway, and that he ought not to be surprised if some day he should get hold of a Norwegian newspaper in which this incident was described. "I don't mind your putting it in the newspapers," he said, "but I won't let you add anything in the letter to my brother." He probably knew from experience that those in Norway who want to emigrate care less about warnings against emigration which they read in the public papers than about that which their relatives write to them. As I have said, this is only one illustration out of many.

Controversy awaits the minister

WRITTEN ON A RETURN VISIT TO NORWAY*

August 1845

Recently I returned to my native country because I felt that from here I would be able to work for the ecclesiastical benefit of our emigrated fellow countrymen in more ways than I was able to do in distant America. The first step I must take to accomplish this purpose is to urge theologians and young clergymen in Norway to consider whether there may not be someone among them who may feel a call to go as minister to the Norwegians over there, in order to replace me and continue the work I have begun. Well aware of my own shortcomings, I have had a good opportunity to get a clear impression of the qualifications that would be expected of the man who devotes himself to such a task. Christian love, a pure, unselfish interest in the cause which shuns no sacrifice, besides a clear understanding of matters of doctrine, peace of mind based on faith and profession, firmness in adherence to objective church fundamentals, ability to handle those who dissent from pure doctrine, strength and determination combined with endurance and thoughtfulness, patience, and steadfastness – these are the main qualities to be looked for in the one who is to hold his own on the battlefield of controversy that awaits every honest Lutheran minister over there.

It should always be remembered, however, that the Lord's power works its purpose through weakness, and that the one who trusts in Him and works with sincerity and prayer in His name shall not suffer disgrace. I myself have experienced how an unworthy instrument may be blessed in his imperfect but honest endeavors. If it is God's will that I shall go back to America, I dare not disobey the call. Rather than see the church which was established among our emigrated countrymen destroyed, rather than imagine the beloved distant congregation without pastor and wholesome spiritual nourishment, I would return to America for a shorter or longer period of time. But if someone with Christian faith in his heart, a clear churchly view, and with God's living word on his lips will go in my place, then my conscience will not be uneasy if I . . . continue my efforts at home for the spiritual welfare of our countrymen out there, since I now have fulfilled the obligation that I undertook and reached the goal of my journey.

* *Morgenbladet* printed this letter August 16, 1845.

Confused by silly notions of liberty

WRITTEN ON A RETURN VISIT TO NORWAY*

March 19, 1846

In *Bratsberg Amts Correspondent* No. 19, which I received a couple of days ago, are some excerpts from a letter by the carpenter Niels Hansen Nærum, who emigrated to America in the spring of 1844 and who has stayed in the Muskego Settlement in Wisconsin Territory. Nærum relates—which must of course be pleasant news for his friends and relatives— that he is most happy in his emigration. In this happiness of his, however, he directs some bitter attacks at me because, to the best of my ability, I have not been able to find the condition of the Norwegian emigrants as good and fortunate as he describes it, and because I have permitted myself to express my opinion of the Norwegian settlements in America in *private* letters, of which some have from time to time been published in various newspapers in this country. Just as I have not, after my return to Norway, undertaken to reply to any of Mr. Reiersen's attacks on me in consequence of my letters, just as unnecessary and futile should I have considered it to reply to any of Nærum's letters were it not for the fact that I feel obligated to pick up my pen because of Nærum's mention of *ecclesiastical* conditions among the emigrants.

It is quite true, as Mr. Nærum writes, that the most important lack among the Norwegian emigrants is adequate church facilities and spiritual guidance from good and competent pastors endowed with Christian strength and firmness in matters of ritual. It is also correct that there would be enough work over there not only for three or four but for four or five ministers. But it is likewise true that the economic condition of the Norwegian settlers is such that it is in no way correct to affirm, as Nærum does, that these ministers would be able to make a modest let alone satisfactory living for themselves, unless the churches of the emigrants receive support from their native country.

With regard to Pastor Clausen, that fine and zealous servant of the Lord who has offended Nærum and several other persons who desire to have a church ritual without wanting to submit to the regulations that are necessary to such a ritual, I may say that Clausen's "strictness," as Nærum calls it, simply consists of his having in Muskego, to which

* This letter appeared in *Bratsberg-Amts Correspondent*, March 27, 1846.

colony he was originally called as pastor, demanded that those who wanted to belong to a *Norwegian Lutheran* congregation would have to submit to the *ecclesiastical* regulations found in the ritual of the Norwegian Lutheran church, to which also Clausen is bound by his oath as ordained minister. On these conditions both Nærum and the others had first entered the Norwegian Lutheran congregation founded in Muskego by Clausen. But when some of them, confused by silly notions of liberty, took it into their heads to reorganize the church community and Clausen, of course, neither could nor would have ecclesiastical regulations dictated to him by these authorities, these individuals became very disgruntled. I suppose it is this disgruntlement that vents itself against Clausen and myself, though I must of course be completely agreed with him in this ecclesiastical firmness, even if Nærum calls it "strictness."

For that matter, it is strange that several of the accounts of the splendid conditions in America recently published should come from persons living in the settlement of Muskego, which colony, even in Mr. Reiersen's judgment, is one of the most unfortunate places for a Norwegian settlement. As Reiersen puts it, it is "a flat, swampy stretch of land with a thin layer of mold over a layer of clay, where the emigrants are not able to feed themselves by the cultivation of the land they have cleared." And yet, despite these published statements of Mr. Reiersen's on this settlement, the emigrants from this colony, who described everything over there in such glowing terms and of whom many know no other place than their own settlement, like Nærum are completely agreed with Reiersen in his account of America. Thus Reiersen will of course describe Texas, where he has gone from what I have heard, as Nærum does Muskego, where he is living, as *the best place.*

We had to move into a one-room cabin

WRITTEN AT MUSKEGO, WISCONSIN*

October 15, 1846

After spending all of Sunday in Milwaukee, on Monday, [September] 21, we set out and arrived here the following day. Nothing at all had been prepared for our arrival. Clausen had left this place at the end of

* Originally this letter was published in *Bergens Stiftstidende*, December 17, 1846.

July, since he had to take over the other congregation to which he had been called. The obligations my congregation had assumed toward me as a result of the conditions on which it had called me, namely to buy land and build a house for me, had not been fulfilled. Things had gone here the way they do everywhere when there is no energetic, determined person to lead and guide people of whom some want to go forward while others want to go back. People here have waited and waited until the land that had been designated for me before my departure was bought up by a speculator who hoped to trick us to his own profit later. Consequently we had to move into a small, open one-room cabin to which had been added a little annex made of thin boards that serves as kitchen. If it had not been for one of the families in my congregation that was more thoughtful than the others, we should have had to go without the necessities of life the first days. For several nights our beds consisted simply of fresh straw strewn on the floor on top of which we put our mattresses, until we got some bedsteads put together. Gradually we have arranged things a little more comfortably in our small home, however, and after considering our situation for a while, some of the members of the congregation have brought us the most necessary victuals like flour, potatoes, and a little bacon, which, together with some prairie chickens that we received as presents, have made up our meals thus far.

On Sunday, September 27, I held the first divine service in one of our small churches, and afterward there was a meeting of the members of the congregation who were present. Most of them seemed to be very happy that I had returned to them and expressed their regrets that the obligations of the congregation toward its pastor had thus far been fulfilled so poorly. But you know that for one thing it takes a very long time before many people get around to thinking and for another there is a great deal of illness here at present. There is hardly a family, nay hardly a house in the whole settlement, that does not have sick people in it, indeed some are very dangerously ill and several have died, so that this autumn there is general misery among the Norwegian settlers. The same condition prevails in the other Norwegian settlements.

The old, bad Norwegian custom of drinking

WRITTEN AT KOSHKONONG, WISCONSIN*

January 29, 1847

We wrote to you about the middle of October and told you that we had arrived up here safe and sound, but that nothing had been prepared against our arrival – no land bought, no house built – and that therefore we had to live in a beautifully located but cold little cabin until our own house was ready. A few days before Christmas we were fortunate enough to be able to move into our new parsonage, a small, fairly well equipped log house with living room, bedroom, study, and kitchen, everything very small. Our furniture is extremely simple: in the living room a table and four wooden chairs, in the bedroom two camp bedsteads and two chairs, in the study a table and a bench, both made by myself, and also two wooden stools.

The parsonage, which is surrounded by a few knotty oak trees, is located at the outskirts of the prairie on the twenty acres of land bought by the congregation. The site is not as beautiful as one might have wished, but it is a convenient location for the members of the congregation, as it is halfway between our two small churches and at the same time practically in the center of the congregation. I have a distance of three or four English miles (about half a Norwegian mile) to either church. The worst thing is that it is difficult to get both water and firewood here. At present you have to drive an English mile for water, but this situation will probably be improved when we get around to digging a well that is deep enough. Thus far we have not been able to get water twenty feet down. We have to pay half a dollar a week for water delivery. Firewood costs us about a dollar a week. There is much talk about buying more land for the parsonage, but nothing comes of it but talk, since for one thing the money is lacking and besides there is no longer any convenient land available in this neighborhood. As a matter of fact, I am afraid that in a few years many of the settlers will suffer lack of wood, since most of the forest around here has either been cut down or bought up, and there is, as far as I know, no peat, which might serve as a substitute.

God be praised we have been in good health all the time, apart from a few minor colds, but of course we too suffer in many ways from the

* This letter appeared in the *Stavanger Amtstidende og Adresseavis*, April 10, 1847.

general illness and disease which make life so difficult for the settlers. There is a great lack of money among people, and as a consequence of this I have only received a very small part of my salary for the first term. On the whole I cannot, much as I would like to, see much change for the better in the temporal conditions of the settlers since I was last here. My congregation has increased considerably in number both since the time I left it and after my return here. At present it consists of 1,076 registered members, while at the time of my return to Norway it counted only 575 souls, but I doubt whether it has gained correspondingly in spiritual and economic strength.

I am sorry to say that as is the old, bad Norwegian custom, the deplorable desire for drinking and rioting has held sway in the congregation, especially during Christmas but also at other times. Besides the attitude of most people is one of apathy and indifference. But otherwise it must be truthfully admitted that once it recognized its obligation to provide the pastor with a house, the congregation has made greater sacrifices than might be expected at a time when conditions are so unfavorable. Three hundred and fifty dollars had been assessed for purchase of land and construction of the parsonage, and of this amount about two hundred dollars have now been paid up. Arrangements for the building of the house were made with contractors after the congregation had provided the lumber. But the result of this was that most of the contractors did a bad job; the roof in particular is so poor that both snow and rain come through and for several days we have not been able to keep dry in our rooms. It is a good thing, however, that the contractors have not received their full payment, for in this way we can force them to improve the quality of their work.

Gifts of Christian charity

WRITTEN AT KOSHKONONG, WISCONSIN*

June 7, 1847

But do you not, then, have anything good? you might ask. Oh, yes indeed, very much, God be praised! My congregation also consists of

* *Nordlyset* (Trondhjem) printed this letter September 17, 1847. Only a portion of it is given here. Dietrichson has been enumerating various troubles with neighbors at the point where the excerpt begins.

many Christian and honest members who are deeply and sincerely devoted to me. On many occasions they give me proofs of their love by presenting me with gifts of Christian charity, thus trying to stave off the want that we should otherwise often suffer because of my scant salary. I see clearly now that I cannot expect to receive the salary which the congregation has promised me — that is, \$300 — at least not for this year in which there has been so much illness and misery. I suppose I might obtain my salary through legal process, insisting on the rights that every contract offers, but I do not want to, needless to say. This first year has also brought me many unforeseen expenditures. Therefore, it was most welcome when the government granted me 200 specie dollars, though I realize that I cannot expect to receive more than 94 specie dollars of the sum, as the rest will have to be spent for payment of my debt. Though the resolution states that the sum granted me is to be regarded as "contribution toward payment of my traveling expenses," I still feel justified in regarding the grant as help toward the payment of my expenses in general during my stay here.

We have a newspaper, nothing less!

WRITTEN AT KOSHKONONG, WISCONSIN*

August 23, 1847

But if nature this summer has thus far withheld its flora, culture has begun to burgeon forth here among the Norwegians in the West and has produced a blossom whose color and scent will undoubtedly become the joy of many an emigrated Norseman: We have a newspaper, nothing less! Its name is *Nordlyset*, and it has for its motto: "Having done our duty, we turn to useful reading, in order to return to our duty with renewed vigor." † This paper is printed in Muskego (which has now been given the name of Norway), where Mr. Søren Bache has established a printing press. Mr. J. D. Reymert is the editor, and one year's subscription costs two dollars. The purpose of the paper is as follows: "Besides information about the constitution of this country and reports from

* This letter appeared in *Nordlyset* (Trondhjem), November 19, 1847.

† See my chapter on "Launching an Immigrant Press," in *Norwegian Migration*, vol. 2, pp. 277–299.

Scandinavia, historical, agricultural, and religious news, we intend to bring contributions from private individuals and everything else that is suitable and useful for the information and entertainment of our readers. The editors will make every effort to preserve the strictest possible neutrality in matters of politics and religion."

This quotation from the second issue of the paper (only two numbers have appeared thus far) makes it clear that the editors have very ambitious plans. Although it would undoubtedly in many ways be a good and useful thing for the Norwegian emigrants to have such a paper, and although I wish the editors all possible success in their enterprise, I still fear, and, basing my judgment on the first two numbers, apparently with some reason, that the editing of this kind of paper may prove too much for the ability of those who have undertaken it. I am taking the paper, hoping for better times for it, and I consider it my duty to do everything I can for its improvement and continued existence. But I am very much afraid that this paper will suffer the fate of the paper *Scandinavia* in New York, which had to cease publication after fifteen or sixteen numbers had appeared.

Taylor has been elected president

WRITTEN AT KOSHKONONG PARSONAGE,
WISCONSIN*

November 30, 1848

A blissful peace reigns in my congregations, and this peace, so beneficial to both our inner and outer life, has now lasted a year. We hope that it will daily be strengthened and our church order, developing through it, become more firmly established.† You may believe that I thank the Lord for what He has accomplished, and I rejoice the more I am confirmed in my hope that I have not been working in vain. On April 1, 1850 – that is only a year from next spring – my period of service with this congregation will end. The way things have developed this year, I might be persuaded to take over the ministry here for a longer

* This letter appeared in *Christiania-Posten*, February 8, 1849.

† Somewhat less tranquil times in Dietrichson's congregation are described in my *Norwegian Migration*, vol. 2, pp. 145–146, and in Marcus Lee Hansen, "Immigration and Puritanism," in *Norwegian-American Studies and Records* (Northfield, Minn.), 9:19–20 (1936).

period of time – if only I could get more clergymen from Norway who could serve the many remote settlements which I am able to serve only rarely – but I long acutely for my native country and would even more willingly serve as a minister there. What a beautiful calling the minister has!

At Rock River and Pine Lake I met, as had been agreed, Pastor Stub, who unfortunately has been ill but now, God be praised, is well again. My hope that he might take over these two chapels was disappointed, since he, at least for the coming year, will not be able to do so. It was arranged, however, that to enable the congregations to have divine service more than the four times a year that I am able to visit them, he as my curate will call on them twice a year.

Of political news the most important is that General Zachary Taylor, general of the Free States in the last war against Mexico, has been elected president. He was the candidate of the Whigs; Cass was the candidate of the Democratic party. A third political party, which has developed this year under the name of Free Soil Men and is said to be opposed to the spreading of slavery to the new territories of Oregon, California, and Mexico, had nominated Van Buren, the ex-president, as its candidate. Before election day, I had daily canvassers from all three parties who wanted me to persuade the Norwegians here to vote for their respective parties; but I considered it the correct thing to remain neutral.

With regard to the harvest, the winter wheat was not very good, but spring wheat and other grains yielded good crops. There is potato blight in most places; we got about forty bushels (*ca.* ten barrels) of potatoes after sowing three bushels; but they rot quickly here. From wild grapes we have made an excellent wine.

Two weeks ago, we had a fire at our house; but we escaped with only the scare and the loss of the roof and some clothes. It is strange that this kind of thing does not happen more often here; for the houses are covered with pine shavings, and instead of brick chimneys we have stovepipes that are very thin and, therefore, quickly get red hot. Some of the clay around the pipe had probably fallen down so that it touched the roof, which immediately caught fire. Through a slit in the floor of the loft the fire was discovered from the kitchen. By the time we were alerted, the whole roof was on fire. Some clothes were burned; but by means of quick aid from the neighboring farms, the fire was put out before it reached the walls. Fortunately the wind was not blowing.

Journeying toward New Horizons

TO New York eyes the "sloopfolk," when they reached the American metropolis after their fourteen-week voyage, were a "novel sight," but as the sailing vessels of the 1830's and 1840's landed thousands of immigrants from the north of Europe, the novelty vanished. The arrival of folk of strange speech and costume became routine. And as the traffic increased in volume, the immigrants, after quarantine and after scrubbing their clothes, landed in a hubbub of runners and agents ready to direct them to "boarding houses" and to supply them with tickets for the West – ready also to separate them from their money.

Before the emigrant traffic swung away from New York to Quebec in the early 1850's, the travel route to the interior normally was by way of the Hudson to Albany, then by canalboat to Buffalo, and thereupon by Great Lakes vessels to Milwaukee or Chicago. As railroad lines were extended, the emigrants became less dependent than they had been in earlier days on transportation by river and canal. Thus in 1845 some three hundred Norwegians made the trip from New York to Buffalo in what one of them described as a row of "wonderful closed wagons with windows," each passenger paying a fare of $3.50. An engine, the emigrant recorded, hauled fifteen cars loaded with people and baggage, stopping the first night in Utica and the second in Rochester. "Since the nights were dark," he wrote, "we stood still."

The journey inland, by river, canal, land, and lakes, revealed many of the wonders of America, and the immigrants looked with curious eyes at the land of their choice. But to most of them the trip was no pleasure excursion. Many were ill or weak after long and stormy ocean voyages. Few had much money. Crowded, with their children and baggage, into cramped quarters, they often had little taste for the beauties of the country they passed through. A newcomer of 1851 tells of "ten long, rough days" on the Erie Canal, thrust with his friends into small space and "treated like so many swine." Death traveled with the newcomers, and burials on land succeeded earlier burials at sea. Nor were conditions on board lake vessels any relief from those on canalboats. The torment of crowding plus weariness and illness left deep marks on those who survived. The introduction to America was an ordeal, but, as Professor Carl Wittke suggests, "it must not be forgotten that thousands upon thousands survived, and that these counted the cost lightly, in view of the new opportunities open to them in America." *

The physical rigors of the journey were bad enough, but to them were added the impositions of what Dr. Wittke calls "beasts of prey in human form" – the runners and agents who swarmed and fought over the immigrants when they arrived in New York, cheating and defrauding them at every opportunity.† Not infrequently guides and interpreters who seemed friendly and helpful disappeared with their money, sometimes on the pretext of aiding them in the business of money exchange. As a consequence, for many the high hope of getting out to the rich lands of the Middle West was postponed, and instead they were forced to look desperately for jobs in such cities as Rochester, Albany, and Buffalo, or to throw themselves on the mercy of successful immigrants of an earlier day, men of the stamp of Lars Larsen in Rochester, whose kindness and generosity have become an honored part of the American immigrant tradition.

As time went on many efforts were made to improve the unregulated conditions of earlier decades of the century. A Board of Commissioners of Emigration was established in New York, and in the middle 1850's Castle Garden became the official place of landing for immigrants, with the "beasts of prey" forbidden access to the newcomers. Efforts were made to help the immigrants exchange their money fairly and to buy tickets for the West without being cheated. This move was denounced as unwarranted governmental interference with private business, but the public interest prevailed. Many evils continued, however, and as they were exposed, states and cities, churches and private societies came to the aid of distressed immigrants, and in time the Scandinavians

* *We Who Built America* (New York, 1939), p. 118.
† *We Who Built America*, p. 119.

themselves formed societies—for example, in Boston, Chicago, and La Crosse, Wisconsin—to help the indigent and ill among the thousands who were seeking haven in America.

As the immigrant tide shifted to Quebec, the character of the long journey westward changed. First there was the river trip to Montreal; then people went by train or steamer to Lachine; and then, by various modes of transportation, to Lewiston, Niagara Falls, and Buffalo or other ports of the Great Lakes, whence steamboats carried the immigrants on to the receiving stations on Lake Michigan. Though the immigrant saga reveals journeys that were relatively pleasant, many of the evils that marked the New York story were repeated in Canada, with cheating less common than it was in New York. Yet poverty, disease, crowding, and filth went with the immigrants, and sometimes disaster on the Great Lakes ended all hope of an American future.

In this chapter no attempt is made to gather up from thousands of immigrant letters the extracts that, in composite, would portray the westward journey, but throughout the volume letters may be found that touch upon the episodes of travel and record both the miseries and the memorable or pleasurable aspects of the way west. Only three documents comprise the present section. One is the narrative of a Norwegian sea captain, Johan Gasmann of the *Salvator*, who in 1844 made for himself the trip to the American interior which so many of the emigrants he transported from Norway to America had taken. His long letter, describing in detail his observations and experiences, was published in full in several Norwegian newspapers. It gave to the people of Norway a circumstantial picture of the long way west and, though it does not catch up the dark aspects, is a valuable historical record from the American point of view today. Its interest is increased by the fact that the captain was a brother of Hans Gasmann, who was then pioneering in Wisconsin.

To this narrative is added a letter of 1852 recording a journey from Quebec that ended in tragic disaster on Lake Erie. This is of interest not only for its description of the tragic sinking of a steamboat crowded with immigrants but also because of the detail in its account of travel from Quebec to Buffalo. The sad plight of the letter writer and his friends touched the generous interest of the people of Milwaukee, when the survivors reached that city, and one can understand the spirit of the immigrant who wrote, "Although I have lost all my possessions, I have not lost my courage." The third and last letter of the section is from 1851, by a thoroughly disillusioned immigrant who, by the time he wrote, had got no farther toward the West than Buffalo. He warned against easy optimism and made it clear that roasted pigs, with knives and forks stuck in their backs, were not running about the streets.

Everything appears so vigorous

FROM JOHAN GASMANN, IN AMERICA,
TO FRIENDS*

1844

On several of my long trips I have recorded much of what especially attracted my attention, and so also I did on this journey, not for the purpose of publication but only for the perusal of my friends and acquaintances, and more particularly for my own future satisfaction. I had about fourteen days to spend, for after having completed arrangements for a cargo for the ship in New York, I found that I could not get it loaded in less than two or three weeks. I spent this time seeing a little of America.

I took passage on the steamboat *Knickerbocker* from New York to Albany, a distance of about twenty-three Danish miles up the Hudson River. This is one of the largest vessels sailing on the Hudson and certainly is the finest. It is 290 feet long with cabins on three decks. To describe its entire arrangement is impossible, but it is a beautiful floating hotel or palace which can offer commodious quarters for nine hundred to a thousand passengers. We were nine hours en route and paid $1.50. The Hudson is one of the most picturesque rivers in the world. Its banks reveal alternating landscapes, beautiful estates, and pleasant rural villages, together with various larger towns such as Poughkeepsie, Kingston, Catskill, Hudson, and Newburg.

After passing for a considerable distance through a very hilly region, which greatly resembled a Norwegian sound, we came to West Point,

* Originally published in *Bratsberg-Amts Correspondent*, February 3, 10, 27, March 3, 6, 10, 1845, and in *Christianssandsposten*, February 7, 14, 28, March 13, 17, 1845, this letter was translated by Carlton C. Qualey in "From New York to Wisconsin in 1844" in *Norwegian-American Studies and Records* (Northfield, Minn.), 5:30–49 (1930).

where the river widened into a large fjord encircled by the most picturesque landscape, with stretches of level country, hills, and in the background, heights resembling mountains clothed with beautiful forests. Immediately to the left, on the western bank, is West Point, which has a number of fine buildings like palaces. This is the United States war school or military academy and is also the arsenal for the state of New York. The place has a most attractive location. To the right one sees two larger towns; one of them, Hudson, lying on a height, is charming. To the left, farther ahead, are the Catskill Mountains, which are about 4,000 feet in height and extend to a steep precipice beside the Hudson, from which they rise about 3,000 feet. At a height of about 2,500 feet, there is a hotel that looks like a patch of snow. People from New York go there in the summertime. At few places can a more beautiful view be found. The sides of the mountain are clad with light-green woods to over half its height and even above that it looks green. On the top, snow lies until far into the summer. One can scarcely find anything so lovely in Europe, for in the southern lands in Europe the hills are not wooded and appear brown and scorched. Here, on the contrary, everything is lively and green.

On the whole, that part of America which I have seen has a greener and fresher appearance than any country in Europe. Everything appears so vigorous. The Hudson River swarms with steamboats and sailing vessels. There is activity everywhere, both on land and water. The steamboats with their star-spangled flags and long smoke streamers whiz past each other, filled with thousands of well-dressed and attractive-looking people. The music of horns and other instruments comes over the water from them. Schooners, sloops, and numerous smaller vessels skim about like flies on the broad surface of the water. All this is so grand, so beautiful, that anyone who enjoys living must be glad and cheerful – and the more so when one recalls that about a hundred years ago there were only a few miserable wigwams or Indian huts here, and on the river only solitary birchbark canoes wherein bloody Indians sat with their tomahawks and scalping knives, ready to torture and to murder their enemies. What a transformation in such a short time! If all this does not rouse a man's enthusiasm, then the greatest human enterprises have no value. I confess that as a seaman, after a long sea voyage, I perhaps found everything more wonderful than it might appear to me if I remained here for a longer period of time. But is it not so everywhere? The most beautiful landscape loses its attractiveness in our eyes the longer we see it. I have, however, seen so much that I can make comparisons. I have seen nothing so beautiful as the Hudson unless it might be the Bosporus at Constantinople, but even that does not come up to this. And what a difference in the people who live there!

I arrived at Albany where the steamboat navigation ended. Albany, a town of about thirty thousand inhabitants, is fine looking, with wide, clean streets. The main street is, in my opinion, finer than Broadway in New York. At the upper end of this street is a stately building with a cupola. This is the meeting place for the representatives of the state of New York and is the capitol of this state. The governor resides here, and this palace is also called the capitol. It is a fine building of cut stone, with a pillared façade of white marble. From Albany I went by rail to Buffalo, at the eastern end of Lake Erie, a distance of seventy-five Danish or three hundred English miles. If one has time enough, it is cheaper to go by the Erie Canal on a canalboat drawn by horses. The cars in which one travels on the railroad are very comfortably furnished. Each is about 25 feet in length, 9 feet in width, and 7 feet in height, and has windows the full length of the car as in a coach. One sits on cushioned seats placed crosswise in the car, one row on each side so that two passengers sit beside each other. In the middle there is an aisle. At both ends there is a door with a balcony or platform outside which has an iron railing around it. Here, with the conductor's permission, one may stand outside and look about. Every third hour we stopped to take on fuel and water, and now and then at a near-by elegant restaurant, or rather two, one for gentlemen and one for ladies, where all possible kinds of refreshments stood in readiness – but the stop was only for fifteen minutes. At noon and breakfast time a person had, on the contrary, a good hour. As a precaution, one or two baggage cars are always placed between the locomotive and the passenger cars in order to prevent accidents in case the steam engine jumps the track.

The route from Albany runs first through extensive stretches of level land, past many rural villages and farms. There is well-cultivated land everywhere, with fields and meadows as far as eye can see. There are wooded areas here too, largely made up of oak and other deciduous trees. Fir and other evergreens are less common. The rural villages and the solitary farms are for the most part built up of wood. The houses are roofed as are ours, and the buildings are usually painted white and red. Many of the solitary farms resemble our Norwegian farmsteads, painted red with white window frames. Everywhere one sees orchards and flowers about the houses. Everything has something new – something distinctive about it. It is not England, not France's straw roofs, and not Norway, but something distinctly new. In appearance the country is like Denmark with its level land, but the orchards display the luxuriance of France. The people resemble the English in dress and manners but are, like the French, more courteous and sociable.

The Americans usually roof their houses with shingles which they coat with a composition of some kind so that they resemble slate, as at first I took them to be. The churches are also built of wood but are of various styles, some with steeples, some with cupolas, and some without steeples. All are painted white. The Americans roof the churches with heavy galvanized sheet iron, which shines and glitters in the sunlight and gives a beautiful effect amidst the green woods. At Schenectady one enters upon a broad valley called the Mohawk Valley, which extends eighteen miles westward toward Rochester. This valley is everywhere well cultivated. Through the middle of it flows the Mohawk, which has a rapid current and at one place several considerable falls. Here the valley is compressed between high mountain ridges so that it is only a little wider than the river itself. Otherwise the width of the valley varies from one-half to one mile – yes, occasionally more than that. Several tributary valleys lead into it, and the view is changed greatly thereby. The valley rises higher and higher on both sides until very high mountain ridges limit the view. The whole constitutes a lovely and colorful landscape. But unfortunately, night came all too soon and darkness shut off the view, so that I was unable to see everything no matter how much I wished to do so. I am often tempted not to venture out upon the monotonous and boresome sea, which never offers any prospect more diverting than seeing one black swell followed invariably by another in consecutive endlessness – not a very cheerful or soul-inspiring view. After one has traveled through this valley, one comes up on higher land, which again stretches out in prairie and hills.

I arrived at Rochester at night and left again at dawn so that I was able to see little or nothing of the town. But since I stayed there a whole Sunday on my return trip, I shall briefly note something about the town. Rochester is situated beside a river which within the town itself has a fall of over 90 feet and which is utilized to operate mills and other machines. In the town a stone bridge has been built over the river, and there is a long wooden bridge above the town. Rochester is a very beautiful city, with broad, fine streets and remarkably fine buildings, scarcely inferior to those of New York itself. The houses resemble those of France more than those of England, have tall windows, and are decorated with cornice work and other ornamentation. The town has about 30,000 inhabitants. There are seven beautiful churches and many large and elegant hotels, the latter being necessary because both the Erie Canal and the railroad pass through Rochester. Not far from Rochester is Lake Ontario, the widespread surface of which one sees just before entering the town.

After a three-hour journey thence, I arrived in Buffalo. The route leads across areas which are partly overgrown with forests, miles in extent. The land appears virgin or only just coming under cultivation, for tree stumps still remain in many places. I suppose that the soil here is not of the best, for pine trees grow here in large numbers, especially firs, and the soil appears sandy. It was, at all events, the poorest country I saw on the whole trip. The city of Buffalo is situated beside a small bay of Lake Erie, which forms a fairly good harbor. The lowest part of the town lies so low that it is subject to floods in times of heavy storms from the northwest, but the larger part lies on the slope of a hill. It has a wide main street which extends about one English mile right through the town and is lined by large and beautiful buildings. Here, as in Rochester, there are many huge hotels for travelers. Therefore, as soon as one arrives on the train at the large shed or station, one is immediately surrounded by servants or footmen from the various taverns or hotels, and one must hold fast to one's luggage so that it is not seized by these eager individuals, not that they wish to steal it but that they want to convey it to their respective employers' houses. Light wagons and carioles stand ready to take the traveler anywhere he wishes. Each of these servants or footmen recommends his master's hotel as well as he can. German menservants especially are employed in this way. One cannot say that it is expensive to lodge here. The taverns or hotels are just as elegant as in the larger towns in France. The furnishings are more French than English, just as, on the whole, America is more French than English. There is a mixture of both, however, and also something distinctive. The Americans certainly are not less advanced than either of the nationalities mentioned.

Buffalo has about 18,000 inhabitants, but it is not so attractive as Rochester. There is a great deal of activity and life here. All goods from the western states are landed here; travelers pass through by the thousands; the harbor is full of freighters, brigs, schooners, and sloops which sail the larger lakes. Along the shore are large wooden warehouses painted white (resembling in that respect Bergen's harbor). Here there were large numbers of seamen, among whom I met many Scandinavians and Frenchmen. The prodigious number of flour barrels and provisions which are loaded here on the canalboats to be taken to New York makes one realize at once that fertile lands surround these lakes. Americans are perpetually active and always seem to be in a hurry; indeed, a more enterprising people cannot be found anywhere. One sees few people out walking merely for the sake of walking, for everyone has something to do. It is only in the evening, a little after sunset, that gentlemen and ladies fill the streets. Buffalo is not far from the Canadian boundary. Just outside the town there is a fort with a little garrison, the soldiers of which, like the English, have red uniforms. In three hours one may travel from Buffalo to the remarkable Niagara Falls, where a tremendous volume of water is precipitated from a height of 160 feet, but time did not permit me to see this.

As one looks out from Buffalo over Lake Erie, it is scarcely credible that this is only a lake, for no land is visible on the horizon, and ships cruise by each other here as on the ocean – and yet this lake lies more than 600 feet above sea level, and consequently almost as high above the Hudson River and the Erie Canal. The railroad also mounts in the same degree over a distance of about seventy-five miles.

Upon my arrival at Buffalo, I looked up Hughes and Company, who are the leading owners of steamships on the Lakes or else the directors of them as well as a large number of sailing vessels and other ships. Hence, a large part of the immigrants pass, so to speak, through their hands. I asked these gentlemen to take care that our countrymen be transported in comfort and not crowded together too much in the schooners. I explained to them that our farmers, in spite of their shabby appearance, are good and upright people, and this they admitted, adding that they had noticed that they are much more modest than the Germans and far more orderly people (*but very ignorant*). They complained that the emigrant agents in New York, with whom the whole journey to Wisconsin is arranged, often sent these same people to several of their commissioners in Buffalo, where, in order to save money, they crowded them onto ships without regard for their comfort.

I left Buffalo for Wisconsin on board the steamboat *Illinois*, Captain Blake commanding. This trip took four days. The ship's commander was very kind to me. Himself an old salt-water seaman, he was pleased to have me as a passenger, and consequently I obtained free passage both going and returning. On board this steamboat, I also made the acquaintance of an English lawyer, a Mr. T. Penyon, a Cornishman. Being acquainted in Cornwall, I found it very interesting to talk about his birthplace. Moreover, we talked of a great many other things, and I could not help laughing at him whenever he sought to point out England's pre-eminence over America and the superiority of Englishmen to Americans. As we were on neutral ground, he was able to get from me my opinion that the English boast too much of their country and that that opinion is common even in Europe. He agreed to this in part and we were good friends.

The shore to the left, which we followed for some time, was almost level land, not low but at about a forty- to fifty-foot elevation, with yellowish corn cockle toward the lake. No hills or bluffs are to be seen. The land is for the most part overgrown with woods, and only here and there along the shore are there plowed fields. Inland there are said to be well-settled areas. We stopped first at Cleveland, a town situated beside a river which forms its harbor. How large this town is I cannot say, for our stop was only for a couple of hours and the town lies spread out between hills. An old place it cannot be, for the tree stumps still remain standing close beside the houses. It seemed to be a pleasant town. Many ships lay in the harbor, and wheat barrels, potash, and willow stakes in large quantities lay on the wharves, which like ours had wooden bulwarks. The buildings were some of them of wood, some of stone, but all very fine and large. From this town a canal goes far inland, clear to the Ohio River, which as you know flows into the Mississippi. From Cleveland the voyage continued to Detroit Sound, where Lake Erie joins with the little Lake St. Clair. At the entrance to this sound, there are many beautiful little islands with fine farms and grassy meadows whereon we saw many cattle.

Having passed these islands and the sound, two miles long, we came to the city of Detroit. This, like Porsgrund, consists of one street along the waterfront, which must have been more than half a mile in length. Just as all such straggling towns seem emptier than the compactly built ones, so also in the case of Detroit, nothwithstanding the fact that it is supposed to have a considerable commerce, for Michigan, in which it is located, produces a large amount of wheat, oats, corn, potash, and so forth. This town is supposed to be one of the oldest in the western states and was founded by the French when France possessed Canada, but it has not flourished. The reason for this is easily understood, for all the goods from the western regions float past here on their way to New York and land first at Buffalo in order to be carried through the Erie Canal down to the sea. Cities which are located on a sound between two lakes, like cities which are situated beside rivers and not at their mouths or at their upper loading or unloading place, usually do not have a great part in the river commerce. Such is the case with Detroit.

The straits of Detroit separate the United States from Canada and, near the town, are about two English miles in width. On the Canadian side there is a little town called Sandwich, which appeared – and is said to be – very inconsequential and poor. My American fellow travelers exulted a good deal in calling to my attention that there lay Queen Victoria's land. "It is poor looking [they said]; it shows the difference of Gouvernement."

The country on both sides of this sound is so low and so absolutely level that I could not discover the smallest hill as far as I could see, but it is heavily wooded. It was reported to be not swampy, however, and to be good corn land except on the Canadian side, which, when there is a great deal of rain, is subject to flood. A railroad is being constructed straight across country to Grand Haven on Lake Michigan. This railroad was already more than half built, and it was to be entirely completed by the next year. It was expected that travel by this route to Chicago and Milwaukee would take two days less than by steamship. After we had passed through the straits, shallow Lake St. Clair, and St. Clair Straits, we came to the large Lake Huron. On this whole stretch, nothing worthy of remark was noticeable. The only thing which gave the shore along the last-named lake any interest was that on the Canadian side were Indians, for whom an English mission had established a church and a school. Their small log houses could be seen through the trees, and several groups of Indians, who shouted and waved to the passengers on the steamship, were visible on the hills by the shore. But as these Indians had discarded their national costume and were somewhat civilized, we did not lose much by not seeing them more closely.

The country on the United States side was more settled and cultivated, with fine-looking farms, fields, and meadows. For the rest, I must confess that the whole stretch of land I previously had seen, clear from Buffalo to Detroit, was somewhat monotonous, viewed from the deck of a steamboat. The forests which grace the land were so even that one was tempted to believe that all the trees grew to a definite height, above which they were unable to reach. Wherever I noticed cultivated land, flourishing fields and meadows were visible, and I expect that the whole state of Michigan, when once under cultivation, will constitute a single large area of fields and meadows, and that it will become a granary for millions. But it is a poor landscape for the painter's brush. In the northern part of Michigan there are reported to be swamps and thickly grown forests of oak, hickory, fir, tamarack, maple, and several other varieties of trees. There are supposed to be a prodigious number of wild pigeons here. On the voyage up Lake Huron we got our first fresh lake trout, the meat of which was not so red as that of our trout but tasted just as good. The fish were very fat — several weighing thirty-six pounds.

We now come to the Strait of Mackinac, which connects Lake Huron and Lake Michigan. Here the country is composed of high hills overgrown with fir and deciduous trees, but it does not appear especially productive. One could see here that one had come farther toward the north. All the species of trees were the same as in Norway, and it was no longer warm, although this place does not lie higher than Rochefort. It also occurred to me that, so far as the native vegetation or the plants were concerned, this region could not be compared with any European country farther south than Jutland, even North Jutland.

On an island in the strait there is the little town of Mackinac, which resembles a Norwegian seaport town. Near the town is a fort or fortress with a small garrison. I was especially interested in this place because here for the first time I saw real Indians. Near here they have a trading post where they set up their wigwams or tents along the shore, about thirty in number, and near by lay their birchbark canoes or boats. I also saw here a great number of Indians who I believe were called Sioux Indians. As to their appearance, there was nothing especially remarkable. They were quite tall and well-grown people and were somewhat darker in complexion than what is called olive, but I could not call it red any more than one calls a mulatto red. Their clothing was composed partly of undressed yellow buckskin, partly of cloth, and over the whole costume they wore a wide English wool blanket as a cloak. On their feet they wore half-boots of yellow leather, which were called moccasins. The costume of the women resembled that of the men with the exception that they wore short skirts. Both men and women were bedecked with considerable finery such as buttons, buckles, and the like. Some of their clothes were decorated with pearls in designs somewhat in the style of our Telemark country folk. Some men, whom I took to be chieftains, wore feathers on their heads and had painted red and white stripes across their faces. The men also carried in their hands small, highly polished axes. Their tents were composed of several poles put down in the ground in a circle about six feet apart, tied together at the tops and covered with tight robes. In the middle of the tent a fire was burning, the smoke finding its way out through the cluster of pole tops. From the highest point in the middle of the tent hung a hook to hang a kettle on. At the sides were hides to sleep on, some deal boxes, and sticks, and that composed the whole establishment. One finds here remnants of the old French population which have become mixed with the Indians. They still speak a kind of French and have not forgotten how to gesticulate with arms and shoulders.

Mackinac Strait, to get back to my travels, is broad and filled with a number of islands. Lake Huron is very deep, about eighty fathoms, and is dark blue like the ocean. It is quite noticeable that the climate in America, or rather the temperature, is very different from that at the same degree of latitude in Europe. The whole northern part of Michigan lies between 46° and 46° 49′ north latitude – the same as the greater part of France, and yet the temperature here cannot be regarded as milder than in Denmark. In the part of Wisconsin below 43° north latitude the temperature is not higher, according to several reports, than in northern France. When one knows what is grown there, I suspect that this is a mistake, for in Wisconsin corn is grown as far north as 44° and even farther, whereas this variety of grain cannot ripen in northern France — no, not even at Bordeaux. One may to some extent assume that the elevation of the land above sea level has some influence, for most of Wisconsin lies 700 to 800 feet higher than the ocean, and that is more than twice as high as most European countries. Toward the north there is a large continent where there is almost perpetual winter and which is not separated from the southern areas by mountains. When, therefore, the north wind blows, one feels chilly even in the summertime. After we had passed the Strait of Mackinac, Lake Michigan was spread before us with its dark blue surface. This is the longest as well as the deepest of all the lakes. Its depth in the middle is supposed to be almost three hundred fathoms, and it is also supposed to abound in fish.

The northern shore of Lake Michigan reveals on that side a poor and ugly landscape. High sand hills rise several hundred feet from the surface of the lake. As far as I could see, there was no sign of vegetation except a few scrubby pines in the valleys and some brown heather. It resembles the western coast of Jutland, but it is still more bare and desolate. Long sand bars extend several miles out from the shore so that no ship can land. I asked an American if anyone lived in this region, and he answered, "O no Sir, not a raven nor a crow would be able to pick a living here." Farther south, the land seemed to become greener again and the woods thicker. Here also, it was said, a few settlers had begun to establish themselves.

The steamboat now made from the Michigan shore and set its course for Milwaukee. The shore disappeared over the horizon behind us. A considerable swell came against us and also to port, so that the steamboat rolled somewhat, and the outboard gangplank often plunged down into the surface of the water and caused violent tremors in the whole ship. I do not regard these long, three-storied steamships as seaworthy vessels, and the captain on the boat said to me that often in the autumn, when storms occurred, he had difficulty enough in navigating the *Illinois*.

After some hours' headway over the lake, Wisconsin rose over the horizon with its green woods and glinting yellow limestone, like the coast of Yorkshire in England. The land was not so level in appearance as the coasts of Michigan on the eastern side. Hills overgrown with oak woods and tall hickory trees were visible occasionally, although there were no high ones as yet. On the whole, the landscape had a colorful appearance, and I cannot deny that a mixture of emotions stirred in my breast such as those I so often feel when, after long voyaging, I approach old Norway's shores. For I soon expected to see my dear brother and his family again. Moreover, so many of our countrymen, some actually needy and some dissatisfied in other ways, seek refuge in this country, where they land with mingled hope and despair. The future must be uncertain for anyone who sets foot on such a new and foreign land. Genuine courage is therefore necessary, or perhaps it is often replaced by heedlessness. However, I do not consider it so difficult for the Norwegians emigrating hereafter as for those who came first. Now they may find their countrymen to show them the way.

Milwaukee Bay appeared, and soon we hove to at a long wooden pier which had been built for the sole purpose of docking steamboats, since these cannot sail into the river, which is only seven feet deep. Milwaukee is situated beside a river in a flat valley. One could see at once that it was a new town, the houses being quite spread out. There were, however, a few built up streets with stone buildings of three or four stories and with elegant stores. Here supplies might be had in plenty, and there were several hotels for travelers, of which the Milwaukee House and the Temperance House were the finest. The Milwaukee House, in size and elegance, is comparable to similar houses in the larger cities.

As I stepped ashore from the steamboat, I met a Dane by the name of Fribert and a Swede named Petersson. The first I already knew by name, and for his later courtesy, I owe him thanks. When he informed me that he lived near my brother at Pine Lake, we arranged to leave the next morning, it being then too late in the day. I also met two of my brother's daughters, from whom I was exceedingly glad to learn that they all were getting on well in their new fatherland. I lodged that night in a little white-painted inn which bore the sign "Lafayette," the owner of which was a Frenchman. The man had not forgotten his French courtesy, and when I exchanged a few French words with him, he became quite spirited. The lodging was very good and quite cheap. For bed and board, a bottle of Bavarian ale, tobacco, and a pipe, I paid in all eighteen cents.

Journeying toward New Horizons

As arranged, Mr. Fribert, Mr. Petersson and his daughter, and my two nieces and I set out in the morning in a four-wheeled wagon with two horses, which we hired from an Irishman. From Milwaukee to Pine Lake the distance was twenty-six English miles. On this stretch of road the country was composed of level areas, none of which were of any great extent, alternating with hills and valleys, so that the landscape was far from monotonous. Woods covered the greater part of the country, but there were also many fine cultivated areas with beautiful fields and meadows and fine, white-painted farmhouses. We drove past two large gristmills which were operated by waterfalls made by damming up small streams. The forests were made up of oak, hickory, basswood, maple, elm, ash, and acacia trees, and a great many others. The white-painted farmhouses became more infrequent the farther we went. Log and frame houses, constructed as simply and hastily as possible, were visible here and there in clearings in the woods. Round about these small houses, there were fields of wheat, corn, oats, and potatoes, all in the most flourishing condition. At a few places there were fruit trees and flower beds. Tree stumps raised their black heads in the midst of the wheat fields, and in some cases the whole tree remained. But the tree was leafless, for the roots had been chopped and the tree allowed to stand thus and dry out until a more opportune time should come to remove it. The whole landscape appeared quiet and peaceful.

The country about Pine Lake, where I found my brother living in a log house, he and his family well satisfied, is very beautiful. There are four or five small lakes here, and between these the land rises in hills, prairies, and valleys. A part of this land consists of the so-called oak openings, that is, hills whereon trees stand as though planted at long intervals, some in groves or groups, so that it all appears like a scientifically laid out English park. There are also thick woods of all kinds of trees, of which walnut trees, plum trees, apple trees, and grapevines are common. Wild grapevines twine themselves about the trees, clear to the tops. The grapes are small and sour, but can be cultivated. Raspberries, blackberries, and gooseberries are to be found in plenty. Strawberries are also plentiful and cranberries in great numbers in the autumn. Flowers of the greatest variety of colors grow everywhere, on the hills, on the prairies, and in the forests, many of them of the same varieties as we have but many strange varieties too. The small lakes, lying enclosed by hills, are mirrorlike in clearness. Many large and beautiful tree-grown capes and headlands extend out into them. Even though this landscape does not have the elevated character in respect to vistas that we find in parts of Norway and in the Alpine countries, it is nevertheless exceedingly beautiful, bright, and charming.

My brother's house stands on a height beside a small lake, and back of it rises a hill, the highest thereabouts. Many Swedes have settled about Pine Lake and are all very well established. Many Norwegians, of whom I knew several, are also living in this region, all, as far as I could find out, well pleased with what they have been able to accomplish. Their houses are still quite small, but are good enough to protect them from the weather. Then too, the climate here is mild and the winter short, so that these houses are much better to live in than many of our Norwegian farmhouses in the mountain districts. A few people have already built themselves good, roomy houses, and in a few years we may hope that there will be a fine community of Norwegians here. My brother has recently purchased quite a large tract of land, about three fourths of a mile from Pine Lake and established a sawmill on the banks of a river which flows through this land. Work has now begun to break the land and to build houses which he himself expects to live in. The place is called Espen. The timber was very good and the soil, my brother says, very fertile.

It is common knowledge that the foreigners who settle on the new land in North America are subject to ague. That is also the case in Wisconsin, although the condition is not the same everywhere. Those who live in the so-called oak openings, where the country is often hilly and consequently dry, are less subject to the fever. On the other hand, those who live on the prairies are more often severely attacked by it. The abundance of trees, with the leaves and grass which lie and rot in the forests, especially in damp places, is a source of the ague, for people have found that as soon as the land is properly brought under cultivation, the ague ceases. Pure and healthful water is necessary. It is, however, difficult to find wholesome water in the low areas, and the new settlers are not always as careful as they might be in this matter. Every newcomer should take the precaution, if he settles on the prairie, to make inquiries as to whether or not there is good water near by and whether the soil has drainage so that it may be dry during the wet season.

He should also beware of lying on the ground in the evening and morning, of becoming wet with rain and then drying out again in the sun, and should be careful not to be out in the woods or in the high prairie grass immediately after a rain until after the sun has again dried the earth. He must be temperate in eating and drinking. The large amount of pork Americans use is not good for people unaccustomed to such a heavy diet, and it is hardly healthful for the natives. At least, I have heard several Americans maintain that biliousness is often caused by the excessive eating of pork. It is not surprising that the American farmer gives his employees plenty of pork, for it costs him little and is a substantial food. Our farmers from the uplands [south of Dovre] think it is a fine food, but in a warm climate, used in excess, it is very injurious, especially when it is used together with many vegetables. After all, from what I have been able to find out from people who know the country in the West, Wisconsin and Iowa have the most healthful climate. One has nothing to fear from the fever if one does not settle near swamps and marshes, and above all, is careful from the beginning.

The steamboat *Illinois* used firewood in place of coal, and that is the case with all the steamships which sail on the Lakes. Consequently we took on fuel at several places en route on the voyage from Buffalo to Milwaukee.

Over three hundred were drowned

FROM ERIK THORSTAD, AT IXONIA, JEFFERSON COUNTY, WISCONSIN, TO FRIENDS *

November 9, 1852

Our good leader, Captain Olsen, contracted with a company to carry us and our baggage to Milwaukee for $7 for each adult and half fare for the children. On August 14 our baggage was brought aboard a large steamboat, and we left the evening of the same day at five o'clock. At six the following morning we came to a town called Montreal. Our

* This letter, translated and edited by Henrietta Larson, was published under the title "The Sinking of the 'Atlantic' on Lake Erie, An Immigrant Journey from Quebec to Wisconsin in 1852" in *Norwegian-American Studies and Records,* 4:92–98 (1929).

skipper, who had accompanied us to this place, then took leave of us. Shortly after he had gone, an accident occurred; a man from Valders fell overboard as he was bringing his baggage off the boat. It was right pitiful to see how he struggled. And no means were on hand whatsoever with which to save him. Arrangements were finally made for dragging, whereupon he was found, but by then he was dead. This event was all the more tragic since he had a family, which mourned its lost provider.

At this place our baggage was taken in wagons about one English mile, and then we traveled by steamboat for about twenty-four hours. We passed through many locks which we looked at with wonder. Since we could not get a boat the day we reached this place, a town named Toronto, our baggage was unloaded on the wharf, and the immigrants, except myself and a couple of others, spent the night under the open sky. At eight the next morning we left by steamboat, and in the afternoon of the same day we landed below Niagara Falls near the ingenious hanging bridge made of steel cables. Many of us had decided to go near this masterpiece and inspect it, but we had to forego this, as our baggage was immediately loaded on wagons and drawn by horses on a railway for about sixteen English miles. On this trip we had an opportunity to view the great and much famed waterfalls, Niagara.

We came to the town of Kingston late in the evening. There, too, our belongings were placed on the wharf, and the same ones as before found lodging on the wharf, while I and two of my comrades lodged in town. Some of the immigrants left for Buffalo on a small steamboat at five o'clock the next morning. At five in the evening the boat returned and got the rest of us. Buffalo is a very large town and has about 50,000 inhabitants, but I did not think it was really a pleasant place. Along the wharves, especially, it was quite unwholesome. From Quebec to Buffalo some seventy-five poor people from Valders had free transportation. But here they had to remain as they did not have enough money to pay passage across the Lakes.

We left Buffalo on a large steamer, called the *Atlantic,* in the evening of the same day – August 12 – at eight o'clock. The total number of passengers was 576, comprising 132 Norwegians, a number of Germans, and the rest Americans.

Since it was already late in the evening and I felt very sleepy, I opened my chest, took off my coat and laid it, together with my money and my watch, in the chest. I took out my bedclothes, made me a bed on the chest, and lay down to sleep. But when it was about half past two in the morning I awoke with a heavy shock. Immediately suspecting that another boat had run into ours, I hastened up at once. Since there was great confusion and fright among the passengers, I asked several if our boat had been damaged. But I did not get any reassuring answer. I could not believe that there was any immediate danger, for the engines were still in motion. I went up to the top deck, and then I was convinced at once that the steamer must have been damaged, for many people were lowering a boat with the greatest haste. Many from the lowest deck got into the boat directly, and as the boat had taken in water on being lowered, it sank immediately and all were drowned.

Thereupon I went down to the second deck, hoping to find means of rescue. At that very moment the water rushed into the boat and the engines stopped. Then a pitiful cry arose. I and one of my comrades had taken hold of the stairs which led from the second to the third deck, but soon there were so many hands on it that we let go, knowing that we could not thus be saved. We thereupon climbed up to the third deck, where the pilot was at the wheel. I had altogether given up hope of being saved, for the boat began to sink more and more, and the water almost reached up there. While we stood thus, much distressed, we saw several people putting out a small boat, whereupon we at once hastened to help. We succeeded in getting it well out, and I was one of the first to get into the boat. When there were as many as the boat could hold, it was fortunately pushed away from the steamer. As oars were wanting, we rowed with our hands, and several bailed water from the boat with their hats. A ray of light, which we had seen far away when we were on the wreck and which we had taken for a lighthouse, we soon found to be a steamer hurrying to give us help. We were taken aboard directly, and then those who were on the wreck as well as those who were still paddling in the water were picked up.

This boat, which was the one that had sunk ours, was of the kind known as a propeller, driven by a screw in the stern. The misery and the cries of distress which I witnessed and heard that night are indescribable, and I shall not forget it all as long as I live. The number of drowned was more than 300, of whom 68 were Norwegians. Many of the persons who were in the first class were drowned in their berths or staterooms. The Norwegians who were rescued totaled 64, but most of them lost everything. I saw many on board the propeller who had on only shirts. The newspapers blame the command of the *Atlantic* for this sad event and reproach them most severely and accuse them openly of having murdered 300 people.

The propeller soon delivered us to another steamboat, which brought us to a city called Detroit, where we arrived at eight the next morning. After we had got some provisions for our journey, we continued on a steam train. Late in the evening we reached a large town in Illinois, called Chicago, where we spent the night and had everything free. On the trip there, we saw many beautiful farms and orchards as well as many attractive buildings. We left the following morning by steamboat, and after five or six hours we reached Milwaukee. That was on the twenty-second of August. We stayed with a Norwegian, where we remained until the twenty-eighth of the same month. Since the city had taken up a subscription for our support, we lived free of charge, and in addition each person received $11 in money. iWth this money I bought two coats, a pair of trousers, a pair of shoes, two shirts, and a bag.

From Milwaukee I went by steam train twenty to twenty-five miles without charge, and then I footed it, reaching Østerlie's the thirtieth of August. There I have since remained. I am well and have, God be thanked, been in good health all the time. Although I have lost all my possessions, I have not lost courage. The same God who has helped me in the time of danger will, I hope, continued to be my protector.

Here you must do three days' work in one

FROM HANS OLSEN THORUD, IN BUFFALO, NEW YORK, TO FRIENDS *

January 27, 1851

As time now permits me to write, I make use of it in the hope that these lines may find you all in good health. We left Drammen on August 7 last year on the ship *Sjofna* commanded by Captain Hovland, and we arrived safe and sound in New York on September 19, that is to say, after six weeks, a rapid crossing. I was in good health while we were at

* This letter appeared in *Drammens Tidende*, April 23, 1851.

sea, God be praised, and everything went well and very pleasantly among the passengers on board, except that we had seven deaths on the way. On our arrival at New York we drew up a contract with Halvor Poulsson for transportation from this city to Buffalo, for which we paid $2.50 a person, with our baggage free of charge. We were stowed together in the hold of a canalboat and were treated in every way like so many swine. Several of us fell ill. After ten long, rough days we arrived here. Lars Lie and I took lodgings with Christoffer Christensen from Kongsberg, who showed us so much kindness that we shall never be able to thank him enough. He owns a house in Buffalo, as do many other Norwegians who live here.

I am very sorry to have to tell you, dear friends, that America is not at all the country that our countrymen have described it to be, and it is a great shame for such swindlers to entice so many of their fellow human beings and countrymen to come here only to end up as beggars. This is now true of several Norwegians who arrived here last year and who, because of their deficiency in the language, are not able to compete with Americans, although they are very capable people of the middle classes. Dear friends and countrymen, consider carefully what you are doing before you decide to come here. Please do not expect to find roasted pigs, with knives and forks in their backs, ready for anyone to eat. Moreover, the high daily wages supposed to be paid here are nothing but a fable. Daily wages here are from two marks twelve skillings to three marks, with few or no jobs available. The work is very hard, as you have to accomplish in one day here what you get three days to do in Norway. If you go to the western parts of America to buy land, it is uncultivated, and it will take two or three years before it is of any use to you. The distance from the main cities, Chicago and Milwaukee, will then be sixty or seventy miles. Roads are bad, at times quite impassable, and most of the Norwegians and other nationals have lost their money before they reach their destination. Then they can only become beggars. Besides there are just as many taxes here as in Norway: poor tax, city tax, business tax, school tax, and so on. What you are quite sure to get here is a sickly body; Norwegians suffer particularly from the ague.

As to landowner G., I can tell you that one of his daughters married a mountain farmer, that the other is a servant girl in Milwaukee, that two years ago one of his sons made a living as a woodcutter, and that the landowner himself now has nothing but what good people give to him, so you may understand it is not so easy for the great ones to come here. There is not one out of a hundred persons here who does not wish he were back in his dear Norway. But as they have no money, they have to stay where they are, to fight it out with the mosquitoes and shake with the ague.

Ordeal and Debate

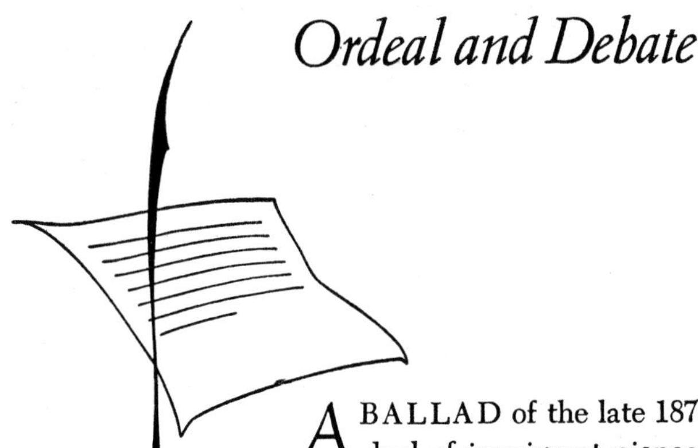

A BALLAD of the late 1870's reviews the ordeal of immigrant pioneering in Wisconsin, tells of the difficult problem of speech when English was "only a meaningless babble," describes a hole in the ground – a sod-covered room – that was house and hearth and home, refers to the difficulty of selecting lands, mentions rocky roads and oxcart travel, and recalls the drudgery of past years. But the ballad closes on a happy note, celebrating success despite early reverses and boasting of schoolhouses, farms, and churches. It sums up the tale in a triumphant line, "We are living right royally here."

Professor Einar Haugen, who has translated this ballad, speaks of the importance of such sources to historians who are trying to "reach the essentially human core of history." * This particular song is interesting because its verses retell, from the immigrant standpoint, the traditional American story of humble and difficult beginnings leading to success and happiness. The ordeal of early days is viewed in perspective, and the view has been amplified in many reminiscences that look back through the haze of decades upon trials long since over.

Contemporary letters give one a close-up of the ordeal that both the songs and reminiscences of a later day recall. They reflect despair and courage, optimism and pessimism, frustration and hope, sometimes resignation over what seems an inexorable fate. Like the narrative ballads, they are personal documents that help the historian to come close to the human core of which Professor Haugen writes. They are perhaps the more valuable because they record the ordeal from its midst and at

* "A Norwegian-American Pioneer Ballad," in *Norwegian-American Studies and Records* (Northfield, Minn.), 15:1 (1949).

the time, when all its details are fresh and when hopes and dreams have not yet been realized in actualities.

The end of the emigrant journey, whatever its hardships, was the beginning of the immigrant pioneer ordeal. Many did not immediately go to lands to carve out farms. They began with jobs – as farm laborers, lumberjacks, sawyers, sailors, workers on inland canals. When and if they took claims or bought land, there was the problem of immediate planting to get crops of potatoes and other vegetables for the coming winter. Shelter was essential and had to be provided at once. It might be a dugout with dirt walls, a sod hut, or a log house, its crevices chinked with clay, mud, or plaster. And sometimes the house was also a barn. Furniture was as primitive as the buildings – log stumps as stools, immigrant chests as tables, and quickly made bunks to sleep in. Then the job of farming began, women joining the men in the many tasks of the day.

These and many related circumstances are the commonplace of American pioneering. Often after a preliminary period of five or six years the promise of life in the New World began to bloom – and not infrequently after such a period the pioneers were ready to move on to new frontiers. Such initial difficulties often were complicated by sickness. As I have written elsewhere, "Many factors let down the defenses against the attack of disease on the American frontiers of the earlier period. The water supply of the settlers was often uncertain, sometimes polluted. Houses were often terribly crowded. New immigrants, recently disembarked from festering emigrant packets, poured into the communities, frequently poverty stricken and germ laden. Sewage facilities were completely primitive. The concept of public health was still a thing of the future. The wonder is not that many died, but that so many survived." *

Malaria, cholera, typhus, typhoid fever, pneumonia, tuberculosis, and influenza struck hard blows at the strength and endurance of the settlers, and their letters are filled with reports of the scourges that robbed them of health.† Muskego, south of Milwaukee, became the

* Blegen, *Norwegian Migration*, vol. 2, p. 54.

† The story of disease among Norwegian immigrants on the midwestern frontiers is told in my *Norwegian Migration*, vol. 2, pp. 53–68, and a more detailed account is given in Knut Gjerset and Ludvig Hektoen, "Health Conditions and the Practice of Medicine among the Early Norwegian Settlers, 1825–1865," in *Studies and Records* (Minneapolis: Norwegian-American Historical Society), 1:1–59 (1926).

famed settlement where many of the "firsts" of Norwegian-American history took place, but it was low-lying ground and its people were decimated by malaria and by the swift-striking, savage cholera. Founded in 1839 and developed rapidly in the years thereafter, it passed through several wretched years. An American minister, an emissary of the American Home Missionary Society, who visited the settlement during the winter of 1843–44, said that the "amount of wretchedness and suffering which prevailed" at Muskego during that winter "was such as absolutely to mock all description." In one family he found eight people, all "prostrated with disease," most of them huddled in bunks filled with prairie hay. The only sign of food that he saw was a "wooden bowl, partly filled with what I took to be shorts, kneaded and prepared for baking." The report that this minister prepared was filled with harrowing details, and he said that the settlement had already suffered a hundred deaths.*

Little wonder that many of the letters of these early years make sad reading. Some of them were seized upon by newspaper editors in Norway who were hostile to emigration, and were printed as contributions to the debates raging in that country over the problem of emigration. But the voices of discouragement or despair are not the whole story. Many immigrants clung to their hopes and saw their ordeal as temporary. Yet others, fortunate enough to escape some of the worst hazards, wrote cheerfully about the American scene. The letters in this section catch up both sides of the story.

They are from the 1840's and open with one by a noted writer of "America letters," Ole Knudsen Trovatten, who had wide influence in his home country because of the glowing pictures that he gave of prospects in the United States. Originally a settler of 1840 at Muskego, he had moved on to the Koshkonong colony, and there, though he had been ill for almost a half-year, he had managed to acquire forty acres of land, he was earning what he considered good wages, his children were learning English, and he declares that under no circumstances would he return to his home community.

The second letter, written in 1844 by one Jon N. Bjørndalen, takes precisely the opposite standpoint. Sickness is everywhere, the climate is bad, the heat of the summers frightful, snakes abound, the woods and

* Milton Wells, "Wisconsin Antique – A Norwegian Settlement – A Tale of Distress," in *Home Missionary* (New York), 17:129–130 (October 1844).

swamps of Wisconsin are ill suited to farming, taxes are burdensome, there is danger of the Mormon religion, few have money, and the work is unendurably hard. Thus the writer catalogues the elements of the pioneer ordeal as he sees them, and he strengthens his argument by including a postscript written by a widow with six children, who tells of the recent deaths of her husband and one son. "Do not let America enter your thoughts," Bjørndalen urges.

Writing about the same time, an emigrant named Tangen, who evidently had a dash of philosophy, solemnly divided mankind into eight classes, for each of which he offered advice. In sum, what he proposed was a plan of voluntary restriction of emigration. Those classes whose chances of success in America he judged to be poor, he advised to stay at home, but to the young, strong, determined, and healthy he issued an unreserved invitation to emigrate.

Inevitably the dismal reports of immigrant ordeal were given wide publicity in Norway, where the debate over America was in full course. It was a period of rising nationalism, and hostility to emigration was linked with patriotic devotion to the homeland. The chorus of antiemigration writings dismayed many immigrants whose courage and patience had not broken under the assaults of illness and suffering.

Early in 1845 eighty settlers in the Muskego Settlement, one of the hardest hit of all the immigrant colonies, banded together in what can only be called a manifesto to the people of Norway. This open letter acknowledged a period of suffering and trial, but denied with simple eloquence that the immigrant woes justified reports condemning America. It recalled the story of the seventeenth-century founders of Virginia, who were beset by illness, hunger, and dangers from both wild beasts and Indians, but stubbornly persevered in their struggles and opened the way for millions of people to enjoy the abundant resources of the land. The Norwegian settlers believed that, with God's help, their venture, too, would be crowned with success in a land more fruitful than any other in the world. This Muskego manifesto, which appeared in the Norwegian newspapers in the spring of 1845, is one of the noble documents of American immigration and perhaps the most memorable of all the Norwegian immigrant letters.

Individuals joined in the protests, including an unnamed immigrant who in the spring of 1845, not without some bitter thrusts at the Norwegian clergy and officialdom, argued the emigration issue on economic and other grounds. And a carpenter named Nærum in the autumn of that year took up the cudgels against the minister Dietrichson, who, indefensibly in the letter writer's view, had termed America a desert. A humble carpenter, in telling words, had no difficulty in exposing the absurdity of the pastor's charge.

Immigrant enterprise in replying to what was considered an unfair and unreliable representation of America took the form, in Chicago, of an organized "Correspondence Society," the purpose of which was to correct "erroneous impressions" of the United States in the fatherland through systematic letter writing. This society was organized in 1848, with a constitution and, in true American fashion, a president, vice president, secretary, and assistant secretary. The officers constituted an executive committee which was authorized to select, each month, a "qualified man to write to Norway upon such matters as the society may order." The group was made up of "Vossings," people from the Norwegian district of Voss. One of the leaders was Ivar Lawson (Larson), who later founded one of the most important Scandinavian newspapers in America, *Skandinaven* of Chicago, and whose son, Victor Fremont Lawson, became the noted publisher of the *Chicago Daily News*. The records of this society include copies of eight letters that were sent to Norway in 1848 and 1849, the first of which incorporated the constitution of the organization and reported that about one hundred Norwegian families then lived in Chicago. A few excerpts from these letters are presented in this section. The eighth and last letter, dated May 1, 1849, complains about the paucity of replies from Norway and makes the very interesting estimate that in 1848 Norwegian immigrants in America had written from four to five thousand letters to their friends and relatives in Norway. One is not surprised to learn that in the 1850's the energetic Chicago Vossings organized what was called the "Voss Parish Emigration Society," for the express purpose of collecting funds to aid "needy and worthy families" to emigrate from Norway to America, and that this new society established a little newspaper that served as a channel for printed letters to Norway.

Immigration is a transatlantic story. The ordeal of the pioneers was reflected in letters that, in great numbers, found their way into newspapers that reached remote valleys in Norway. Exaggeration there was, on both sides of the argument about America, but time was the ally of those who clung to their American hopes. And the time was to come when ballad singers, reviewing the pioneer saga from the perspective of years, could say with truth that the immigrants were living "right royally" in the land of their choice.

In no circumstances would I return

FROM OLE KNUDSEN TROVATTEN, AT VERNON, WISCONSIN, TO TOLLEF OLSEN JUVE*

June 28, 1842

As Knud Aslaksen Svalestuen of Raulandsstranden is making a trip back to his fatherland, and thereby affords me the best opportunity for writing to you, I shall not neglect this chance, but shall acquaint you with my position in my present abode. I hope that my former letters have reached you so that you have at least some information concerning my travels hitherto. I accompanied Captain Ankerson from New York after my arrival there, together with some persons of ordinary position that fall. As I hope that my friends and those of my wife are already on the way to America I cannot communicate with them in this letter. But if I am mistaken in this, then friendly greetings are sent to them in this letter; they must not fail to take the important step of coming over to me.

You, my true friend, together with many others of my acquaintances probably censure me for my emigration considerably, and perhaps even yet believe that I regret having left Ødefjeld. No! not so. In no circumstances would I return to live in Ødefjeld, not even if I could be the owner of half of the Annex. Ødefjeld is such a wretched place that one ought by no means to live there. Every inhabitant would do better by selling his farm to people from Lower Telemark. It seems rather foolish to me to abide by one's ancestors' ignorance of better regions and their fear of emigration and live in so poor a place and upon such barren ground as Ødefjeld. Fertile fields lie uncultivated in America partly for ignorance of the fertility of this land and partly for fear of emigration. Here in America a much better mode of living is open to every honorable citizen, as I hope most inhabitants of Ødefjeld are.

* This letter appeared in *Telesoga,* September 1910. My translation of it was first printed in "The America Letters," *North Star,* 2:75–77 (March 1920).

Every poor person who will work diligently and faithfully, can become a well-to-do man here in a short time, and the rich man, on the other hand, has even better prospects, for he can work out his career with less drudgery and fewer burdens and thus have a much more peaceful life here than in Norway. You may take as an example myself, whose fortunes seemed from the beginning to be bad, for all my money — twenty-eight dollars in silver — was stolen from me in the city of Albany, so that I was able to ward off starvation from myself and family only with great difficulty. You must bear in mind that I lost my money nearly at the beginning of my journey in America, as Albany is not far from New York. In my company there were various persons, and among them the richest were the most unwilling to aid me with a loan. Finally, after a fashion, I was given enough help to reach my destination in Wisconsin. I have now been in Wisconsin about a year and a half. During the past winter my wife and I and our oldest child were taken sick with malaria, which attacks almost everyone, both natives and foreigners, but is not fatal. Still, with me it lasted almost all winter. Despite the fact that I came here empty-handed and have also been sick, I have nevertheless acquired the following property: one cow, a year-old pig, one calf, two two-year-old oxen (which are necessary to everyone for work), and forty acres of land, though I owe eighteen days of work on this land.

This will show what advantages there are for everyone who can work to come here. Though I have been sick almost half a year and have a family to take care of, still I have achieved much more than a worker can in Norway. We are now all well and happy, and my two oldest children have attended the English school so that they understand the language fairly well — much better than I. I have not learned very much of the language, but I can manage when occasions arise, and my wife also. My wages per month are from $16 to $18 and board. I have been in the employ of the same men all the time as I think very highly of them, and they continually do kind things for me. When I was sick, they did much more than my neighbors from my own country. These two brothers for whom I work have said several times that they earnestly desire me to stay with them permanently, and that if I were to leave them they would be greatly disappointed. I may therefore say that I have gained friends here among the natives, even as I had friends in Ødefjeld, and these will regret my departure even as a few there did.

It is by no means my purpose to move now, for I have never lived better than at present. The only thing that I am dissatisfied with is that most of the groups here have no religion. They do not observe the Sabbath, a practice in which some of my own countrymen follow their example. Dangerous religions are also taught here which are altogether pernicious and most likely that antichrist which Christ speaks of. The founder of this religion is living. His name is Joseph Smith, and he calls himself a prophet who speaks much with the Lord, like Mohammed, as he says. I regret to say a number of my countrymen have gone over to this sect. Smith's residence is in the state of Illinois, where he has already begun the construction of a great temple to which he gives the name "the New Jerusalem."

The common monthly wage here is from $12 to $18, but some people, who are lazy, must be contented with $7, $8, or $10 a month. Servant girls get from $1.00 to $1.50 a week. Money is scarce here at present, so that some farmers do not pay their laborers. There is complaint everywhere, therefore, against untrustworthy people, but this is not the truth of the matter. A large part of the drifting laborers are lazy and dishonest so that the farmer will not give them their pay. But I have never heard of an honorable and truthful laborer losing his pay.

Almost all conceivable useful things grow here with the greatest luxuriance, but the crops are greatly different and they are not all equally good. This year the crop promises to be very small, for it happened to be so exceptionally cold here the night between June 10 and 11 that much of the seed froze and some replanting was necessary. This was so unusual that no native had ever seen it before. But it seems to me as if the world were getting older and coming closer and closer to destruction through the many changes in nature. We know by the words of the Savior that the Lord's day will come like a thief in the night, so we ought therefore every moment be prepared to meet our bridegroom and judge. A good many here in America – in New York and Boston – have already determined the time, which will occur next summer, in accordance with the words of the prophet Daniel, and they are continually noising their views about it both in printed books and in newspapers. But every wise man can believe the words of Jesus when he says that no one knows when that day shall come. Let it suffice that we prepare ourselves earnestly and look well to our wandering through this life so that we may reach the goal we have set up. . . .

I find no difference between the climate here and in Norway. To be sure, some days in the summer are warmer here – but the warmth is not excessive. On the other hand I have experienced winter cold as severe here as in Ødefjeld – but it seldom lasts longer at a time than one or two days, at the longest three days. The snow, during my experience as an emigrant, has been at its greatest three or four inches. The snow comes in the latter part of November and disappears in the latter part of March. Toward the last of April the cattle are put out to graze on the new grass which springs up very rapidly.

Both winter wheat and spring wheat are seeded here, and the harvest of the wheat last summer occurred in the first week of July. Almost every kind of grain is planted here and each kind thrives beautifully. The haying takes place in July, but it could really occur in May, for the grass is even then very high.

Few of the native-born have sheds for the cattle in the winter, but they stand always under the open sky and seldom freeze. They thrive exceedingly well both winter and summer, and I presume it is better for them to be without a shed since they are not accustomed to having it. The pigs are not looked after very much, as they must be given food only during the first part of the winter. Every man has a large number of pigs and also chickens. There are some here who have as many as a thousand chickens. The piece of land I have bought is as thickly covered with maple trees as the densest woods in Ødefjeld, so I have the opportunity of tapping as much maple sugar as I please. The tree which they here tap for sugar resembles the Norwegian maple, but there are many varieties of the same.

Do not let America enter your thoughts

FROM JON N. BJØRNDALEN, IN MILWAUKEE COUNTY, WISCONSIN TERRITORY, TO HIS PARENTS*

January 5, 1844

I write you briefly for your information, because several of my countrymen are planning to go to America. I hope that they will not disregard my humble communication.

* This letter first appeared in *Morgenbladet*, May 28, 1844.

I think of my countrymen with tender feelings and remember how they imagine that as soon as they get to America, great glories will open up to them. And how could they believe otherwise, for almost all reports and letters received in Norway from America were good. But this is very wrong; only about a third part of these letters is true. People only write down accounts of the good, although they themselves have had no experience of it. As we traveled up through the country we all had high hopes that we should be happy, but these were disappointed. The first thing we encountered on our arrival in Milwaukee was two of our countrymen down at the wharf. Not until then did we see the good things one acquires in this country – an emaciated body and a sallow face! This is how almost all our immigrants look. The ague and other pestilential fevers were widespread so that one victim could not help the other. All who have this illness become weak, are never safe from it, and daily suffer from poor health. The heavy air is depressing, and people walk around bowed like slaves weighed down by their chains and deprived of their freedom. In the summer the climate is far too hot; during the daytime the heat is so severe that when you work sweat pours out all over your body, as if you had been drenched by rain, and during the night everything is covered by a poisonous fog.

There are a lot of snakes here, five or six different kinds, most of which are unfamiliar to me. They even get into the houses; rattlesnakes, for instance, have often been found on the floor. They are able to burrow down into the ground and thus get into people's houses. The biggest I have seen are as thick as a man's arm. In the short time I have been here I have killed many of them.

The land the Norwegians have settled consists mostly of woods and swamps, of which there are a countless number. They are used for grazing because the woodland hardly affords good grazing as it is so extensively covered with oak bushes and hazel bushes. It looks like land thickly covered with juniper and other small trees. It would be difficult to clear this land because of the big knolls and the roots the bushes put out, and the oak trees are as heavy to clear away as stones. The settlers do not get much milk from the cattle fed with swamp grass in winter unless they add to it kohlrabies, potatoes, and Indian corn.

You have probably heard how light the taxes are said to be here; and it is true enough that the first two or three years the tax on eighty acres of land is only $1. But later a man goes around and puts a tax on your land, on what you have fenced in, on the land you have cleared; if you have built a house, you have to pay tax on that; you have to pay tax on the cattle, on a cart, on a house covered with boards; in short, you have to pay taxes on everything you own. And the value of everything is assessed by the men who travel around and inspect it all. Thus it is estimated that when a Norwegian has lived here long enough to have his road all made and his house and farming tools in good condition, he will have to pay from $10 to $16; that is, $1 out of every $100, to the government. If a man has lent money, he is taxed 1 per cent, so that, in fact, he almost has to pay for his own harvest and work.

I shall have to tell you also about the Mormon religion, which is the most miserable sect you can imagine. The first one to adopt this detestable religion was Ole Olsen Sandvigen. Now he has lured several of his countrymen into this abominable kind of worship, for instance, two of the sons of Lars Folseland and Anne Christiansdatter. There is a whole sect of them in Illinois, where Ole Sandvigen is staying. If he makes more visits to the Norwegian settlement, probably many will be converted. I do not understand this religion, and I do not want to understand it. They believe that their baptism is the gate to heaven, and that it is easy to go there once you have been baptized. They believe that they can cure the sick, even that they can help those of the dead who in their opinion have not been saved to enter heaven by means of their baptism. There are many Anabaptists, but none are so ridiculous and detestable as the Mormons.

Daily wages are much lower now than they used to be. Money is scarce, and you can get practically nothing but trade in kind unless you know the language and travel to distant markets. I do not deny that if one has good health and a happy disposition, in time it will be easier to make a living. But when the Norwegians have to work for Americans, they are at first much too weak to stand their work. You work strenuously from morning till noon without rest. Then when you have gobbled down your food, you have to start work again. I am reminded of the rush in Norway when we tried to save the dry hay from the rain!

Thus, I do not advise any of my relatives to come to America. If you could see the conditions of the Norwegians in America at present, you would certainly be frightened; illness and misery are so prevalent that many have died. One cannot imagine anything more misleading than the tempting and deceptive letters that reach Norway, for these letters have not only taken away people's relatives, but they have almost taken away their lives. One might suppose that the emigrants believe that they are well off, but this is far from true. Except for a few men, all are in misery from illness, starvation, and cold. Most of them lack money and are unable to work – certainly the greatest misery anyone can imagine. I want to tell you briefly how many of those who emigrated from Tind have died: Knud Mærum and his insane son Thore, Tosten Mærum and his wife, Jacob Ejhoug, Ingebret Berge and his wife, Ole Sanden, Østen Eggerud and his wife, Gro Eggerud, Sigurd Vemork, Anne Halvorsdatter Laavekaase, Anne Bøen, and besides many small children, Halvor Jørrisdahl and Gunner from Sjøtvedt; all told sixty-eight grown people and children.

Both my wife and I have been ill with the ague from eight days before Holy-Cross Day to Christmas; but since we feel a little better now, we hope that God will let us live and that in time we shall get our health back. But even if we do get better, we shall have to keep quiet and not try to work for the rest of the winter. So far we have a debt of 16 specie dollars, and we are staying with the Hølje Grimsruds, who are good, congenial people. Time is heavy on our hands, and we are not happy in our emigration. If the Almighty grants us good health and we can make enough money, our greatest wish is to go back to old Norway. When you have neither health nor any pleasures here in America, it is better to live in your native country even if you own nothing. America will always be unhealthful, and no Norseman is ever going to be happy here.

Many persons here in America have behaved very badly, for instance, Knud Svalestuen, who lured so many people out to great misery. The statement in his letter that he was the owner of a great deal of land was the greatest falsehood you can imagine, for he did not own a thing here in America. In the same way, Jan Knudsen Traen inveigled his brothers out to great misery. He promised them that if they would pay the passage for Ole Sanden, he would pay them back when they arrived, but he did not even own the clothes he was wearing or enough food to give them a meal. His sister now lives on charity, for she is unable to provide for her small children. Likewise Jon Nielsen Rue with his deceitful letters so shamefully induced his parents to come here to utter wretchedness. And there are many other such swindlers.

The Norwegians have a good pastor – a Dane – and they have sermons every Sunday. Children are taught both in the Norwegian and the English school and, with God's help, will be encouraged in their Christian religion.

In conclusion, then, my relatives, do not think of coming to America at all. Dear parent and brothers and sisters, and you my dear Halvor Gjøsdal, do not let America enter your thoughts any more. And I do not advise Gro and Gunnild to follow me but to stay in their native country. Time is short, and I shall now stop though I have much more to write about. I send my best greetings and may the spirit of truth be in your hearts and aid you in your several undertakings.

P.S. Please write to me, dear Father, if you get an opportunity; or if you do not write yourself, have someone else do it for you. Tell me how you all are, how the year has been, and what has changed since I left. Good-by. If there is anyone who does not believe my letter he can consult Sjur Jørgenson Haaeim's letters and Bailiff Anfindsen. There he will learn the truth if he does not believe me.

To my dear Parents-in-Law Niels John Nielsen and Groe Madsdatter Bjørndalen: A small note from me, Gunnild Tostensdatter Mærum, to my sister Aslaug Tostensdatter Røsland and her son Tosten and also her daughter: when we put our faith in God's help, we poor human beings shall surely there find comfort and guidance, for God often sends us sufferings and tribulations to test our faith if we have patience both in good fortune and in adversity. How hard and miserable it will be for me, left behind with six small children, to settle on land that has not even been cleared. We have all been ill but feel better now. Knud was ill for eight days before death called him away, and so was our son Thore. They were buried together. My parents died shortly afterward. God grant that beyond the grave we may meet in a happier state, for the world sends us nothing but suffering and hardship. If I could talk to any of you, my relatives, my most fervent plea would be that you never think of America. I would have written more to you if Jon Nielsen had not already written so clearly about all our difficulties. I will write in more detail about everything when I see how things turn out. Many greetings from me to my relatives, friends, and acquaintances.

Not all people, only some, should emigrate

FROM ELLEF BJØRNSEN TANGEN, AT PINE LAKE, WISCONSIN, TO RELATIVES*

January 14, 1844

Your letter of May 19 reached me through Halvor Halvorsen Hogolt, and from it I learn that my letter to you was published in *Bratsberg Amtstidende* and that it has met with several objections, especially from Jørgen Haaeim and in a letter from a German correspondent published in the paper *For the Working Class* put out by Mr. H. Wergeland. Since the varied accounts of returning emigrants will create differences of opinion concerning emigration, I wish once more to give my opinion about my adopted country.

What Jørgen Haaeim has written about his fate in America in *Skiensposten,* Nos. 22 and 24, March 17 and 24, seems to me to show of itself that he messed around without any thought or plan. Surely everyone who thoughtfully reads his account of his doings here will agree that no sane person would be so foolish as to move into a desert far away from other people. When a person actually does such a thing, no one is surprised at the consequences. From this you will get a fairly good idea of what I think of this man, and I shall not waste any more words on him.

Now let me say something very briefly about the paper *For the Working Class,* which mentions an emigrant from Germany who, after staying here for some time, complains so much of the complete dishonesty of the Americans. This I can safely affirm is a great falsehood, for according to my experience, people in Scandinavia can hardly match the Americans in honesty. He also observes that the money here is often no good. This likewise is completely untrue; for what money has better value than gold and silver, the currency most frequently

* This letter appeared in the *Bratsberg-Amts Correspondent,* April 1, 1844. The *Correspondent* characterizes the writer, who had emigrated two years earlier, as a trustworthy farmer with an unusually good education.

used in these states? Paper money is sparingly used, and no one is obliged to take it.

For a more complete description of conditions here, there is no more reliable and at the same time interesting account than Mr. Reiersen's observations on immigation, published in Christianssand and based on his extensive travels in the United States. To write more about conditions here is thus unnecesary, but having started, I shall go on.

Unfortunately I have seen people come here who, once their feet touch the promised land, have ample reason to regret leaving their native country. For the language and customs are foreign to them; surrounded by a numerous flock of children, they have nothing but two empty hands; or because of age or some affliction, they are unable to work and support their families. Add to this the fact that they are surrounded by strangers whose speech they do not understand and who cannot comfort them in their need, and it is not surprising that they sometimes get discouraged when they find themselves needing the charity of their fellow human beings.

To prevent similar mistakes in emigration, I divide the mass of human beings into eight different classes: The first class are the growing youth. (2) Workers under fifty. (3) Nonworkers. (4) Fifty years of age and above. (5) Those who are so poor that they cannot support themselves. (6) Those who are able to come here with ample means. (7) The strong and healthy. (8) The timid and weak.

First class: Come, you youngster, if you have good advisers who can teach you to know God, religion, the world, man, and to love virtue and hate vice. You will not lack opportunity to develop your natural talents for becoming a good citizen and a good human being.

Second class: It is difficult to advise you, my dear friend. You will have to examine your situation carefully and see if any of the other listed points stand against your becoming an emigrant. If not, I trust that, with God's help, and with fortune favoring you, you will be able to make a safer and more secure living here and thus meet old age with confidence.

Third class: If you cannot or do not want to work, then stay at home. But if you are a man of property and have experience in trade, I think you will be able to make a good living here in that field.

Fourth class: Dear old man, you who have spent your strength in working the Norwegian soil, let that same soil become your resting place. Consider that the days of your youth are past and that it would be hard for you to start everything afresh. Consider that you will come to a foreign country, unfamiliar with its language and customs, and that it would be hard for you to see time go by with so little done to make your old age secure. I do not deny that you have many tribulations to bear in your native country, and that a democratic indignation fills your soul when you remember that those who ought to be your protectors are your persecutors. Thus, I cannot give you any better advice – in case you have no children or other relatives whom you can count on to bring you here – than to work patiently in the calling where your destiny has placed you.

Fifth class: Yours is indeed a hard lot, for you really live in true bondage, and every sensitive heart must pity you. If you are not young or do not have children and other relatives to help you, I can give you no better advice than that you must patiently spend the years of your bondage in the conviction that some day the Almighty will, once and for all, deliver you of your suffering.

Sixth class: For you who own some property, it will be twice as easy to cultivate the soil of the New World, and your money will multiply like lilies in the fertile field. Your crops will compensate for the social pleasures you have to do without in the beginning.

Seventh class: By this I do not mean physical strength but good health, a firm character, and ability to plan systematically. These qualities ought to be added for all the other classes. With such a combination you would certainly have prospects of a successful future.

Eighth class: Be satisfied with the talents that the Lord has given you. Consider that you would worsen your situation in such a journey. It is true that you are surrounded by people who are your protectors in name only; you will have to stand up to them as best you can and try patiently to get through life at home.

I shall now leave this matter and address myself to your questions. You must excuse me if I do not answer them as fully as you had expected, but I have little space left. (1) You ask where we generally sell our products. (2) How dependable is the sale? (3) Would I have what I need of forest, firewood, and farm buildings on my land? (4) How much does it cost to plow the land, and how much does the land yield? (5) Is it easier or more difficult to build houses in America; what material would I use? (6) How far away is the nearest mill and sawmill?

1. This, of course, depends on where you live. Here we mostly sell our products to newly arrived emigrants. What is left is taken to Milwaukee, a distance of twenty-eight miles, or four Norwegian miles; you can make this trip back and forth with loaded carts and oxen in two days and a half.

2. In the city mentioned, you can always sell your products because of the shipping on the Erie Canal, which connects Lakes Michigan, Huron, and Erie with the Atlantic.

3. I have as much forest as I need on my land to bring it under cultivation, and this is true of most people here. And you do not need to suppose that there is merely brushwood.

4. The usual price for plowing is $2.50 an acre. You can sow wheat the first year and expect a fairly good crop; the yield varies from sixteen to thirty-five fold, and the other grains are in proportion to this.

5. Houses here are usually built of oak or maple and are very resistant to decay. If you want to build more elaborate houses, it will of course be more expensive as the daily wages are high. But the houses we put up do not cost very much.

6. I live close to four sawmills and two mills; the farthest is two miles and a half away.

Thus you see, dear Ole, how conditions are here, and I do not think anything in my description of these classes goes against your expressed decision to come here. . . .

We the undersigned, your countrymen

FROM EIGHTY NORWEGIANS AT MUSKEGO, WISCONSIN,
TO NORWEGIANS IN THE OLD COUNTRY *

January 6, 1845

Something like a year has now gone by since the hearts of nearly all among us were filled with foreboding and discouragement, brought

* This letter, known as the Muskego manifesto, was published in the Oslo *Morgenbladet*, April 1, 1845, with eighty signatures. The translation, which is by S. B. Hustvedt, first appeared under the title "An American Manifesto by Norwegian Immigrants" in *American-Scandinavian Review*, 13:620–622 (October 1925) and has been reprinted in Søren Bache, *A Chronicle of Old Muskego* (Northfield, 1951), pp. 141–144.

about by illness of various kinds and in part by want of the very necessities of life; a condition which at that time prevailed among us because of the crowding into our midst of large numbers of our poor immigrant countrymen who, lacking funds to continue their journey, found themselves compelled for a while to sojourn here. It was a season of sorrow, such as to try the patience of several of us to the utmost.

A certain few, overwrought in mind, even spread the most thoughtless rumors, accompanied in some cases by curses and expressions of contempt for America, as much as to say that God had no part in creating this land, a land so highly endowed by nature that even its uncultivated condition must be regarded as in effect half-cultivated when compared with the native state of the soil in Norway and many other European countries; a land which for centuries has been a safe refuge for exiles from nearly every state in Europe, exiles who have, almost without exception, found here a carefree livelihood after conquering the first difficulties that beset every pioneer community, provided only that they bent their minds upon gaining through industry and thrift the necessary means of subsistence.

There are some who complain of the trials that immigrants at first must meet; but all such persons should feel a sense of shame when they recall what history has to tell of the sufferings of those earliest immigrants who opened the way for coming generations by founding the first colony in the United States, the Virginia colony. Not only were they visited by contagious diseases and by famine; they had also to fight against wild beasts and Indians. Through such misfortunes the colony was on several occasions nearly exterminated and had to be reinforced. At length, of some six hundred colonists about sixty were left; these survivors, facing certain death from famine, found themselves compelled to leave the shores of the country in boats which they had built in the hope of reaching the banks of Newfoundland and of meeting there with fishing vessels on which they might return to England. But, as it appeared, such was not the will of God. Just as they had embarked they met, at the mouth of the Potomac River, the gateway to the colony, some ships that had been sent out from England for their relief. Thus encouraged they returned to continue the work of settlement that they had begun. So they fought and won their victory; and so they became the immediate occasion whereby it has been made possible for twenty millions of people to find abundant resources in the

United States, a number which is supposed to be capable of being doubled more than once before the opportunities here shall have been exhausted.

Should not we likewise, with brighter prospects than theirs, entertain the hope of winning by perseverance victories like theirs and of gaining what we need to sustain life! Or should God, who in his word has laid upon us the precept "Be fruitful, and multiply, and replenish the earth," not crown such an undertaking with success, inasmuch as He has so richly endowed this land and made it more fitted to produce all manner of food for mankind than perhaps any other country in the whole world; more especially under the present conditions, when over-population in Europe, greater than at almost any earlier time, has made emigration a necessity.

The dissatisfaction that showed itself at the beginning among many of the immigrants at this place had its origin for the most part in an unseasonable homesickness more to be looked for in children than in grown people. It arose from such circumstances, for instance, as that they had to get along without certain kinds of food to which they had been accustomed, that this or that article in their diet did not have the same flavor as it had in the old home, that they suffered from the lack of some convenience or other, or that they missed certain of their friends with whom they had before had pleasant association. By taking such things to heart they permit their minds to be filled with unquiet longings that must remain fruitless. Meanwhile they lose sight of all those former difficulties, of the whole gloomy prospect of material success under which they labored heavily in the land of their birth; and so they now imagine the place where they were born to be that land of Canaan which at one time they supposed to lie in America. One who tries to forget bygone things and to look forward instead, and who pursues his lawful labors in patience and in the fear of God, will surely not find his hopes disappointed if he will only aim, so far as his material needs are concerned, to be content with his daily bread.

We have no expectation of gaining riches; but we live under a liberal government in a fruitful land, where freedom and equality are the rule in religious as in civil matters, and where each one of us is at liberty to earn his living practically as he chooses. Such opportunities are more to be desired than riches; through these opportunities we have a prospect of preparing for ourselves, by diligence and industry, a carefree old age. We have therefore no reason to regret the decision that brought us to this country.

An attempt has been made to prevent people from coming to this country by representing America as a suitable refuge for released convicts or such men as seek to escape the wrath of the law. It is true that many persons of this type have come hither and that here as elsewhere there are altogether too many wicked men. Yet this state of affairs is unavoidable, inasmuch as good men and evil are permitted to come in, the one with the other; nevertheless, assault, robbery, and theft are much less common here than in the lands from which such men may have come. At all events, misdeeds of this kind are unheard of among us, and so no one need shrink back from America on this account. Attempts have also been made to frighten people away from this settlement because of the presence of illness among us last year; yet although the summer just past was unusually wet and cold for this latitude, we have not suffered from any epidemic, in spite of certain fears during the spring; and we hope that we shall continue to be spared.

Only a few words more. By reason of the circumstances just mentioned, namely the privations and the sickness that visited our colony and robbed most of us of the gains of our labor, some among us found it expedient to turn to our friends in Norway with a request for assistance in building the church of which we stood in such great need. The response to our request has been so unexpectedly generous that we have been enabled to complete, after a fashion, the church building that for some time has been under construction in this settlement. Wherefore we take occasion to express here our thanks to the honored donors, the following named men:

Mr. T. O. Bache, Proprietor, Walle, Drammen ..	$200
Mr. N. Bache, Drammen	100
Mr. T. Bache, Merchant, Drammen	50
Mr. E. Olsen, Merchant, Drammen	50
Mr. J. K. Lykke, Merchant, Trondhjem	10
Mr. Simen Svendsen, Lier	15
Mr. Tollef Mörch	5
	$430

The newspaper editors of Norway are hereby respectfully requested by the undersigned, their countrymen, to publish this account in its entirety and without change in their daily press, and to append our several names.

Well pleased with public administration here

FROM A NORWEGIAN IMMIGRANT IN WISCONSIN TO A FRIEND AT HOME *

September 4, 1845

After I have thus told you about those things that concern us privately, I suppose I ought to add a few general observations which you, my friend, may insert in *Christianssandsposten* or in the magazine *Norge og Amerika* if you like. I have been told that this magazine is published in Arendal, but thus far we have not received any issues of it here, as far as I know.

In the following lines I intend, to the best of my ability, to give you a clear idea of the prospects that an emigrant may reasonably hope for here, compared to those he might expect in Norway during a similar period and under normal conditions. Let me add that the following remarks are based on the experience I have been able to acquire during my stay here and also on conversations with several persons who have lived in this neighborhood for a fairly long time and who have supplied me with information about the progress they have made since their arrival here.

Let us assume that a young, able-bodied man from the country, who has saved up a small sum of thirty or forty dollars, leaves Norway with the intention of emigrating to America. He then presents himself in the *Great West* with a few dollars in his pocket. His intention and wish must consequently be to get work, the sooner the better, and this he will soon be able to do by consulting those of his countrymen who arrived before him. Depending on the time of year and other circumstances, his daily wage will be from 60 to 100 cents (one cent approximately equals one Norwegian skilling). In the winter he will get 60 cents, in the spring 80 cents without board, and during the summer and autumn, when the harvesting of grain and hay requires many workers, 100 cents ($1) plus free board. Thus his average pay will be 80 cents, out of which he must subtract 30 for good board and clothing, and in this way he has saved 50 cents a day.

If we figure that the number of working days is 250, at the end of the year he will have saved up $120. If he gets permanent employment he will be paid by the current wages here, $10 – often $12 – a month plus

* This letter appeared in *Norge og Amerika,* 1:97–101 (January 1846).

good board, and will thus get $120 a year, from which he must subtract the price of the clothing he will need. It is easily seen that after two years, this young man will have saved up $200, and consequently, for $50 he can buy one sixteenth of a section, or forty acres of land. . . . For the rest of his money he will build houses, buy animals, farming tools, and so on. Thus at the end of two years he has become an independent man and is in a position to marry without having to worry for himself or his family, and in all probability he may look forward to a pleasant and carefree future. Since some of you may not be familiar with the term *acre*, let me just observe in passing that an acre of land contains 9,000 square *alen*, and if you want a clear idea of the size of forty acres, you may get it right away by measuring out 4,800 average paces for the length and 3,000 paces for the width.

Now, if this young man had stayed in Norway, I do not think it will be necessary to attempt to prove my contention that at the end of the two years, he would have been in about the same position as he was in the beginning.

For a laborer who has a wife and children the prospects are about the same. By washing, knitting, and other indoor work, the wife will always be able to make enough to support herself, and if she is good at this kind of work she can make much more. As soon as the children are in their teens they will be able to find suitable jobs, so that a wife and numerous children are not to be regarded as a burden but rather as an advantage.

As to emigrants who have a skill or trade before they leave Norway, like smiths, ship's carpenters, carpenters, sawyers, coopers, shoemakers, tailors, and so on, it goes without saying that these will be able to work ahead to an independent position faster than the simple laborer, since they are paid relatively better because of their skill. And when they have acquired a small capital, they may use it either for buying a quarter of a section of land – 160 acres – or for getting established in a city. Every year new cities are founded, as the country becomes increasingly inhabited, and these offer fine opportunities for beginning artisans.

As to *bønder* or people from the cities who are lucky enough to have some capital on their arrival here, it is evident that these may buy a quarter or a half of a section depending on the size of their capital. And as their money enables them to carry on the cultivation of their land efficiently, soon their uncultivated land will be changed into fertile fields.

We are well pleased with public administration here, for no taxes or other burdens are weighing heavily on us. For a piece of land of forty acres a yearly tax of something over $1 is paid. We know nothing about road laws and transportation laws. The construction and upkeep of roads are paid for by the public, and stagecoach stations have been established at necessary points where the traveler pays for the transportation he uses. We have no poor people here and consequently no relief system. The conduct of officials is, as might be expected in a *truly free* country, obliging, gentle, and polite to everybody, not the aristocratic, haughty, repelling kind of address that I met with on several occasions in my old native country, where the common man, if he has any business with the officials, must often be prepared to be treated with an authority and smugness that clearly indicate that they consider themselves creatures of the utmost importance.

I notice now that I have neglected to mention religion, which, since I consider it of the highest importance to every well-regulated community, ought to have been foremost in my thoughts. But I hope that this neglect on my part will not be resented by the clergy, a hope which I trust will be fulfilled, so much the more since on several occasions it has seemed to me that religion was not of quite so much importance to them as the emoluments. *But perhaps this is the illusion of an imagination that is frequently misleading me [written in English].* Therefore I freely admit that my impression in this respect may be wrong. "Judge not, that ye be not judged." But I cannot deny that the tact with which I observed several ministers in Norway – especially in the country – conduct divine service made an impression on me and many of the listeners which is the exact reverse of the impression that every pastor, who wishes to fulfill his duties as such, ought to endeavor to convey to his congregation.

We have no Norwegian minister in this neighborhood, but several of us who have lived here long enough to know English fairly well do not feel the lack of one. We go to the Episcopal, or Protestant, church, which agrees with the Lutheran in practically everything. I have attended divine service there several times now, and I have witnessed with great pleasure the fervor, the devotion, and the propriety with which their service is conducted. Thus, we do not intend to write for a Norwegian minister, the more so as an attempt made in this respect by another settlement did not lead to a happy result. No! there are very few things that we can import from our old Norway which could be of benefit to us, and least of all – Norwegian officials.

Many opportunities for investment

FROM NILS HANSEN NÆRUM AT MUSKEGO, WISCONSIN, TO J. H. NÆRUM, PORSGRUND *

November 16, 1845

From Christiania morning papers I have seen Pastor Dietrichson's letter to Norway, which is said to have created a good deal of irresolution and caused many people to change their decisions to come over here.

It caused nothing but mirth here that such a man could write in this almost childish way. But as I hope that you may also have seen the letter of Mr. Reiersen in which he criticizes Dietrichson (on the whole Reiersen's views agree with my own experience), perhaps it will be superfluous to try to refute him in this letter, too. But surely it does not take a man like Mr. Dietrichson to judge a new country and the situation of its inhabitants – a man who all his life has been in the best of circumstances and who has never experienced personally what it means to have to support yourself by work in Norway. Nor has he taken the trouble to familiarize himself with the lot of the common people in Norway, which he should have done before he took it upon himself to give an account of the Norwegians in America and of the American nation in particular.

He complains of poor roads and miserable huts. Still the roads are good enough to make it possible to carry mail all over the country in stagecoaches drawn by four horses, except in the most recent settlements, where one cannot expect this. As to the houses, you have to build simply at first in the newest places to get a shelter while you grow something on the land and try to build a better house as soon as possible. In the areas where the land has been inhabited for some time, you

* This letter was published in *Bratsberg-Amts Correspondent*, March 5, 1846, much of it being omitted, the editor explained, because it covered ground already familiar. Nærum had emigrated in 1844. The letter of Pastor Dietrichson to which he is replying is that on p. 144 of this book.

will find houses as beautiful as those in Norway – and even more beautiful. That Mr. Dietrichson should have permitted himself, in his sermons, to call America a desert is almost indefensible. For one might expect a man like him (especially as a theologian) to show more appreciation of God's providence than to call a country a desert which has been so richly endowed by nature. The oldest inhabitants of Wisconsin have only lived here ten or eleven years, and the majority not half that time, yet the land can already feed the population of the numerous bigger and smaller towns and the many thousands of people who arrive every year. And it is said that as early as 1842 forty thousand barrels of wheat and wheat flour were exported from Wisconsin. Since that time the land has been improved to more than the double of this capacity, because the difficulties which beset the first immigrants especially have gradually been almost completely overcome.

We have also many other advantages which one must value highly: all sorts of honest trades are open to everyone who has a liking and ability for them, and there are many opportunities for investment which pay off well if you go about them carefully and in the right manner. As soon as a man has become known as honest and dependable, he is just as much respected here as anyone. Farmers and artisans are just as good as merchants and officials. They all have practically the same manners, and the appearance and dress of people are usually the same as they are in Norwegian towns, with the exception of the Norwegian mountain people, who stick to their old customs to some extent.

The English language is spoken everywhere, with the exception of a few smaller areas, settlements or colonies of Norwegians, Swedes, Germans, or French. In these settlements people usually speak their native language when they are among themselves, but this habit will generally die out with the second generation.

Though the degree of freedom is very great here and the nation is made up of people from almost all European countries, crimes are very rare. But if a crime has been committed it is punished according to the laws, which are very hard and explicit. The criminals do not have to wait long to be sentenced, and when sentence has been pronounced, it is carried out as soon as possible, for all business both public and private is dispatched quickly and is as little of a burden to the public as possible. Begging in the streets is not known here and would not be tolerated either, since everyone who can and wants to work will find plenty of jobs and will be able to make a decent living for himself. But those who for some reason or other are in need receive sufficient support to enable them to live fairly well.

Yet no country or place can be or become so perfect that several drawbacks cannot be found. This has never been otherwise and will never become so, and God's wise providence has ordained that it should be so; but I hope that some of the things one might object to here will be changed before long. For several reasons people have not moved in among us Norwegians thus far, mainly because of the situation of the emigrants in the beginning, and the fact that the areas where the Norwegians have made their homes were too thinly settled previously.

There is a very great lack of good ministers, since we only have one by the name of Clausen, a Danish "seminarian" who was ordained after he came here. He is a very intelligent young man, but several persons bear him a grudge because of the rigor with which he observes the Danish-Norwegian church ritual. And since he alone has to serve the Muskego, Koshkonong, Jefferson, and Rock Run settlements and the Norwegians in Chicago and Milwaukee plus the settlement at Rock River, and as all of these places are far apart, I suppose that there would be enough to do here for three or four Norwegian ministers. These would be able to make a decent living if, supplementary to their clerical office, they owned some land.

I suppose that competent theological graduates who are good Christians would be best suited for this, preferably such persons as have acquired a sound knowledge of the conditions of the Norwegian common people and who would not in the beginning expect to find everything very comfortable here with large, elegant buildings, and so on. If they arrived shortly after graduation, they could be ordained here and might thus, when they took the oath of office, be exempted from pledging loyalty to the Norwegian church ritual, which in its entirety and severity, especially with regard to excommunication, is not very applicable here. For cases that call for excommunication should first be judged by a higher clerical authority, and besides direct application of it is against the law of the land. This was brought out clearly by Mr. Dietrichson's procedure at Koshkonong Prairie Whitsunday this year. He had excommunicated a man by the name of Halvor Funkelien (as far as I recall), and as this man would not submit to sitting in a chair of disgrace that had been placed for him at the door of the church, Mr. Dietrichson ordered the sexton to put him out of the church. The man offered resistance and said that he intended to stay inside, but then Dietrichson himself came down, and the man had to leave. But shortly afterward he had Dietrichson summoned before court, which fined him $50 for abuse of his authority.

I have thought a great deal of Pastor Bruun, who served the congregation at Gjerpen for Pastor Rode last year, and I have often wished that he were here. And if he came, I trust that here too he would win the hearts of many people, and do much good both for the earthly and spiritual welfare of his congregation. And I am sure that he would not lack the necessities of life for himself and his family in the future.

Freedom is drawn in with mother milk

FROM THE VOSS CORRESPONDENCE SOCIETY OF CHICAGO TO "FRIENDS IN THE FATHERLAND" *

September 30, 1848

Since many erroneous impressions exist in our fatherland concerning the political as well as the religious situation in America, particularly as relating to the emigrated Norwegians, and in order that these may be dispelled through correct advices from the immigrants here, which can be brought about only through a systematic correspondence, we have agreed and decided as follows:

I

That to attain the end sought we form ourselves into a Correspondence Society of Chicago, Ill., for the mutual purpose of meeting the costs which will ensue upon writing to Norway, and, possibly, of obtaining correspondence therefrom.

* The handwritten book of the secretary of the Voss Society, containing copies of the eight letters it sent to Norway, was obtained by Mr. Knut A. Rene of Madison, Wisconsin, from Mr. Edward Williams of Chicago. Mr. Albert O. Barton has translated parts of the letters and given an account of the society in "Norwegian-American Emigration Societies in the Forties and Fifties," *Norwegian-American Studies and Records*, 3:23–42 (1928). The following excerpts are from this translation.

II

The officers of the society shall be a president, a vice president, a secretary, and an assistant secretary, who together shall constitute an executive committee. It shall be the duty of the president to preside at meetings of the society and in his absence the vice president shall do so. The secretary and the assistant secretary shall keep a careful record of the meetings of the society, its correspondence and business, and publish such matter as the society may determine. It shall be the duty of the executive committee to appoint each month a qualified man to write to Norway upon such matters as the society may order. No such writings shall be sent without the approval of the committee, the members of which shall subscribe to them in the name of the society.

November 1, 1848

Every friend of the common people in Norway has for a long time been distressed to witness how the Norwegian government has sought, both directly and indirectly, to frighten the working class away from America and thus hinder emigration, well knowing that by taking such a haughty stand the few could retain their servitors and thus insure to themselves unbounded ease and power. However, we hope the time is not far distant when everyone, be he high or low, will take the truth as neighbor.

After careful investigation we find that the Norwegians here in Chicago have a population of from 600 to 700 and enjoy a general prosperity. Yes, we have the greatest cause to be thankful, since many among us who, on our arrival, did not own our own clothes are now in comparatively independent circumstances—yes, even have several hundreds of dollars out at interest. And this has not been brought about by any chance stroke of fortune, but as a result of industry and economy.

December 1, 1848

Ivar Larson Boe has also acquired a considerable amount of real estate in the city and a fine home. Besides, he and his brother are half-owners of a sailing vessel which he and another Norwegian bought for $1,800, and he is also employed at the post office and has now a wage of $25 a month.

January 1, 1849

Here it is not asked, what or who was your father, but the question is, what are you? . . . Freedom is here an element which is drawn in. as it were, with mother milk, and seems as essential to every citizen of the United States as the air he breathes. It is part of his life, which cannot be compromised nor surrendered, and which is cherished and defended as life itself. It is a national attribute, common to all. Herein lies the secret of the equality everywhere seen. It is an American political creed to be one people. This elevates the lowly and brings down the great. . . . It would be far from our purpose to rouse a spirit of discontent, but as American citizens who have tasted the joys of being free of the yoke which tyrants ever bear with them, and having in common with you the Norwegian temper, love of liberty, and warmth of heart, we would say to you who dwell amid Norway's mountains: Show yourselves worthy sons of the north. Stand as a man for your liberties. Let freedom and equality be your demands, truth and the right your reliance, and the God of justice will give you victory.

May 1, 1849

We recall with gladness the day we left the chill cliffs of Norway and praise the Lord whose wisdom guided us so that our lot has been to dwell in a land where liberty and freedom prevail, for here we can enjoy all the privileges to which men are rightfully entitled.

Appraising the American Scene

THE immigrant discovery of America in the nineteenth century was aided by thousands of travelers who came to the United States as tourists in search of adventure or under the impelling urgings of a curiosity that was all-European in breadth. Not a few foreigners embarked on missions of serious investigation, exploring American political, economic, and social life or attempting to fill out the Old World understanding of the American land and its varied and stupendous resources. Some saw America only from car windows or on polite and comfortable tours that never penetrated the hinterland of the seaboard. Inevitably there was a torrent of books in nearly all the languages of Europe picturing America in its changing phases and mirroring the reactions of European observers to the New World scene. These reactions were often incredibly shallow and superficial, of little interest or importance to historians as compared with the critical self-examination by Americans themselves as they advanced, decade by decade, into national maturity. But occasionally if rarely there were European observers who managed to see more than blurring flashes of car-window vistas and to view the larger American scene with some degree of objectivity and insight. In any event, however, the European thirst for information about the world across the Atlantic was unslakable. Good or bad, there could not be too many books about the United States of America.

Many books by European travelers not originally written in English have been translated and made available, and not a few anthologies have been published bringing together excerpts from such writings. Some of the curious Europeans did not publish their accounts in book form, however, but reached the public of their home countries through newspaper reports and letters which were read alongside the letters from the immigrants themselves and thus contributed to the image of the New World forming in the minds of thousands of people to whom "America" previously had been little more than a name. Relatively few of such accounts are widely known to American readers.

Ole Munch Ræder, a well-educated Norwegian jurist, was sent by his government to the United States in the late 1840's to study the jury system. The three-volume work that Ræder wrote on the jury system in the United States, Great Britain, and Canada was duly published in the 1850's and was influential in bringing about later judicial reforms in Norway. That scholarly and weighty book has been forgotten, however, whereas the sprightly and informing travel letters, contemporaneously printed in newspapers, have become well known, thanks to the Norwegian-American Historical Association, which published them in full in an English translation by Gunnar J. Malmin in 1929.

In the following pages some selections from Munch Ræder's letters are offered. Here are sharp observation and critical and judicious commentaries. The sweep of the reports and the interests they reveal are catholic: the conditions of immigrant travel, the burgeoning life of the towns of the frontier, the struggles of homesick immigrants in the newly founded settlements of the West, the nature of linguistic transition of immigrants quick to adapt themselves to a strange environment, the social and religious scene at mid-century, economic problems viewed in a national as well as a local setting, the perplexing problems of Americanization, the working of frontier "club law," ill-informed American attitudes toward immigrants and toward Europe, the basic experiment of American democracy, the future prospects not only for the pioneers but for the whole country, and the slavery question as viewed more than a decade before the Civil War. Never far from the mind of the writer are the repercussions of European events upon the American mind and the lessons of America for Europe – and especially Norway. In passages not included in these selections Munch Ræder writes about the possibility of a Scandinavian "United States," with a government taking its inspiration from the constitution of the United States.

Let them be American, but stay Norwegian

FROM OLE MUNCH RÆDER, IN WISCONSIN TERRITORY, TO HIS COUNTRYMEN *

September–October, 1847

The trip on the Erie Canal, from Albany to Buffalo, costs only $7.50, including meals, and lasts a day longer than the journey by rail. This price, however, is only for ordinary travelers. The spirit of speculation has led to a rather material reduction in the price for immigrants. Some canalboats, I believe, transport them and their belongings for $2.00, but they have to provide their own food and the journey of eight or ten days becomes extremely monotonous.

The railroads, too, have made an exception in their case to the general rule of having only one class. Sometimes a large box car is added to the train, labeled in huge letters "IMMIGRANT CAR," and here the immigrants are piled together in grand confusion, with all their trunks and other belongings. In New York there are companies which arrange the entire journey for immigrants, making their profits through the large masses they transport, as well as whatever they can make through cheating—by dropping them off halfway, and so on.

The consul general at New York has made a splendid arrangement for the immigrants whereby they may deposit a sum of $6 and are then transported to Wisconsin by one of the most dependable companies, which is paid by the consulate upon notification from the immigrant that the company has faithfully discharged its obligations. This plan is announced to the immigrants upon their arrival in New York, but they are so suspicious—or perhaps so unsuspecting when it comes to the Yankees and their agents—that they seldom make use of this splendid means of securing a journey that is both cheap and safe. They cannot resist the temptation of an offer to transport them for a few cents less. The immigrant companies have in their service Norwegians and Swedes who carry on a very profitable business.

Up the Hudson to Albany, as well as on the Great Lakes, there is

* These letters were published in *Den Norske Rigstidende* from November 6, 1847, to July 3, 1848; some of them were reprinted in newspapers in Drammen and Stavanger. The present translation, with some minor changes, is by Gunnar J. Malmin, who has assembled and translated the entire series as *America in the Forties: The Letters of Ole Munch Ræder* (Minneapolis: University of Minnesota Press, for the Norwegian-American Historical Association, 1929).

only one means of travel, for immigrants as well as for others, and that is the steamship. Very few, except the immigrants, of course, are satisfied to be packed away in the space below deck; steamships, as a rule, do not follow the practice of the railways in having only one class. Often first class is on the upper deck, second class on the lower, and third class, for immigrants, mostly underneath the decks. The American steamship is quite different from the European. Imagine the deck of a European steamship turned upside down so that what was underneath now comes on top, and vice versa, and you will have some sort of idea as to what an American "steam-palace" is like. Instead of masts there are merely three or four iron rods on top of the structure, fastened together by wires; on top of these rods there are often gilded balls, American eagles, or the like. The part that towers highest is often the machinery, its pistons rising and falling with great regularity high up in the air. The elegance of such a ship is quite remarkable.

And now, finally, to get at a very important item, both the food and the service, provided by Negro servants, were as good as can be found in the best hotels; and the cost was remarkably small, only $10 for the whole voyage from Buffalo to Milwaukee, which took four days.

Now, at last, we had arrived in Milwaukee, the flourishing emporium of a large part of the West, so richly blessed by nature. It is said to rank first among American cities for the energy and the rapidity with which it has grown; a few years ago it was merely a nameless spot in the wilderness.

Milwaukee has a population of eleven or twelve thousand, about a dozen churches, a beautiful courthouse, a Land Office, a bank, seventy lawyers (!), and so on. The price of lots is said to have increased fivefold or more during the past five years. There is only one other American city, namely, Rochester, New York, which has been compared with it for rapidity of growth.

One of the first things we did in Milwaukee was, naturally, to look for fellow countrymen. It was easy to find them, and in large numbers, too. Just a few steps from the hotel we found a group of people whose language and appearance revealed their nationality. We soon heard, as we have since become so accustomed to do, complaints of sickness, hard work, and homesickness, alongside of expressions of satisfaction with the good wages and the low cost of provisions, as well as the hope that their condition, on the whole, would become better.

The next day, which was Sunday, a driver called for us in the morning with a coach drawn by two horses and, after a drive of a couple of hours towards the southwest, we arrived at the Norwegian settlement at Muskego Lake. The first people whom we met were a couple from Tinn, both of whom seemed greatly pleased with the visit.

We next visited, among others, Even Heg, who seems to be one of the leaders among the Norwegians in these parts. He is said to be a Haugean and he was away attending a devotional meeting when we reached his house. He, too, seemed satisfied with the state of his affairs. He did not feel very friendly towards Reiersen, who, in his opinion, had given exaggerated accounts of the unhealthful conditions at Muskego and had thereby frightened the later Norwegian immigrants to such an extent that they not only would not settle there but they even went miles out of their way to avoid going through the place. Here they published the Norwegian-Wisconsin newspaper *Nordlyset,* edited by Mr. Reymert. It is without doubt a very good idea through such a medium to maintain a cultural link between the Norwegians here and the mother country, as well as among themselves. Every one, indeed, who would like to see them preserve their national characteristics and their memories of their native land as long as possible must, first and foremost, turn his attention to the problem of preserving their language by keeping it constantly before their eyes and ears.

As you know, I cannot convince myself that all these countrymen of ours, as they leave our own country, are to be regarded as completely lost and as strangers to us. Let them become Americans, as is the duty of holders of American soil, but this need not prevent them from remaining Norwegian for a long time to come. The American character is not yet so fixed and established that it excludes all others.

There are, even now, so many of our people out here in the West that they already appear as a group and thereby are protected against influences foreign to themselves, because their relationship to one another is stronger than their relationship to other races. But if this condition is to be at all lasting, there must be more intelligence among them; they must realize that this instinct of theirs is quite consistent with good sense and honor; they must learn to appreciate their own nationality more than they do and to cause others to respect it, too. For these reasons the establishment of a press among them is undoubtedly of the greatest importance.

I have already suggested how desirable it would be for the Norwegians to see their language frequently in somewhat pure form, not only in their religious literature, but otherwise as well. I had in mind particularly the great ease with which they learn the English language and, unfortunately, the equal facility they have in forgetting their own as soon as they cease to use it every day. In this respect they seem in no way to differ from their ancestors who, when they had settled in France, forgot their native land and their native tongue so rapidly that it has been an object of considerable astonishment to historians and literary scholars. The habits of speech among our countrymen in America are surely very likely to lead to such results, it must be admitted. They do not bother about keeping the two languages separate, so that they may speak Norwegian to their countrymen and English to others; instead, they eliminate one word after the other from their Norwegian and substitute English words in such a way that the Norwegian will soon be completely forgotten.

Such a practice, to be sure, is rather common among uneducated people who emigrate to a foreign country, but the Norwegians seem to have a special knack at it. The first words they forget are *ja* and *nei*, and, even if everything else about them, from top to toe, is Norwegian, you may be sure they will answer "yes" or "no" if you ask them any questions. Gradually other English words, pertaining to their daily environment, are added. They have a "fæns" about their "farm" and have probably "digget" a well near the house so that they need not go so far to get water to use on their "stoven." Such a well is generally necessary, even if there is a "læk" or a "river" in the vicinity, because such water is generally too warm.

The ease with which the Norwegians learn the English language has attracted the attention of the Americans, all the more because of the fact that they are altogether too ready to consider them entirely raw when they come here. "Never," one of them told me a few days ago, "have I known people to become civilized so rapidly as your countrymen; they come here in motley crowds, dressed up with all kinds of dingle-dangle just like the Indians. But just look at them a year later: they speak English perfectly, and, as far as dress, manners, and ability are concerned, they are quite above reproach." Of course I tried to explain to him that their original mode of dress certainly could not make Indians out of them and that they were not entirely devoid of culture or those habits of diligence and regularity which one expects to find in a well-ordered and civilized society, even among the poorest classes out in the country, but he seemed scarcely disposed to make any concessions on that point.

It is, on the whole, quite remarkable how quickly our farm girls improve when they are among strangers. Their English is quite correct, but as soon as they start to speak their mother tongue, it generally sounds broad and clumsy enough. No matter how much patriotic love you may profess to feel for the various dialects of our language, you cannot deny or at any rate avoid the feeling that the harmony is broken, even if the unfortunate expression comes from the fairest mouth or is animated by the friendliest smile. I believe that most of them are not conscious of the peculiar impression made by their way of speaking Norwegian; at any rate, they are too goodhearted and too happy in the recollection of their native land to be bothered by such a trifle. One can scarcely say as much for the Norwegian boys; at any rate, I have heard the opinion expressed that as soon as they have learned "to guess" and "to calculate," they at once become strangers to their less fortunate countrymen and are very loath to admit their Norwegian origin. This fact (and I am inclined to believe it is one) furnishes new proof of the need of improving the cultural conditions among our countrymen here and, at the same time, of increasing their national pride so much, at least, that they will not feel themselves tempted to deny their own country. I do not believe that any cultured Norwegian has ever felt any tendency to do such a thing; on the contrary he is all too apt to boast of the fact that he comes from the "land of the heroes."

About three thousand Norwegians as yet do not belong to any religious organization. Such a situation is rather serious, and yet no worse than among the Americans themselves. The complaint is frequently heard here in the West that religion has few adherents and few ministers, but it must at the same time be admitted that progress is being made in this respect almost everywhere. Even if the situation is by no means what it was among the Puritan settlers in New England two hundred years ago, when a church was the first thing to be provided for, nevertheless spiritual needs do assert themselves even out here in the West, as soon as the first severe struggle with nature is over. Many a person who never has experienced the influence of religion in a thickly populated, civilized country, learns to appreciate, out here in his loneliness, how deep an influence religion exerts upon the soul of man.

Americans who live near the Norwegian churches attend services at times despite the fact that they are not Lutherans and do not understand the language. They say, however, that since they know that an act of worship is taking place, it does them good to be present. This is not at all surprising, as Pastor Dietrichson conducts the services in such a beautiful and dignified manner that it will naturally make an impression even on a person who is not able to derive benefit from the actual meaning of the words. I have never heard Pastor Clausen but he, too, is said to be a capable speaker and to be otherwise well qualified for his work. Pastor Dietrichson has been requested to preach occasionally in English. I do not believe he will venture to do so; and, although it might be desirable in so far as it would enable him to do more good, and, through establishing an American congregation alongside the Norwegian, he would gain prestige both for his church and for himself, nevertheless, for my part, I hope it will not be done. It would tend to Americanize our countrymen too soon. Let us rather keep the church, as well as the language, to ourselves at first; through them alone can we hope to preserve our nationality.

I hope you are not looking to me for any account of the economic conditions among our good countrymen in Wisconsin – this vale of tears – this Land of Canaan. You will have to be content with the quite general remarks that Wisconsin is a fertile territory, the land is cheap, and farm products also are cheap. The last is almost self-evident when one considers the fact that grain, in order to reach New York, has fifteen hundred miles to travel, and that on this journey, it has to pay high enough freight rates to make a paying business of the navigation on the Lakes, the Erie Canal, and the Hudson River, and then the canal tolls as well as the merchants' profits, commissions, and the like. From New York it still has three thousand miles to travel before it reaches the European market, where it has to compete with English, Russian, Danish, and Austrian products. It is true that a great deal is consumed in the United States, particularly in the South, where cotton is the chief crop, and in the East. It is estimated that New England, which is largely industrial, feeds two million stomachs on wheat from the West and New York and Brooklyn's half-million get their wheat from there also. But, as it is a fact that huge portions go to Europe, it is obvious that the prices even in New York and Boston must be somewhat lower than in the European markets, and recent events have proved conclusively that they are quite dependent on the prices in England.

It is obvious, then, that the profits of the farmer cannot be very great after he has paid high wages to his workers and with difficulty has managed to have his produce hauled to town over the wretched roads. The price at Milwaukee has been as low as 50 cents a bushel for wheat; this year, however, it has scarcely gone below 60; and, at present, when many ships are waiting for loads, it is from 80 to 85 cents. Here in Madison people do not raise more wheat than they need for local consumption, as it really does not pay to haul it to the lake shore, and the six hundred citizens of the town, most of whom are farmers themselves, do not buy much. They find it more profitable, therefore, to cultivate Indian corn, root crops, and the like, for their cattle. The farmers did not make any considerable profits as a result of the hard times in Europe. Since the Lakes and the canals are frozen during the winter, the farmer must hasten to sell his produce immediately after the harvest. Thus it happened that it was already in the hands of the merchants before people had any idea how bad conditions were in Europe. And, as navigation could not set in until late in the spring, you will readily see that what was shipped from here would not arrive in England until shortly before the harvest season. The circumstance that navigation must ordinarily cease until late in April and hence most of the shipping must occur in the fall naturally tends to increase the freight rates; and, if one gets his crops to town too late, he naturally gets a still lower price because they will have to lie over during the winter and bear the storehouse expenses and all kinds of risk.

Even if his produce does not command a high price, it means much to a farmer to be able to provide with ease practically everything he needs in the way of food and clothing. I could easily put myself in the place of a farmer, who, as he ate his simple meal, patted himself on the stomach and exclaimed: "I must say, the food here is fine; we never need to be afraid of starving." That means a great deal. Hunger is an enemy from which many of our highlanders in Norway never feel safe. Even if parliament and the administration manage the ship of state to perfection (and they do, of course, as you know), nevertheless they can never succeed in bringing it to anchor south of latitude 43° any more than they can toss overboard the fearful ballast of naked rock which encumbers it. Just think what an impression it would make on a poor highlander's imagination to be told that some day he might eat wheat bread every day and pork at least three times a week.

I must add that, among all the people I have talked with – and they are not a few – I have found very few who said they were dissatisfied and wanted to return to Norway, and with some of these it was more a matter of talk than of a real desire to go. One man said he wanted to return home because his wife did not like it here; another, who said he was a Quaker, was dissatisfied with the schools. Both of them had been talking in this vein for a long time, without making any real move in that direction but rather the opposite. A little merchant from Drammen, on the other hand, seemed to mean it seriously; he has been rather unfortunate, for which I am sorry, as he seems to be a very fine man. And it is not strange if there are some who have been ruined through their emigration. The emigration fever spread through our country districts like a disease, paying no heed to age or sex, rich or poor, the diligent worker or the lazy good-for-nothing. Naturally, many have emigrated who are totally unfit for the strenuous life here, which demands so much energy, common sense, and endurance if one is to succeed. It is equally true that many have made a mistake in buying or claiming land before they had either the necessary understanding or means to proceed with its cultivation. The fact that there have not been more wrecks than there have, in view of all the mistakes made, gives evidence both of the inherent strength of character of our people and of the excellence of the country itself.

I do not mean to imply that few complaints are heard. Quite the contrary. In addition to the fact that many, indeed most, admit that they had expected the land to be far better than it actually proved to be and that they had been fooled, to some extent, by the false reports contained in letters, there are many other complaints; but all of them are of such a nature that time and habit will presumably remedy the situation. Some complain that the work is too strenuous, others that there is so much ungodliness, others that there is too much sickness. One woman complained that there seemed to be less real nourishment in the food here than in Norway; no matter how much good food she gave her husband, he simply would not gain in weight. Possibly, she thought, and very likely with good reason, this was due to the severe heat which, coupled with strenuous labor, sapped his energy.

The worst complaint of all is homesickness; everyone experiences that, of course. But time can heal even deeper wounds than that of having been severed from one's native land. Furthermore, most of the immigrants seem to cherish more or less consciously a hope of returning some day to their native land, having realized only after they had broken away how strong were the ties that held them there.

In contrast to all these troubles and complaints, I found, particularly among those who had owned considerable property in Norway, a quite general feeling of satisfaction that they had come, built rather on their hopes for the future, to be sure, than on what they had already achieved. Among those who have worked their way up from poverty this feeling of satisfaction is so great that they are likely to overestimate their present prosperity. A certain Lars Hedemarken (or Rollo, after the farm by that name in Ringsaker) is now a well-to-do man and is highly esteemed for his uprightness. I mentioned one of the largest farms in Ringsaker and asked him how he would like to trade his present farm for that one. He said he would not do so under any circumstances, chiefly because the farm in Ringsaker would prove far too small for all his sons, while here the whole prairie was theirs. His house was one of the better kind. Very few Norwegians have yet built comfortable houses. The great majority live in log cabins of the sort that can be erected in a day.

A very profitable business consists in buying up large stretches of prairie land, taking part of it into use for oneself, and then parceling the rest out into farms for sale, building a log cabin on each, and plowing up an acre or so. Immigrants are glad to pay a fairly good price for such a farm, as they like to have a house ready to receive them when they arrive and to find the work of cultivation already begun. I know many Norwegians who have made good profits in this way, and I have met no one who denied that it was a paying business.

As there are everywhere people living on land which they have not paid for, it is necessary for the immigrant to be careful to avoid getting into trouble. Even if the map at the Land Office designates a piece of land as unoccupied, there may be someone living there, and one will either simply have to let well enough alone or else pay him whatever people decide is fair. This is in accordance with the famous "club law" which the people have established as a protection against a clause in the act of Congress by which it is specified that if a person is not able to pay for a piece of claimed land after a year he loses all rights to it. The people have organized themselves to oppose this clause and they arrange things as they please between the buyer and the holder of such a piece of land. The buyer runs the risk of being seized and forced to waive his right to the property and to write out a deed on whatever conditions they dictate. Many Norwegians are members of such organizations, but they often get into trouble because they are not so clever at it as the Yankees, who know how to introduce a certain appearance of law and order even into a practice which in the nature of the case is the direct opposite of law and order.

Recently a Norwegian in Milwaukee bought some land occupied by a Norwegian at Koshkonong. When he came to take possession he was seized during the night by a group of people with their faces blackened, whose speech and actions revealed that they were Norwegians. They mistreated him more or less and forced him to give a written promise that he would make out a deed. This he later refused to do, of course, and even succeeded in having them fined. The trouble was that they had gone ahead on their own initiative without consulting the president of the organization and letting him arrange matters according to the rules.

What has annoyed me most in my associations with the Americans is their prejudice against Europe, which they regard as hopelessly lost in slavery and wretchedness. Three fourths of the people in the East and ninety-nine hundredths of the people in the West are fully convinced that the other side of the Atlantic is nothing but a heap of medieval feudal states, which, indeed, show some slight indication of reform here and there, but have not made much political progress and have not enough vitality to rise from the abyss of misery and corruption into which they have fallen as the result of centuries of ignorance and despotism; their doom is inevitable. If one tries to dispute any portion of this creed of theirs, they simply point to the foreigners: "What further evidence is needed than these immigrants who swarm into our country by the hundreds of thousands every year with the traces of suffering unmistakably written on their faces and curses in their mouths at the tyranny they are escaping?"

If the Americans hear of any scandal from some European court or of corruption in some European government, both of which have been rather plentiful this last year, they at once use it as a weapon against the monarchical system itself. It is a rather big job to defend all Europe; and I have on various occasions declined to do so, no matter how agreeable it might be once in a while to lay aside my little Norwegian, or even Scandinavian, patriotism and to pose as the champion of a whole continent. It does not help much to reject this constituency of two hundred million people, because people here do not recognize many differences among the various nations; every European is responsible for the whole thing. They have a special grudge against England, to be sure, in return for the English prejudice against them. Even the strong resemblance between these two nations and the common origin of their institutions only tend to irritate them the more. The Englishmen, who regard their own laws and institutions as quite ideal, naturally consider the development which has taken place in America a degeneration and perversion. The Yankees, on the other hand, if possible even more proud of their own, consider the English institutions to be antiquated and impractical because they have not kept pace with the improvements and progress made in America.

It is just as true, then, that an American utterly fails to understand England, as is the reverse. Indeed, no European nation need expect a fair judgment in America – but this is not necessarily reciprocal. Experience has shown that Frenchmen are able to view American conditions without any prejudice. The Americans themselves realize this and De Tocqueville's book is as highly esteemed here as in Europe. The same can also be said of the writings of a considerable number of French scholars and literary men about America, while the English accounts are generally treated with the utmost indignation and disdain.

If I remember De Custine's account correctly, the Czar has declared that he can as easily understand a democratic republic, where the people rule, as an autocracy, but that the so-called limited monarchies are a complete riddle to him – they appear to be built on deceit and corruption. This idea fits in well with the American attitude. Both the Russian and the American forms of government are absolute, the only difference being that in one case the majority takes the place of one man. Half the population minus one is just as dependent on the will of half the population plus one as the Russian people minus one is dependent on the will of that one man. Even the word "liberty" is used here almost in the same way as in Russia – that is, only with reference to slavery; the abolitionists are called the "Liberty Party." The word "sovereign," on the other hand, is constantly heard; the voters are spoken of as "sovereigns," both in jest and in earnest.

But let us not push the parallel too far. Even if the rule of the majority is not always so favorable to the interests of the minority, it is nevertheless obliged to be somewhat moderate, if only in its own interest. Its laws must as a rule be for the welfare of all and must treat all alike; the members of the party generally have somewhat the same interests as other citizens of the state and its leaders must beware of weakening their party's strength and thus endangering its prestige through unreasonable measures. Their own interests naturally urge them to strive for growth and progress, and even their mistakes rarely have a significant, and never a lasting, effect. The principles of such a government are grounded in the hearts of men and will live long after that form of government which gives the power to one man has been undermined and shattered by the force of the new ideals of civilization.

And what a wonderful example America gives the world of a large number of states living side by side in peace and order! What a marvelous sight, without equal either in the past or the present, to see one state after the other, with hundreds of thousands of citizens, spring up as though out of the soil and then peacefully take its place among its sister states, renouncing the use of arms and pledging allegiance to a common tribunal!

Everything here bears evidence of life and progress; no narrow, selfish consideration can stem the tide. It has been estimated that if the population continues to increase as it has – and there is every reason to suppose that it will – in a few years it will amount to 30 million and in 1900 it will be 135 million; that does not take Mexico into account. Europe may view this growth calmly enough because a republic such as America can never conquer territory on the other side of the Atlantic, and it would not if it could, because it would not know what to do with it; this is clearly seen from its present predicament as to Mexico. Of course it will become a great naval power, but Europe is already accustomed to having a master on the sea. And for all save England it would merely be a question as to which master would be the better. Besides, its location at the very center of the commercial world, midway between Europe and the Orient, will give it such a great advantage over Europe that it will not need to use might and insults against other nations in order to reap the benefit of a world trade. Furthermore, the sentiment here as well as in Europe is opposed to restrictions on trade, and this will probably be the case in the future also. America's power on the seas will be useful to Europe as long as it balances England's, because it will protect European nations against the injustice that they have so often experienced at England's hands. And when America finally gains the upper hand, one of the results will probably be that the European states, through dread of the consequences, will be led to follow America's example and establish a union of their own.

People living on the western frontier, many of whom have gone there to make up for failures or misplaced investments in the East, quite generally give up for the time being those pleasures and social observances which usually accompany a higher civilization. Some of them take a liking to the simple life which they have been obliged to adopt and allow their suspension of luxuries of every kind to continue "without day," but others introduce their accustomed refinements as soon as they are able. In a number of homes at Madison, Elkhorn, and Janesville, I found all the comforts and all the elegance that we generally associate with the upper classes in Europe. In some of these homes I even saw candle-snuffers and handkerchiefs in use. People no longer sit around spitting at the stove as is the fashion out here in the West; tobacco-chewing is restricted if not altogether outlawed, and cuspidors protect the floor and the carpets.

What I have said about the use of handkerchiefs must not be taken to mean that such articles are an unknown commodity out here but only that they are used rather economically, after the major operation has been performed with the fingers. Women are not guilty of such a practice, but even the most elegantly attired gentlemen are often very proficient at it. As far as the absence of candle-snuffers is concerned, I must admit that I first thought it was total and I was very agreeably surprised when I found one at Jefferson. One learns to appreciate the value of such things after he has had to get along without them for some time, as I had. Although the specimen I found at Jefferson was in such shape that it took two men to repair it, I could not help regarding it as one of the masterpieces of modern civilization. Here along the Mississippi there are candle-snuffers, but their form bears evidence of the fact that their manufacture and use have long been forgotten arts and have but recently been revived.

Generally speaking, I believe that Wisconsin has acquired more European flavor than most of the other districts in the West. This is due partly to the fact that the Norwegian, German, and Irish immigrants provide a class of servants more obedient and less exacting than the Yankees but not servile and thoughtless as the Negroes. Furthermore, most of the Americans here have come from New England and New York, where the greatest culture and refinement is to be found. Among these people there is none of that coarseness which one meets so often in the southwestern states, in spite of the smooth, polished exterior. It finds abundant nourishment there in the slavery system, at all times and all places an abomination, despite all arguments to the contrary.

And what a difference there is between an American and an English court dinner! As far as the food itself is concerned the difference is evident from the fact that the former costs about a Norwegian mark and the latter more than two *specier*, not including the cost of wine. In England the party is made up of the counsellors alone, as the judges generally eat by themselves, and the attorneys as well as clerks and other officers of the court are excluded. Here at Wisconsin all without exception, jury, witnesses, defendants, and so on, gather about the dinner table at the hotel while court is in session. The English counsellors eat their dinner in the evening, after the toil of the day is over, while the Americans take an hour and a half at noon, but they devote only a small part of it to gulping down their dinner. The Englishmen enjoy their dinner; the Americans just eat it. The Englishmen lay aside their professional dignity together with their gowns and wigs in order to drown their cares in champagne and burgundy with song and merriment. The Americans change neither their clothes nor their manners, drink their water in silence, and consider how they are going to tackle the case that comes on at 1:30. In England, not only does the exclusive flavor that attaches itself to such a small, select group tend to give it a somewhat higher tone, but the knowledge of the strict code of honor that prevails among them as well as their broad general culture and the outstanding abilities that have elevated them to positions of trust and honor—all these factors tend to purify the atmosphere about them, so to speak, and give a visitor the agreeable sensation of being in particularly good company.

Here, in this section of America especially, there are many of the lawyers who do not particularly command one's respect, either for their natural abilities or for their culture and training. When a lawyer in the East finds the competition too sharp for him, he generally goes west. The same is true of many young men who hesitate to begin their careers too close to their home communities, where everyone knows them. I have spoken with some lawyers of this kind, who knew so little about European conditions even in their own special field that they thought the English common law was in force in Norway. One of them was greatly surprised when I told him that we not only had our own laws but our own government as well; he had the impression that we were subjects of Queen Victoria! The lawyers out here do have their merits, however. They certainly are kind and obliging to strangers. Furthermore, many of them play trumpets, trombones, flutes, or other musical instruments; these come together and organize bands which enliven things very considerably as the court visits the different towns. One of my good friends is an excellent piccolo player.

America herself has become a mighty nation

FROM OLE MUNCH RÆDER, IN BOSTON, MASSACHUSETTS

May 1848

Americans are as interested as ever in watching developments in Europe. Every time the telegraph brings the news that a steamship is in sight off Boston harbor, or that one has arrived at New York, the streets are filled with people curious to hear the latest reports. All flock to the newspaper offices, and there is great competition among the various papers as to which one shall reap the profits of satisfying the public. An army of little boys waits impatiently outside the newspaper offices. As soon as the papers are out they rush off in every direction noisily crying their wares. Posters are put up here and there, giving brief summaries of the most important news in huge letters painted with brush and ink – for example, "War! War! War! Cotton goes up. Attempted overthrow of the provisional government."

Great as is the interest in European affairs now, it can scarcely be compared with that during the first French Revolution, when even the political campaigns centered in European rather than American problems. Nowadays the situation is quite different. America herself has become a mighty nation and she looks across at what is going on in Europe rather with an eye to her own profit than because she feels herself a member of the European family. Many seem to rejoice in the rise of democracy in Europe, which they attribute largely to the example of America. Everywhere people express the hope that much European capital will now be put into American bonds, as a result of lack of confidence in the credit of the European nations.

Most Europeans find that their hatred of slavery diminishes when they visit the slave states themselves. With me the opposite proved to be the case, although I visited slave-owners who showed the greatest kindness in dealing with their "property." One of them, for example, told me that he would never try to recapture a slave in case he ran away. Another owned a preacher to whom he granted almost complete freedom to study and travel. Those slaves whose moral and intellectual powers have been held at the lowest stage of development, almost like animals, are contented enough, and this contentment on their part is held up as a splendid argument against the fanaticism of the Abolitionists. The sight of such degradation was all the more painful to me because I felt that many of them, in spite of their obvious ignorance, had some slight consciousness, at any rate, of the fact that they were the victims of a shameful oppression.

The Transatlantic Gold Rush

THE thrilling news of gold in the Far West reached Norway in the summer and autumn of 1848.* By the following year a miner who had dug gold in California had actually returned to Norway, and newspapers carried many stories about his adventures, betraying a special curiosity about a mysterious chest, presumably of money or gold dust, that he was said to have brought back with him. Emigration, stimulated in part by the exciting news from the West, leaped from 1,400 in 1848 to 4,000 in 1849. A bark was announced for a trip direct from Norway to California in the spring of 1849, and other vessels during the next two or three years went to Panama or all the way to the gold country. In 1850 a Norwegian expedition of gold-hunters was organized, a ship chartered, and in October of that year more than a hundred Argonauts, high of hope, sailed out from Trondhjem for San Francisco by way of Rio and Cape Horn.†

"California" soon became a familiar name in Norway. Books came from the press with such titles as "The Gold Thirst, or California Fever in America," ballads about the wonders of the golden land were composed and sung,‡ and in due time letters written by immigrants in California appeared in Norwegian newspapers. These first-hand reports were supplemented by the return of gold-hunters, some

* See the chapter on "Emigrant Gold Seekers" in *Norwegian Migration*, vol. 1, pp. 267–286.

† The story of this expedition, with detailed references to specific sources, is told in *Norwegian Migration*, vol. 1, pp. 272–280.

‡ See, for example, "To an Expedition of California Gold Seekers" and "El Dorado" in Theodore C. Blegen and Martin B. Ruud, *Norwegian Emigrant Songs and Ballads* (Minneapolis, 1936), pp. 131–145.

of them "decorated," as one newspaper put it, "with massive rings, breastpins, watch chains, and similar expensive gold trinkets." *

What kinds of pictures of California and the West did the immigrant gold-hunters lay before the people of Norway? The following pages offer fair samples, starting with a story of a journey west via Panama, with a report of earnings in California, some mention of the Indian menace, and a good account of the workings of frontier justice. "Every man here," wrote the international forty-niner tersely, "is armed with a gun, pistols, and knives."

The immigrants experienced the ecstasy of the gold mania, but not all of them sought out the gold fields. One, after traveling around Cape Horn, admiring the beauties of Valparaiso, and pushing on to San Francisco and Sacramento, took work as a carpenter at fifteen dollars a day. He had earned only a humble ten cents a day in Old World Bergen, but nonetheless he was dissatisfied, for "every time some gold-miner returned," he wrote, "we all went crazy."

He was not the only one who found other ways of making money than panning gold. One letter writer who in the summer of 1850 concluded that the "best time is undoubtedly over," took a job at $150 a month "plus board and lodging." Anthon Lassen, another immigrant, tried his luck at mining, but promptly "decided on Oregon" after he learned of the opportunities for land and farming in that rich region to the north. In the spring of 1851 he reported in detail from Portland, where everything, as he said, was new. Yet another, at Bidwell's Bar, turned to canal-digging and bought a share in a company engaged in that business. He warned his friends not to expect to see a "bigwig" when he returned, but still, he suggested, he might have "a little capital in gold dust." One writer, penning his letter on board a ship about to depart for Australia, said that in gold-digging, everything depended upon chance, though he also believed that "if you have money, you can make money."

Strange, indeed, were the fortunes of the gold-seekers who sailed in the chartered ship from Trondhjem in 1850. Because of a faulty vessel, the expedition broke up at Rio de Janeiro, and the stranded gold-hunters became tropical farmers in Brazil, with crops of coffee, cotton, oranges, bananas, and other products as foreign to their experience as they were to the soil of Norway. One writer in this settlement tried to comfort his wife and children in Norway with the hope that in three

* Quoted in *Norwegian Migration*, vol. 1, p. 280.

years he might return to them. Another, however, found that he could not settle down in Brazil, for, he wrote, "the idea of California was always on my mind." Ultimately, after many adventures, the idea got him to San Francisco, where, before starting for the mines, he strolled about the streets, fascinated by the many gambling houses, where he saw money piled high on the gaming tables. Later he reported gloomily that life in America was drudgery, but he did not forget to mention that he had saved a tidy sum of money.

Thus, the general picture is rounded out in the letters. "Come, and you will regret it – do not come, and you will also regret that," wrote the philosophical Carl Nordbye of Drøbak in 1852. Looking to the future, this observant immigrant outlined some of the opportunities in California for grocery-keepers, farmers, fishermen, and tradesmen – and even appraised the wonders of the region as a study ground for naturalists.

The letters do not disclose fabulous fortunes made at the mines, but occasionally they point to success along lines of traditional competence in Norway. Thus a letter in 1854 names one Nortvedt, or North, a Norwegian immigrant, as the "best shipbuilder in California." A year later another writer tells of starting northward for the Oregon boundary where, among other things, he hoped to be able to plant the American flag at the top of the highest mountain on the Pacific Coast. "California," he wrote in a valedictory judgment, "is a rough country to live in." However rough a country might be, the lure of gold was irresistible, and when the Fraser River gold discoveries became known in 1858, Californians, including not a few Norwegian-Californians, set out for the newer El Dorado. One letter, written from "Whatkom" – now a part of Bellingham, Washington – describes vividly some aspects of that gold rush as viewed in midsummer of 1858. The selections close with a contemporary account of two immigrants who had gone on from California to Australia, but in 1863 returned to their native land to become farmers, golden chains around their necks, "very heavy rings" on their fingers, and fortunes of "several thousand dollars" in their pockets.

Here are documents of the kind from which the people of Norway read about the Golden West in the 1850's – letters faithful in their detailed reports of personal experiences and observations. Taken as a whole, they are not without historical interest as fresh and first-hand records of the gold rush; and, read from another point of view, they afford some insight into the reactions of the immigrant mind to the realities of the El Dorado whose wonders stirred not only America but the mid-century world.

Gold is found almost like fish scales

FROM A FORTY-NINER IN CALIFORNIA TO HIS FAMILY *

July 15, 1849

Once more I have the pleasure of writing you, though I am a thousand miles away from you and more than two hundred and fifty miles from the coast. At present I am staying in the Sierra Nevada Mountains in California.

You will recall that I told you that I had decided to go on to California. As a result of this decision, I left New York on February 1, and after a very pleasant voyage of eight days on board the steamship *Falcon*, I arrived with three hundred other passengers at Havana, where we stayed one day. From there we sailed to Chagres – a four days' voyage. Here we left the *Falcon* and took another steamboat up the lovely river Chagres, which is from sixty to a hundred feet wide but very shallow. As the steamboat could not go up more than about twenty-five miles, we had to continue our journey in canoes. These are from twenty to eighty feet long and in proportion to their length are paddled by from one to eight naked Negroes. I was in one of the smallest canoes with only one Negro. These Negroes are extremely good-natured, honest people. They excel in particular in the exceptional endurance and strength with which they paddle the canoes up against the strong current all day long without resting, except when they eat their simple meals.

After spending forty hours in the canoe, I arrived at Gorgona, a small town of about fifteen hundred inhabitants, where four of my friends and I pitched our tent to wait for the arrival of the rest of the company. From here it is about twenty-three miles through very mountainous country to Panama. Transportation of baggage is very cheap here. We bought six horses at from $14 to $25 apiece, and a friend of mine and

* This letter appeared in *Christiania-Posten*, November 15, 1849.

I thus transported all our baggage to Panama. On the whole the state of health was very good here, though it had been proclaimed terrible in the New York newspapers. During my whole journey I heard of very few cases of illness.

On March 10 we left Panama on board a steamship bound for San Francisco, where we duly arrived on April 1, exactly two months after we had left New York. Since this city, to judge by all indications, is some day to become the greatest emporium on the Pacific, I shall try to give you a description of it. The city is located on the southern side of the entrance from the Pacific at the first large bay, part of which is called Santa Clara Bay. For the main part, the city has been laid out in a small valley between two rows of hills. Its appearance from the anchorage is completely American, except for the lack of church steeples, of which American cities always have a very large number. The surroundings of the city are quite barren. There are two hotels in town where you pay $5 a day, and a great many gambling houses, where thousands of dollars are lost every day. The population is about five thousand.

After four days' stay in San Francisco, I once more boarded a small vessel and went about 120 miles up the Sacramento River. Here we took three wagons drawn by oxen to carry our baggage to the mountains, where we hoped to make our fortune by washing and digging for gold. After four days' troublesome journey on foot we arrived at our destination, but for two reasons we discovered that we could not make our fortune right away. In the first place, the water in the river where we hoped to find gold was too high, and besides the hostility of the Indians presented a serious obstacle. On one occasion the Indians had killed five people and burned the bodies. The angry gold-diggers, about forty in number, got together and set out to find the Indians. They did find them, killed about fifty, and took sixty prisoners, who were all released, however, except seven. The next day these were taken out of their prison, one to be shot and the others to watch. But as soon as the unfortunate creatures were out in the open, they tried to run away. Shouts of "Shoot them! Shoot them!" were heard. Guns were fired, and three of them fell on the spot, three others threw themselves in the river, but all were shot. One fell only a few steps from me riddled by six bullets, another by three. This shocked me very much, and I also think that it is wrong to shoot them wherever you catch sight of them. As a rule the Indians are both cowardly and cunning. If one of them can find an opportunity to shoot an arrow – they are extremely skillful with bow and arrow – into the heart of a white man, he does so. Besides they steal a lot of horses, which they kill and eat.

Every man here is armed with a gun, pistols, and knives. My six-barreled pistols which I bought in New York for $12 I have sold here for $100. To give you an idea of the prices of various things here and of the cost of living in this place, I shall give you a list of the current prices of the most necessary and common articles. A horse costs from $200 to $500, an ox $100, and a sheep $16. Hard bread (for there is no soft bread here) $1.25, flour $.75, dried apples $1.25, ham $1.25, all a pound. Molasses $4.00 a bottle, sugar $.80 a pound, tea $5.00 a pound, etc. Boards cost $700 for 1,000 cubic feet, and three small boxes of matches are $1.00. Potatoes are $1.25 a pound. A pair of boots that cost $2.50 in New York are $20.00 here. A pair of shoes that were $.75 in New York are $8.00 here, and so on. These are high prices, to be sure, but if you work hard you can still make money. In May I saved $223, in June $295. Yesterday alone I made $35. All my earnings from May 1 to July 14 amount to $750, which is $120 more than the cost of the journey here.

The work is extremely hard. I start at four o'clock in the morning and keep on till twelve noon. After that I rest for three or four hours, for at that time of day the heat is unbearable, and then I work again till eight o'clock in the evening. The nights here are exceedingly cold. We live in tents; I have not been inside a house since April 1. The ground is our bed and a saddle or something like that our pillow. This kind of life agrees with me, and my health is excellent. We live a free life, and the best thing of all, that which I have always considered one of the supreme blessings of existence, is that no human being here sets himself up as your lord and master. It is true that we do not have many of the luxuries of life, but I do not miss them, with the exception of cigars, which are too expensive here, as you only get three for a dollar.

Fine order and peace prevail here. It seems to me as if one person were afraid of the other, since he knows very well that an insult will usually be paid back with a piece of lead. Thefts and robberies have been very rare, up to the last two weeks, when a lot of horses were stolen. Everyone may safely leave his tent, without having to fear in the least that something has been stolen when he returns. But if this does happen and the thief is caught, all the neighbors assemble and elect a judge. If the thief is found guilty by the judge, he is punished with a certain number of lashes and is given a respite of twelve or eighteen hours to enable him to clear out of the mountains. If he is still there after the respite has expired, he is shot. This is the usual procedure, but three Frenchmen who had gone a little too far were hanged to a tree without further ceremony.

It would be too detailed a matter to describe to you how the gold is found. I hope that Almighty God, who so far has guided my way through life with the greatest love and goodness, will grant me the happiness to see you and all my dear ones again; then I will tell you everything that I now have to leave out of my writing. Here it must be enough to say that the gold we find is almost completely pure. The size of the nuggets varies. In some places pieces have been found that weighed up to seven pounds. Here at the river where I am staying, it is found almost like fish scales, very thin and in all kinds of forms. You obtain it by washing out the dirt in a machine which looks like a roller, and that is what it is called. You throw the dirt in one end of the machine which is somewhat higher than the other, and start the machine, all the time adding a certain quantity of water. By this process, lighter particles like dirt and pebbles are washed away, and the gold is left behind together with a sort of fine black sand which consists mainly of iron particles. This is taken out of the machine and carefully washed out in a pan.

Under a tree, my boots for a pillow

FROM A MAN FROM BERGEN, NOW IN SACRAMENTO CITY, CALIFORNIA *

June 14, 1850

This time I am writing to you from a city whose name is at present only known from the newspapers. It is true that it is a long time since I wrote you last; but in the meantime I have made a long and dreary journey and spent a most miserable winter, so that I can honestly say that I have not felt inclined to write to a friend, even from a place like this, which seems to amaze the whole world. In European newspapers I have read the most exaggerated stories which have already brought, and in the future will bring, thousands of families to ruin and an early grave.

* This letter appeared in *Den Frimodige* (Trondhjem), September 14, 1850.

A few Scandinavians have already arrived here and more may come. I wish, therefore, to give you as truthful an account as I can after almost one year's stay here. First about the trip from New York: you can now travel to Chagres and over the Isthmus, and from Panama to San Francisco; there are enough steamships and ships for both voyages with the total passenger fare at $250. But last year not enough ships were available, and I had to go around Cape Horn, a voyage I do not advise anyone to make, not so much because of the danger – we were not exposed to any, although several vessels did suffer considerable damage – but imagine being cooped up in such a small space as a ship, living on bad food, and passing through all four seasons in the course of one month! Surely a strong constitution is needed to stand that.

But the arrival in Valparaiso compensated us for all our sufferings. Truly, it was the most beautiful morning in my life when we approached the coast of Chile: the impression made on you is enhanced by the country that arises out of the sea, clothed as it is in lush, green tropical beauty. As I have said, we had endured a great deal, but nature made it up to us during our ten days' stay in Valparaiso. Not only the abundance of fruit but the romantic scenery – mountains and hills (which instantly reminded me of old Norway) –refreshed and encouraged us. Nature has been very generous of her gifts here, offering a great variety of views: in the background you see the snow-clad Andes, whose summits have not yet been climbed by any human being; and when you lower your gaze, scenes of southern agriculture and fertility, and also of volcanic destruction, meet the eyes. I strolled around here the way you and I used to do in the old days on our trips in the Norwegian mountains; and it was with heavy hearts that we left all this behind when the captain ordered everybody on board.

The voyage now became more unpleasant to us than it had been before. As we approached our destination, the goal of our desperate gamble, we began to consider things more carefully. None of us knew whether there really was gold to be found in California; rumors to that effect might have been started by the government to induce people to emigrate. And even worse, we did not know if there were housing and food enough to keep so many adventurers alive. But we put such worries aside, and the ship sailed on, although slowly, because the trade winds north of the equator were against us. We tacked almost over to the Sandwich Islands and after that swung about to San Francisco, where we arrived 156 days after our departure from New York.

I was very eager to get ashore, and when the ferryman charged $6 for half an hour's ferrying, I thought: here there must be work I could do. Ashore I could learn little about the mines; they were far away in the interior, and one account contradicted the other. But a laborer in the city had made $16 a day and was now making $12; and that was good enough for me. So far so good; but the food, though abundant, was bad, and there was no housing. Some of the passengers had been prepared for this and had brought tents from New York, and I was accommodated in one of them together with four others. This soldier's life in open camp did not agree with me in the beginning, but now I am accustomed to it and can sleep quite comfortably under a tree with my boots for a pillow. I worked for the city and for the government and made $13 a day as a carpenter; but I couldn't get the thought of the mines out of my head. I therefore quit my job as a carpenter and went up the river to Sacramento, which is the center of the mines. Here I saw people who had returned from the mines, which were fifty to three hundred English miles away and to which you travel on foot. The accounts now became more reliable and reasonable. Carpenter's wages in this city were $15 a day in gold dust, with a real value of $17. I now reconsidered everything soberly and settled down in this city.

The $15-a-day work lasted only two months. Can you believe that I, who at one time back in Bergen was working for ten cents a day, was not even satisfied with this royal pay? For every time some gold-miner returned and displayed his find, we all went crazy. Three times I got ready to set out for the mines (for you have to carry everything with you). The first time I fell ill; the second time my traveling companion did; and when for a third time I was getting ready to start, the rainy season began and I had to stay here. And I am glad that I did, for I have done better than most miners. Thus, I have not been to the mines myself, but in talking to people who stayed during the whole mining season at the so-called *diggings*, I have decided that as long as I can make $8 a day in the city, this is better. But those who know no trade have to go to the mines, and unaccustomed to labor, they suffer unspeakably, until Bacchus and company speed them out of this world.

I will outline the life of a miner for you. Arrived in this city, he has to rid himself of everything that he cannot carry on his back, for the rental of a trunk* would be too costly. Off he trudges, then, from thirty to four hundred miles. In the cold, wet nights he has no other house than a tree, if there is any. The heat during the daytime is terrible, and the sand is a foot deep on the plains. When he has left these behind, he climbs the mountains, some of which are as steep and difficult as Ulrikken at Bergen; and these he has to climb carrying his provisions, his blanket, and mining equipment. When he arrives, he has to get to work moving masses of stone three to four feet in diameter, carrying dirt and mud, and often standing knee-deep in water all day. Then night falls with its chilling raw air. Tired and hungry, he has no house; he must spread his blanket on the ground for a bed. As to his food, he must cook it himself, which is easy, for last year the only things he could get were salted bacon and slapjacks (sailor's pancakes) and black coffee. If he falls ill, no friend is near him, and only death brings relief. Add to all this the fact that a digger's earnings are very uncertain, varying from $1 to $12 a day. A few out of thousands have made fortunes in a short time, but most of them have not and will not.

Life in the city is better, though I have had to live in a tent all winter. But the food is better here, at any rate, and the city is developing rapidly. Provisions arrive in abundance, and houses are shooting up in such numbers that it can truthfully be said of San Francisco and Sacramento that they are the greatest wonders you ever saw. One must admit that the Yankees are a progressive people; and how strange it must be for the other nations of the Pacific to have got such neighbors!

We – for now I have become a Californian myself – have added another star to the American honor – the flag, I mean.

It is very hot in the mines

FROM A MANDALITE, AT BENICIA, CALIFORNIA †

June 27, 1850

On March 26 I arrived in San Francisco, where the ship stopped for four days. During this time I tried to get work, which I found extremely

* The trunk would be to store his things in.

† The letter from which this is an excerpt appeared in *Den Frimodige* (Trondhjem), October 1, 1850.

difficult because of the huge crowds of people. I therefore went on with the ship to Benicia and helped unload it there. After that I found employment with the government at $150 a month plus board and lodging. The work I do is not very hard; it consists of rowing boats, unloading ships, and the like. Benicia is about thirty-five miles up the San Francisco Bay and is a depot for the army and navy. I have decided to stay in this job as long as I get the same pay and will only try the mines if my pay decreases. The comments I hear on the mines are contradictory, however, both as to the advantages and the dangers and hardship you are exposed to. After talking to many of those who are coming down from the mines, I cannot estimate their profits at more than $4 or $5 a day on the average. It is true that some make strikes worth hundreds of dollars, but many can hardly pay their expenses. As a foreigner I will have to pay $20 a month for permission to dig for the precious metal.

As to the climate here, it is very hot in the mines but not unhealthful; the diseases that you may contract are caused mainly by bad food and irregular living. Here in Benicia, as everywhere on the coast, the air is pleasantly cool since we always have a fresh breeze. I do not advise anyone to emigrate to California now; the best time is undoubtedly over, and year after year things will grow worse. How long I shall stay here I cannot say as it will depend on circumstances. During the rainy season it is hard to find work. The monthly pay for sailors is now $75.

I decided on Oregon

FROM ANTHON LASSEN, IN PORTLAND, OREGON,
TO HIS FAMILY *

March 26, 1851

I packed my clothes and left the ship as soon as possible to take the first job I could get. I left all my things at the house of a Danish grocer who hired me as a carpenter. The second great fire broke out the fol-

* This letter was printed in *Drammens Tidende*, June 27, 1851, together with an excerpt from the law governing public lands in Oregon. Anthon Lassen, the newspaper says, emigrated from Drammen in 1849. He sailed first to New York, a journey of seven weeks, and then spent nine months and twelve days in travel to San Francisco via Cape Horn. He arrived in California June 10, 1850. The excerpt given above picks up the story at this point.

lowing day, and most of my things and some money I had left there were lost. Everything in the city was in a state of confusion for some days, and so I took a job on board a ship in the harbor. I worked at loading lumber, and in a month I made 80 specie dollars, which was then the usual pay.

With this money I went up to the mines and spent about $40 on the way for food and transportation. I immediately started hunting for gold, which was very hard work as we had to dig almost fourteen feet down before we found anything. I had no luck and made only enough to pay expenses for two and a half months, which was almost longer than I could stand it there, working hard in the unbearably hot weather. I did see many others, however, who were so lucky that they were able to wash out $30, $40, or $60 worth of gold a day for a long time. But most of them made only $4 to $6 a day. October came, and with it the rainy season. I could not sleep out of doors any longer, so I left the mines and went to San Francisco with many others. I stayed at a coffee house and paid $2.50 a day for board and lodging—only a third of what the price had been a year ago.

I read in the newspapers that both in California and Oregon I could claim a whole square mile of land for nothing. At once I decided on Oregon, went down to the harbor and arranged with a captain that he should take me there for $50, which was all the money I owned. I went on board at once, and we weighed anchor the following day. The voyage lasted eighteen days, during which we had very stormy weather that gave many of us an ague from which I suffered severely for eight days and which left me so weak that I was unable to work the first days after the landing. After that I got work right away as a carpenter repairing the house of a minister; this job lasted eight days, and I earned $20. With this money I left the city to take a farm about fifteen miles from Portland. Since I swore allegiance to America more than a year ago, I can (according to the enclosed law) claim a square mile of land when I have complied with the regulations.

Oregon has a very good and healthful climate; we never have more than eighty degrees heat (Fahrenheit) in the summer and rarely more than three or four degrees of cold during the winter. Even this much cold is extremely rare—I noticed last year that the water froze only seven or eight times, and it was always thawed out the next day by the sun. There is very little snow here, and it only stays on the ground a day or so. Three or four months of the winter are very rainy; but during the summer there is little rain, but enough for the vegetation.

All kinds of grain and vegetables are harvested in abundance here. Wheat yields from ten to forty fold, potatoes from ten to twenty, sometimes more; all other vegetables the same way. A barrel of wheat costs $10.00; a barrel of potatoes this spring $12.00; one pound of wheat flour $.08; one pound of bacon $.10 and meat $.08, farther up in the country three or four cents more; eggs $.75; one pound of butter $1.00; cheese $.40; and other groceries accordingly. Compared with other products, clothes are cheaper than anything else.

The hogs are out in the woods both winter and summer and get their food from acorns and roots; at any time when they are butchered, they are as fat as if they had been fed on grain. The cows are not fed in barns either, but graze in the fields all the year round. From time to time, they are given a little salt to keep them attached to the home place.

With the new discovery of gold mines four hundred miles from Portland, Oregon, the prices of all kinds of food will go up in the near future and will probably remain high for a period of two or three years. The work of the spring starts in the middle of March, and harvest time is in the beginning of August. Daily wages will be very high here during the summer and are likely to stay high for a couple of years. I have made $2 a day regularly since the middle of February and can now get $3 a day all during the summer. During harvest perhaps I will earn even $5 or $6, including meals; for most people here are leaving their farms and going to the mines, which are said to be very rich. Perhaps I shall try the mines myself after I do a little sowing and planting on my *claim*, even if I had bad luck in the mines of California. But there everything had already been worked, while everything here is new. That makes all the difference in the world.

I do not regret that I left Norway, though both my money and clothes were lost in the course of the journey and I now have to work up again from the bottom. For I figure that in my land I have considerably greater value than in the little money I lost. Apart from the many hardships that I shall probably still have to meet, I can look forward to a pleasant future here, which I could not do in Norway. Already I live better and more happily here than I did at home; and, perhaps, some day I shall return a rich man.

Coffee and bananas all year round

FROM A MAN FROM LEVANGER, NOW IN DONNA FRANCISCA, BRAZIL, TO HIS FAMILY, RELATIVES, AND FRIENDS *

July 2, 1851

How often I am moved when I think of you, dear ones, and how often I wish that I might hear how you are! Now I shall tell you how I am. From South America, I have written two letters, one from Rio, the other since we came to the German colony here which was founded recently by the firm Schrøder and Company in Hamburg. This stretch of land has been given to the Prince de Joinville in France by the Emperor of Brazil.

Now I must tell about our prospects and the reason we came here. After all chance of continuing the journey to California was gone because of the bad condition of the ship and lack of funds to pay for its repair in Rio, where everything is very expensive, and also because this was the worst season in the yellow fever area, after many deliberations and a five or six weeks' stay in Rio, the decision was made to come here. Consequently we embarked on a small American schooner and left Rio on March 4. We were five days at sea. During this time, we were not very comfortable since we had to lie or stand on the deck most of the time. As soon as we had cast anchor, we went to a small town called Sao Francisco. On the same day a German passenger ship had landed the first settlers at that colony, a group of one hundred and seven. We were seventy-three.

By boat we immediately left for the colony, which is about one Norwegian mile from the lake. You may well believe that we did not get here without a lot of thought and without many trials and struggles. But I have always found peace in the reflection that the Lord must surely have His hidden plans for human beings, though it may not seem so to our limited understanding. A group of five of us have now decided to buy a piece of land and cultivate it. In Norwegian coin we paid about fifty cents for a hundred feet square. We have much forest to clear away and many roots in the ground. But as soon as the trees have been cut down and burned you can plant rice, corn, and potatoes between the roots. And when the land is clear, you can sow and harvest all the year

* This letter appeared in *Nordre Trondhjems Amtstidende*, November 4, 1851.

round, planting the next crop when one has been harvested. The way the Lord has arranged everything in nature is wonderful; and it is an interesting sight for us to see the growing of coffee, cotton, rice, oranges, lemons, and bananas all year round. Six weeks after we came here, we planted some potatoes, but a great part of the crop was damaged. We did eat some of it, however, after two months.

We have had many difficulties and much hardship, and it took a long time to complete our purchase of land. Since the manager of the colony, Mr. Schrøder, fell ill and was ill for six weeks, everything was at a standstill. For a while we were ill, especially with dysentery and fever. Out of seventy-three persons, only four died, however – S. Hansen from Helgeland, L. Stensem from Ytterøen, Luthersen from Horten, and Nordby from Laurvig. L. Stensem was in our group and on his deathbed requested that his property be sold and the proceeds sent to Lorentz Møen at Ytterøen, which will be done by a bill of exchange to Hamburg, if circumstances permit. The disease has now abated, and everybody is well again. Apart from a few minor attacks, I have been well all the time, God be praised.

Now, how are you, my dear wife, whom I can never forget, and my little children? How I wish that I had a letter from you telling me that you and the children are well and happy, trusting in the Lord and that you are contented in spite of all the sorrows and worries of life. Above all, my dear, do not grieve and worry about me and my situation. It is true that we are far apart now, but we can still be together in spirit. And if it is God's will that we are to see each other again sometime, then nothing is impossible; for He who has carried us so safely over the stormy seas has also the power to bring us back home again, sooner or later. I have not made any definite decision, but I do plan to return to my native country in three years; I hope to get a letter from you before that time, however, but now I shall have to see how things turn out.

We do not know, as yet, what the profit of our stay here may be. To begin with, we have tried to cultivate a little land and build a few houses. Our nearest neighbors are Johannes Eide, Johannes Nerland, Knud Kjesbo, Johannes Munkrøstad, all in one group. They are building houses opposite us. In our group are L. Kjelstrup, Johannes O. Aagaard, Laurits Flotten, Johannes Hallen. All these ask me to send their best greetings to their friends and relatives and say that they are well and happy.

At present we are clearing away forest and sawing boards. When we have arranged for the most necessary things, have built a house and got a little seed in the ground, some of us plan to make a trip up to the mountains to a river where the Brazilians claim that there is gold. We have cleared the site of our house at a river where we thought that we had found a little gold dust, but it did not amount to anything. But then this river has not been searched carefully. Otherwise, fourteen of us plan to put some effort into gathering some dyewood, for instance, brazilwood, sandalwood, fustic, and guaiacum. We have planned to gather these and try to make a profit by shipping them to Europe with rice, sugar, and cotton. At the present time, we are busy building houses, since at any moment ships are expected from Germany with passengers who are to use the houses that we are living in now.

We associate here with Brazilians, Germans, and Frenchmen, and it is very difficult for us because of our trouble with the language. We shall have to make an effort to learn it. Here is no church or minister; but now a church is to be built and soon a minister will arrive from Germany. May the Lord hold His hand of grace over us and sustain us in faith and patience as we struggle every day with humble devotion and trust in the Lord, holding everything as nothing compared with winning His love and resting in Him. Johan O. Aagaard from Værdalen requests that you give his best greetings to his parents and tell them that he is now well and happy, but a while ago he was ill and very close to death. Hs asks his parents to write him. The Lord be with you, young and old.

The best time is undoubtedly over

FROM LARS HANSEN, AT BIDWELL'S BAR, CALIFORNIA, TO THE EDITOR OF FREDRIKSHALD BUDSTIKKE *

August 26, 1851

I left San Francisco in the beginning of March this year and arrived at the place mentioned above, where, with some of my countrymen, I

* In printing this letter, the editor of *Fredrikshalds Budstikke* relates that Lars Hansen, from Fredrikshald, had shipped in 1849 as a ship's carpenter on the brig *Louis de Geer*, but during the course of the voyage had deserted the ship in order to go to California and hunt for gold. The letter was reprinted in *Christiania-Posten*, November 20, 1851, under the title "A California Traveler."

started digging for gold with meager results. On the opposite side of the river, however, a dam-building company was working. Three brothers named Johnsen from the Christianssand district had been interested in this company for more than a year. Through these brothers we were offered a share on what seemed to be very reasonable conditions, and I, with four other Norwegians, therefore joined the company. Among the latter are Julius Abertus and Niels Olsen Kjetelsen from Fredrikshald. Since that time – after April 1 – we have been busy digging a canal to change the course of the river.

I must admit that this has been a trying time. The work was extremely difficult, involving mining and cutting through rock; and besides most of my money was spent, without my knowing if I would ever get a penny in return for my expenses and time. At present I have, however, a fairly substantial hope that I shall not have done this work for nothing. The last couple of weeks we have been working in the river and have no reason for complaint, the profit having been from $200 to $400 a day, which in Norway would seem to be a fortune but in this country, where equipment and everything is so terribly expensive, is considered a trifle, especially as it is to be divided into twelve parts. Therefore, people back in Fredrikshald should not expect to see me return as a "bigwig" but perhaps with a little capital in gold dust. For I have decided that if I can make some money during the autumn, I shall travel via Panama and the United States and be home in March or April next year.

A goldsmith's apprentice Thoresen (from Fredrikshald) came to California from New Orleans about a year ago, and after traveling around in several places trying his hand at prospecting, he arrived at the mines in Bidwell's Bar about the same time as I. Ever since we started work here, he has been with me. But he is not planning to return home right away, as he wishes to earn a small fortune before he leaves the land of gold.

Hans Hoel (a mate from Fredrikshald) came up to the mines with me, and we worked together at first; but since I got into this construction company, he has been the trusty comrade of Sigwardt Baastad (from Fredrikshald). As far as I know, these two industrious young men earned quite a bit for a couple of months, and I hope that once again they may strike some little shining nugget or other that might enable them to leave at the same time I leave. From the experience I have of California, I certainly do not advise anyone to come here. The best time is undoubtedly over, and I can safely affirm that ninety-nine persons out of a hundred wish that they had never thought of California.

Gold has also been discovered in Australia

FROM A MAN IN SAN FRANCISCO,
TO FRIENDS IN NORWAY *

November 14, 1851

Probably you have heard in Norway, too, that gold has also been discovered in Australia (New Holland), and since I, with many others, have on the whole been disappointed here when I recall the glowing reports we heard at home, I have decided to try my luck in Australia.

I do not blame California, for there is money to be made here. But it requires a fairly long time to earn a little capital. It may seem somewhat rash to leave so abruptly a country where you have a chance of making money, but my main reason is that the mines in Australia are newer and consequently not so nearly exhausted as here. I got here a little too late, and I shall now try to get there in time. I have several reliable reports from Australia which I consider much more exact than those I had from here. Several letters have arrived from families in Sidney who urge their relatives to come there, the sooner the better, because they will be able to do better there than here.

I have worked about six weeks in the mines without having earned much more than the cost of my equipment and food, and the last two weeks I worked for others at a pay of $3 a day and board, making more that way than if I had worked on my own. Everybody is waiting for the rainy season to get water, and then there probably will be more to do than under present circumstances. A good constitution is required for all kinds of activity here, for the work is hard and strenuous. No one should imagine that it is as easy to make money here as people assume; everything depends a great deal on luck. Nor should one have too much faith in the glowing reports of the newspapers about all the gold to be found here. There is no denying that someone may, now and again, make his fortune in a short time. But one must remember how many thousands of people here make no more than they spend. This the newspapers are

* This letter appeared in *Lillehammers Tilskuer*, May 11, 1852.

reluctant to let people know about. As a matter of fact, I know people who arrived here with money and who have grown poor; for if fortune does not favor you, you may work a long time without finding a thing. In gold-digging everything depends on chance.

For craftsmen, on the other hand, I believe that there are good opportunities here, since they are always sure of making a good day's pay. I suppose that the following craftsmen are the ones needed most: goldsmiths, watchmakers, joiners, carpenters, wheelwrights, and painters. But there is not much work for tailors and shoemakers yet, for clothes and shoes are imported in large quantities and cost less here than at home. Clothing expenses are a trifle compared with earnings.

The greatest difficulty of the emigrant is undoubtedly his deficiency in English, for as long as he does not have a command of the language, he cannot hope to make money by starting a trade of one kind or another in the city. In thc mines he can get along after a fashion, but it is very difficult. If I had a good command of the language, I should hesitate to leave California; but since I do not, I shall go on to New Holland, hoping during the course of the passage to become more familiar with the language by listening to the Americans. The trip will start next week and the fare is $50. I have already moved on board and get my meals here, and at any rate I shall be far more comfortable here than I was on the *Amerika Paket*. We are scheduled to touch at the Sandwich Islands and the Friendly Islands, and the voyage is expected to last about two months. Originally three of us Norwegians from the mines planned to travel together, but the other two are not yet quite sure that they will have enough money to go. Yesterday six of my countrymen who arrived here on the same boat as I came down here, and these will probably go with me. Most of the passengers who came from Norway would like to leave for Australia if only they had money; and daily people come down from the mines to go there.

The suit brought against the company of *Amerika Paket* was settled with little compensation to the passengers; but including all expenses, this trial cost the company about $3,000, so that it did smart a little for its inconsiderate action. All the sailors immediately jumped ship without the company getting any of them back. The day before yesterday the ship left for China, having mustered a new crew.

Bruun and Brøndalen will stay here since they do not feel like leaving yet. I have promised to write to them and to other countrymen; and if things are better in Australia, I suppose they will follow. Aided by a Norwegian, Brøndalen got one-fourth share of a mine with some Frenchmen, and they may be lucky enough to strike gold.

I met many countrymen up in the mines, among others Steenshorn. I spoke to Gustav Madsen from Drammen every day; he has made some, but not much money. When I returned down here I also met a person from Kongsberg, a son of the late mine superintendent Samuelson. He has been ill but is better now and is planning to return to the mines. My own health, God be praised, has been excellent all the time, although I slept under the open sky most of my time at the mines; but at this time of the year the climate is very wholesome here. The days are still very hot, but the nights are cold. Anybody planning to come here should bring with him only the clothes that are absolutely necessary. For if you are going to the mines, you are likely to move from one place to another, and it is not wise to have too much to carry. No one should bring any tools, for the implements they use here perform the work much more quickly.

Here as everywhere, if you have money, you can make money, and this is even more true here than elsewhere, for there are many opportunities for investment. The safest and most profitable thing is undoubtedly farming. Everybody says so. Uncultivated land costs nothing; but you have to have it fenced in, make a down payment for equipment, farm hands, and seeds. If you have the capital for this, you are sure to make money in a short time.

California is a wonderful country for its liberty, and during the time I was in the mines I neither saw nor heard about a single fight. From theft you are safer here than at home, for you can leave your things in the open field and be gone for several days and they will remain where you left them. The punishment is severe for a thief; if he is caught, he is hanged at once, or his head is shaved and he is chased out of the mines.

There are several towns near the mines, and food and other things are easy to buy. The prices of the several provisions are as follows: 100 pounds of wheat flour $10 to $12; butter $1 a pound; coffee about 2 marks (Norwegian) and potatoes 1 mark a pound; heads of cabbage $.50 to $1 apiece; fresh meat 14 skillings a pound; milk 3 to 4 marks a pot; eggs $.50 apiece. Thus you see that food prices are high; but if you cook your own food and are economical, you can live for $.50 a day. In the restaurants meals cost $8 a week, but then you eat very well indeed. The Americans work with great endurance, but they also eat very well. Their meals are substantial with hot foods both for lunch and for supper.

Gambling houses with large, elegant rooms

FROM T. S. STØP, IN SAN FRANCISCO,
TO HIS PARENTS *

January 18, 1852

I have been away from my dear home for a long time, among strangers and foreigners, and have traveled from one place to another, until now finally my first wish has come true – as you may see from the address given above.

As you know, I traveled to the colony of Sao Francisco in Brazil. I stayed there three weeks, but as there were no prospects of work for me, I went on to Rio de Janeiro, where I was ill in a hospital for a short time. Since I got out I have been very well and strong, although I have gone through a great deal.

I then shipped on a Hamburg brig to Valparaiso, working my way. I had a job in Valparaiso for three months at two and a half specie dollars a day; board and lodging cost four and a half specie dollars a week. I was quite comfortable there and learned a little English, but even there I felt no peace because the idea of California was always on my mind. I hired out on a three-masted schooner for five specie dollars a month, but I also had to pay five specie dollars to get this job.

Thus, in friendly companionship with two other Norwegians of the unfortunate party, I sailed from Valparaiso on November 28 on the American three-masted schooner and arrived in San Francisco in California on January 14, was discharged, and went ashore on the sixteenth.

Here I can get work and earn five to six specie dollars a day; lodging costs ten a week. But first I want to visit the mines, and tomorrow or the day after, together with J. H. Bakke and L. Buch, who are the two Norwegians I have already mentioned, I shall take a steamboat up the Sacramento River to try my luck in the gold mines. I leave with high hopes. But if I have bad luck at the mines, I shall return to the city, take work in a shop until I have saved up a little fortune, and then return home. My only wish is to get home as soon as possible. However comfortable I may be with my boss and my board and lodging, I much prefer to return with a little money to my dear home, where I can make out better with two specie dollars than I can here with ten.

Last night to amuse myself I walked around in the streets to have a

* This letter appeared in *Trondhjems Stiftstidende*, April 24, 1852.

look at things. I went into several gambling houses, where large elegant rooms were furnished with tables, and on these were big heaps of gold and silver coins. Gold pieces of fifty, sixteen, and eight specie dollars were piled on the tables; without exaggeration, there were several thousands on each. At the gambling tables were scantily dressed sailors in the company of their masters, and the gold coins were changing hands at a brisk pace.

The prices of ready-made clothes of all sorts are much lower here than at home, and up in the mines you can also make good bargains. When you have read my letter, dear parents, please do not wait too long before writing me. My address is as follows: Antwerp Place, Corner of Montgomery and Pacific Streets. C/o J. B. Sommers.

Since I have nothing more to report, I will finish with warm greetings to all my friends and acquaintances. Tell them that I am doing well and am in good health. But above all I send my greetings to you, dear parents and brothers and sisters, from your ever loving son and brother.

I had to take a job as a dishwasher

FROM A CLERK OF DRAMMEN, NOW IN SAN FRANCISCO, TO FRIENDS [*]

May 1, 1852

What could I write about that would be new from a country the newspapers have described? About the gold mines? I have not been there. About the appearance of the country? Of this I am just as ignorant as you are, for I have not yet been outside the city limits of San Francisco. About social conditions? I do not think I am qualified to do that. About what then? I only want to write you a few lines about very ordinary things and about myself.

Having arrived here on September 9 last year, I stayed in San Francisco to look around for a job, as I did not feel like going to the mines. At first I had to endure some hardships to get ahead. I had to take a job as a

[*] In printing this excerpt in *Drammens Blad*, July 4, 1852, the editor writes: "A couple of years ago the Chief Clerk, Bing, from Drammen, left for California. Since we realize that many of our readers who made contributions to this journey, which Bing so urgently wished to make, will be interested in knowing how he is doing we print below an excerpt from a letter of his."

dishwasher and developed a leg ailment because of long hours of standing. For a man not accustomed to it will find it hard work to stand from four o'clock in the morning to nine in the evening without a chance to sit down. Cured of this leg ailment, I was lucky enough, to get a job as a clerk in a lawyer's office at a monthly salary of $100, which is considered rather poor here, as board and lodging cost $10 a week in the cheap places and twice as much in fashionable hotels.

I have now been in this position since November 15 last year and have managed to save a couple of hundred dollars, with which I have bought a fourth of a share in a house on which at the present time I take in $40 a month – an interest that we are not accustomed to at home. But because of fire hazards, rents are very high here.

Since I have learned a little Spanish so that I may start translating old Spanish documents, I expect a raise in salary of at least $30, and I hope thus to be able to save $100 a month, which is not bad. It is not easy for those who have no trade or skill or who are not accustomed to hard work to save money. To qualify for office jobs you must be an accomplished linguist, that is to say you must be able to speak Spanish, German, and French, apart, of course, from having a good command of English; but even so it is very difficult to be successful in this field because there are so many applicants for such jobs. Probably people at home think that if only you know English you have mastered all the wisdom of the world and need no more. But in this respect things here are exactly as they are at home, where you expect a clerk to know not only Norwegian but also other foreign languages; and this is even more true here because so many different languages are spoken within the country itself. Consequently, a command of several languages is a good thing to have. If one is unfortunate enough to come here without this or without knowing a trade, or if he is unable to stand hard work, it is very likely that he will starve to death, for nobody has any use for him. He may go to the mines, it is true, and if he has good luck there he will be able to manage all right. But if he has bad luck, it will be hard for him to pull through.

Just as I advise people who have the necessary knowledge and abilities to emigrate to this country – undoubtedly the best country in the world in which to build oneself an independent future – just as strenuously do I warn those who do not have the abilities required against coming here. A capable worker in any trade whatsoever will be paid better for his work here than anywhere else in the world. A man that has a small capital and knows how to place it in the right way will be able to increase it many times here in a short while. Anyone with useful practical knowledge (Greek and Latin or philosophy and the like would not bring him much profit), for instance, in languages, music, painting, lithography, mathematics, trade, and so on, will find that this knowledge will benefit him more here than anywhere else. But in spite of all this, he must not expect to step into his chosen field the minute he sets foot ashore. On the contrary, he must expect hardship and adversity in the beginning before he becomes familiar with conditions here. Even so, he need not fear poverty if he wants and is able to work. For there are many ways here in which he can make a living. The best one is to get employment in one of the numerous restaurants and hotels, and most of the people who arrive with empty pockets resort to this. But one requirement in this kind of work is that the applicant be able to speak at least the English language.

Above all I warn old people who have no one but themselves to rely on against coming here. Only young, healthy people are fit to travel to California – I have seen many instances of that. It is strange to see how thoughtlessly some have created only misery for themselves. Old people at home who have got into straitened circumstances, either through their own fault or by bad luck, set out for California on the spur of the moment in the firm belief that they will find a land of milk and honey there to supply their wants. They do not stop to think that one has to work to acquire these riches. Perhaps some of them do realize that they have to work, and come here with that intention. Most of them do not know what work is until they have tried it here, and then they are terribly disappointed. Though young people may not have been accustomed to hard work, they at least can get into the habit of it; but it is physically impossible for aging people of fifty, sixty, or even sixty-five to stand regular day labor. They are to be pitied; at home they might have lived supported either by their family or friends. But here! I do not mean to imply that they starve to death here, but they have to beg their way among their countrymen and they live miserably. I feel very sorry for them, and I am indignant at their folly in leaving their families at home.

My realization that I was not an ordinary laborer made me stay quietly here instead of going to the mines, as almost all the others did. And the outcome proved that I had done the right thing, for I was able to support myself with the little money I had until I got a job, while my friends who were just as unaccustomed to work as I was spent all they had on the trip to the mines before they were able to earn anything. Some came back sick and helpless, some who had money went to Sidney—this was perhaps even more foolish, and they will probably come to regret it; among them was Jørgensen who worked for Bryde and C. Borch in Drammen. Others are in poor circumstances and are making shift up there as well as they can, and four or five have become downright tramps. The few who took up farming will probably be the most successful, for farming pays off well and quickly here. About the mines, I only want to say that some seem to make a good profit there; but on the whole work in the mines is a gamble, and many workers there have to slave for relatively poor daily wages. To win success in mining, as in all other occupations, experience and insight are needed. People ought to remember that.

Immigration to this country increases daily, with people constantly arriving from all corners of the world. A great many Chinese are pouring in; every week five hundred of these strange people land in this city and tramp about the streets, a very strange sight, you may well believe! But people are beginning to hate them, for they are no good to the country. They spend nothing, and when they have earned something, they go back home.

Life in America is a life of drudgery

FROM T. S. STØP, AT YUBA RIVER, CALIFORNIA, TO HIS PARENTS *

September 6, 1852

I sent you a letter in January this year which I hope you received a long time ago. In it I wrote you that I had spent more than five months in Valparaiso in South America and gave you the reason why I traveled to California right away to start in the mines, where I have now been working for eight months. During my first time in the mines, I worked together with three Norwegians; but that soon stopped, and since then I have been working alone among people of all foreign nationalities. To date I have earned more than $800 cash. I suppose that next year I shall be able to make another $1,000, and when I have earned enough to live independently in my dear Norway, I intend to return home. For I assure you,

* This letter appeared in *Nordre Trondhjems Amtstidende,* December 21, 1852.

my dear parents, that life in America is a life of drudgery. I am in good health, and it is my intention to be thrifty and return as soon as I can. I write this letter in a hurry; but the next time I write you I shall write you a long letter and tell you everything about California. Do write me as soon as possible and tell me how you are. In the meantime, I hope that you are all well at Støpsvaldet by Levanger.

Panning gold is a poor source of income

FROM CARL NORDBYE OF DRØBAK, NOW IN SAN JOSÉ, CALIFORNIA, TO FRIENDS *

September 1852

Letters from Norway indicate that some people still intend to emigrate from Norway to this place. Because of this, I believe that I can be of help to many by describing briefly the main conditions here, that is, those which I think it most valuable for the emigrant to know before he sets out on such an important undertaking as emigration to a new and foreign country.

My chief reason for doing this is that I know from experience that public reports on California are generally unreliable, since much in them is exaggerated and much has changed the last couple of years. Nor do I find that such official accounts describe the conditions of everyday life in sufficient detail; they only treat thoroughly the more general situation, which is of less importance to the emigrant. During my nineteen-month stay here I have had a chance to find out both about the gold mines and about other sources of income, and what I say is based on facts, not on exaggerated and misleading rumors.

With regard to panning gold, I may say that it has sunk rather low as a source of income, since practically every place that yields as much as $4 net a day has been claimed. To be sure, someone may be lucky enough to happen upon a better place, but this is rare since the crowds at the mines are too large for the better places to have been passed by or overlooked. Almost everybody who arrives here rushes off to the mines but has to leave them after looking long and vainly for a claim or for work. Work in the mines is very hard; the difficulties are many and great; and

* This letter appeared in *Morgenbladet,* December 6, 1852.

diseases – especially fever and dysentery – are common. To live in the mines costs about $1 a day, while during *prospecting* (looking for a claim) the expenses are $4 a day. This, I suppose, answers the main questions of those who plan to go to California to pan gold.

The fastest and easiest way to make money is no doubt by trading, especially in groceries. Trade, carried on even by retail, yields a very good profit. At first one generally establishes a small *grogshop* for the sale of wine and liquor, etc., by the glass. Here a glass of beer, wine, or liquor costs $.12½ to $.25, which at the lowest price, amounts to $4 for a gallon of liquor that can be bought at $.25 to $1 a gallon wholesale. At the end of a month such a store is usually stocked with groceries and dry goods, and the profit, of course, rises rapidly. In the smaller places, as is the case everywhere else, the goods are the most expensive and the risk the smallest. The credit system is not used here; but in spite of this one's risks are greater here than elsewhere, since no kind of property can be insured. It is hoped, however, that this difficulty will be removed very soon.

Farming provides a safe and pleasant living, and I prefer it to all other sources of income in this country. But though the land may be obtained for practically nothing, a sum of about $1,000 is required for the fencing in of property, buildings, animals, and implements. Government land can be bought at $240 for 160 acres and has to be redeemed within three years from the time of purchase. Wheat and barley can be harvested after a first sowing for four to twelve years; oats grows wild. Vegetables fetch higher prices than grain and potatoes. Wages are from $50 to $70 a month plus board and lodging.

So many people are occupied in the shipping business that at present there are few openings in that field. The so-called *clippers* completely outsail other vessels, making the passage from New York to San Francisco in two to three months, while other ships require five to six months for the voyage.

So far, fishing has only been carried on a little in the rivers and in San Francisco Bay. It is likely that there is profitable fishing both in the rivers and along the coast, but the solid boats and equipment that are needed require several thousand dollars in down payment.

Hunting is practiced only by a few people, but successfully; game commonly hunted includes wild geese, reindeer, deer, and bear.

In Lower California and in the southern part of Upper California tanning would be a very profitable business, especially combined with the butcher's trade. For in these tracts live a great many Mexicans whose wealth consists of millions of cattle which they sell at very moderate prices – not over $20 a head.

The price for the hide, when bought separately, is $1; by sending it to the States raw, one gets $7 for it – that is 700 per cent.

Wages in the jeweler's and watchmaker's trades are high. A good worker in these occupations is paid from $8 to $12 a day.

Other trades are still undeveloped, since carpenter's products as well as clothes and tools are imported from the States and sold as cheaply here as in Europe.

Experts affirm that the botanist would be able to acquire here a considerable collection of rare flowers, plants, and trees; and some of my countrymen, who know the zoological collection of the University in Norway, inform me that several of the local reptiles, butterflies, and animals of the field are not found in Norway. Undoubtedly, the natural scientist would find work in California highly rewarding.

It is true that the voyage here is somewhat troublesome but still not to the extent that people imagine. Of the ships that put in here, the English packets are the best equipped and have the most pleasant accommodations. I myself arrived here on an English vessel and recommend the English packets to everyone who plans to undertake this voyage. For in addition to the many other advantages that the trip on these ships offers, you get an opportunity to learn the English language, which it is absolutely necessary to be able to speak on your arrival here.

I think the above may be of interest to everyone who plans to come out here. I dare not attempt to talk anyone out of or into trying his luck in the New World; but come, and you will regret it; do not come, and you will also regret that. You cannot suffer want here; but neither can you at home if you want to work; and orderly living and industry are more necessary here than anywhere else.

Nortvedt is the best shipbuilder in California

FROM A MAN IN SAN FRANCISCO,
TO FRIENDS *

1854

At the present time Nortvedt, or North as he calls himself here, owns a new schooner which he has built himself and which is said to have cost him $17,000. He has now sent it to Australia with freight and will sell it there if he can. On its trial trip it proved itself the fastest ship in the harbor, and for fifteen minutes made a speed of seven English miles, the best speed ever made as far as is known. The newspapers have praised the vessel highly, much to North's credit.

North's ships are noted not only for their beauty but also because they can load a considerable cargo. They are quite flat-bottomed and have a center keel that enables them to put in at very low water. His schooner is of two hundred and fifty tons and has a displacement of only seventy-two inches at full cargo. North is regarded as the best shipbuilder in California. He plans to return home when he gets his affairs settled here. Without doubt he will be a great asset to his native country, for he will provide Norway with the best – and to shipping most profitable – ships in the world.

Here in San Francisco there is general complaint of bad times and poor business. In the meantime the city is developing with surprising vitality. Everywhere you see stone buildings, one larger and more elegant than the other, being erected. Stone buildings as large as the castle in Christiania are raised several yards because of the raising up of the streets. This is done by means of machines and only a few men are required to do it. I have seen stone buildings raised four or five yards from the ground with people and everything inside the house – they did not even have to move out.

Ole Bull is in California at present and has given several concerts before crowded houses.

* This letter appeared in *Christiania-Posten*, November 7, 1854. A prefatory note says that Nortvedt, or North, once was a worker in a Christiania shipyard. Dr. Kenneth Bjork is preparing a volume on Norwegian immigrants on the Pacific coast, from California to Alaska. His monograph, to be published by the Norwegian-American Historical Association, will discuss later aspects of the western immigrant story but will include an account of immigrants in the gold rush. Also of interest is *California Emigrant Letters* (New York, 1952), edited by Walker D. Wyman.

The army worms and locusts devoured everything

FROM PETER HELGESEN, IN NEVADA, CALIFORNIA, TO HIS BROTHER *

November 20, 1855

Once more I take the opportunity to send you these lines to let you know that I am still happy here and in good health. I still share the farm with Mr. George B. Smith. This year we suffered a considerable loss because of the great many insects that infested the country. They destroyed everything or nearly everything for us, so that personally I lost about $500 this summer in addition to the time I wasted. We have had about twenty different kinds of insects this summer. The worst were the army worms and the locusts. The locusts came last and devoured what the army worms had left. They came in such numbers that when they flew up they looked like a cloud hiding the sun almost completely. I never saw such large ones before; some weigh a pound. They actually settle in the trees and make a "barking" sound. All we have left is a few heads of cabbage, some pumpkins, red beets, and potatoes, which we sell in small quantities at eight cents a pound.

I think I shall quit farming in California. In the mines I made money rapidly, but I lost it just as rapidly in farming. I plan to go to the mines again as soon as I have sold the little we have left on the farm. I intend to go up to Shasta near the Oregon border about two hundred and fifty miles from here, since it is considered a very good mining district. I have also another reason for wanting to go up there. I intend to have a try at planting the flag of the Union on the top of the highest mountain on the Pacific coast. I have been offered $1,000 for that job. Snow and ice lie all the year round on the top of this mountain. The last two years many have tried to reach the summit but have been very far from succeeding. I think I shall succeed; I want to try anyway.

The Shasta mines offer the advantage that there are only a very few workers up there. Down here there are far more. The reason fewer men go there is that the Indians up in that district are cruel. There have been several clashes with them this summer, and at night the whites gather in log cabins to seek shelter from attacks.

California is a rough country to live in. You may tell the Norwegians

* This letter was reprinted in *Stavanger Amtstidende og Adresseavis*, May 13, 1856, from *Emigranten*.

who plan to come here that they must be prepared for all sorts of things, for they will not get either sweet milk or cream to live on out here. No, my friend, we have to chew old rancid ham and Spanish meat which is so hard and tough that you might well be able to cut shoestrings out of it. You might ask them how they would like to come out here where they have to go to sleep on the rocky ground and crack butternuts to stay alive. I have now stayed here in the gold mines for two long years, and because of my bad luck in farming I shall have to stay another two years. If I had had better luck I would have gone home this spring, but now I shall have to try to make up for the loss.

The blows of hammer and ax all day long

FROM A MAN FROM BERGEN, NOW IN WHATKOM COUNTY, WASHINGTON TERRITORY, TO FRIENDS *

July 12, 1858

I reached here after a pleasant journey of five days by steamer from San Francisco, a distance of eleven or twelve hundred English miles. On our way we stopped at Victoria, the capital of the English possessions or of the Hudson's Bay Company, which is located on Vancouver Island. Over four thousand men had recently arrived there, most of them from California. They were camping out under their tents, since there were not enough small steamers or other vessels to take them up the Fraser River. Only one steamer was available, which carried merely two or three hundred passengers at a time. Under these circumstances I, with several others, preferred to walk to Whatkom, which is located on American soil. This town, not quite two months old (before this time only two or three houses were here), had sprung up so quickly because this point is conveniently located near the new gold mines, which will be easily accessible from here both by water and land as soon as the new road through the woods is completed. The above-mentioned trail is finished for a distance of a hundred and fifty English miles. According to the last reports they hope to complete it up to Thompson River in two or three weeks. It is

* This letter appeared in *Stavanger Amtstidende og Adresseavis*, September 30, 1858. The translation is by C. A. Clausen, who has published it in "The Fraser River Gold Rush," *Norwegian-American Studies and Records* (Northfield, Minn.), 7:47–52 (1933).

new and very interesting for me to note the life and activity connected with the building of hundreds of houses, and to observe the energy with which trees are cut down and burned to make room for the new town and new farm lands. Every moment one of the mighty trees crashes to the ground, causing trembling and roaring like an earthquake.

I have now stayed for almost two weeks in Whatkom with a Norwegian by the name of Severin Gullicksen, who is a gunsmith by trade and a partner of Klipzey. I knew him in San Francisco. Gullicksen has been in Whatkom a month and a half, or almost since the founding of the town. As yet he is practically the only gunsmith here, and has during this short time earned more, according to what he himself says, than a whole year's strenuous work would have netted him in San Francisco. Certainly if Whatkom becomes one of the large cities (as there are reasons to expect), he will become an independent man merely because of the building lots which he was so fortunate as to secure at the outset for a mere trifle. The people who came a week before Gullicksen secured lots for nothing except the promise to build on them. To give you an example of how easy it is to earn money in this country if one merely has a little cash and some initiative, I will mention that Gullicksen has been offered $3,000 for the lot alone on which his newly built house stands. However, he has declined. Six weeks ago it cost him $50. I have unexpectedly fallen in with the musician B——. He also wants to go to the gold mines to dig for gold.

Washington Territory and the adjoining English possessions are exceedingly fertile and beautiful country. High mountains covered by fir and spruce trees, besides all other species of trees that grow in Norway, such as birch, maple, and so forth, give the land a northern and homelike appearance. The blows of hammer and ax are heard all day long until far into the evening, and consequently houses spring up in a few days as if by magic. This town presents a peculiar view at present. Here and there by the side of large wooden buildings tents are pitched. In places tents are so numerous that a stranger would at once conclude that soldiers were encamped there. Immediately below Gullicksen's a doctor took up residence in a tent day before yesterday; and in front of an adjoining tent he has had these words painted in big letters: MEDICAL OFFICE. Every day steamships come and go, bringing passengers from San Francisco. Most of the passengers have hitherto landed in Victoria. Still there is at times so great a jam in the main street that a person finds it difficult to elbow his way through. In short, all signs indicate that the story of 1849 will be repeated. Three days ago two steamers from San Francisco landed no less than three thousand passengers in Victoria in one day. As soon as the trail is completed the migration will undoubtedly flow into this town. No less than five gambling houses have been in operation every day, including Sundays. They were, to be sure, closed last Sunday as a result of protests and complaints brought by a number of citizens to the sheriff, who is still the highest civil authority here.

There are Indians in great numbers round about Whatkom. They are peaceful and good-natured. Many of them are big, good-looking, well-built people. Some of the men have dressed up in coats and trousers. The rest, both men and women, go about wrapped in fiery red blankets. They are particularly fond of these startling colors. The site upon which the town is now being built seems to have been especially favored by the Indians, because their huts are still standing in many places. It strikes one as queer to see these Indian huts entirely surrounded by clusters of houses; but very soon they will disappear into the outskirts of the town. It is illegal to sell or give whisky to the Indians; nevertheless some of them are seen under the influence of firewater. They are then entirely transformed from good-natured beings into noisy and uncontrollable semisavages. One sees them gambling all day long in front of their huts; and they are well supplied with gold and silver money. I myself saw two Indians sit and play for $60 in gold, consisting of three $20 pieces. There are said to be Indians who possess several thousand dollars, presumably secured by gold-mining, because here there is gold everywhere, yes, even under the ground. It is well known that gold can be found anywhere in the area where Whatkom is now being built if one only wants to dig, but it is so fine and so meager in quantity that it does not repay the trouble.

A couple of miles from Whatkom a new town is also being built, which is called Schome. At this place the water is deeper and the ships can lay to. Halfway between these two towns there is a rich coal mine, so this territory has all possible advantages and will become a wealthy land. The weather is exceedingly fine. One is free from the unpleasant wind that always arose every afternoon in San Francisco.

Today I am setting off with three good companions whom I have been fortunate enough to meet. It will be a trip of about two weeks to reach the gold mines. I will not have time to write any more.

Each wears a golden chain and heavy rings

FROM A MAN IN TYSNÆS TO THE EDITOR OF STAVANGER AMTSTIDENDE OG ADRESSEAVIS *

1863

Niels Ørjansen Geigland and Johannes Gregoriussen Teigland from Tysnæs clerical district left their home in August 1854, intending to go to California and dig for gold. They went as passengers on a steamship from Bergen to Hamburg, where they went on board an English ship going to North America. Arrived there, they shipped on an American ship to California. Everything went well on the trip, and finally they reached their destination, where they planned, as the proverb says, to become self-made men in a hurry. But their hopes were immediately disappointed, for at that very time there was a tremendous influx of people and the profit of the gold-digging was so uncertain that prices of provisions rose terribly high. Moreover the greatest disorder and lawlessness prevailed among the workers in the mines, and theft and robbery, everyday occurrences, went unpunished.

Frightened away by all this commotion, they went on the same ship back to North America to try if they could possibly get from there to Australia. Having shipped on board American vessels for almost three years, they finally arrived in Australia. They started digging for gold at once and soon found enough to encourage them to continue digging. Since they had a prospect of making money, they wrote home and assured their parents that if they made good money they would return to their native country in a few years. Thus several letters were exchanged between them and their parents over a period of three years. After that the parents got no answer from them, and everybody thought that they were no longer alive. This was not the case, however. The reason for their silence was that their letters from Australia had not reached the parents, while those of the parents had not been received in Australia.

But still love for their native country was not dead in the gold-diggers from Tysnæs. On the night of April 30 this year they arrived in their home completely unexpectedly. No one recognized them – neither their parents nor their brothers and sisters – as their complexion, hair, and beards had changed greatly since the time they left. It is easy to imagine the surprise and happiness of their family on seeing them again, after so long

* This account appeared in *Stavanger Amtstidende og Adresseavis,* June 15, 1863.

and dangerous a journey, dressed like distinguished persons and covered with gold. Each of them wears his golden chain around his neck and very heavy rings on both hands. Both chains and rings consist of gold in its natural condition, though the nuggets of which the chains are made have been fastened together by a goldsmith. The biggest finger rings consist of one whole nugget with a hole drilled through it.

Although they have not made any definite statements about their profit so far, there is every probability – according to a few hints they have dropped – that they have made several thousand dollars. Now each one plans to buy a good farm and stay in this country. After their return they have behaved in exemplary fashion. They speak their native language the way they did before, are courteous and obliging toward great ones and little ones, and at the first holy communion held after their return they were among the communicants.

During their stay in North America they made several trips inland to the Norwegian settlements. They became convinced that many of the Norwegians are not doing quite so well as they claim in their letters. From the experience they acquired there, they advise everybody who does not know the English language against going to America. And although they personally know the language very well, they did not want to make their homes there.

Cheerful Voices at Mid-Century

IN Norway, as in other parts of Europe, there were violent differences of opinion about America – a psychological state that has not disappeared in times remote from the days of lonely frontiers and struggling pioneers when immigrant letters reflected conflicting emotions and judgments. Svein Nilssen, a pioneer collector of immigrant stories, records that in the earlier years of migration from northern Europe, "opinion was divided." He writes, "Some saw everything pertaining to the world across the sea in rosy colors, while others were astounded that anybody should venture to emigrate to a land full of poisonous snakes, bloodthirsty animals, and even more dangerous wild men. . . . Imaginary pictures furnished the stuff for the most exaggerated accounts of America's glories, while the enemies of emigration drew from the same sources materials from which they put together terrifying stories of the sorrow and misery which awaited the foolhardy persons who, despite warnings, went to meet their certain doom." *

Ordeals there had been and were, but the land and rich resources of Midwest America were a reality, and neither preachers like Dietrichson nor nationalistic Norwegian newspapermen could brush them away with emotional rhetoric. And gradually the immigrants began to surmount initial difficulties. Muskego drew away from the pitiful malaria and cholera era. Lands were cleared, houses were built, and the days of unrelieved misery began to recede into the background. Not that later letters did not carry tales of woe to the homeland. They did, for

* *Billed-Magazin,* 2:237–238, quoted in Blegen, *Norwegian Migration,* vol. 1, p. 148. Nilsse interviewed settlers in the 1860's and recorded his interviews in a series of interesting articles.

frontiers shifted, and swarms of new immigrants to some extent repeated the experiences of the older immigrants. But settlements took root. Muskego and Koshkonong had offshoots to the north and west, time lessened the pangs of nostalgia, and the processes of adjustment and adaptation went forward year after year, with changes in outlook of which many of the immigrants themselves were scarcely conscious. The mirroring of change gives to the immigrant documents no small part of their historical significance.

Letters out of Wisconsin in the late 1840's and early 1850's offer interesting comparisons with the narratives of Muskego in its initial years. The tone of underlying confidence reflected in the Muskego manifesto is echoed in the letters from this later period. The poignancy of individual suffering, never wholly absent from the American frontier experience, finds its way into the record, but the worst agonies are in the past, and there is a new note of cheer and buoyancy in the voices that sound from the Middle West.

It is appropriate to open the section with the letter of a young woman who made her way to America in 1847 as a maid for an immigrant family. There is an air of sprightliness about her. She enjoys the ways of the New World and has both humor and a quick adaptability. Her early wages are a trifle unusual: she receives the fruits of three acres of land for a period of three years. Making her way in Wisconsin, she leaves a log cabin in the rapidly developing Koshkonong Settlement to take a job in Madison at a dollar a week, with hopes of rising to a dollar and a half. To many immigrant girls, America initially meant service as maids before they married and made homes for themselves. Jannicke Sæhle of Koshkonong Prairie and Madison speaks for this segment of immigrant America. Henrietta Jessen, an immigrant of 1849, did not have the sprightliness of Jannicke Sæhle, but she had courage. With her husband desperately ill, this young wife and mother nursed him through many weeks of anxiety. Her letter leaves no doubt that the pain of homesickness was present in full measure, but she found consolation in her religious faith and in her hopes for her children in "a fruitful land, where God's blessings are daily before our eyes." Her letter records the helpfulness of neighbors and friends, and in the midst of her trials she writes objectively about the prospects for people in the old country who are thinking about emigration to America. The third letter of the series, written by Ragnil Omland from Blue Mounds, Wisconsin, in

1850, and signed both by her and by two of her sisters, is a paean of praise for America, of special interest for the intensity and assurance with which the writer urges relatives to join the throngs of emigrants. The appeal, made in words direct and persuasive, was directed especially to a brother. The "immigrant image of America" was created out of many sources, but it is doubtful that any were so powerful as the thousands of letters written by people who had themselves emigrated and reported their triumphs in early or in later years. One reservation marks this particular letter, and that is a warning against being "so foolish as to go to the warm Texas."

The note of elation runs through another letter, this one written by an unnamed immigrant at Beloit, Wisconsin, late in November 1851. An interesting part of his letter is that in which he describes a "wonderful dish" called *pai* – something, he says, "that glides easily down your throat." But apple pie is only one of the many wonders of the New World, in his view. He finds the Americans admirable people – enterprising, deeply interested in education, and possessed of a "strict sense of morality." And he grows almost lyrical as he writes of the land and its fruits. "You ought to see the Indian corn," he exclaims, "this majestic plant." His letter was printed in a leading Norwegian newspaper, as was a letter similarly ecstatic in tone, written at Milwaukee in the summer of 1853, which described the Americans as a "proud and liberty-loving people" and declared that "no country in the world" had "so many churches, schools, universities, teachers, and ministers" as America. Of interest also is this writer's references to the famous violinist, Ole Bull, then on a great concert tour.* This series of Wisconsin letters closes with one from Blue Mounds in 1854 which tells, with some elation, about an appeal made by Norwegian ministers to the immigrants "to help relieve the need of the poor people in Norway." The writer expresses his pleasure in responding to such an appeal and ironically suggests that the best help would be free passage to America and that this kind of help "would annoy those in Norway who live by the sweat of the poor."

* The tour took Ole Bull as far west as California. See a reference in a California letter, p. 250.

A superabundance of food here

FROM JANNICKE SÆHLE, AT KOSHKONONG PRAIRIE, WISCONSIN, TO JOHANNES SÆHLE *

September 28, 1847

It seems to me that in my last letter to you, written from my former home in the Old World, I hoped that from my new home in the New World I should be able to write to you with even greater happiness and contentment, and God has fulfilled my wish. As I wrote you, we did not leave our dear native land until April 24, as we were held up eight days at Holmen in Sandvigen waiting for a number of passengers who had not yet arrived.

We sailed in the morning at seven o'clock, with fair wind and weather, and we had lost sight of the shores of our dear fatherland by half-past three, when the pilot left us. I remained on deck until six o'clock in the evening; then as the wind was sharp and cold I couldn't stay there any longer, but had to go down to the hold, where general vomiting had been going on for a long time. And after five minutes my turn came, also, to contribute my share to the Atlantic Ocean.

Still, what can I say? Not in all eternity can I thank God enough that the America journey was not for me what it was for many others. It seems now like a faint dream to me and as if through God's providential care I had been carried in protecting arms, for I was sick only four days, and even on these I went on deck now and then. I was not afraid, but slept as peacefully as in the little room that I had so recently left behind. My traveling companions were just as lucky as I; but a number of passengers had to keep to their beds nearly the whole journey, for the weather was stormy almost the entire voyage and besides it was so cold that there were few days when we could remain on deck for the whole day. But the wind had a good effect on conditions in the hold, which was well aired, and warmer weather would have been less desirable. So, as we went steadily onward we hoped for the best, and our hopes were not disappointed.

By May 14 we had already reached the Banks, where the captain and the skipper caught nine great cod; and for dinner on the Seven-

* My translation of this letter was first published in "Immigrant Women and the American Frontier," *Norwegian-American Studies and Records* (Northfield, Minn.), 5:14–29 (1930).

teenth of May we ate fish, though it was such a stormy day that we had to steady our plates with our hands, and not infrequently we were jerked backward with our plates in our hands.

In mentioning the skipper I can greet you from an old friend of our younger days, John Johannessen, who used to be in the service of Captain Fischer and once worked in his little fishing vessel. He is now much more alert as a seaman and looks much better than in the old days, but he is plagued by a long-standing malaria that he cannot get rid of, despite all the medicines he is said to have used. His wife is dead. He has one married and three unmarried daughters. This was his fourth trip to this country—and the fastest.

As the wind continued favorable, we expected to reach Staten Island, one mile from New York, by Whitsunday; but late in the evening before Whitsunday there was a calm, and a thick fog covered everything, so that it was necessary to keep up a constant ringing and shooting in case other sailing vessels should be in the vicinity. Later the fog lifted, and we saw several vessels. In the afternoon, about four o'clock, the captain saw a sailboat that resembled a pilot's vessel, and when he looked at it through his glass, it turned out to be so, to our delight, for the captain had not expected to get a pilot so late in the day. It was not long before the man was on board, and the next day near dinner time we anchored on American ground. The foggy weather continued, and we were able to see only the delightful island, with its many lighthouses, pretty forts, and buildings, which stood out majestically among the charming stretches of woods.

After the good old doctor had come on board and we had all had the good fortune of being able to walk smartly past him, he gave his permission for the vessel to proceed immediately in to New York, where we arrived in the evening at five o'clock. The next day we made ready to go up to the town on the following day to look about, but as we had the children with us and the day was very warm, we did not get very far. The skipper accompanied us as a guide who knew the place and as an interpreter.

First we came to a large and beautiful park for pedestrians, outside of which were a great number of fruit dealers and pleasant carriages for hire. We immediately hired one of these and had ourselves driven for a mile through the streets, for which we paid six pennies each, about the same as six Norwegian skillings. The next day we went to the museum, which we thoroughly enjoyed. Here we saw animals and birds, from the largest to the smallest, and many things, some of which I understood, some of which I didn't, portraits of all the generals that there have been in America, and finally an old man with a richly braided uniform who stood on a pedestal. After we had looked about us at this place, we learned that a drama was being played, and when we reached the theater we saw a representation of Napoleon's funeral, which was very beautiful. This ended at half-past five. Another play was to be presented from seven to ten, but we were already satisfied. We paid about thirty skillings.

On May 20 we left our good ship *Juno* with its brave crew, who said good-by to us with a three-times repeated hurrah. The captain accompanied us on board a steamer that was to carry us to Albany. He showed us around. It was like a complete house four stories high and very elegantly furnished, with beautiful rugs everywhere. Then he left us with the best wishes. Captain Bendixen treated us more as though we were relatives than passengers. He was very entertaining and courteous.

The rest of the journey was much better than expected. Things went merrily on the railroads. Once in a while the passengers, when we neared some of the noteworthy sights that we rushed past on the trip, would stick their heads out of the windows to see everything, but one after the other of them had the misfortune to see his straw hat go flying away with the wind caused by the speed of the train.

On June 3, after we had passed several cities which for lack of space I cannot tell about, we reached Milwaukee, where we remained three days. We left Milwaukee on the seventh and came to Koshkonong on the ninth. Torjersen, after having made the acquaintance here of a worthy family named Homstad, from Namsen, who settled here last year and found this land the best after long travels, has now bought a little farm of forty acres of land, with a fairly livable log house and a wheat field of four and a half acres. This has brought him forty-five barrels of winter wheat, in addition to potatoes, beans, peas, more than a hundred heads of cabbage, cucumbers, onions in tremendous amounts, and many other kinds [of vegetables]. He paid $250 for this farm and four humble pigs that went along with it.

After having lived here and having been in good health the whole time, I left on August 16 for Madison, the capital of Wisconsin, which is situated twenty-two miles from here. There I have worked at a hotel for five weeks, doing washing and ironing; and I enjoy the best treatment, though I cannot speak with the people. I have food and drink in abundance. A breakfast here consists of chicken, mutton, beef, or pork, warm or cold wheat bread, butter, white cheese, eggs, or small pancakes, the best coffee, tea, cream, and sugar. For dinner the best courses are served. Supper is eaten at six o'clock, with warm biscuits, and several kinds of cold wheat bread, cold meats, bacon, cakes, preserved apples, plums, and berries, which are eaten with cream, and tea and coffee – and my greatest regret here is to see the superabundance of food, much of which has to be thrown to the chickens and the swine, and to remember my dear ones in Bergen, who like so many others must at this time lack the necessaries of life.

I have received $1.00 a week for the first five weeks, and hereafter shall have $1.25, and if I can stand it through the whole winter I shall get $1.50 a week, and I shall not have to do the washing, for I did not think I was strong enough for this work. Mrs. Morison has also asked me to remain in her service as long as she, or I, may live, as she is going to leave the tavern next year and live a more quiet life with her husband and daughter, and there I also could live more peacefully and have a room by myself, and I really believe that so far as she is concerned I could enter upon this arrangement, provided such a decision is God's will for me.

I am well and so far I have not regretted my journey to this country. I have now been with the Torjersens for four days and have written to Bergen and to you, and tomorrow I shall journey up to the Morisons', where I find myself very well satisfied. I have had the honor of sitting at their daughter's marriage dinner, and I ironed her beautiful bridal gown. She was in truth a lovable bride, beautiful, and good as an angel, and she has often delighted me with her lovely singing and her playing on the piano. She was married on September 16 and left on the seventeenth for Boston with her husband to visit her parents-in-law. And now, my dear Johannes, I must say farewell for this time. God bless you. Do not forget, I shall give you Torjersen's address, so that you may write me here. I greet you affectionately. Do not forget to thank God, on my behalf, who has guided me so well. I cannot thank Him enough myself.

I have now received from Torjersen for my services, three acres of land for cultivation for three years, and it is now planted with winter wheat – if God will give me something to harvest.

God's blessings are daily before our eyes

FROM HENRIETTA JESSEN, IN MILWAUKEE, WISCONSIN, TO ELEANORE AND "DOREA" WILLIAMSIN *

February 20, 1850

Fate has indeed separated me from my native land and all that was dear to me there, but it is not denied me to pour forth my feelings upon this paper. My dear sisters, it was a bitter cup for me to drink, to leave a dear mother and sisters and to part forever in this life, though living. Only the thought of the coming world was my consolation; there I shall see you all. Of the emigrants from Arendal, I think, probably none went on board with a heavier heart than I, and thanks be to the Lord who gave me strength to carry out this step, which I hope will be for my own and my children's best in the future. So I hope that time will heal the wound, but up to the present I cannot deny that homesickness gnaws at me hard. When I think, however, that there will be a better livelihood for us here than in poor Norway, I reconcile myself to it and thank God, who protected me and mine over the ocean's waves and led us to a fruitful land, where God's blessings are daily before our eyes.

When you have received these lines, dear No and Do, I must ask you to write my dear mother as quickly as possible and tell her that I have had the joy of receiving her letter by the post. That was the greatest day of happiness I have had since I came to America. Greet Mother and Ma and Georgia and say that they must not expect any letter from me before midsummer. Tell Mother that I have not received the letter she sent by the brig *Juno*.

Since we came to America neither my children nor I have been sick abed a day, for which God is to be thanked, who strengthens my body and my poor soul. I have not had so pleasant a winter as I might have had. My husband fell ill in the middle of September and had to keep to his bed until eight days before Christmas. Then he began to sit up a little and now he is up most of the day, but he is so weak that he cannot think of beginning to work for two months and perhaps not then. The doctor calls the sickness dysentery. Yes, my poor Peder has suffered much in this sickness. The doctor gave up all hope of his life

* This translation was first published in my "Immigrant Women and the American Frontier," *Norwegian-American Studies and Records,* 5:14–29 (1930).

and we only waited for God's hour, but at twelve o'clock one night his pulse changed and the doctor said that now it was possible that he would overcome the sickness, but he said that it would be very stubborn and [the recovery] slow.

That sickness I can never forget. Think, in one terrible day and night my husband lost eight pots of blood. That was the night before he was near death, and I was alone with him and my children. But afterward there were a few of the Norwegians who were so kind as to help me for a time watching over him, the one relieving the other. For seven weeks I was not out of my clothes.

From these lines you will see that I have experienced a little in America; but now that the worst is over, I thank the Almighty Father from my innermost heart, who has cared for us and met our daily needs. We have lacked nothing. Good food and drink we have had daily. I believe I may say that even if I had been in my own native town I would hardly have received the help I have had here, and I get $2 a week (that is, in goods). I will not speak of my own kind family, what they would have done for me, but I mean the public. There are four Norwegian families living quite near who have been very sympathetic with me in my misfortune and have proved their faith by their works; they have given me both money and articles for the house. Among these four families there is a man named Samuel Gabrielsen, who has been like a rare good brother to me. I will not say how much that kind man has given us, for he has told me that I should not tell anyone. "I give to you now because I know that it will be a help to you, but I do not give to be praised." He knows my brother-in-law well; in fact, Gabrielsen says that Williamsin is the best man he knows in the world, and all the Norwegians whom I talk with say the same.

There are a large number of Norwegians here from the vicinity of Farsund, most of them seamen. It is the sailors who are paid best in America. All the sailors get rich. Here an ordinary seaman gets from $18 to $25 a month. Clerks have gone without work here this winter; carpenters and shoemakers are the artisans that are best paid. Glass workers and tailors are not able to make a living for their families. This is easy to understand when you know that you can get window panes of any size at small cost, and it does not take much intelligence to put in a pane.

My dear sisters, when I last wrote to Farsund it was farthest from my thoughts that I ever should be separated so far from my native land and my home. How often I think of you and of your innocent angels, whom I never have seen and never shall in this life; but in my thoughts I seem to see your innocent little ones. From Mother's letter I learn that all is well with my dear ones in Farsund, and this gives me much happiness. I hope that you all, with God's help, will be strong and in good health when these lines reach you.

Your butter tub, Norea, I have used daily since I came to America, but it has not held butter since I left my native land. It would not be well if I should lack needed articles in a foreign country where I have neither mother nor sisters to comfort me in dark times such as this winter when my dear Peder was sick, and I suppose I have often wished that I were surrounded by my dear ones. I suppose it is a little strange to receive a dress in Norway and not to thank [the giver] for it before one comes to America, but better late than never. I will therefore, dear Dorea and your husband, thank you both for the dress that you gave me last summer for my Georgine S. She still has it in good condition, and when it can no longer be used it will be put away as a remembrance of Uncle Perneman and Aunt Dorea in Norway. The greatest pleasure I have is talking with the children about their grandmother and aunts and uncles in Norway; that is our daily talk, and what pleases me so specially is that from the smallest to the largest they answer me with a happy smile as soon as I begin to talk about home in Norway, about grandmother and aunts.

Seval greets "Aunty" Norea, but he says he cannot remember aunty. He received the blue socks from Aunt Norea, and he is so glad to look at them when I unlock the chest; then he is quick to ask if he may see his little socks. I shall not praise my own child, but I surely believe that if I live he will give me happy days, he is so tender and understanding toward me. And Søren is an unusual little fellow for his age; he has kept us supplied with wood this winter and works like a little horse. George is a little rascal; Georgine is large for her age; everybody asks if they are twins.

Tell Mother that I long since looked up Christiane Lydeman. She is well off and greets Aunt. I am often with Christiane; she is kind and pleasant to me.

The winter here in America is just as long as in Norway and much colder, but the nights are not so long. At Christmas time we had light until five o'clock in the afternoon. Ask Margaret to tell Peder Mekelsen that I advise him to go to New York and from there by canalboat to Buffalo and then by steamboat here to Milwaukee. Nels Klaapene, the sailmaker, lives here in the vicinity; his wife's name is Ingebaar.

I am writing with a pen and the paper says stop. And now in conclusion I ask God's blessing upon you all. God guard you from all evil in your peaceful homes. A thousand greetings to you, Norea, with your husband and children, and you Dorea, with your husband and children, from me, my husband, and my children.

Greet my dear mother a thousand times, M. and her children, and Mrs. Hal and Mrs. Ramlu, with their husbands and children. Good-by, good-by, all my dear ones. God bless you.

Here you can get to own much property

FROM RAGNIL, SIGRI, AND GUNILD NICOLAIS DATTER OMLAND, AT BLUE MOUNDS, WISCONSIN, TO THEIR BROTHER TELLEF NICOLAISEN *

November 18, 1850

Now I will no longer put off writing you a true account of our trip to America. You know that we would like you to come over here, but if you should become more unhappy here, then we would rather that you stayed at home. But we all fear that after working so long on the farm in Norway you may eventually end up poor. If you sold the farm you might be able to come here with some money. And even though you should come without money, we would think you fortunate if you came owning only the clothes you wear. Remember that you are young and that in a year you may earn enough to buy a farm much better than Omland.

We have also heard that you are afraid of the diseases here. Do not be, for Blue Mounds is not only the most healthful place in all America, but we do not hesitate to call it as healthful a spot as any found in Norway. The air here is pure and clear and there is plenty of water, both rivers and brooks. We ourselves have not been ill for one single day

* The original Norwegian of this letter is printed in *Agder og Amerika: En Samling Gamle Amerikabrev,* with introductions by Tolv Aamland and Ingrid Semmingsen (Oslo, 1953).

since we came here, and this is also true of those who have arrived this year and last.

The soil here is as fertile as any you can find in America, and our daily food consists of rye and wheat bread, bacon, butter, eggs, molasses, sugar, coffee, and beer. The corn that grows on large cobs is rarely eaten by people; it is not tender enough for that, but is used as fodder for the animals. Thus you can understand that we have had no trouble making a living and have not had to ask others for help. My brothers and sisters and I have all acquired land, and we are happy and content. This year we have produced so much foodstuff that we have been able to sell instead of having to buy, and we all have cattle, driving oxen, and wagons. We also have children in abundance. Gunild has given birth to two girls, Sigri and Anne, and I have also had two here, a boy called Terje and a girl called Sigri. But Ole and Joraand have no children.

Our old father, who is in good health, received the $200 in June. My sister Sigri worked for twenty-five weeks in a town forty miles from here and got $25 for that. Guro has traveled thirty-five miles from here down to Koshkonong Prairie to be confirmed; she will not return till next spring.

Since I love you, Tellef, more than all my other brothers and sisters, I feel very sorry that you have to work your youth away in Norway, where it is so difficult to get ahead. There you can't see any results of your labor, while here you can work ahead to success and get to own a good deal of property, even though you did not have a penny to begin with. I wish that you would sell the farm now for what you can get for it and come here as fast as possible. I and all the others with me believe that you would not regret it. Our old father would tell you the same thing. He has heard that you do not feel like leaving, and he says that you are so young and inexperienced that it may be best for you to try your luck in Norway first. Then later you will be very glad to come here. If you do come, we hope that you will not be so foolish as to go to the warm Texas. It is true that Reiersen praises it highly, but when my mother asked him how conditions were in Texas, he himself told her that it was so hot there that if you put a pan with bacon out on the street, it fries by itself. Then, of course, we were frightened at the thought of such a hot climate and were afraid to go there. And when they say in Texas that a man can get a completely satisfying meal out of a cob of corn, we conclude that this must be because the people there are so sickly and unhealthy that they cannot eat very much. We are to blame for not having written about this before, but the reason was that we had not expected that our brothers and sisters would want to go to Texas. We are a little surprised to see that our relatives do not seem to love us so very much, since they want to travel to such a remote place, as if they were afraid of meeting us again. But it is just the same to us; if they can get along without us, we can get along without them, but I do know that none of us would have acted in this way. We have talked to a man by the name of Kjøstel, from Holt, who had traveled far into Texas with Jørgen Hasle, but when he saw the way people lived there he returned. They have neither wheat bread nor butter there, only the coarse corn foodstuff, but we here in Wisconsin would not be satisfied with such hog's feed.

Much attention is given to education

FROM AN IMMIGRANT LIVING IN BELOIT, WISCONSIN, TO FRIENDS *

November 29, 1851

Everywhere I have traveled in Wisconsin the land is on the whole flat, alternating with bigger and smaller hills, little valleys and fairly wide stretches of swamp, then again large plains or prairies and woodland. Along the rivers or where the soil is moist there is always wood, mostly oak but also linden and aspen. There are also said to be a great many ash trees here. The hazel tree likewise grows here, but it is not so tall as in Norway. The tallest I have seen must have been about two or three yards. It covers the fields like bog myrtle and has nuts in abundance. The fir and the spruce do not grow here but are found farther north. Oak, linden, ash, and maple are cut into boards and planks and sold at one cent (about one skilling) a square foot.

Strawberries, raspberries, and blackberries thrive here. From these they make a wonderful dish combined with syrup and sugar, which is called *pai.* I can tell you that is something that glides easily down your throat; they also make the same sort of *pai* out of apples or finely

* This letter appeared in *Stavanger Amtstidende og Adresseavis,* June 12, 1852.

ground meat, with syrup added, and that is really the most superb. There are not many fruit trees here yet, since the land is too new. But they are being planted here in great numbers, and in many places I have seen large orchards with apple trees planted in rows like potatoes, one yard or farther apart, depending on their height. Such orchards are called nurseries. When anyone wants fruit trees here, he buys them and pays from twenty-five cents to fifty cents apiece. The apples that grow here are big and have an excellent taste. Consequently they are still very expensive and cost one or two cents apiece. Most of them come from Ohio. Here in Beloit there are both apple and cherry trees, but I have not eaten cherries since last year in New York, and I did not think the cherries there had the same good taste as those in Norway. Of the domestic grasses clover and timothy are grown here. The hay is sold at $3 or $5 a ton, which corresponds approximately to two thousand Norwegian pounds. Some flax is also grown here, and it yields a good profit. You ought to see the Indian corn, this majestic plant. It has a stalk and leaves. The stalk is more than an inch in diameter or thicker than the handle of a rake, and the height of the plant is about four yards. It is planted in rows with two feet or more between the plants and is hoed like potatoes to keep it free of weeds. Yes, if you could see a field with a nice crop of Indian corn, I think you would be surprised. Indian corn is usually fed to the animals, but a little is ground and sometimes forms a part of our meals.

Wheat is a staple among the grains here and it grows well. But many years it is ruined by rust, which was the case this year around Beloit — many fields were actually rotting away. But not all kinds are affected by this rust. Barley is also grown but is used for malt exclusively. It does not have as full a kernel as in Norway, since it is too hot here for the proper ripening. A good deal of oats is grown here, but it is only used as fodder for the horses. It does not get very thick, but is more like the Swedish oats. All grains have to be sown very thinly, otherwise they will be spoilt, and the soil rarely yields as much here as it did in Norway. I imagine that "Løeageren" at the Levig farm is about an acre in size. On this you could average a harvest of ten barrels of oats. Since an acre in America only yields twenty bushels (four bushels to a barrel), there is a considerable difference. Potatoes have to be planted in the same way — if they are put too close together nothing comes of them.

The houses are built of brick and another sort of stone dug out of the earth. One yard under the surface of the ground the rock begins and ranges out in all directions, and all you have to do is break loose the stones. This sort of stone is also used in making mortar. Besides, houses are built of small, round boulders placed in rows above each other, and these houses are a fine sight. Finally, houses are also built of timber, in the same way as the seaboard sheds in Norway, although they have more posts here. Everything is made ready on the ground, then it is erected and made secure with nails. A covering of boards is put up on the outside, and inside some strips of board one and a half inches wide, which you get ready-made at the sawmills. These strips are fastened with nails at appropriate intervals, and then a heavy plaster is put on and next a coat of whitewash. Then the houses are finished. These buildings are warmer than one would think. No tiles for the roofs are used here but instead thin shingles of fir, which serve the purpose very well.

The enterprising spirit of the Americans reaches out in many directions. If you think you can make money in any one particular business, you can try it. Those who are wealthy undertake several projects, for here a man can carry on as many trades as he pleases. Rich businessmen travel up and down the country looking for places suitable for the laying out of towns. They buy up the surrounding land, build mills and sawmills and rent these out, and sell the land as building lots. In this way they make huge profits.

Rents are extremely high. Here in Beloit you pay from $100 to $400 a year for shop premises, but this is nothing compared to what you pay in larger cities. But in proportion to this, rent for a family is not too high, since you can rent a house in an out-of-the-way street or in the outskirts of town, and so on. For board you pay $6 a month here. This is the cheapest rate for a single person, and in addition to his board he gets free laundry and a bed. A meal costs from twelve to fifteen cents and a bed the same, all depending on the time and the nature of the place.

I imagine you would like to hear something about yellow California gleaming with gold. The gold fever has affected both Americans and Norwegians severely, and they outdo one another in dreaming and raving. Many leave and some return. Most of them make huge sums of money, while others have nothing to brag about. Recently eight Norwegians that I know left for the land of gold.

The Americans are a most educated people. On the whole I do not think that one will find anywhere a more educated people than here. Much attention is given to the educational system. Both children and adults go to school. Boys and girls usually go to school until they are twenty years old, and this is particularly true of girls who want to become schoolteachers themselves. For both women and men are employed as schoolteachers, and the former are preferred since they can be had at a lower salary than the latter. In the schools the following subjects are taught: spelling, reading, writing, and arithmetic. The schools consist of classes, and each class has its special form. Here the children learn to spell. The teacher pronounces the word, and the student spells it out. Perhaps you think that this is not difficult, but I say that it is. For such lessons suitable books are used which begin with the letters of the alphabet and simple words of one syllable. Later they become progressively difficult and use instructive, edifying, and amusing stories. In such schools no religion is taught, but each of the denominations to which the parents belong has its Sunday school where religion is taught. Sunday school starts at nine o'clock and finishes at half past ten, the time for people to go to church. It is always held in the church, and not only children go to it but people of all ages. Since both a farmer and a man from the city teach their children that which befits their position, it follows that one is not inferior to the other in education, and the man from the city does not consider himself any better than the farmer.

The Americans also have a very strict sense of morality. The Sabbath is observed with an almost pharisaical severity. Yet I do not believe that it is the same way in all cities as it is here in Beloit, where everything seems so sanctimonious. Sunday passes peacefully and quietly, and few people are seen in the streets except those on their way to and from church, which happens three times every Sunday, namely in the forenoon, afternoon, and evening. Besides, divine service is held every Thursday evening and singing school three times a week, and he who wanted to play or dance on a Sunday would first be regarded as a breaker of the Sabbath, and after that he would not be respected much any more. From the little insight I have acquired, I really do not know what to say about these people. I am much inclined to believe that many of them are "whited sepulchres"—if there were not a few tares among the wheat, it would be almost too good to be true. Some of the Yankees say prayers every day, in the morning and in the evening, by reading a chapter from the Bible and after that offering a prayer of their own making. During the prayer they kneel down, and so on. Others do not read a single word of God with any devotion but instead devote themselves the more diligently to the newspapers and things that appeal to the senses. There is much interest in singing here, and I have often gone to their church to listen to the beautiful hymns.

The Norwegians here have ministers that were properly ordained in Norway. On January 5 last year they were assembled at Rock Prairie together with a great many deputies from all the Norwegian Lutheran congregations. This assembly, which is called a synod, agreed on binding decisions for the church and its teachings. The church was named the Norwegian Evangelical Lutheran Church in America, and Pastor Clausen was elected bishop. He is functioning in that capacity this year, but a new bishop is elected each year. At present there are six ministers here, but even these are too few. The Norwegian Evangelical Lutheran Church is respected by the other American denominations, of which there are a great many.

Here a minister has to be a minister in the truest sense of the word, for to encompass all sects and their adherents within your confines is more difficult than many people in Norway can imagine. The most difficult in this respect among the Norwegian sectarians are the Ellingians and those who are adherents of Unonius, Paul Andersen, and Ole Aasen of Luther Franklin's synod. The last three have their congregations in Chicago and Illinois. Paul Andersen has studied here in Beloit and now belongs to Franklin's synod, mentioned above. Andreas Scheie from Sandeid is minister in their service. As yet he does not have the authority to administer the sacraments, but may only preach and baptize. The Ellingian congregation selects its ministers out of its own midst, and, besides, the congregation is presided over by four elders. Between these and the Lutherans there are disagreements on many points and constant discord and quarreling both orally and in writing. I agree just as much with the Ellingians as with the Lutherans. Ole Aasen's congregation accepts no one unless he states publicly that he has been converted or is on his way to conversion. The Norwegian ministers are watched suspiciously day and night by all the sectarians, since some of the sects contend that the Norwegians are not moved by the spirit of God but solely by lust for gain.

A minister has much more to do here than in Norway, and in church he has to preach God's word very purely. If he does not do this, he may expect to get fired. Now you may ask: "Who is so wise that he can judge a minister?" I would reply that there are many such persons here. There are quite a few minds here who consider themselves the equals of a minister as to knowledge of God's word, and they are not afraid to tell a minister very frankly what his deficiencies are. Thus a minister here has to work like a minister, live and teach like a minister.

Pastors Clausen, Preus, and Dietrichson publish a paper of religious content called *Maanedstidende.* This was printed in Racine by Knud Langeland, the editor of *Democraten.* But since he has moved, the Norwegian ministers have got in touch with others interested in the project and plan to buy the printing press of Knud Langeland for $500. They intend to print Bibles, testaments, books of sermons, hymn books, and other things that might be needed. Very likely we shall also get a permanent Norwegian newspaper started. The two earlier ones have ceased publication, partly for lack of subscribers, and partly because subscribers did not pay for their subscriptions.

Here where so many live separated from the mother who bore them under her heart, nursed them at her breast, and tended them with loving care as children; here where so many are separated from brothers and sisters, to whom they were attached by many ties of affection, ties that remain until the last abode is made ready for them and the roof is covered with earth; here where no old friend or relative can be found anywhere — here your mood often grows heavy and all your privations are sorely felt. But let us not trouble our hearts with the things of the earth and sow only in the flesh, for then we shall only reap corruption of the flesh. But let us sow in the spirit, then we shall reap eternal life. From now on let us wander on the road of the pious, all the time we have to live on this earth, faithfully trusting that God in His grace will let us enter His heavenly dwelling, whose bliss and glory no mortal can describe.

A railroad from the Atlantic to the Pacific

FROM CARL THORSTEINSEN, IN MILWAUKEE, WISCONSIN, TO HIS FATHER *

July 19, 1853

I have been in good health ever since I came to America, not ill a single day, and things have gone well with me. The greatest difficulty for the Norwegian is his deficiency in the language. This usually lasts one or two years before one has made enough progress to make oneself understood. Personally, I did not have too much difficulty in this respect, for I had learned a little of the language before I left Norway, and therefore it has been easier for me to make good. It will be easy for a young man who arrives here without having learned any craft, but who has had fairly good schooling, to find employment in trade where he can serve his countrymen who do not understand the language. Such has been my main occupation thus far. Immediately after my arrival here, I got employment as a merchant's clerk; and in this position I have been able to familiarize myself with the English language, which I now speak almost as fluently as my native language.

Another means I used to increase my knowledge of English considerably was by going to church diligently, which I have done two or three times every Sunday since my arrival. In America the Sabbath is observed very rigorously, that is to say, among the native Americans; and I therefore believe that God has blessed America and ordained it to become the biggest, wealthiest, most powerful country on the earth.

The Americans are a proud and liberty-loving people, but in all their prosperity they have not forgotten that fear of God is the strength of nations. There is no other country in the world that has so many churches, schools, universities, teachers, and ministers as America. As proof of the high education of the people it may be cited that the clergy is not regarded, nor indeed regards itself, as better than the common people. The minister dresses just like other members of the congregation. He wears no cassock in church, as in oppressed Europe, to call attention to differences of station in society. The same thing is true of lawyers and government officials. I have not yet seen an official dressed differently from a common man. Thus everybody is equally free, equally respected,

* This letter appeared in *Morgenbladet,* November 28, 1853. A prefatory note says that Thorstein Olsen, the writer's father, is a smith.

whether he be an official or a farmer, a grocer, or a craftsman. America has an army of two million men, but I have not yet seen a soldier or an officer in uniform in this country, though I have traveled thousands of miles here. Time and money are not wasted here on the vanity of a useless uniform and on drill. In the event of war, every honest man is a soldier. Every workingman, whether he has learned a trade or is only able to use the ax, the pick, or the spade, can make his daily bread in America free from care. He who has a little money and is accustomed to farming will also do well to continue this work here.

It has now been proposed to build a railroad across America from the Atlantic to California or the Pacific, and the cost is computed at a million specie dollars. Many railroads are being constructed in Wisconsin alone, so there is, and always will be, an abundance of work here for the emigrant. The American does not want to travel by stagecoach and be shaken and jolted, or spend four weeks (as I did once) on a ship to cover a distance like the one from Christiania to Christianssand. You can now travel from Milwaukee to New York – 1,700 miles – in forty-eight hours, and from there to London in ten days, and on to Christiania in two or three days. Thus, in less than three weeks you can now speed across half the globe. From this you can understand, dear Father, that it will not require very much time for me to come and visit you.

When Ole Bull was here last spring, I and four other countrymen arranged a ride four Norwegian miles into the country for him. There was plenty of champagne and other good things, and we had a wonderful time. Bull gave two concerts here which, of course, were applauded and admired by everybody. A Norwegian mountain tune that he played seemed to please even the Americans more than anything else. The first night tickets were 2 specie dollars and the last night 1 specie dollar; he had crowded houses on both occasions. Ole Bull invited all his countrymen to the concert the last night, and many had also been given free tickets for the first concert. My wife and I went both times. On his arrival here, Ole Bull was received on the quay by a committee consisting of the oldest Norwegian citizens in town, and as I knew Bull a little I functioned as spokesman. At his departure we showed him the same kind of attention. Toward the construction of a new Norwegian church in Chicago he gave a concert the proceeds of which were 700 specie dollars. He has also promised to contribute to a new church in Milwaukee.

Martin has a good job in a shop close to where I work, so we see each other every day. I am sure that he will do well here, for his chief gives him a raise every time Martin gets angry and says that he wants to quit. As for me, I have every reason to be satisfied. At the beginning of May I was promoted to inspector of customs for the customs district of Milwaukee at a regular salary of 40 specie dollars a month, and all told the job pays 600 specie dollars a year.

The harvests were very rich last year

FROM N. ARNESEN OMLAND, AT BLUE MOUNDS, WISCONSIN, TO HIS SON *

June 4, 1854

I received your letter of February 12 on May 25 this year, and we were all happy to hear that both children and friends in our old native country are well. We hope that this may continue to be the case till the end of your days and that you may win eternal happiness in the Beyond. Fortunately I can tell you that we here are also in good health. Your mother and I are still so well and strong that we are able to manage our own household. It is not very large now, as Guro was married last spring to a bachelor by the name of Johannes Olssen. They are doing very well, which makes us happy, but sometimes we feel lonely, mostly because the thought of you children who are in Norway and of those who are in Texas is forever on our minds. Still I have the constant happiness to see that my children here are doing well and show their love for me. I am very thankful to God for this, for I brought them here; and if they had been dissatisfied here, it would have been a great sorrow to me.

You write in your letter that you sent 70 specie dollars, but you do not say whether you sent them to me or to someone else, nor do you say whether you sent them by bill of exchange or in some other way. As it is such a long time since I had any news about this, all I can do is to write you. I do not know where to inquire, so as soon as you get this letter you must write me and tell me what the situation is.

* The original Norwegian of this letter is printed in *Agder og Amerika: En Samling Gamle Amerikabrev*.

I assume that you sent this money to me, and if this is so it gives me great pleasure. If I get it, I shall be able to get along for quite a period of time, if God will let me keep my health, which is and has been good for a long time, though my strength diminishes much every year.

You do not have to send any more money to me unless I write you and ask for it. If this should happen, I will write in good time, but now you must think of paying Jorand, Gunild, and Guro their shares of the inheritance. They do not want to let it lapse any longer, and I can do nothing more about it.

I have greetings for you from Ole Knudssen Fladeland the younger. He requests that you please notify his father, orally or in writing, that at present he is living here at Blue Mounds, that he is in good health, and that he made good money last winter. Three days ago he had a letter from his brother in Texas. He, too, is in good health and is doing well.

I have some interesting news for you: The good Norwegian ministers that live here have appealed to us to help relieve the need of the poor people in Norway. I am sure that both I myself and most of the other Norwegians here would be very happy to do so. We should like to see poor, industrious, honest, and able-bodied persons given free passage over here, and we should be very happy to contribute toward the payment of the traveling costs to the best of our ability. In this way we could be sure that the poor would benefit by our help, not only for a month or a year but during their whole life. If this should happen it would make all charitable Norwegians in America rejoice. And it would annoy those in Norway who live by the sweat of the poor.

The harvests here were very rich last year, and wheat has rapidly risen in price so that it now costs $1 or 100 skillings a bushel or a quarter of a barrel. The fact that it is shipped to Russia is said to be the reason for this rise, and this has been very fortunate for America, so that the masses of the people have been able to improve their lot greatly. The prospects for this year are very good too. I have sold more than twenty bushels of wheat and forty bushels of oats, and I have enough wheat for my own household until the fields yield more. Since I make no other demands on life, I live here quite free from financial troubles, and as I did in Norway, I here enjoy the company of many close friends. I do not really deserve to have so many friends, but I thank God for them.

Some time ago Guro wrote a letter for your mother to Arne. She would like to know if you have received it or not. Please write us also if the letters that we send from here can be addressed to Omli and how much it costs to redeem a letter. The letters we receive here and which have not been stamped we redeem for thirty-six cents and sometimes more. You asked me in a letter how people live here, and I can truthfully say that people here live much more decent lives than they do in Norway. There is no drunkenness, no slandering, bickering, and quarreling, which were so common in Norway.

I cannot think of anything more to write, and I shall therefore conclude my letter with much love from all here to you dear children and brothers and sisters. Greet Wrol and Kari and thank them for their letters. We wish you all good in worldly and especially in spiritual matters, and may you win eternal happiness in the Beyond.

P.S. Write something about the poor, if there are many of them. Let us also know about the conscription for the war [the Crimean War] and what education is like in Norway these days. Are the letters we write sent to Omli? In this settlement there are more than two hundred farmers, and we have only two poor persons who need help. They do not even have to leave their houses to get the things they need, as supplies are brought to them. Our religious arrangements are very satisfactory. We pay a minister to visit us from time to time, and the Norwegian church ritual is used. Now we expect to get a permanent minister soon. No one is forced to become a soldier here, but soldiers are paid so well that there are many who want to enter the services. I have been told that you doubt that Ierul Tvedt was in America a second time, but do not do that. He was here when he returned from Texas, and he had suffered much.

More Than a Ballad

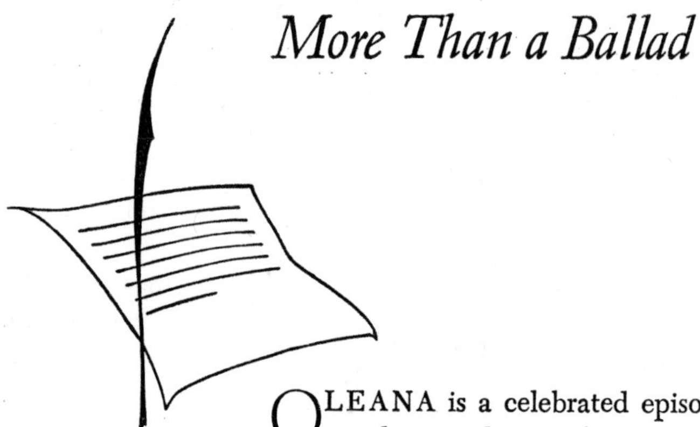

OLEANA is a celebrated episode in American history, but its fame derives less from its connection with the glamorous violinist Ole Bull and the colony he established in Pennsylvania in 1852 than from the fact that it inspired the satirical ballad "Oleana," still remembered and still sung a century after the violinist's paternalistic schemes collapsed like a punctured tire.

Oleana was, of course, more than a ballad and an ironical laugh. It was an organized colonization project born in the mind of a musical genius. Ole Bull first came to America in 1843 and gave concerts extensively throughout the country, reaping fabulous rewards. His idea of buying a huge tract of land in the United States and using it to establish the colony "New Norway" seems to have developed from rage over criticism in Norway of his Bergen national theater, coupled with a desire to impress the people of his country with an act of magnificence. There was anger as well as benevolence in his mind, plus a generous enthusiasm for America. Nor should one forget that he planned his "colony" in a period when many Utopias were being hatched in the New World.*

In any event, Ole Bull bought, or thought he bought, 120,000 acres of land in Potter County, Pennsylvania, in 1852, and he promptly invited Norwegian immigrants to settle there, with promises of wages and food for their work in clearing the heavily wooded lands of his tract.

* A brief sketch of the Oleana colony is in the *Dictionary of American History* (New York, 1940), vol. 4, p. 171, and I have written more fully about the colony in *Norwegian Migration*, vol. 1, pp. 287–307, with full references to sources. The reader who desires more detail is also referred to a series of articles by Torstein Jahr in *Symra* (Decorah, Iowa, 1910), vol. 6; Oddmund Vik, *Ole Bull* (Bergen, 1890), pp. 287–344; Sara C. Bull, *Ole Bull, A Memoir* (Boston, 1883), pp. 198–213; and M. B. Smith, *Life of Ole Bull* (Princeton University Press, 1943).

Emigrants soon arrived, and Ole Bull dedicated the enterprise with a flourish, declaring that the colonists were establishing "a New Norway, consecrated to liberty, baptized with independence, and protected by the Union's mighty flag." There was a burst of enthusiasm in Norway, and songs and ballads were composed in honor of the great benefactor. In the very same year a whole book appeared in that country under the title "America, Ole Bull, and the New Norway," * which included a jubilant song:

Come, hail the Music Master
  Hurrah for Ole Bull!
To cheats he's brought disaster,
  Their cup of woe is full.

And the labor newspaper of Norway celebrated the event with a paean of praise:

Good men of Norway, strong of arm,
  If fortune's barbs have torn you,
Behold a friend whose heart is warm,
  A man who will not scorn you.
Better he than gold or fame!
Ole Bull – yes, that's his name.†

The hopes of immigrants ran high, but the letters voicing Utopian dreams were soon succeeded by others that breathed only disappointment and disillusionment. As the bubble burst, the witty ballad of "Oleana" appeared and was seized upon with a shout not only by the shrill critics of Ole Bull but by all who fancied that the tales of America and its opportunities had been greatly exaggerated.

It turned out that the violinist had fallen into the hands of land speculators. Not only was the land difficult to clear; not only were promises of wages to the immigrants broken; but in the end it appeared that Ole Bull did not even have clear title to the land itself. Cheats had brought disaster to him. The colony, with the village of Oleana as its center, disintegrated. Some settlers stayed on, but most of them moved elsewhere in the East or made their way to the Middle West. Ole Bull himself was busy with still greater dreams that included vast additional land, the opening of a polytechnical school to be staffed with European profes-

* The book appeared appropriately in Bergen. See Theodore C. Blegen and Martin B. Ruud, *Norwegian Emigrant Songs and Ballads* (Minneapolis, 1936), pp. 176–182.

† The full text of the song appears in *Norwegian Emigrant Songs and Ballads*, pp. 183–186.

sors, and other splendid details; but the enterprise faltered and failed. A series of concerts given by Bull with Patti and Strakosch failed to revive it; and meanwhile the satirical ballad was taken, both in Norway and in America among the emigrants, as the final word about it. Oleana was sung out of existence. The letters in the present section need to be prefaced by the famous ballad, and I present it in a verse translation that I wrote some years ago.

I'm off to Oleana, I'm turning from my doorway,
No chains for me, I'll say good-by to slavery in Norway.
Ole – Ole – Ole – oh! Oleana!
Ole – Ole – Ole – oh! Oleana!

They give you land for nothing in jolly Oleana,
And grain comes leaping from the ground in floods of golden manna.

The grain it does the threshing, it pours into the sack, Sir,
And so you take a quiet nap a-stretching on your back, Sir.

The crops they are gigantic, potatoes are immense, Sir,
You make a quart of whisky from each one without expense, Sir.

And ale as strong and sweet as the best you've ever tasted,
It's running in the foamy creek, where most of it is wasted.

The salmon they are playing, and leaping in the brook, Sir,
They hop into the kettle, put the cover on, and cook, Sir.

And little roasted piggies, with manners quite demure, Sir,
They ask you, "Will you have some ham?" And then you say, "Why, sure, Sir."

The cows are most obliging, their milk they put in pails, Sir,
They make your cheese and butter with a skill that never fails, Sir.

The bull he is the master, his calves he likes to boss, Sir,
He beats them when they loaf about, he's never at a loss, Sir.

The calves are very helpful, themselves they skin and kill, Sir.
They turn into a tasty roast before you drink your fill, Sir.

The hens lay eggs colossal, so big and round and fine, Sir,
The roosters act like eight-day clocks, they always tell the time, Sir.

And cakes come raining down, Sir, with cholera frosting coated,

They're nice and rich and sweet, good Lord, you eat them
  till you're bloated.

And all night long the sun shines, it always keeps a'glowing,
It gives you eyes just like a cat's, to see where you are going.

The moon is also beaming, it's always full, I vow, Sir,
A bottle for a telescope, I'm looking at it now, Sir.

Two dollars for carousing they give each day, and more, Sir,
For if you're good and lazy, they will even give you four, Sir.

Support your wife and kids? Why, the county pays for
  that, Sir,
You'd slap officials down and out if they should leave you
  flat, Sir.

And if you've any bastards, you're freed of their support, Sir,
As you can guess since I am spinning verses for your sport, Sir.

You walk about in velvet, with silver buttons bright, Sir,
You puff away at meerschaum pipes, your women pack them
  tight, Sir.

The dear old ladies struggle, and sweat for us, and labor,
And if they're cross, they spank themselves, they do it as a
  favor.

And so we play the fiddle, and all of us are glad, Sir,
We dance a merry polka, boys, and that is not so bad, Sir.

I'm off to Oleana, to lead a life of pleasure,
A beggar here, a count out there, with riches in full measure.

I'm coming, Oleana, I've left my native doorway,
I've made my choice, I've said good-by to slavery in Norway.
    Ole – Ole – Ole – oh! Oleana!
    Ole – Ole – Ole – oh! Oleana! *

* The original of the ballad, by Ditmar Meidell, with the music, may be found in *Norwegian Emigrant Songs and Ballads*, pp. 187–198. The translation appears in *Common Ground*, 5:73–77 (Autumn 1944); *Norwegian-American Studies and Records* (Northfield, Minn.), 14:117–121 (1944); and *Grass Roots History* (Minneapolis, 1947), pp. 50–53.

The greatest benefactor of the North

FROM H. LARSEN, IN OLE BULL'S COLONY, PENNSYLVANIA, TO HIS COUNTRYMEN *

1852

The stretch of land is located fifty or sixty miles from Wellesville, Genessee station, in so-called Potter County in Pennsylvania.

Together with many others I have traveled through and examined this land, and I am happy to be able to assure my countrymen that nowhere in the United States is the climate fresher and more healthful. The inhabitants enjoy the pure, clean air of the highland. Brooks of fresh, wholesome water wind around the hills. This and the pure air enable the inhabitants to have good health and a long life, and besides, it is said that every disease can be cured here without the assistance of a doctor. The land is covered with primeval forest everywhere. The soil, consisting largely of clay combined with fallen leaves, branches, and huge trees that have been rotting for generations and now are blended with the earth, is very easy to cultivate and so extremely fertile that it will yield rich crops for many years without manuring. Even the hills contain the same kind of soil and may be cultivated way up to the top. Flat areas, many hundreds of acres, are found both on the slopes and on the top. Everything is excellently suited for agriculture and sheep breeding.

So-called tableland is also found here. It is elevated and flat, comprises many thousands of acres, is best suited for farming, and has the same kind of fertile soil described earlier. The bottom land is lower, located along the rivers and in the valleys. With its soil of black mold mixed with a little clay, it is exceedingly fertile. The soil contains the same elements for a depth of several yards, even in the highest places. Maize, tobacco, hops, and all European grains and fruits are cultivated more profitably here. A great wealth of coal and iron lies in the big hills. Coal has been found at a depth of only a few yards. Likewise salt has been found, and it is said that this land contains many other valuable products not yet unearthed.

The forest consists mainly of the so-called hemlock (*Abies canadensis*), a kind of fir tree which may be sold very profitably – and the seed

* This letter was reprinted by *Bergens Stiftstidende* from a New York newspaper and then printed again in *Morgenbladet,* December 7, 1852. It is credited to a gardener named H. Larsen.

is also of great value. Also there are oaks and many beeches; birch trees in untold numbers; sugar maple (*Acer saccharinus*), from which is drawn the well-known syrup which supplies excellent sugar (such a tree may yield from three to six dollars' worth of sugar a year); white pine (*Pinus strobus*), very valuable as timber for houses and ships; and white wood (the tulip tree), excellent for all kinds of carpenter's work. Besides there are walnut, chestnut, plane, chokecherry, wild apple, and cherry trees here—a great many grapes and untold quantities of all kinds of edible berries. The land is rich in rivers. Construction of a railroad line will be started soon.

We all know the greatest artist of the North, my dear countrymen, but soon we shall get to know the greatest benefactor of the North! He has left his beloved native country and has generously sacrificed many advantages for himself in order to provide his countrymen in a foreign, distant continent with a new and happy home. He has bought so much land that he will be able to receive his countrymen here for many years to come, even if the number of emigrants should increase by several times over what it is now; and every industrious and honest man may safely count on a happy home free from care here. Yes, my dear countrymen, his great name and generous acts will survive in the memory of our last descendants.

Everywhere Mr. Bull goes he arouses enthusiasm. Wherever his train stopped, Americans came out to see the great man, as they called him. At the request of many people, Mr. Bull in several places gave small concerts which were enthusiastically received by everybody. In many of the towns we came through, the Norwegian flag and the flag of the American Union were flying from omnibuses, and even the ladies came out and greeted us with honorary salutes. In the valley where Mr. Bull plans to found the first town is a large two-storied house which, along with the surrounding valley, was called Oleana. Here the Norwegian flag was hoisted on top of the house.

In the evening Mr. Bull came out on the balcony and played the Norwegian national anthem and gave many excellent speeches, each one followed by repeated cheers. Some of Mr. Bull's friends, very wealthy Americans, also welcomed us in cordial speeches. All this and a grand illumination (for the trees had been cut down on several acres in the neighborhood and set on fire) gave a romantic appearance to the whole scene. At the sight of Mr. Bull sitting on the balcony playing the Norwegian national anthem, surrounded by the sons of old Norway, and at the sound of the dear Norwegian language spoken all around, memories of days gone by and of the beloved valleys of Norway were awakened in the breast of every man. As roused from a dream, you saw yourself removed to this distant but beautiful, romantic country, and this made an impression and aroused feelings which no pen can describe.

In conclusion, my dear countrymen, I ask you to excuse my imperfections in writing, which has never been my business. But I had to write because I was so enthusiastic about this splendid, noble, and beautiful project.

But Ole Bull is no businessman

FROM PASTOR JACOB A. OTTESEN, AT OLEANA, PENNSYLVANIA, TO FRIENDS *

1852

On September 17 at five o'clock in the morning we disembarked here in New York, and at the steamboat we were met by Ole Bull and Holfeldt, who was to go along as cashier. The steamboat only took us across the Hudson River, a trip of one or two minutes, to New Jersey, where we entered the railroad cars. These are like large drawing rooms, have about twenty couches on either side of a yard-wide aisle, with doors at both ends. On each couch there is ample room for two persons, so that each car accommodates about eighty persons. One more person could easily be seated on the couches, as sometimes happened. The backs of these couches can be turned to either side, so that four persons can sit facing each other and have something like a small drawing room to themselves, and this is what we did. The captain, Ole Bull, his cashier, and myself made up the whole company. But will you believe it, not a soul recognized Ole Bull! We did have the most expensive accommodation on an express train, which is the fastest; and I think there were six or seven cars, that is to say, about five hundred persons of the fashion-

* This letter appeared in *Den norske Tilskuer*, November 20, 1852. Jacob Ottesen was a well-known pioneer minister; he was on his way to Wisconsin when he joined Ole Bull.

able world, out of whom no one knew the famous artist. No, here is neither art, poetry, nor science; here are dollars and steam – that is all.

In the state of New Jersey, which we traveled through first, and also in the portion of the state of New York which we entered next, we saw the richest and most fertile vegetation you can imagine. Here were the orchards, vegetable gardens, and milk-supplying farms of New York. And when you know that fruit is part of the most frugal meal here, you realize that large supplies are needed. Melons, watermelons, and peaches were served in all the restaurants along the railroad, also apple pie, several kinds of jam and excellent pastries, since wheat, sugar, and fruit or berries are so common here. Can you believe it, in fields of two to four acres planted with maize (which is called Indian corn here), there were also sowed pumpkins, which grew by the thousand, a pumpkin of eight inches in diameter between every two plants of corn. And for what is all this used, did I say? As fodder for the animals.

At every railroad station a table was laid for about five hundred persons, where for twenty-five cents you could get beef, poultry, turkey, ham, and coffee or tea. But the coffee is as weak as tea and the tea as weak as water, and you do not often get cream, only milk. From seven o'clock in the morning till seven-thirty in the evening we covered 367 miles. Beautiful weather and beautiful, rich land everywhere. Here were plains and hills with small streams and canals and scores of villages with beautiful two-storied houses and lovely gardens.

At Genessee we got off the train and drove from there to a small place called Wellesville, where we stayed for the night. Upstairs there were twenty bedrooms, I believe, and each of us got a room of his own. Yes, we lived like gentlemen, and I would never have accepted this from a stranger if it had not been for the fact that Bull wanted me to hold divine service in his colony on the following Sunday. You may believe that is what decided me. In this way, I was traveling in the capacity of minister, and on these official journeys you get your traveling and subsistence expenses paid.

We then had to leave Wellesville on the following morning at five o'clock and drove on in a calash. We now got into wooded districts where houses and fields were getting scarcer but fir trees correspondingly more frequent and bigger – diameters of about one yard were not unusual. At the resting places in these districts there was always a *table d'hôte* laid with cakes and jam. About four miles from the railroad we arrived at a small village, Coudersport, capital of Potter County,

Pennsylvania. It had a population of about four hundred. But a newspaper four times as big as *Morgenbladet* appeared weekly, and there were two churches and a courthouse which had cost from ten to twenty thousand dollars. At the hotel a *table d'hôte* was laid for about eighty persons, and on the occasions we ate there, for twenty cents (about twenty-four Norwegian skillings), there were twenty or thirty guests.

After a trip of a few miles, we came to the outskirts of Ole Bull's property here in Potter County, Pennsylvania. It is 120,000 acres, where with Norwegian emigrants he wants to found a colony called New Norway with a town, for which the first foundations have been laid, to be called Oleana. Here he has a flag with the Norwegian and the American colors, and supported by the capital of some very wealthy American speculators, he is starting out in grand style.

About two thirds of our emigrants came here. They get paid $15 a month (that is to say, if they are good at the work of clearing the heavy forest) and board and lodging for themselves and their families. Later on he plans to sell each acre of land for $3 the first year, after that for $5, and then for $10, and at the end he probably expects to get this whole area of impenetrable forest and steep ridges turned into arable land inhabited only by Norwegians. No one should let himself be influenced by my word alone either to come here or to stay away, for I do not know enough about the project to tell whether he *can* keep his fine promises and realize his great plans. For poor people the conditions our fellow travelers got seem to be very good, if they want to work for him daily. But I dare not say yet whether it is advisable to buy land there. It is now expected that a couple of railroad lines will soon cross his property, and this of course will facilitate the development of the colony. Otherwise it seems to me that the forest is so thick and the ridges so steep that the land can hardly become very rewarding in farming, but it is suitable enough for cattle-breeding, especially for goats. Wild cherry trees grow here in abundance, almost a yard in diameter, and a sort of fir called the hemlock, with a circumference that it takes three men to span.

It was very pleasant to see my dear fellow travelers again. Both men and women cried when they saw me and the captain again, and I was happy to be able to sanctify their new home "by the Word and the prayer." I believe that they all liked me. On board the ship I had held divine service every Sunday, and this was perhaps the last one I was to hold for them. I preached on the text "No man can serve two masters," and urged them to "seek first the kingdom of heaven." They were all very much moved, and I hope that the Lord may bless one or two of my words and let it find its way to their hearts.

I certainly believe that Ole Bull means very well. But he is no businessman, and, besides, political-democratic schemes on a large scale are involved. Oleana is located sixty miles from the railroad.

There are now 250 persons in the colony

FROM C. J. KRABY AND J. HAARSLE, AT NEENAH, WISCONSIN, TO FRIENDS *

December 27, 1852

Probably most Scandinavians already know that our famous countryman Ole Bull has bought 128,000 acres of land in Pennsylvania with the intention of founding a large colony for Norwegian, Swedish, and Danish emigrants. Seven years ago, when Ole Bull visited America, he discovered how disadvantageous it was to his countrymen to go to the distant Far West. It is true that land could be had out there at the fixed government price of $1.25 an acre, but the market was bad and in most cases money was so scarce that people had to barter their products in exchange for other goods. On his return to America last year, Bull decided to investigate the possibility of acquiring a large area of land in one of the eastern states, where the fertility of the soil would be comparable to that of the western states, but where, in addition, the emigrants might have the advantage of being able to take their products to America's main market, New York.

With this plan in mind, Bull traveled extensively in all the eastern states, and at last his attention was called to Potter County in Pennsylvania. Here he was told that speculators held vast stretches of land, and had been holding them for more than fifty years, convinced that in the course of time new railroads constructed in the neighborhood of the large cities of New York and Philadelphia would rapidly and greatly increase the value of the land. Two years ago, before the New York–Erie Railroad had been completed, it was not possible to settle this land,

* This letter appeared in *Arbeider-Foreningernes Blad*, February 12, 1853.

since the Allegheny Mountains to the north completely shut it off from every market. But now this obstacle has been removed, and in a few years you will see farms with cultivated land where at present there are only vast forests. At present the Erie Railroad is about sixty miles from the colony, but work is in progress on a side line which is to extend from Corning, a stop on the Erie line, down to Coudersport, which is the main town in Potter County, and from there it is only twelve miles to the colony. This railroad is expected to be opened up next summer, and then people from the colony will be able to travel to New York in less than eighteen hours. The connection with Philadelphia will be even closer, since the Philadelphia-Sunbury Railroad will pass through the southwestern part of the colony up to Lake Erie.

In order to make sure that there will be a stop in the colony, Mr. Bull has bought $50,000 worth of stock in this railroad on condition that he may employ as many men as he pleases in work on the railroad in the neighborhood of the colony and in the colony proper. For the first two years he will, in this way, have enough work for all newly arrived emigrants the whole year around at a dollar a day. This railroad is expected to be completed in two years, and then we shall have only a trip of ten or twelve hours down to Philadelphia.

According to the report of the Danish gardener Mr. Larsen the soil is supposed to be very fertile everywhere, which is readily understood when you consider that for centuries the leaves shed by the trees and old rotting trunks have blended with the surface of the earth. The whole country is covered with heavy forest. The trees are rather far apart but are huge in size. In the plains are found the following varieties: walnut, cherry, maple, and various kinds of oak; on the hills mainly hemlock and fir.

Everywhere you travel, the landscape alternates between fairly high hills and intervening valleys cut through by larger or smaller streams, so that many places offer good opportunities for the construction of water mills. At present there are two sawmills in the colony, and during this winter it is planned to build two more. Besides, a Danish millwright has bought land where there is water power and intends to build a grain mill. Since it is thus very easy to get the lumber cut into boards, which are shipped to New York and Philadelphia and sold there at considerable profit, it is believed that the money made on the lumber will pay not only for the clearing of the land but even for the land itself.

Old settlers who live near the colony are unanimous in declaring the climate there exceptionally healthful, which was to be expected, for there is found the kind of pure fresh air which is so characteristic of the highlands. Wherever you go you see little springs of clear, fresh water gushing from the bottom of the hills.

Mr. Bull did not get his project under way till the beginning of September, and already on the fourteenth of the same month he engaged a whole shipload of Norwegian emigrants arriving in New York from Christiania on the brig *Incognito* commanded by Captain Christophersen. On the same brig was also Pastor Ottesen, who was traveling to Manitowoc. As Ottesen was staying for a while in New York, Mr. Bull asked him and the captain to go along up to the colony, since the emigrants would be very happy to see both of them again. At the colony they found that the emigrants had arrived a few days earlier, all well satisfied and happy that Mr. Bull had completed his arrangements before their arrival so that they might benefit by his generosity. Pastor Ottesen held the first divine service in Norwegian in the colony. With God's help they will be able to hold weekly services by next summer, as it is planned to call a minister from Norway, and Mr. Bull's partner Cowan has offered to build the first Norwegian church in the colony at his own expense.

Later another brig arrived in New York with Norwegian emigrants, so that all told there are now about 250 persons in the colony who feel quite content there. They have claimed land, and many of them have already built houses. The others who have not yet finished their houses live in two large buildings that belong to Mr. Bull and are used to accommodate the emigrants immediately after their arrival.

The land is measured out in lots of fifty acres, for half of which, twenty-five acres, each settler pays by working two days a month for three years. Fifty acres are paid for by working four days a month, and if someone wants to pay cash, the price is \$3 an acre. The settler has the right of purchase on the other half for five years, and if he wants to buy within this period, the price is \$5 an acre, and he can get a credit arrangement by paying 6 per cent interest. The first two years every settler who is not working on his own farm can get work from Mr. Bull at a wage of a dollar a day. The name of the colony is New Norway, and the emigrants have already begun to build two towns, Bergen and Oleana, which are about six miles apart. Later another town will be founded farther south, where the stop is planned on the Sunbury Railroad, which is expected to pass through the colony.

Land enough to choose from

FROM JENS SKØIEN, AT NEW BERGEN, PENNSYLVANIA, TO FRIENDS *

January 16, 1853

Soon after we had arrived, Holfeldt and Bull came on board to see us and offered us land in Pennsylvania on very good conditions. Bull has bought this land and plans to have it colonized by Norwegians, Swedes, and Danes. Everybody was to have fifty acres of land at $3 an acre. We were to pay for the land by working two days a month for three years, and furthermore we were to get $15 a month plus free board and lodging. This was later changed to $1 a day, and we have to supply our own food.

Two thirds of the passengers agreed to Bull's proposal, and we left New York the third day after our arrival there. The first part of the way we traveled by steamboat up a river and after that by steam carriage to a place about twenty miles from here. The last part of the way the women rode in freight cars, and most of the men had to walk. We got off the train at a small town called Wellesville where the road to the colony begins. About twenty-five miles from Wellesville is a town called Coudersport, and there we spent the night. The distance from New York to the colony is about four hundred miles, and the trip takes three days and nights. The fare from New York to Wellesville for my wife, Sophie, and myself was 10 specie dollars, while the baby did not have to pay any fare. Every passenger is allowed to bring luggage weighing one hundred pounds for the same price, but I had so much luggage in excess of this that I had to pay $10 more. I cannot say with any certainty what the cost of traveling from Wellesville up here would be, as we got free transportation the rest of the way, but I believe that the price for a full wagonload is about $15.

I have selected a claim for myself and believe that I have made a

* The letter of which this is a portion appeared in *Arbeider-Foreningernes Blad*, April 30, 1853.

good choice. There is land enough to choose from, since Ole Bull owns 300,000 acres here, and much of it has not been claimed yet. As soon as the snow disappears from the ground next spring I shall build a house. At that time Bull will make arrangements to have a lot of cattle driven up here at his expense. Of these cattle every pioneer may select two or three head which he will pay for in work; agricultural tools may be obtained on the same conditions.

For three or four years at the very least there will be enough work here at a dollar a day, since plank roads are being constructed in all directions. It is also planned to construct a railroad through the colony. We have started building two towns; the one I live in is called New Bergen, the other New Norway. The distance from this town to New Norway is about a Norwegian mile.

The Sunday after our arrival to the colony, Captain Christophersen and Pastor Ottesen arrived to see how things were going. Ottesen held divine service, since we have neither minister nor church here. Next summer, however, a church is to be built, and we shall try to get a minister from Norway.

I like it very much here, and I can tell you in all honesty that I would ten times sooner be here than in Norway, even though I were the sole owner of Thronsgaard. Those who can and want to work make good money. I advise those who want to come here to sail with Captain Christophersen and to bring their own food for the voyage. They will need to bring potatoes, whey cheese, flour, herring, and a good supply of bannocks. Do not take too much ordinary bread. The boxes for the provisions must be made as thin and small as possible to avoid weighting the ship too much; they should be well put together and have good locks. You should bring all your clothes, and heavy clothing especially is called for. The winter begins a little later here than in Norway, but we have not had much cold until today. There is now a foot of snow on the ground, the most snow we have had so far.

Where is Ole Bull?

FROM OLE L. SORKNÆS AND O. PEDERSEN, IN CHICAGO, TO FRIHEDS-BANNERET *

March 11, 1853

Since the undersigned have now for six months been working for Ole Bull, we believe that through *Friheds-Banneret* we may fulfill a duty toward our countrymen by making known the real present conditions in the colony. In September last year we arrived at Ole Bull's colony and started work there. On October 15 Mr. Ole Bull arrived at the settlement for the second time, and even then almost everybody was dissatisfied and demanded a settling of accounts. The people in Oleana were paid with money, those in New Bergen with promises. Ole Bull promised to return in eight days and satisfy everybody, but neither Bull nor any money arrived, and since that time he has not been to the colony. He had also promised the people that they would get provisions at wholesale prices, but this promise was not kept either.

The appointed steward of provisions, one Larsen, a tailor, who was to deliver victuals and subtract them from the wages, did not keep his word either. He would not let the people have butter and other provisions without payment in cash, for he said he knew that there still was money among the people. Finally the people got angry and vowed that they would not work any longer. For one lie followed upon the other. Now it was said that Mr. Ole Bull was on his way here; now he was to have written from such and such a place; now he was expected on such and such a day, until the people finally ceased work.

Some went to Williamsport to Ole Bull's partner, the American Cowan, but did not get to see him. Possibly he had been notified of their arrival and had hidden away somewhere. They went on to New York, and there they were told that Cowan would come to New York, pay the workers, and settle everything. Cowan finally did arrive but declared that he did not have enough money to pay everybody. In the meantime, he would pay something on the workers' account out of his own money. Some got a little, others nothing at all. Single persons got $15 and married persons $25. But think of it, they had to travel all the way to New York to get what was coming to them, and the agent in the colony subtracted the traveling money from the pay!

* This letter was reprinted in *Stavanger Amtstidende og Adresseavis*, May 6, 1853.

We do not want to attack Mr. Ole Bull's character, but we contend that at his last stay in the colony he knew about the complaints of the people without making any attempt to satisfy them. And his long absence can in no way be justified. Everybody is asking, Where is Ole Bull, and why does he not come back? The people are still attached to him, and we fervently hope that these unpleasant conditions may be remedied.

As to the land here, it is full of steep hills and deep valleys through which brooks flow here and there. It would take many years of hard work before it could feed its inhabitants.

One of us got some traveling money, and the other did not get a single cent for all the work during the six months' period.

We repeat, Where is Mr. Ole Bull? To whom should we address ourselves to get what is owing to us? We do not believe that it could have been Mr. Bull's intention to let his countrymen work in the colony for nothing! Where do we find Mr. Ole Bull?

Would Mr. John Holfeldt, who calls himself "agent for Ole Bull," perhaps be able to give us some information?

Most of us decided to leave the colony

FROM JACOB O. WOLLAUG, AT COUDERSPORT, PENNSYLVANIA, TO FRIENDS *

April 10, 1853

Our crossing to America was a long one, nine weeks and a half, but otherwise very fine. The weather was good and calm, and we did not have much seasickness, though three little children died during the voyage. On our arrival in New York on September 11, we were all engaged to travel up to Ole Bull's new colony in Pennsylvania, where everybody was to get work at $.50 a day plus board, or $1 a day without board. The artisans were to get more, from $.75 to $1 plus board. Everybody could select land as he pleased, from twenty-five to fifty acres at $3 an acre, and the land was to be paid in three years at a rate of $2 a month. Bull would make advance payments on all necessities, houses, and so on, to be paid for in monthly installments. You may well

* This letter appeared in *Christiania-Posten*, May 25, 1853.

understand that this impressed everybody and that Bull was a great one for making promises and conceiving grand plans.

On our arrival, our expectations were disappointed, since the land looked quite miserable. The road to the colony, which is about ten Norwegian miles from the railroad, was wretched, and it got worse the farther we went, until at the end we found ourselves surrounded by very high mountains and narrow valleys cut through by small rivers and brooks. Because the forest was so thick with trees about a yard in circumference, everybody realized that it would take a generation before you could get a suitable piece of land cleared for a farm that could feed a family.

The first month went by quietly, with everyone working as hard as he was able, until on October 15 Ole Bull arrived at the colony and with him about forty new emigrants from Christiania, among whom was the wheelwright Berg, whom you know. Then we were offered work for $.50 a day on our own board. You can imagine how the colonists felt at that sort of talk: to drudge away there at hard work simply to get the daily food for yourself and nothing for your wife and children, as all provisions are very expensive here, though we had been promised that we would get everything at wholesale prices. Everybody then made ready to depart immediately, since we could not possibly stay here on those conditions. Then we were made another offer, which was for $.75 a day on our own board, but the workers were adamant. Then finally Bull appeared in person and promised that everything was to be the way it had been agreed upon in the beginning: we were to have permanent work for the winter, and in the spring everybody was free to take land or not, just as he pleased.

In this way time went by smoothly enough until New Year. Then the workers wanted money, and Bull was expected to arrive every week and every day to pay us. But Bull was away and he stayed away, and no money arrived. By this time the people lost patience and demanded payment for the work that had been done, and besides they quit working. Finally at the end of February Ole Bull's partner, an American by the name of Cowan, arrived. He declared that Bull had not sent him any money but that to satisfy the people he would pay us something out of his own funds. I got $25 and had to be content with that, others got $15, still others $10 or $5 of what was owing to them. I still have more than $50 coming to me.

As our prospects of getting what was due us seemed very poor, most of us decided to leave the colony and try our luck somewhere else. A few single persons went to New York to get their money there, as Cowan had promised them, but these, too, were disappointed and none of them got a single skilling. Some went to Chicago, some to Buffalo, and my wife and I went to Coudersport, a small town four Norwegian miles from the colony. Wheelwright Berg and others are also here, and all of them have found work. I intend to stay here for a while to learn something of the language. I get $.75 a day and free board for myself and my wife, but I have rented a house and we want to keep house for ourselves. Prices of all victuals are about the same here as they are in Christiania, but wheat flour costs 3½ skillings a pound here. If I pay my own board I get from $1 to $1.25 a day.

When I left Norway many persons asked me to inform them about conditions in America, as they felt like leaving. But I do not wish to do this, since such a journey involves so many difficulties that the decision must be left to everyone to make for himself. I do not advise anyone either to come here or to stay at home. Deficiency in the language is a great obstacle to overcome, especially for older people. You are often cheated when you do not understand what is said or cannot make yourself understood. But I have found out this much: he who has a pair of strong arms, who wants to work and can work, will make a better living here than in Norway. At present there are sixteen Norwegians here in Coudersport, most of them artisans. The Americans are well pleased with us and make all efforts to persuade us to stay here.

As I intend to remain for a while, I wish you would write to me and address the letter to Coudersport Hotel, Potter County, Pennsylvania. My wife and I are in good health, God be praised. And although in the beginning everything did not meet our expectations, we are satisfied and have no cause to regret that we left Norway.

May 17 we had splendid fireworks

FROM HELGE K. MØKLEBYE, AT KETTLE CREEK, PENNSYLVANIA, TO HIS WIFE [*]

June 8, 1853

I have received your kind letter of February 16, and I was happy to hear that you are all in good health. Knud and I are also well and in good spirits; my only wish is that I had you and the children here with me.

Some time ago I had the bad luck to cut myself with my ax, which prevented me from working for six weeks. Therefore, it would have been impossible for me to send you money for the passage if the kind, good Mr. Bull had not helped me, may God bless him for it. You may well believe, dear wife, that Mr. Bull has a good deal to take care of. He owns about 200,000 acres of land, and at present a new town is being built with a bathing house and many other useful things. We have a fine doctor now, but fortunately no one is ill at present.

The country here is very beautiful and resembles Norway with its alternating hills and valleys. I shall send this letter from New York, since the bill of exchange will be enclosed there. The amount will probably be around $160. You should try to go either via Quebec or New York, as Bull has agents in both places.

May 17, the day Bull arrived here, was celebrated in a very solemn and festive manner. Many Americans were present on this occasion. Several of them had traveled about thirty miles to get here. We had splendid fireworks, triumphal archways, a climbing pole on which had been hung several prizes, and other things that added to the festivity. America's Day of Independence, the Fourth of July, is also to be celebrated in a grand manner. Guests will arrive from New York, Washington, and many other distant places.

When you get to this country remember to put on warm clothes, for the trains are often very cold. You must also have food for the time you spend on the train. In a year or two a railroad line from New York will run almost way out to our colony. By the way, when you get to this country you must be sure to take good care of your luggage.

[*] The letter of which this is a portion appeared in *Arbeider-Foreningernes Blad* July 30, 1853.

High hopes of the new Norway were crushed

FROM A FORMER RESIDENT OF KONGSBERG
TO FRIENDS *

February 2, 1856

I immediately got work at my trade in New York and kept my job until the great man Ole Bull arrived in this place and told us that he had bought a stretch of land which he planned to make into a new Norway, where his countrymen might live in a freer and better way than in the old country. Almost all Norwegians around here agreed to go there. I therefore went up to Mr. Bull one day and asked him about the conditions on which he would receive us in his colony, and I was satisfied with these when I left his house. Happy and content, I went home and told my wife about all the promises this world-famous man had given me, and she also was well pleased. We now decided that I would go there alone at first to get everything arranged properly, and then I would have her join me.

About a week later, with several others, I went up to Bull's colony. But how surprised we were on our arrival! It seemed to us that we had come up to one of the mountain districts in old Norway! All the plans we had made on the way were upset at one stroke. The high hopes I had had about the new Norway were crushed, and I almost completely lost my good spirits and courage.

Early the next morning some of the people in my company went back to New York, but I took fresh courage and decided to stay in the colony until Ole Bull's arrival, so that I might learn what he really thought about the project. I therefore put my ax to my shoulder and went to the woods to cut timber, since this was the only kind of work we could get there. As I was unaccustomed to this, my fingers were soon raw, and I felt that this work was very wearing. But at the end of two or three weeks my hands improved. I developed calluses and gallantly attacked the old spruce and fir trees. After all, I was not among the worst in this lumberjack company of Bull's. In it could be seen many a bankrupt merchant, artisan, and perennial student afflicted with large stomachs, leg trouble, or other hereditary diseases which made it almost impossible for them to learn the art of lumber-

* This letter appeared originally in *Morgenbladet*, June 17, 1856. It has a prefatory note dated Kongsberg, June 12, ascribing the letter to a former resident of that city.

ing. I must add that the company did not consist of Norwegians alone but of people from all Scandinavia.

At the end of a month Mr. Bull arrived. "Now," he said, "is it not beautiful here? This is where we want to live and make our homes. How pleasant we shall make it for ourselves and for those who come after us." But we did not think so. He seemed to think that Norwegians were unable to live in places that did not have mountains and rocks. There were many among us who had traveled extensively in America, and these now told him what a great mistake he had made in buying this particular stretch of land, when there were millions of acres of good land in America. At that he got angry and said that they did not understand anything about good land. After that he paid us and promised, at our request, to pay us every month. He stayed with us for a while and encouraged us with fresh promises; then he left and promised to be back in a month. But Mr. Bull stayed away for a long time. He left in October and did not return until May 17 next year. At that time not many people were left in his colony, for most of us had gone away during the winter. It was not until February that I left and went to a town thirty miles from here and started to work in my trade. I stayed almost a year there, and after that I went to a bigger town where I am now doing well.

I had expected to see Bull return and pay the people who are still left in his colony, but this has not happened yet. If he has forgotten or if he has no money, I do not know. But it is serious neglect on his part, and this cannot be forgiven. The people who are left are poor *bønder* from Gudbrandslen and Solør who are unable to break away on their own means. We do not hear anything of Bull. God knows where he is, poor man. After all, he has lost a lot of money on this speculation – his losses are said to amount to $70,000.

A Humorist in Canaan

FRITHJOF Meidell, a brother of the brilliant Meidell who wrote the ballad of Oleana, was a spirited and ironical soul who observed the turbulent life of the frontier in the 1850's with an alert eye to its comic aspects, but also with an understanding that was not wholly masked by his gay and extravagant exaggerations.

He was the son of an army officer, received a good education in Norway and in Scotland, and turned up in Springfield, Illinois, in the summer of 1853. The originals of many of his letters, written chiefly to his mother, were made available to me for copying in Norway; except for a single one they have not previously been translated. If the letters from manuscripts and contemporary newspapers were presented in full they would make a volume, and only a few of them can be brought together in these selections.*

The debonair Meidell tried his hand at many jobs and enterprises in what he described as "this highly praised Canaan, where the hedges consist of sides of bacon and tobacco." He worked as a carpenter's apprentice in St. Louis, a clerk in Iowa, a railroad hand, and a laborer in a lumberyard and a grocery clerk in Springfield. Later he bought farm land in Kansas, and in the early 1860's he was a gold-miner in Calaveras County, California. His career came to a quick end, for, having returned to St. Louis from California, he died in 1864, probably from cholera.

In Springfield Meidell, as recorded in his letters, was oblivious of the existence of a fellow townsman named Abraham Lincoln, but of the

* The manuscript letters were put in my hands in Norway by Gudrun Steen, a daughter of Ditmar Meidell, and I then turned the collection over to the Historiografisk Samling in Oslo. Mrs. Steen later wrote an interesting biography of *Ditmar Meidell* (Oslo, 1944).

things he knew and saw, he wrote with interest and candor. He was sensitively aware of the problems and reactions of newcomers, and he pictured them with ruthless irony. He looked with curious eyes at the prairie town where he lived, and occasionally he strolled out into the countryside, where he met botanizing cows and pigs. His opinion of American women was as unflattering as it was superficial. He found them lazy and pampered, and he ridiculed what he regarded as their latest fashion, that of an absurd affectation of illness. He satirized the metamorphosis of Norwegian servant girls into ladies who changed their ways as well as their names with "incredible speed," but underneath his satire was a solid layer of truth.

Late in the summer of 1855 he described the rise of American towns on the frontier. His details reflect the play of a lively imagination, but the total picture is not far from basic fact in an era and in a region of a frontier optimism that caused some people to voice mock concern lest all the land of America should be taken up by towns and cities, with no land remaining for farming. In another letter he sings the praises of the inventive and shrewd Yankees and, by way of illustration, tells a typical frontier tall story. If Meidell at one time was exuberant about the promise of prosperity in the booming West, he soon knew the meaning of panic and depression, for in 1857 he recorded "hard times," blaming them upon unrestrained extravagance and insane land speculation (in which he himself participated). Disillusioned, he set out for California in 1858 and tried his luck as a miner after the "opulent, golden days" were gone. In the Sierra Nevadas he finds time to enjoy the magnificence and beauty of mountain scenes that touch his imagination. His purpose as a miner was "to grease his joints," but high success eluded him, and he returned to the Middle West only to find an early grave in Missouri, the promise that he held of fortune and fame in America unfulfilled. In his letters this immigrant lives again through his exuberant phrases, and he catches something of the fervor of young America and its frontier hopes.

The hedges consist of sides of bacon

WRITTEN AT SPRINGFIELD, ILLINOIS *

June 1853

This is the way things have gone with me so far in this highly praised Canaan, where the hedges consist of sides of bacon and tobacco, so that you may lie in the shade of the bacon and smoke the tobacco. I started my career, as I have told you, as a carpenter's apprentice in St. Louis. But since I was not treated very well, I did not stay more than three weeks with my master, and besides I thought that it was too slow a way of getting ahead in the world just by edging my way forward.

After I had left the carpenter I went to a small town in Iowa. Here I stayed for some time looking around for a job as a clerk in a shop. But I did not find one, and tired of walking around with a clerkship on my mind, I appointed myself a free American laborer, a position that pays just as royally as similar Norwegian occupations. I worked at this for some time. It was very hard work, and in the extremely hot weather I dared not work without stop. You have to be very careful here during the summer, since a great many fevers are epidemic and nearly all newcomers are liable to attacks from them. Personally I am in good health and have been ever since I came here.

A couple of months later I worked on a railroad and got $1.15 a day. Work here is something very different from work at home in Norway. Here a man is always watching you, and if you do not work ceaselessly you are fired. Then the air, too, is very different from what it is in Norway. It seems difficult to breathe here. If you had the fresh, healthful climate of Norway here, this would be a wonderful country. But all the same I like it here and advise every young man who wants to work to come over here. But he must be prepared to work, for God help him if he thinks that he will be able to make out better here without working. But if he is not ashamed to work, he will make a good living here and also will be treated much more politely.

What I missed most of all was a friend. I did not lack fellow countrymen, however, for I worked with some Norwegian farmers. But it so

* This and the following two letters were printed in *Aftenbladet* (Christiania), May 29, 1855. All the letters included in this book were written by Meidell to his mother.

happened that these were just as dirty as they were lazy and sanctimonious, full of quotations from Scripture, which they spouted as soon as you came near them. The Norwegian farmer does seem to become a little more enterprising here than he is at home. All the same, if a poor miserable skilling happens to find its way to his hands, it is usually, according to the custom of his forefathers, put away in the bottom of the coffer he has carried with him from his homeland, in which the Norwegian spirit of enterprise seems to have been locked up from time immemorial. But in general the Norwegians do quite well here and are well pleased with everything. I believe that the good food they get is usually the cause of the diseases they contract. When a poor Norwegian mountain farmer comes here with his stomach used to porridge and bannocks, and stuffs himself with the rich American food, it is no wonder that he gets ill, when you remember that at home the food also serves as a belly filler and that he wants to consume the same quantity as usual for his money.

From his clothes you can tell immediately that a man is a newcomer here, and as newcomers are generally despised, everybody at once gets himself a suit of an American cut. The huge number of German and Irish immigrants of the very lowest classes have created the general contempt in which the Americans hold immigrants. They are so dirty, ragged, and stupid when they arrive that it is no wonder Americans are tempted to treat them like cattle. Germans and other peoples, except the English, are called Dutchmen. But the strange thing is that no one makes more fun of these poor Dutchmen than their own countrymen. When a German has been here a couple of years he no longer wants to acknowledge his relationship to them but laughs at them and calls them Dutchmen. There is another reason why the Germans are so despised, namely their cowardice. Americans are always ready for a fight, but the Germans are always ready to let themselves be thrashed. It was a "nice" crowd working on the railroad. Most of the workers carried some kind of weapon, and it happened that one worker would fire a gun at another. Sometimes I had to fight with them to protect myself, and I was thrashed. But I did manage to give some of them a couple of black eyes to prove I was no Dutchman.

The town is situated on a large prairie and has about eight thousand inhabitants. It would be very beautiful here if the streets were paved. But picture to yourself a town laid out on the blackest mold without pavement; add to this that swine, Irishmen, cows, and Germans walk around loose in this slush and you have a pretty good idea how the streets look.

The town has six churches, a statehouse, and several other public buildings. Among the churches is a Negro church which has a colored minister. It is not easy to reproduce what he says, for his sermon consists mostly of such screaming that one might expect his liver and lungs to shake loose in his body. These yells are accompanied by the most furious gestures. You ought to see the little Negro children. Every time I meet one of them I simply have to go and scratch his head the way you do with little black kittens.

A while ago there arrived here in Springfield thirty pieces of Norwegian beef enveloped in homespun and sacking. The beef consisted of human beings of both sexes and smelled strongly of old cheese, smoked food, and other such national delicacies. They have all settled around here and are well satisfied. Among them was also a schoolteacher who has to work at odd jobs like everybody else, though he is able "to teach the young both catechism and explanations."

The women look, and are painted, like angels

WRITTEN AT SPRINGFIELD, ILLINOIS

May 1854

Yesterday was Sunday. I went to church in the morning. I had decided to use the afternoon for letter writing and already had pen in hand when the sun came out so beautifully and invitingly that I could not stay inside any longer. So I went for a walk out on the prairie to enjoy the grass. I believe I told you once before that Springfield is situated on a large prairie which borders on woodland. It was beautiful out there. It had rained the night before, and the grass looked so fresh and green that I almost felt like tasting it. But there were no flowers except white clover. The Americans say that nothing can be compared to their flower-covered prairies in June, but I have not seen the flowers yet. It is strange that virtually no flowers here have any scent, even jasmine and lilac give off only a very faint scent. But there is a tree here which they call "locust." Its leaves look like those of the laburnum, and the flowers are white and toward evening give off a wonderful odor. The roses are almost without fragrance, and I have not even seen reseda.

I walked far, far out into the vast grassy plain without meeting a single human being—people were probably in church. The only creatures I met were a botanizing cow or pig. People here are too lazy to care for walking. When they cannot make money on a thing, it does not interest them.

Just now I was interrupted as a man came in and bought a codfish, and as these have a rather homely smell you may well understand that it dissipated the rest of my prairie fantasy. You asked me how the ladies look here. As everywhere, they are very much like angels. But they dress in bad taste, since all they are interested in is to have very expensive-looking clothes. Besides they are unforgivably lazy, truly pampered creatures. All day they sit quietly in a rocking chair and rock themselves, and then they sew a little once in a while by way of change. In my opinion they are the rudest persons I have ever met among civilized people, but of course they may very well look like "angels" in spite of that. If you do them a little favor they very seldom thank you for it but treat you as if you had only done your duty and there was no need for them to think of theirs. At present the latest fashion among the ladies is to be ill. One has a pain in her back, another a pain in her side, and a third one has it in her head, but I believe that the most fashionable seat of illness is the chest.

God knows if this ailing condition is not something they have hit upon to ease their bad conscience concerning the unspeakable amount of paint they use to freshen up, with a make-up of rosy red, the color of their skin which may otherwise look a little bit too much like a buttercup yellow. Probably as a result of this extensive use, the paint is very expensive here, especially if it is to be the genuine article. Those who want to be in the competition but cannot afford to get the genuine, unadulterated "milk and blood" color, therefore have to content themselves with a substitute, which unfortunately will not stick to the cheek. So when they get warm the whole "daub" runs off, which makes them look as if they were crying bloody tears over their own and the world's vanity. Still further down in society the women cannot even afford to buy the adulterated paint, so here they have to try the most desperate means, for red they must be. What do you think they do? I have not happened to see it, but it is generally said that they pinch their own cheeks, and if they can get away in private where no one sees or hears them—something that is not so very easy in America—rumor has it that they do not hesitate to box themselves on the ears, and by so doing produce the most natural blooming complexion you can imagine. These boxes on the ears are the most well deserved I have yet heard about. But despite these attempts to aid nature, there can be no doubt that the American ladies really do look like angels, and perhaps the similarity is increased by the daub, since for so many years of grace we have seen nothing but painted angels.

You ought to see our Norwegian peasant girls and servant girls here You would not be able to recognize them or ever think that these lovely creatures had been transplanted from the rocky ground of Norway to this tropical soil. Big-heeled, round-shouldered, plump, good-natured cooks who at home waddled about in all their primitiveness in front of the kitchen fire between brooms and garbage cans here trip about with a peculiar, affected twisting of parasols and fans and with their pretty heads completely covered by veils. Aase, Birthe, and Siri at an incredible speed become changed to Aline, Betsy, and Sarah, and these ladies like to have a little "Miss" in front of their names. Their English is just as incomprehensible as the language of the native Indians.

Speaking of Indians, the other night I went to see a troupe of real Indians "perform." Their performance consisted of dancing, yelling, beating of drums, and producing a most disagreeable stench. I do not exactly blame these sons of the primeval forest for this, but enough is enough. In short, the stench immediately drove me away from these typically American national performances, and thus I am unable to give you any description of the degree of development that the dramatic art of the Indians has achieved.

Five cents plus an empty stomach

WRITTEN AT SPRINGFIELD, ILLINOIS

April 30, 1855

Recently I made a trip down to St. Louis. I went for two reasons, partly to visit C. and partly to see if I could find a better job. I did not find one that I liked, so I went back. I had decided that I would not write to Springfield for money but just manage on what I had brought with me plus my two arms. Well, I started my trip back, and after traveling half a day I arrived in a town whose name I have forgotten, with five cents in my pocket. Now, as you may know, five cents is not exactly big capital here. It is about two skillings in Norwegian money. Take five cents and add to that an empty stomach and see how much is left when the stomach has been filled. I went out to various bakers' shops and asked the prices of all the things I saw there. Water buns are not found here nor the delicious Trønder skillingcakes, let alone Christiania cinnamon cookies. After I had carefully learned the prices, I took my five cents out of my pocket, threw them on the counter, and got a cake which – to be brief – disappeared.

Now Richard was himself again. I went out in town to dig up some traveling money. That is, I inquired about jobs. After I had been through town a couple of times, I discovered an old dried-up looking man with spectacles on his nose. He was sitting on a load of boards and looked very learned. I asked him if he happened to know someone who needed the assistance of a fellow human being in some kind of work or other. He said no, like all the others. But he added that if I would go with him to the town where he lived, I might be fairly sure that I would get work there. It was about eight miles to the town. The man looked so withered and dried-up that I thought things rattled in him when he moved. Well, I turned around, looked once more back at the baker's shop, jumped up on the load, and off we went with the bespectacled creature for driver. In the afternoon we arrived at his home. I was received very hospitably by his family. Here I worked for four days planting a hedge around a large garden. My pay was $1.25 a day plus board and lodging.

From there I came back to Springfield, where I got a job the day after my return. I am working at a lumberyard, where I get $400 a year. The work is not very hard except when we receive a fresh load of wood. But my boss is a decent man who hires laborers to do the hardest work. My job consists of measuring and selling boards and planks, and when my boss is away I look after the other business. At six o'clock in the evening I am my own master.

It is already terribly hot here. Peach, cherry, and apple trees have been in bloom the last couple of weeks. You cannot imagine how beautiful the orchards look at present. The peach tree has such pretty red blossoms, and when the white cherry blossoms are scattered among them here and there, the whole orchard looks like one big bouquet of flowers. Everything promises very well for a good year, and we need it. Prices are three times as high as last year at this time; and many things, potatoes, for instance, are six times as much. Our farmers are getting prepared to supply Europe with grain, more so this year than other years because of the war.

A quart of whisky, without batting an eye

WRITTEN AT SPRINGFIELD, ILLINOIS *

August 7, 1855

Hansine's letter came a couple of days ago, and I was indeed glad to hear that all of you are getting along so well. The same is true of Christian and me; both of us are feeling fine. I have tried many a ruse to get him to write home, but all in vain. A real porker, that fellow! You must thank Hansine ever so much for her letter. It was very interesting. I sent her a letter about two months ago by a man from Arendal who was returning home. Likely she has received it by now. I must admit that I felt quite flattered by her praise of my epistles, and least of all did I expect that Ditmar would find anything in them worthy of printer's ink. But there you see: do not judge a tramp by his rags. How pleased I should be if I could only secure copies of *Aftenbladet* from time to time. Could not this be arranged? In the Norwegian paper *Emigranten*, which is published in Wisconsin, I find many articles from *Aftenbladet*. In the same paper I also see that you now have both railroad and telegraph. Hurrah for old Norway!

How is the railroad getting along? Here in America it is the railroads that build up the whole country. Because of them the farmers get wider markets and higher prices for their products. They seem to put new life into everything. Even the old apple woman sets off at a dogtrot when she hears the whistle, to sell her apples to the pas-

* The translation of this letter, which is by C. A. Clausen, has been published in "Pioneer Town Building in the West," *Norwegian-American Studies and Records* (Northfield, Minn.), 9:45–53 (1936).

sengers. Every ten miles along the railways there are stations which soon grow up into towns. "Soon," did I say? I should have said "immediately" because it is really remarkable how rapidly the stations are transformed into little towns. I can but compare it with the building of Aladdin's castle by means of his wonderful lamp, only that things move still faster here, where it is not necessary to sit and rub a rusty old oil lantern. Here you can buy houses all ready to be placed on the freight car, and in half a day's time they can be nailed together.

Since I have nothing else to write about this time, I shall attempt to describe how these towns spring up. First — that is, after the two old log houses that stand one on each side of the tracks — first, I say, the railroad company builds a depot. Next a speculator buys the surrounding one hundred acres and lays it out in lots, streets, and a market place. Then he graces the prospective town with the name of an early president or a famous general — or his own name — holds an auction, and realizes many hundred per cent on his investment. A young wagonmaker who has just completed his apprenticeship hears about the station, that it is beautifully located in a rich farming country, is blessed with good water, and, most important of all, that it has no wagonmaker. Making a hasty decision, he buys the barest necessities for setting up in his profession, hurries off to the place, rents one of the old log houses, and is soon at work. One absolute necessity he still lacks, however: a sign, of course, which is the most important part of a man's equipment here in America. The next day he hears that there is a tramp painter aboard the train; he gets him off, puts him to work, and the very next day the farmers are surprised to see a monstrous sign straddling the roof of the old log house. The sign is an immediate success, for the farmers rush to the shop and order wagons, wheels, and the like. The poor man is overwhelmed with more work than he can handle for ever so long. He is about to regret that sign notion of his, but suddenly he has another idea. He accepts every order, and no sooner are the customers away then he seizes his pen and writes to the editors of three different newspapers that three good apprentices can secure steady work with high wages in the "flourishing town of L." Within two days he has help enough, and the work goes "like a song."

The train stops again, and off steps a blacksmith who went broke in one of the larger towns. He saunters over to the wagonmaker's shop as unconcerned as if he only wished to light his cigar. In a casual way he inquires about the neighborhood and wonders what its prospects are, without indicating that he intends to settle there – by no means! But the wagoner, with his keen Yankee nose, soon smells a rat and starts boosting the place with all his might. This inspires the smith with ecstasy; he starts jumping around and making sledge-hammer motions with his arms. Off he goes and rents the other log house and nails a horseshoe over the door as a sign. The horseshoe, to be sure cannot be seen any great distance, but the smith has a remedy for this, and he starts to hammer and pound away at his anvil so that the farmers for miles around can hear the echoes. They immediately flock to his door, and there is work enough for the blacksmith. Within a short week a carpenter, a tailor, and a shoemaker also arrive in town. The wagoner orders a house from the carpenter and rents the second story to the tailor and the shoemaker. Soon the blacksmith also builds a house, and things progress with giant strides toward the bigger and better.

Again the train stops. This time two young fellows jump off, look around, and go over to have a chat with the blacksmith. One of them is a doctor, the other a lawyer. Both of them rent rooms from the blacksmith and start business.

Once more the locomotive stops. But – what's this getting off? Be patient! Just let it come closer. It is nothing more nor less than a mustachioed, velvet-frocked German with an old, overworked hurdy-gurdy strapped to his back. On the hurdy-gurdy perches a measly little monkey dressed in red. The German goes over to the blacksmith shop and begins to crank his music box while the monkey smokes tobacco, dances a polka, and grinds coffee. But the German receives no encouragement for his art, nor does the monkey – except some rusty nails which the smith tosses to him. The artist realizes that his audience is unappreciative, and the poor man's face is overcast with sorrow. Then he looks about inquiringly as if searching for something and steps up to the doctor to ask if there is a restaurant in town. On receiving a negative reply, his face brightens again, and after a short conversation with the doctor and lawyer, he steams off with the next train and jumps off at the first big town, where he sells his hurdy-gurdy and monkey and buys a barrel of whisky, another barrel of biscuits, two large cheeses, tobacco, cigars, and sausages – miles of them. Thereupon he engages a painter to make an appropriate sign, and in three days he is back again in the new town. Now he rents the blacksmith's old log house and rigs it up as a shop. Soon the sign swings over the door, the whisky barrel is half empty, and the sausages are dispatched by the yard. But how could it be otherwise? Our clever German calls them *egyptische Brautewurste*, an irresistible name, *nicht wahr*? And what of the sign? *Polz tausend noch einmal.* In the center rests a large barrel adorned with the magic word *Lagerbier.* On one side of the barrel is a large cheese and on the other a necklace of sausages. Between these German Valhalla delicacies we read in large yellow letters, *Wirtschaftshaus zur deutschen Republik, bei Carl Klor.* Fortune smiles upon the German innkeeper.

His best customers are the railroad workers, most of whom are Irishmen. They discovered the shop one Sunday afternoon while it was closed. But fortunately two Germans in the crowd were attracted by the sign and interpreted its mysteries to the Irishmen, who at once burst into frenzies of joy and started to dance about to the accompaniment of war whoops. Then they stuck their thumbs into their mouths and pulled them out with popping sounds like the uncorking of bottles, after which they hammered at the door. The German immediately opened both his mouth and his door and began murdering the English language and tapping whisky. He is now well on his way to becoming a capitalist, because these fellows have tremendous capacities and swallow a quart of firewater without batting an eye. I believe I must have mentioned them before. They consist mostly of the worst riffraff of Europe, to whom America is a promised land where you earn a dollar a day and are not hanged for stealing. When these roughnecks get together it is a pretty dull party unless there are a couple of fights and someone gets a good hiding. As you go along a railway under construction it is easy to detect the places where they have had their frolics by the torn-up sod, the tufts of hair, the broken bottles, pipes, pants buttons, blood, and so forth, which they have left behind them. I imagine that if the most brutish hog in the world could express himself he would do it something like these fellows.

But to get back to my town again. The German, the blacksmith, and the tailor do a rushing business. The train stops again, and this time it is a printer who makes his appearance. He gets in touch with the doctor and lawyer; an old printing press is for sale in the next town; they buy it, and with this new event we can really say that the town has "arrived." Some little trouble there is, to be sure, concerning the political affiliations of the paper, because it develops that the lawyer is a Democrat, the doctor an Abolitionist, and the printer a Whig. But a compromise is soon reached and the paper announces itself as "independent." The lawyer volunteers to write the editorials, while the doctor promises a wealth of death announcements, and the German and the blacksmith undertake to fill the rest of the paper with advertisements. Within a few years the town is very large. The wagonmaker owns practically half of it. The German deals only in wholesale. The lawyer is mayor of the town, and the blacksmith does nothing but smoke cigars, for he is now a man of affluence.

I sent Hansine's letter to Christian as soon as I had read it. I shall not let him know that I am sending this letter. Probably this will help induce him to write.

From Hansine's letter it appears that I may expect letters both from Ditmar and Gyritta. It certainly would be a wonder if Ditmar should write to me. I have waited patiently for the long letter he promised me months ago. Has he been to Leven yet? When you write to Trondhjem you must greet Gyritta and her family for me. Tell her that I expect a letter soon. Every time I receive a letter from you folks back home I get lonesome to see you all again. If I can only retain my present resolution and health for a few years more I shall make a trip home. I wrote to Hansine about sending me some newspapers through a company in Boston, Massachusetts. If this can be done then be sure to send me some numbers of *Aftenbladet* – and I believe you once mentioned that Ditmar had written a comedy. Send it also if it is not too big and weighty. Address the package to M. L. Shubart and H. Lyen, care of C. H. White, No. 50 Court Street, Scollays Building, Boston, Massachusetts. Farewell for this time. Greetings to you all.

Many new inventions in this country

WRITTEN AT SPRINGFIELD, ILLINOIS *

August 10, 1856

I received your letter about two weeks ago, and I ought to have written you an answer a long time ago, but I have many excuses for my slow-

* The original letter of which this is a portion is in Historiografisk Samling, MSS., Oslo, A. L. S.

ness this time. My chief, through whom I once sent you a letter, has left me without any help but an old baker who is more in my way than he is of any use, so you may well believe that I am busy and do not have much spare time. Our store trades in groceries and bread. Last week I sold more than three hundred dollars worth, and since most sales are for only five, ten, or twenty-five cents at a time, you can imagine that I have had enough to do.

The wheat harvest has just ended, and in most places it was very good. The harvesting of wheat is mostly done by means of machines here. Two men with two horses and a machine can harvest twelve acres in one day. Incidentally, machines are used for almost all kinds of work in this country. The ease with which a man can work his way up and become independent, the fertility of the soil, and the low cost of living make it necessary to find substitutes for hired help, that is, work-saving tools or machines. If you add to this the fact that the inhabitants here consist of peoples from all over the world who bring new and different ideas and concepts with them, I think you will understand the reason why so many new inventions are made in this country. Unquestionably necessity is the mother of invention.

More particularly it is among the Yankees that most inventions are made. When people in Europe say "Yankee" they mean every American. Here it is different. The word *Yankee* is an Indian corruption of *English* or *Anglais*. By Yankees in this country are meant the inhabitants of the northern states. If a man is a cunning businessman and knows how to get the better of you in a bargain, he is called a Yankee. What we call a jack-of-all-trades in Norway is a Yankee here. It was a Yankee who first discovered how to cut nutmeg from a simple fir tree. And have you ever heard about the famous patent for a "hen's nest"? This too was a Yankee invention – but I must describe it to you, in order that dear old Norway may benefit from at least one Yankee invention, although of a lower order.

With what patriotic feelings I write these lines! My feet are beating the time of "Sons of Norway" and my imagination has brought me back from an "egg-inspection-trip" in my dear native country. I have found every farmer, cottager, and widow in possession of one or several patented hen's nests. Every storage room, cellar, and pine cottage is full of fresh eggs. Eggs are no longer sold by the score, but in bulk. Deep in the mountains I heard the trolls making eggnogs, and in one place

I saw a pixy and a brownie bombarding each other with eggs. On almost every hilltop I saw a wood nymph stuffing herself with a huge omelette.

And now for my description of this "hen's nest." It has two compartments, one above the other. The bottom of the upper compartment is constructed in such a way that it opens as soon as the hen sits down. In this manner the egg slips down into the lower part of the nest. A poor, naive, unsuspecting hen, which knows nothing about the wicked inventions of men, sits down in the nest, lays an egg with great diligence and labor, gets up and cocks her head to have a look at the results of her industry. She has started to cackle before she discovers, to her amazement, that the nest is empty. Crestfallen and blushing for shame – for the rooster has seen her – she sits down to renew her efforts.

It happened once – where I do not remember, but that makes no difference since the story is true – that a woman had a hen. The story does not say whether she was related to the woman who owned the hen that laid the golden eggs. The woman I am talking about had shut a hen up in one of these nests, early in the morning. In the evening when she returned from the city, she went in to see how her hen was doing and she found – well, what do you think? No hen was to be seen, but in the lower nest were eighteen lovely, fresh eggs – and in the upper nest she found, to her great grief, a beak, two claws, and a handful of feathers. Was that not terrible?

The Yankees excel especially in a variety of patent medicines, any of which can cure any disease. One of the newest inventions is a heating device for a traveler. He places a heating pan under his legs, puts a mustard plaster on his head, and then the plaster, of course, draws the heat from the pan up through his whole body. . . .

A cozy Christmas, with beer and punch

WRITTEN AT SPRINGFIELD, ILLINOIS *

January 11, 1857

I suppose that this letter should have been sent to Hansine, but when I write to one of you I mean all of you. I received Hansine's letter the day before yesterday, and many thanks to Hanseman for it. I read it

* The original of this letter is in Historiografisk Samling, MSS., Oslo, A. L. S.

four times and once more when I went to bed, so that I had the pleasure of dreaming about my dear home all night. I ought to have begun this letter by wishing you all a Happy New Year, but you know that I wish that without my saying it. Christian visited me at Christmas and stayed here for about a week. He looks very healthy and well and is the same gay, singing Meidell that he always was. He promised me that he would write home some time soon when he got an opportunity. We had a cozy Christmas, drank beer and punch, thought of rice porridge, and talked of the old days. This letter is rather thin, but I do not feel like writing today; it is too cold.

Ole Bull was here and gave a concert in October; of course, he had a crowded house. As I was about to go home, he called me out into the hall. A German had told him that there was a Meidell in town. I talked to him for a while. He was very kind and invited me to call on him in the morning, but I did not have time to do so. You cannot imagine how he has changed. He looks very old, and his face shows only too clearly that he has gone through many difficulties. I have not seen anything of his son Alexander. I believe that Ole Bull is in New York at the present time.

Although it does not pay very well, I shall stay at Springfield at least another year, since I do not feel like moving around too much. Christian and I are talking a little about buying a section of land (640 acres) in Kansas next spring. We would let this land lie for a year and then turn farmers. I do not know if anything will come of it, but I have tried to talk Christian into it. Even if we should not move to the land and live on it, it would rise in value and it would be a better and safer investment of our money than any other use we could make of it.

Concerning my return, I am not quite sure when that will be; but I have no doubt that I shall come back in a couple of years or so. It all depends on my luck. I do not have any great desire to come back poor, since it is far easier to make money here in America than in Norway and consequently far better here for needy people.

The Sierras, with their crowns of snow

WRITTEN AT MILL VALLEY, CALIFORNIA *

December 1, 1859

You may be sure that I am still well. As a matter of fact, I have never enjoyed better health, and as far as personal safety is concerned I now live in a country which is very different from what it was a few years ago. One is in no greater danger here than anywhere else. I am an almost full-fledged miner now, but I have not been so lucky as to find a good-sized nugget yet. And even if I should never strike it rich, I shall not be disappointed, for my ideas about California never caused me to entertain any very extravagant expectations.

I am now living in the Sierra Nevada Mountains, and you cannot imagine a more romantic country, rich as it is in the most magnificent scenery. I wish you could make a trip up here in the spring and see the flowers that cover every inch of ground. I had gathered quite a few seeds which I meant to send to you, but a mouse stole the package one night on a little "prospecting trip." I had always thought that our Norwegian field flowers, for color and scent, were inferior only to those of the tropics, but now it seems to me that their sisters here in the Sierra Nevada Mountains win the prize. Most of the time I have a bouquet of them in my cabin, and that is the only ornament it contains. On Sunday, which is here the busiest trading day in the week, you often see the hardy miners on their way to the grocery store with bouquets of these flowers in their hands. Arriving at the store, each miner compares his bouquet with those of the others, and if there is a lady present, which is rarely the case, she is immediately chosen as judge of the flowers. But the prize for the finest bouquet is, it grieves me to report, whisky.

I shall never be able to forget a walk I took last spring on a Sunday morning. For hours I wandered about without following any road or trail, until I was completely overwhelmed with admiration of all the splendor and glory that surrounded me. I sat down in order to enjoy the glorious view. Everything was as fresh as if God had just created it. Probably no human foot before mine had ever trodden on this splendid carpet of flowers He had spread out here, and I was probably

* The original letter of which this is a portion is in Historiografisk Samling, MSS., Oslo, A. L. S.

the first man to see the beautiful cedars and evergreen oak trees He had planted here and there to provide shade for the flowers and a cool place for the birds to sing in. There was no trace of a human presence, and not even the smallest indication of an Indian trail could be found in this sacred spot. A strange feeling came over me. Never before had I felt God's greatness and omnipotence as strongly as I did here. None of His servants can describe in words His boundless goodness as well as He Himself had done it here with His flowers, birds, and natural beauty. One gorgeous range of mountains rose behind the other, and on to the horizon towered the still higher summits of the Sierras with their crowns of snow. I was alone with my Creator, and a feeling of awe and gratitude arose in my breast that I should have been given so much for nothing. I prayed to God without realizing that I did so.

Please do not believe now, dear Mother, after reading this, that I have grown melancholy in any way. I am in good spirits and full of courage, but my pen ran away with me, and I believe that the lonely life I lead here is to blame if I have shown any faintness of heart.

I had really planned to write a long letter to Ditmar, as I have several things to relate which I think would amuse him, but I do not have any more paper now. But I promise, my dear Ditmar, that you will hear from me soon. As far as your writing to me "at once" goes – that will do to tell the marines.*

I fell in love with a black-eyed widow

WRITTEN IN SAN ANDREAS, CALAVERAS COUNTY, CALIFORNIA †

March 29, 1861

You are right in saying that my letters have been lost. I wrote one letter on October 14 and one on December 9 – perhaps you have received them now. One of them contained an account of our brother Christian's nonmarriage. What a happy outcome that was! Imagine a nobleman marrying a simple commoner! We have reason to be happy,

* The phrase "tell the marines" is in English in the original.

† The original of this letter is in *Historiografisk Samling*, MSS., Oslo, A. L. S.

I should think, that he did not contract a disgraceful misalliance. And, will you believe it, I almost did the same thing. Yes, indeed. I fell in love (halfway, you understand) with a black-eyed widow staying at the same hotel as I in Springfield, but unfortunately love does not provide a person with dresses, potatoes, or trousers but only with an increased need of these things. So I left my "black-eyed darling." That was too bad, for we were such great friends; but I suppose I must resign myself. I meant well. It is written, I know, that one should take care of widows, but perhaps this does not apply to noblemen. The worst thing of all was, however, that exactly a week after my departure, she married someone else. What the deuce am I to do? I mean what should a nobleman do in a situation like this? Do write and advise me about it. Do not forget it. Should I send him a challenge? It is not so easy to be a baron, I find. Are triangles something that I should not, as an aristocrat, occupy myself with? Do send me some rules of etiquette. Remember now.

I suppose that I should have begun this letter by wishing you Happy New Year, but perhaps as a nobleman I may be excused for the slip. But God grant you all a carefree year, health, and good spirits. Just keep on living, Mother, and then perhaps we may still meet some day. It is true that the prospects are very uncertain, but I cannot stand the thought that I should never see you again in this world. No day passes by without my thinking of you, no evening without my praying God to keep and bless you all at home. But we should all be thankful that we are well, and that through letters we may sometimes hear from one another.

I had a letter from Christian and Niels a short time ago. They are both well and are occupied in the same kind of work as when you heard from me last. I am still well and carrying on with my gold-digging. Lately things have gone fairly well; a few projects did not succeed at all, but I am content. The opulent, golden days in California are over. There are very few here who are doing at all well. My mine pays me more than that of anyone around here, and I do not get much out of it. I shall probably stay here another year, but then I shall leave.

We have had terrible rains here the last few days. The Calaveras River overflowed its banks, and several houses were washed away. Yesterday you could have seen a very peculiar sight here, people busy fishing Chinamen out of the river. They had climbed up into trees along the banks when they saw the floods approach, and some of them sat there all day until white people arrived with ropes and "lassoed" them out.

Well, the letter is finished now, so good-by for this time. Do write soon to your loving son.

P.S. Thanks to Hansine and Ditmar for their kind letters. I will write to Niels about the diary. I will try to write more often from now on.

A Lady Grows Old in Texas

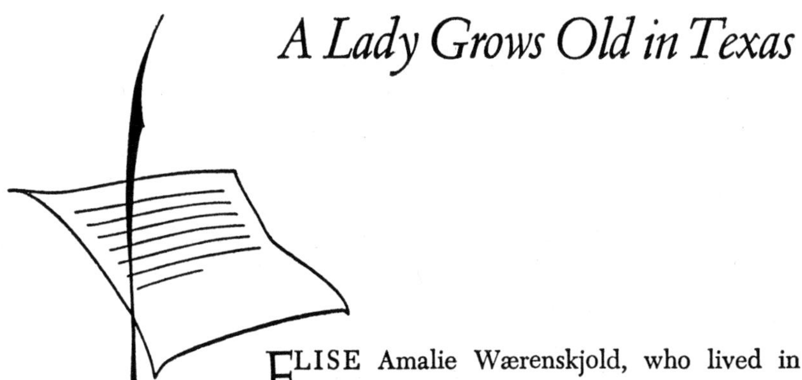

ELISE Amalie Wærenskjold, who lived in Texas from 1847 until her death in 1895 in her eighty-first year, was a woman of cultivation, courageous convictions, and forceful pen. The daughter of a clergyman, Nicolai S. Tvede, she had the early advantages of a home of books and cultural interests. When only nineteen years old, she established a private school for children in the town of Tønsberg, Norway, which she conducted for three years. In the late 1830's she married Svend Foyn, who became the builder of the modern whaling industry of Norway and ranks as one of the outstanding figures in the nineteenth-century history of that country,* but this marriage, after a few years, resulted in a friendly separation initiated by the wife, a bold and courageous step for her to take in a period when divorce carried a serious stigma. She soon set about launching another school, this one a training school in handicrafts for girls, in the village of Lillesand. Seeking accommodations for this enterprise in one of the public schools of Lillesand, she was rebuffed by the mayor and crustily told that no woman should bring forward a proposal of such a nature. She was not subdued by this reverse, but established her school, and it continued successfully until she left for America. Meanwhile, she interested herself in temperance and in 1843 published a cogently written brochure on the evils of alcohol. This booklet was remembered a century later when Hartvig Johnsen published a short life of "Elise Tvede" as a pioneer in the temperance movement in Norway. †

* See Arne Odd Johnsen, *Svend Foyn og Hans Dagbok* (Oslo, 1943).

† Mrs. Wærenskjold's brochure was published at Christianssand, and a copy is in the library of the University of Oslo.

In the early 1840's this pre-modern woman found herself deeply interested in the United States, probably as a direct result of the agitation carried on by her friend Johan R. Reiersen, and in 1846–1847 she edited the magazine *Norway and America*, which he had started in 1845. Then, in 1847, she herself emigrated to Texas and shortly thereafter married again, this time J. M. C. W. Wærenskjold, one of the leaders in the Norwegian settlements in Texas, in whose party she had left Norway for America.*

From Texas Mrs. Wærenskjold wrote numerous letters, some to newspapers in Norway in defense of Texas and America, some to personal friends. In the late 1860's she wrote an extensive magazine article presenting the history of the Norwegian colony in Texas, and at various times she contributed briefer articles and letters to the Norwegian-American newspapers. Toward the end of her life she was engaged again in writing the story of the Texas settlements, but that work was left unfinished and seems now to have been lost.

In 1925 many of Mrs. Wærenskjold's personal letters to an old friend in Norway, Thomine Dannevig, were published in the Norwegian newspaper *Tønsberg Blad* (May 11–26, 1925), and these, together with various newspaper letters and articles, have been translated into English by the Verdandi Study Club of Minneapolis. From these translations, supplemented by a few letters located by Dr. Qualey in later Norwegian-American newspapers and a dozen original manuscript letters of Mrs. Wærenskjold preserved in the archives of the Norwegian-American Historical Association at Northfield, Minnesota, I have drawn the extracts presented below – a series of letters and writings extending from 1852 to 1894, all of them written at her home in Four-Mile Prairie, Texas. Ultimately a separate volume recording the full texts of the Wærenskjold letters and articles will be published, and the precise source of each item will there be documented.

Meanwhile, in these pages, although much detail has necessarily been omitted, the reader is drawn into the circle of the Texas home and family of Elise Wærenskjold and with her can look out upon a Norwegian colony in the South, as well as upon events on both sides of the

* On Mrs. Wærenskjold and the Texas settlements, see my chapter on "Southern Colonization and the Western Settlements," in *Norwegian Migration*, vol. 1, pp. 177–195. An interesting account of Mrs. Wærenskjold is given by R. B. Anderson in his *First Chapter of Norwegian Immigration* (Madison, 4th edition, 1906), pp. 379–386.

Atlantic, as reflected in her sensitive mind. Here are her commentaries on people and events, on foods and drink, on beliefs and religion, on special celebrations and humdrum affairs, on the place of books in the immigrant life, on sickness and death, on family and community life, on failures and triumphs, and occasionally on political and other happenings in the old country. Good times or bad, she never wavered in her devotion to Texas, and she was ever ready to spring to its defense. Her interests were not bounded provincially by state or region, however, and in her later years she turned more and more to reading, following alertly and critically the newer writers who were appearing in her native land.

Most people here are Methodists

December 27, 1852. I should like to have various kinds of fruit stones and seeds sent over here to be planted. We have many good things in Norway that are lacking here; but it is not the fault of the land, for we could hardly expect to harvest what we have never sowed. Such a simple thing as ale I haven't been able to get up till now because of a lack of yeast; but since the last emigrants brought yeast with them, almost all of us have now brewed ale for Christmas, and it has never tasted so good to me as now. I haven't tasted a glass of wine in four years. If I could get fruit, I would certainly have wine and [fruit] juice too. It is certain that when one is suffering from fever thirst, one misses refreshing drinks, especially since cold water is looked upon as harmful.

Last summer there was quite an unusual amount of sickness here. We were spared for a long time, but then Wilhelm got the fever, and since there was no quinine in the store or anywhere else in the neighborhood, he couldn't break it. Anne, the maid, had to do part of his work, so she got it too, and then when I was left alone, Otto and I got it also. After a few days had passed, however, we were lucky enough to get some quinine. It is wonderful how quickly and surely one can break the fever with quinine. In the shops it was soon sold out to the doctors, and so the Norwegians got little. The result was that nine people died, most of whom surely could have been saved if they had had this remedy. A widow who lives in our old house had fever every day for several weeks and at last grew so weak that we feared for her life, but finally she got hold of some quinine, and from the moment she took it, she was entirely free from fever.

My husband had sent out an invitation to people to pledge an annual contribution for a Norwegian Lutheran minister, and in a half-day something over $70 was pledged by only half of the settlement's inhabitants, so it seemed likely that the matter would progress satisfactorily, but these many deaths have so depressed most of the people that the matter has come to a complete standstill for a while. We are now expecting Gjestvang and ten or eleven families from Hedemark. If they should settle down here it is possible that something may come of it. There are all kinds of religions here, as you no doubt know, but most people are Methodists. They hold various kinds of meetings, of which their camp meetings deserve to be noted. They are held preferably in the fall and last for several days, when a number of ministers preach day and night, baptize adults as well as children, perform marriage ceremonies, and administer the holy sacraments. People assemble then from many miles around; some live in wagons, some in tents, and some in lodging houses that have been erected at the place where the camp meetings are held. There is no church there, but an open shed serves as such; into it some benches are brought which are perfectly in keeping with the building. People bring food with them in abundance and are most hospitable.

There is nothing unusual about their sermons or hymns, or their baptism or the sacrament of the Lord's Supper, which are administered about as with us; but in the afternoon all the men go to one side and all the women to another for private prayer. There they alternate song and prayer, which one of the women says in a very loud voice. During these long and vehement prayers, they kneel at first, each in his own place, but gradually as they become more and more excited soon one, then another, will begin to scream and cry out, clap his hands, strike those standing nearest him, throw himself down on the ground, and on the whole act as one who is crazy or possessed by a devil. The others press around the inspired ones and continue singing and praying. The same noise takes place in the evening after the sermon and after the minister's most zealous incitement. It seems as if they believed they could not get into heaven unless they took it by storm. There was no edification for me in this. Several of the Norwegians have abandoned their Lutheran faith. Andreas and Mads Vincentz have been baptized and have gone over to the Carmelites, Marie Grøgaard to the Episcopalians, Mother Staack to the Methodists, and her brother to the Baptists. I wish very much that we could soon get a good Lutheran minister.

The Fourth of July was celebrated by the Norwegians in the settlement, one and all, and each person contributed either food or money. Wærenskjold gave half an ox and fifty cents. They gathered in the morning and continued celebrating a good twenty-four hours. They ate and drank lustily. A very few danced a little. Wærenskjold made a speech. As for me, I would rather have had nothing to do with the whole riotous affair, but such things are just what Wilhelm likes, especially when he can be at the head of the whole affair. Of what we are accustomed to call amusements I have few or none. My greatest joy is Otto, and then I also have a great satisfaction in seeing our various domestic animals thrive and multiply. Now you must soon send me a letter again. To get letters from Norway is one of my greatest pleasures, but with the exception of Gjestvang almost no one writes except when emigrants are coming; then we usually get a lot of newspapers too and a few books, which we read over and over until the next year when emigrants come again.

Cattle-breeding is our principal livelihood

January 6, 1857. You no doubt know that cattle-breeding is our principal means of livelihood. We do not plan to sell the cows, but only the steers until we can acquire about two hundred calves a year. This spring we can expect about seventy. Cows and calves are now $15 each, and a three-year old untrained ox costs the same. When it is trained for work, it costs much more. We have four mares, a horse, and a mule. The latter is unusually gentle and sure-footed. It is the children's and my riding horse. Niels sits in my lap and Otto behind me. We do have a four-wheeled carriage but very seldom use it.

We have sixty-two sheep, and this month and next we are expecting many lambs. I help clip the sheep, but I am not very good at it. I can clip only one sheep while the others clip two. Wilhelm can keep up with anyone. He is very quick at all kinds of work. I do not know how many pigs we have, not because we have so many, but because pigs are so difficult to keep track of.

Since I hate liquor, it is a great joy to me that Wilhelm never tastes it. He has organized a temperance society in our settlement, and since that time the community has become so respectable and sober that it is a real pleasure.

All of us Norwegians, about eighty persons counting young and old, can come together for a social gathering without having strong drink, but we do have coffee, ale, milk, and mead, and food in abundance at our gatherings.

In the older Norwegian settlement there is a disgusting amount of drinking, among both the Norwegians and the Americans. A young Norwegian boy shot himself as a result of his addiction to drink, and recently an American was stabbed to death by another American, likewise because of drunkenness. Drinking, quarreling, and fighting are common there. Yes, liquor destroys both body and soul.

We have organized a reading club

February 26, 1858. Even though we Norwegians find ourselves content and happy in our new home, which is thousands of miles away from our mother country, we still cherish in our loving hearts the memory of old Norway and our countrymen over there. Every possible link with the beloved land of our birth is important and precious to us. For that reason, we Norwegians, Swedish, and Danish immigrants of this little settlement of Four-Mile Prairie have organized a reading club. As the group comprises only sixteen families, the total fund for the purchase of books is very small ($22). We are presuming, therefore, to ask our countrymen who may be interested in their distant brothers and sisters in Texas, for a gift of some books, to be delivered to the publisher, Jacob Dybwad, of Christiania. We should appreciate it if the kind donors would write their names in the book or books which they are good enough to donate. We shall gratefully welcome each book whether it is new or old. Because I am personally acquainted with several of the publishers, I am taking the liberty of appealing to them for a small donation. They must have many volumes that will not be sold out.

Many good books of the older authors have perhaps now little or no value in Norway as they are supplanted by the more recent writers. That is not the case here, where we so rarely have the opportunity to procure Norwegian books, as very few had the forethought to take books with them when they left Norway. The various editors would do us a great service if they would reprint these lines in their respective newspapers.

In 1854 a theological candidate, A. E. Fredrichson, was called as pastor to Four-Mile Prairie. That same year, a small, simple church was begun in the settlement and was dedicated immediately after the pastor's arrival the following year. Each member paid from $3 to $8 yearly toward his salary, not including the festal offerings and fees for baptisms, funerals, and the like. Some widows and spinsters subscribed $1 or $2. As Pastor Fredrichson plans to return this winter, it would be very desirable if a Chirstian-minded theologian would come to us. He assuredly must not come for any temporal gain, because he could not count on more than $300 annually and a simple house, from all three settlements.

Neighbors here are very kind to one another

October 16, 1858. You probably heard from your brother, to whom I have written a couple of times this summer, that I again expected a little boy, and now I can tell you, God be praised, that the baby arrived happy and well the fourth of this month. I cannot express to you how glad I was that everything went well because, after all, I am no longer young and, therefore, I was worried for fear I might have to leave my beloved children. Neither Wilhelm nor I have a single relative in this country, so it isn't easy to say what Wilhelm would have done with the children if I had died, because it is absolutely against the custom in this country for a white girl to keep house for a widower – and as to a stepmother, well, they are seldom good.

But, thank God, I am entirely well again and hope that the Almighty will grant me yet a few years with my sweet little boys. The little one shall be named Thorvald August after your dear Thorvald and a little German friend I had on the emigrant ship. I can truly say that the neighbors here are very kind to one another on occasions such as this, for they look after and provide one another with food. That is to say, our neighbors in the country; the city women, on the other hand, follow the American customs.

They have organized a temperance society

March 24, 1860. This winter we had a visit from a minister, Elling Eielsen, who was ordained in Wisconsin, where he and his family live. He is a Haugean, to be sure, but a particularly capable man who is an untiring worker, although he is an old man. He visited all the Norwegians and preached every day and nearly all day. Thus, the day we had communion, he preached an especially good sermon first, then gave a long talk to the communicants. In the afternoon he first talked with the people about organizing a religious school and managed to arrange for us to have a Sunday school. Following that, he took up the temperance question, in which he is keenly interested.

He spent the most time in the Norwegian settlement at Brownsboro, where the Norwegians are great lovers of intoxicating drinks. He and my husband have again organized a temperance society there, since the one which my husband started five years ago died out almost immediately, partly because they had completely misunderstood the rules and thought that one might drink liquor if only one did not become intoxicated, and partly because there was no one who took charge of promoting the cause. This time we hope that with God's help it may fare better, as they seemed to be deeply moved by the minister's presentation and admonitions.

He confirmed four adults who had not wanted to be confirmed when Frederichson was the minister here. One of these was a married woman.

Eielsen undertook this long and difficult journey without arranging any guarantee of compensation for his expenses and his time, in fact, without the slightest indication that he expected that anyone should pay him. He does not accept offerings. Of course, they paid him something, but I very much doubt that his expenses were covered. I presume that he received about a hundred dollars in the three settlements.

It was the general wish that he would move down here to be our minister, and I think we could not find anyone better fitted to work here.

We had snow four times this winter, and three times it lasted for several days. The poor starving cattle, which had nothing to eat, were nearly covered with ice. A great many cattle, swine, and sheep died this winter, and people have had a very costly lesson not to be so completely unconcerned about winter. I do not know a single person who had so much as stacked his straw. We had all left it on the ground, where it spoiled. We still do not know for sure how much we have lost, for we have not yet collected our livestock. Spring is very late this year, and the old saying "While the grass grows, the cows die" has been literally fulfilled, for most of the cattle have died after the grass began to grow.

Many who had no work in Norway are doing fairly well here. There are nineteen Norwegian families in our settlement. They are all satisfied, and I know of no one here who wishes he were back again. They are all prospering. My husband recently had a letter from a man who moved away from here to Wisconsin. He says that he often calls himself a fool because he sold his land and moved away from Texas. There is scarcely any doubt that it is now more profitable to come to Texas than to go to the northern states, according to what all those who come from them say.

A Haugean, but untiring in his religious work

March 25, 1860. I suppose that Wilhelm has told you that Otto and Niels go to Sunday school, where they are taught catechism and the testaments of the Bible. "That school is fun," Niels said the first time he attended. It was certainly needed here, as many children grew up in complete ignorance of the teachings of religion. It was started by Pastor Eielsen, who visited us last winter. Perhaps you have heard people talk about him, and hardly in a complimentary manner, as he is a Haugean who was ordained in Wisconsin. But he is a capable and unselfish man, untiring in his religious work. He is not trying to make money on his religion, and his manner shows that he does not consider himself better than others, which our former pastor did. He has now returned to his home in Wisconsin.

The Negroes are free now

November 18, 1865. All the children have learned little or nothing during these years of war, as we have had no school here and there have been so many other things to take care of. School has been held here since last spring; but now it has been stopped for almost four months because a new school building is being erected. Though this building is ugly beyond description, it takes a very long time to complete it. God only knows how our husbands could be so indifferent toward a project which is of so very great importance to our children. In a society where the spirit of cooperation is lacking, nothing can thrive and prosper.

I have not lacked help during the war, which was the case in many families whose men and sons were fighting in the army. I had a very nice German maid all the time, and in addition a Negro woman a good deal of the time. We usually rented out the farm or else we hired a Negro to work it for us. The mulatto whom we hired last year is still with us. We pay him $10 a month, but then he is very capable and trustworthy. I suppose you know that the Negroes are free now. Of course this is a good thing for many of them. But for a while at least things are going to be more difficult for many women with small children than they used to be. Think of it, dear sisters-in-law! Many thousands of people suddenly left to their own resources, without anything to start out with. They hardly have enough clothes to cover their bodies, and that in a country which has been terribly devastated by war! This may not be so in Texas, but it is true of most of the other slave states.

Prices of all agricultural products, with the exception of cotton, are very low. It is well-nigh impossible to get cash for your products. This summer we have sold eighty-two wethers at $3 a head, but we have not received one cent of the money yet. Later we sold fifteen head of oxen, and all we have received for them thus far is $25. But I hope that after a while conditions will improve, when we shall all be able to settle down a bit after all the upheavals caused by the war, and when we grow more accustomed to the new relationship between the colored people and the whites. Many wealthy families have suffered terrible losses at the emancipation of the Negroes; I know of a man who lost $200,000 by the change. Much as I have always wished for the Negroes to be free, I cannot help thinking that it would have been better, for their own sake, too, that their emancipation had been brought about a little more gradually.

My sweet little Thorvald is gone

June 22, 1866. You surely know that my sweet little Thorvald is gone. It was so absolutely unexpected for me and came so suddenly, like lightning from a clear sky. Our neighbor's daughter had her wedding January 19, and since their house was very small and they wished to invite about two hundred guests, they got permission to have the wedding in our house. Perhaps the abundance of cakes and fresh meat provided for this occasion, which lasted several days, was harmful to Thorvald. Yet he didn't seem to be ill. Sunday afternoon, January 21, several people who were staying with us, my husband, Thorvald, and I went over to visit a Danish family who live a mile and a half from us. When I wanted to go home to bring in the sheep, all the others thought it was too early; but Thorvald wanted to go with Mama and on the way chatted quite cheerfully with me. We had gone just about ten steps after he last spoke when, without a complaint, without a sound, he sank down at my side; he spoke no more until Wednesday morning when he regained consciousness and could speak a few words and gave Mama the last kiss. I was so happy then, for I believed he would recover, but that was not to be. At four o'clock he died, and he was buried on Friday. Yes, little did I think the Friday before, when the house was filled with gay wedding guests, that the next Friday I should lose the dearest thing I had on earth. My little Thorvald was such a sweet, lovable boy, and all who knew him loved him. I cannot really enjoy anything, and my only desire is to be with my Thorvald once more.

I must, however, tell you a strange question my little Tulli (that is what he called himself) asked me the night before he took sick, just as though he had a premonition of his impending death. He asked me if I didn't think it would be sad if he died now. Since I didn't think there was the slightest danger that such a thing could happen, I was merely surprised and asked why. "Oh," he said, "if I died now I would always keep this wicked spirit I have now." He thought, that is, that the new body we shall get after death will be exactly like the body we have when we die. I told him that our new body in all probability will have a certain likeness to our earthly body, but that it will be free of all defects and imperfections. He asked me then much about resurrection and the next life, much more than I was able to explain to him. Now my little angel knows all that he wished to know and what is still a mystery to us. Otto and Niels are well. If only they could learn something and be confirmed!

A little over $300 a year has been subscribed here for the salary of a pastor, and a letter has been written to a Norwegian pastor, Rasmussen in Illinois, to procure one for us. It is uncertain whether or not the attempt will be successful.

I have lost my husband

April 15, 1867. When this letter arrives, you will doubtless have heard that I have lost my husband, the loving father of my children. Only God knows which of us will be next. If I should be taken away from the children before Otto, at least, is of age, it would be very hard for them in many ways. However, God's will be done! It does no good to worry about what may happen to one. It would be quite different if I were in Norway, for there I have both relatives and faithful friends whom I know I could count on. Here I am alone in a foreign land where I have no assurance that anyone would assume the responsibilty of providing a Christian training for my children or safeguarding their inheritance. During the war my husband made a will, so that I have full authority over everything and can administer our affairs as I see fit.

Thank you so much for the photographs. Is it possible to get views of landscapes or are they expensive? I should like to have a view of Lillesand and my birthplace, the Dybvaag parsonage. You surely must have seen it from the sea. I was eight years old when we moved away from it, but I remember every detail about it so clearly, much more so than Moland or Holt where we lived afterward.

We subscribe to three newspapers – a Norwegian, a German, and an English one. I rarely have an opportunity to read any French except in the French books I brought from Norway.

Most difficult to get hired help

June 9, 1869. You talk about peasants living as cottagers. Such conditions are unknown here where everybody, even the poorest Negro, is too independent to submit to such a state of dependence on others. It is even most difficult to get hired help for months at a time, since they who do not possess land of their own prefer to rent land. He who owns the land then has to supply buildings, working animals, tools, seeds; he also has to feed the animals and pay for the maintenance of the fences. For all this you get half the harvest. It is mainly freed Negro slaves who take land in this way. Many of them are lazy, cruel to the animals, or so careless with the tools that they cause you a lot of trouble. This year we have twenty-two acres of cotton, fourteen of corn, six of rye, and seven of wheat. The rye and the wheat have already been harvested. Plums and blackberries have been ripe for several weeks — is that not early? Otto has eight acres of cotton, and all he can harvest on that piece of land he is to have for himself. Niels's main job is to look after the cattle and the hogs. We have somewhere between two and three hundred hogs, and last winter we sold about $300 worth of hogs and bacon. We got $.05 a pound for live hogs and $.11 a pound for smoked bacon. We have also sold some oxen and ninety-three wethers. Prices were $10 for a four-year-old ox and $1.50 for a wether. It used to be $3. In addition to this I sold turkeys last fall and got $25 for them, all told. Now that I have paid off my debts we are able to manage fairly well. I do not know as yet how things will work out with regard to the sum of money that is owing to me. It is an annoying affair.

Better to come to Texas[*]

For some time several persons in the district of Christianssand had given particular attention to the emigration problem when it became

[*] The original of the narrative from which this excerpt has been translated was published by Mrs. Wærenskjold under the title "Beretning om de norske Setlementer i Texas," in *Billed-Magazin*, 2:58–60, 66–67, 75–76 (February 19, 26, March 5, 1870). The full translation by the Verdandi Club will be included in a projected volume on Mrs. Wærenskjold to be issued by the Norwegian-American Historical Association. The magazine in which the original appeared was published at Madison, Wisconsin.

known that Johan Reinert Reiersen, the editor of *Christianssandsposten,* wanted to find a new home in America. In him, people believed, they had found the right man to investigate the situation there and to publicize the facts. Upon the motion of Christian Grøgaard, son of Pastor Grøgaard in Bergen (the author of the *Reader*), he was advised to go without his family so that he could visit the various states in which conditions seemed advantageous for Norwegian emigration. Upon his return, then, he could give a complete report of his findings. For this he was offered three hundred specie dollars. Reiersen agreed and left for New Orleans in the summer of 1843 from Havre de Grace, France.

From there he went to the northwestern states where he traveled and visited the existing Norwegian settlements, after which he wrote a brief account. This was sent from Galena to Hans Gasman, who added his own remarks as footnotes. Pastor Unonius and several others at Pine Lake and Wiota also confirmed Reiersen's report. All of this was reproduced in the *Pathfinder,* which Reiersen published after his return in 1844. He also traveled through Texas, which at that time was an independent republic, and wrote a very favorable description of the country, which may be found in the *Pathfinder,* page 136.

In March 1845 Reiersen left Lillesand accompanied by Christian Grøgaard and Syvert Nielsen, a smith's apprentice from Birkenes parish. At Havre de Grace, they were met by Reiersen's father, Ole Reiersen, the former deacon at Holt, with his oldest daughter and his son, the watchmaker Reiersen, together with Stiansen, a carpenter from Christianssand. The latter had gone by way of Arendal – they could not all go by the same ship because it was too crowded. From Havre they boarded an American ship for New Orleans. Upon their arrival there, they learned that Texas was to be annexed to the Union, so then and there they decided to head for Texas. At home they had agreed that they wanted to choose a milder climate than Wisconsin's, but they wavered between Missouri and Texas.

In New Orleans Deacon Reiersen bought a land certificate for 1,476 acres which gave him the privilege of choosing that amount of previously unclaimed land anywhere in Texas. He also received a letter of introduction from the Texas consul to Dr. Starn in Nacogdoches (the oldest town in Texas) requesting his help in staking out the purchased land. Among the Norwegians whose acquaintance they made in New Orleans, James Trumphy of Bergen must be mentioned. He still lives there and carries on an important and flourishing business. This man has shown unusual generosity toward the Norwegian immigrants and has several times assisted them with money when they had too little to reach Texas.

From New Orleans they continued by steamer up the Mississippi and Red rivers to Natchitoches, from where old Reiersen, the editor himself, and Lina Reiersen walked overland to Nacogdoches, arriving the Fourth of July. The Reiersens remained in Nacogdoches several weeks, since the surveyor was unable to go any earlier to his district, which lay about ninety miles northwest. Their companions, C. Grøgaard, Gerhard Reiersen, Stiansen, and Syvert Nielsen, had continued their journey up the Red River to Shreveport and thence overland to Marshall in Texas, where they stayed in the meantime, the last three having obtained work.

Toward fall Reiersen went out to seek land and selected as his home a place several miles north of the Neches River where no one had settled. Here they had their 1,476 acres surveyed as well as a claim of 640 acres. At the same time a few American families, and an old Norwegian bachelor, Knud Olsen, who had come from the northern states, took land in the same vicinity. This was the first meager beginning of a Norwegian settlement in Texas.

In the beginning of 1848, the foundation of a Norwegian settlement was laid at Four-Mile Prairie in Van Zandt and Kaufman counties, about thirty-six miles from Brownsboro. As the name signifies, the prairie dominates, although there is no lack of woods, consisting entirely of leaf trees and some cedar. In its natural aspects, this country resembles Denmark closely and is very pretty. Brownsboro, on the other hand, is more like Norway, as the land is very hilly and even has high ridges and large pine woods. It was really beautiful when the Norwegians first settled there. The forests were without underbrush, and there were a few small prairies of luxuriant grass, but these prairies were later overgrown with an almost impenetrable thicket, just as the bushes have shot up everywhere among the leaf trees.

Again Reiersen was the first Norwegian at Four-Mile Prairie as he had also bought a place there early in 1848, and in June of the same year, Wilhelm Wærenskjold from Fredrikshald moved in as well as the aforementioned Mr. Staack and a Norwegian widow. The last two had come to Texas the previous year. This was the region of the so-called Mercer's Colony, where every family which had settled previous to 1849 obtained 640 acres, and a bachelor, 320 acres, paying $2 for the land certificate plus the cost of surveying.

Meanwhile, the Norwegians in Brownsboro had regained their health, were contented, and had begun to realize what great advantages Texas had to offer the poor immigrant. Several had written glowing letters back to Norway. Consequently fourteen more families, mostly from the Ombli Parish, as well as several unmarried persons, arrived in the fall of 1850. Some located in Brownsboro, others in Four-Mile Prairie. A few had come the same summer with Andreas Ørbeck, who had been on a visit to Norway. Ørbeck emigrated with Christian Reiersen and was the son of the deceased merchant at Lillesand. Two of his family accompanied him back, and later his stepfather, the merchant Bache of Lillesand, and the rest of his family followed. Among those who came with Ørbeck was a young man from Holt Parish, Terje Albertsen, who is now perhaps the richest Norwegian in Texas. He carries on a considerable business in partnership with his younger brother, Elef Albertsen, in Tyler, Smith County. Elef Albertsen is especially well liked by everyone for his willingness to help.

In 1851 a couple of families came from Wisconsin, where they had immigrated in 1845. They were very discontented, remained only the one summer in Brownsboro without looking around further, and so returned to Wisconsin where the fathers of both wives lived. No doubt these two families were responsible for the cessation of emigration from the Westland, or more correctly the Ombli Parish, since this was their native parish. In their letters they must have complained about everything in Texas and said that the land and the conditions absolutely were not so good as the older settlers had represented them.

In Brownsboro there are sixteen Norwegian families, and a few of these, including Aslak Terjesen, are well off. They have considerable property besides money on loan. The settlement got its name from the little town Brownsboro, founded by an American named Brown. Christian Halversen from Næs Foundry once lived there, but he moved to Clifton in Bosque County. Reiersen, Wærenskjold, and a Gundersen from the vicinity of Christianssand established in 1859 a steam sawmill in Brownsboro on Aslak Terjesen's land, but the last two sold out to John Hansen from Næs Foundry. When the pine wood was cut down, the mill was moved to another county. I shall not tell any more about the settlement at Bosque now because one of the oldest settlers there has promised to write an account of it. I merely want to point out here that the capable machinist Ole Knudsen, or as he spells it himself Canuteson, was one of the first to settle there and apparently has contributed to its rise by importing threshers and reapers which he himself assembles.

It was in Bosque that old Cleng Peerson died, but he was also well known in eastern Texas. He had often made long visits to the Reiersens and Wærenskjolds, where he was always a welcome guest. He had a great fondness for Texas, which he always considered the best of the states to which the Norwegians had emigrated. An old Norwegian, by the name of Nordboe, who first had lived in the northern states, had located in Dallas County long before the Reiersens came to Texas. In spite of his not having seen any of his countrymen other than his own family for years, he had kept alive such a great interest in them that though he was nearly eighty years of age, he walked to Four-Mile Prairie tc visit the Reiersens and Wærenskjolds. He was a man of means, but he was too weak to go horseback riding and his sons, who did not share their father's interest in their countrymen, would not drive him. He was an interesting old man who had seen, read, and thought much.

The Norwegians in Texas have felt a great lack in not having had a Norwegian Lutheran pastor for most of the time, and they tried early to fulfill this need. At the suggestion of Wærenskjold, the people in Four-Mile Prairie were agreed that they should write to Norway for a pastor. Early in 1855 Reverend A. E. Fredrichson arrived, and he was also elected to serve as pastor in Brownsboro; but after three years he left for the North. We have been without a minister since that time until Reverend O. Estrem came to Bosque this year in June. He located there but has promised to spend a couple of months of the year in each of the other settlements. He has held confirmation already in Bosque, and many of the confirmands were married people. In the short time he and his wife have been here they have won the affection and respect of everyone. They themselves also say that they are most content here, so we shall hope to keep them for many years.

The state is a paradise for poor people; because anyone who will work can get a good job in every season, and children are no burden but a great help to their parents. In the fall children can make good money picking cotton, which pays them $.75 per hundred pounds, plus board. A good worker can pick two hundred pounds a day, and as it is light work, it can easily be done by children. Land is still very cheap but is rising in price. Anyone who cannot buy land can easily rent a field for half or two thirds of the yield, depending upon whether the owner or the renter supplies horses, equipment, and seed. All foodstuffs are inexpensive. A four-year-old beef costs $10.00, a sheep $1.50, fresh salt pork $.05 a pound, corn and sweet potatoes $.50 a bushel, and wheat $1.00. This year wheat has even risen as high as $1.75, since last year the wheat was destroyed by grasshoppers. As a consequence of the difficulty of getting seed wheat the crop this year is smaller than usual for so much less was planted. A cow and calf, which always are sold together since the calf sucks the mother, who otherwise would not come home, cost $10.00.

I have no doubt that immigrants would do much better by coming to Texas than by going to Minnesota. I am strengthened in this view because a Norwegian and Dane, both of whom have lived here but now live in Minnesota, have written that they want to return to Texas this winter.

You can pick cotton from August to January[*]

Anyone who has little or nothing to start out with had best build a log house, since he can improve that as he goes along. But anyone who can afford to buy boards right away is wiser to build a frame or box house at once. I have a fairly large house (box) on the same estate where a Norwegian-German family is living now. This family has rented one of my fields. One of my chimneys is built of stone [granite?] and the other of brick, and I have a kitchen range and a stove. For these stoves we only use iron pipes that go up through the roof.

Most people also have a smokehouse for the smoking of meat and bacon, a granary, and a stable for the horses, all built of oak logs. The stable is then only for the horses you use every day or for the horses of guests who may stay overnight. Many horses are never kept in the stable and never fed; they find their own food all the year round. I also have a kind of house for my sheep (completely open to the south and east) and a chicken coop, but are an extravagance in Texas.

* This letter probably belongs to the year 1870.

The courtyard is always fenced in either by rails or some other kind of paling, and all the land you plan to cultivate is also fenced in with rails to prevent the cattle and hogs from getting in there and ruining the crops. Rails are hewn from oak trunks which are cut off to a length of about eight or ten feet and are then whittled down to a convenient thickness with an iron wedge and wooden club. After that the rails are placed across each other in this way * eight or nine rails high, and in each corner are placed two rails supporting each other with one rail on top of them. A good rail splitter can make two hundred rails a day, and his pay is $.75 or $1 per hundred plus board.

The plowing preparatory to the planting of corn and cotton can be done at any time during the winter; they are planted in rows with about three feet between the rows. The corn is planted from the end of February to May, though the beginning of March is the best time. The cotton is planted from April 10 to May 10. After both of these plants have come up, a furrow is plowed at either side of the plants, and then the weeds and some of the cotton plants are hoed away. After this the whole middle area of the field is plowed up once more and is gone over again with the hoe, and the field is then ready to be harvested. At the second hoeing all the corn and cotton which is in excess of the desired quantity is removed. The corn plant grows up with a very tall stem with broad leaves and usually two ears. In August the leaves are picked off, dried, and used as fodder for the horses. During the plowing period the working horses are fed with corn and fodder (leaves of corn) and sometimes also with oats.

The cotton plant grows to be quite tall, too, but it branches out more, like a tree, and has large yellow flowers which turn red before they are shed. On the same plant you may often see both yellow and red flowers. The cotton is picked off when the ripe seed capsule opens, and the seed is then separated from the fibers of cotton in a cotton gin. You can pick cotton from August to Christmas, yes, even in January. It is easy work that pays well, from $.50 to $1 per one hundred pounds; and a person can pick from one hundred to three hundred pounds a day, depending on the skill of the picker and the quality of the cotton. You can mow as much hay as you please out on the prairie, which is open to everybody. But the Americans do not want to take that trouble, and if you cannot mow the hay yourself, you are unable to hire anyone

* In the original there is a drawing here of rails laid in a crisscross design.

to do it for you. The Negroes say that it is too hard work and that they do not want anything to do with it.

Twenty degrees, the coldest night we have had

March 18, 1870. In the part of Texas where we live all land has been claimed, as far as I know. The land which had not already been seized by land speculators was given to settlers many years ago — 640 acres to families and 320 acres to single persons. But vast stretches of land here (some of it very fine) are still uninhabited, as the owners live far away and have never shown themselves here during the twenty-two years that I have been living at Four-Mile Prairie. If one went to a little trouble one could probably find out where they live and buy land from them. It is also possible to buy smaller tracts rather cheaply, partly improved, partly unimproved. A good and beautiful piece of land containing a small field and a little log house was recently sold in my neighborhood at $2 an acre.

We had a severe frost in the beginning of this week by which our hopes for a rich harvest of plums and peaches were crushed. The winter has been very hard, but this is the driest spring I have ever experienced in Texas. Last Tuesday morning the thermometer showed twenty degrees, and I believe that is the coldest night we have had this winter.

The price of land is rising

May 1, 1870. The price of land is rising, however, because of the good times, and many people migrate to Texas from other states. Where vacant land (which belongs to the government) is available — and vast areas of this exist — every emigrant may obtain 160 acres if he is married and 80 acres if he is single, all this free of charge. In our immediate neighborhood there is no vacant land, however, but good land may be bought at $2 an acre. If there are buildings on the lot and the land has been tilled the price is higher.

If you come, bring your own bedclothes with you. The feathers that are used in featherbeds cost $.75 a pound so that a featherbed will run into some $20. Cotton cloth is cheap, $.12½ a yard (a yard is one and a half *alen*) for a nice calico material; thus clothes are not expensive. Furniture (nice) is expensive and hard to get, but I imagine that the cost of transportation would be too high if you were to bring your own furniture from Norway. Yet I would bring at least a chest of drawers or a chiffonier. It is a good thing, however, that simple, everyday chairs cost only $1.25 apiece.

Bring a few trees with you from Norway

May–July, 1870. I should be very happy if you would bring a few trees with you. Of pear trees the following: Empresses, Bergamottes, and gray pears. Of apples these: Gravensteiners, glass apples, and pigeons. Of plums the following: green plums and St. Catherine plums, and some good cherry trees. Bring also some gooseberry and currant bushes. It goes without saying that I will pay for the trees and for their transportation here, and I will give you a good cow for your trouble. Speak to a gardener.

Later on we had coffee and cake

May 24, 1871. I suppose that you have received my last letter with Ophelia's picture for old Grandmother, but I imagine that she does not see very well any more. I have certainly got a beautiful, gracious, and pleasant daughter-in-law. Otto was married on March 2, and they are living with me until he can get a house built, which I hope will be sometime this summer. They plan to build a little to the north of my place. The wedding was held at the house of the bride's parents, of course, and was followed by a party in the evening. The following day we had a dinner at my house and in the evening there was a dance for which a hundred and thirty persons had been invited. We butchered two hogs, three turkeys, and twelve chickens. It does not cost as much to give a party in this country as it does in Norway, since people here usually do not use any other beverages than coffee, milk, and water. We do not have as many different courses here either. At this dinner we only had roast, stew, several kinds of cake, and pie. What was left over from the dinner was served cold in the evening with coffee, and later in the night we had coffee and cake for the third time. Everybody seemed to be having a good time.

A horse disease that spread all over

May 12, 1873. I have not only a great deal of property but also great expense with but small income, and this winter has been especially difficult for all those who have livestock. In the first place, the end of summer and all of autumn was so dry that the animals became very thin when the grass withered. After that, winter came early and was extremely cold, and at Christmas time all the horses had a disease which spread over all the United States. All these things taken together caused the death of horses, cattle, sheep, and hogs, even though we used a great deal of grain besides our hay in order to keep them alive. My loss through the death of my animals and the extra grain consumed was over $200 without taking into account what Otto and Niels lost. To help Otto get started has naturally cost me a good deal too.

I milk the cows and look after the garden

June 11, 1876. I have a young widow staying with me, a daughter of one of my brothers. She bore a little boy last winter, and he and your little sister's son were baptized on the same day in our small new church. All the godparents had dinner at my house. Wattne and Bertha were the godparents of Therese's little son. Niels and I share the household expenses, and Therese takes care of the cooking and general housekeeping. I milk the cows and look after the garden. I have planted a lot with potatoes and sweet potatoes, and I look after that myself. Our common potatoes are now ready to be dug, but you do not dig sweet potatoes until you begin to fear the danger of frost. Our barley, rye, and wheat have also been harvested now.

Our pastor wants to move to Minnesota

October 22, 1876. I suppose that we shall lose our pastor soon as he wants to move to Minnesota; but he will not leave until we have another one. We do not know as yet who the new pastor will be. I do not remember if I have told you that we have a church now. Earlier divine service was held in my house. Recently two Norwegians from Michigan arrived here. They are going to rent land very soon, and if they like it here many others will follow them, about a hundred it is believed. If this should come about, then we here in Prairieville and Brownsboro Settlement or congregation could get a pastor of our own, and that would be a much better arrangement. Brownsboro is only a day's journey from here, while Bosque, where the pastor lives, is 120 miles away.

Norwegians are increasing in number in Texas

December 29, 1878. I see that a certain Mr. Larsen reports to your paper "that the Norwegian settlements in Texas have dwindled so much that within a perhaps not very remote future there will probably not be a trace of them left." I should like to say that Mr. Larsen must be badly informed, especially when he states as the reason for this that the Norwegians are not able to acclimatize themselves in Texas. The good man would easily be able to convince himself that the opposite is true if he would visit the Norwegian settlement in Bosque County. I live in the Norwegian settlement at Four-Mile Prairie in the eastern part of Texas, and have been living here for more than thirty years, and I can truthfully say that my health has been as good as I could only expect it to be in the most healthful place on our earth. Yet I must admit that the western part of Texas is more healthful than the eastern, and that is the main reason why several families have moved from here to Bosque. Other reasons are that the soil is more fertile there and that the Norwegian pastor lives in that colony. There can be no doubt that the number of Norwegians in Texas, far from decreasing, is increasing with every year.

Our new pastor came to Bosque last fall; but he has not honored us with a visit yet, though his letter of call stipulates that he is to spend three weeks in our settlement every fall and spring and the same period of time in Brownsboro. This does not exactly look very promising for us.

We had a fairly good harvest this year, but in spite of this, the times are very hard, since the prices for agricultural products are lower than they have ever been. Besides, we have had the driest autumn that I can recall, so that it was very late before people could sow their wheat. And no sooner had the wheat come out of the ground, shortly before Christmas, than we had a severe frost, so that I fear the wheat has been ruined.

What ruins a person is doctors and lawyers

November 10, 1882. This summer I visited my dear Otto again and some old friends in Bosque. I traveled both ways by train, and since the fare has been lowered to three cents a mile, the whole trip cost a little over $9. They had built a plain little house in a very beautiful spot with a charming view, and their sheep, which were their means of livelihood, had done well last winter.

Otto wanted me to move out to his place in Hamilton County, and I had decided to do so next summer, but that is not God's will. As soon as I had left, a disease broke out among the sheep so that Otto became afraid and decided to sell his, and presumably the land and house also, and to move to the town of Hamilton to open a small business. Thus there was no longer any need for me to think about moving. As long as my health is good things go well, and it does not help to worry about the morrow. I hope that God will arrange everything well for us.

What ruins a person here is doctors and lawyers. The former very seldom receive much from me, but all the more do my children have to pay out to them. The lawyers, on the other hand, are to blame for my being poor.

Another bad thing for the farmer is that he cannot hire help except at such unreasonable wages that it doesn't pay. Therefore one must either rent the farm or let the land lie uncultivated. Usually one must provide most of the renters not only with house but also with work animals, machinery, and food for them and their animals; yes, and often clothing as well. If the renters are not industrious and honest, they leave indebted to the owner for a smaller or larger amount. Very often when the time comes to pick the cotton, the renter says that he is so deeply in debt that it will take the whole crop to pay it. Then, if he is dishonest, he goes his way and picks cotton for another man to whom he is not indebted. This is how it was with Niels last year, and so it is this year. One renter left with a debt of $75 and another with a debt of $50. This year a family moved away with a $50 debt and another with an even larger one.

I read everything that pertains to Norway

September 23, 1883. I have read Husher's Travel Letters with the greatest interest, but it grieves me to see that politics in Norway has generated so much bitterness and hatred. It seems very natural to me that in both politics and religion one can have different opinions, but to hate one another because of them seems very unchristian. As I have perhaps told you, Husher kindly sends me his paper free of charge and so does publisher Relling. So I always read everything that pertains to Norway, while I skip everything about the elections in the northern states and the religious controversies in the Lutheran Church in America.

Greet Thorvald from me and ask him if he will be kind enough to send me Jonas Lie's *One of Life's Slaves*. Your son Niels once sent me *A Doll's House*, and Lerche a book which his painter son wrote. It interests me so much to see something from our recent authors, but I cannot afford to buy them. I must certainly thank God, though, that I have good health and daily bread.

Ibsen does not appeal to me at all

July 14, 1884. Some time ago I received by mail six books, which I presume you were so very good as to send me and for which I heartily thank you. I have always enjoyed reading tremendously and still do. One of your most lauded writers does not appeal to me at all, however, and that is Ibsen. The fault may well be mine since he is so generally admired. I like Lie, Jansen, and Kjelland much better and find Gløersen's *Laura* especially interesting. I had not heard of Gløersen before I received this book from Relling, the book dealer; but it is very remarkable how far he goes in championing the cause of women. Relling and Husher are kind enough to send me their papers, *Norden* and *Fædrelandet og Emigranten* free. In them are stories by Norwegian, Swedish, and Danish authors, and currently a story, "Dagny," by Mrs. Aubert, which I like especially. She is also a writer about whom I have heard nothing.

The last newspapers brought us the unexpected news report that Johan Sverdrup has become prime minister. I wonder if it will not be more peaceful in Norway now? I mean that the right wing and the left will not be so hostile and hateful toward each other. It has hurt me so to think of the conditions in my dear fatherland recently, and I should be most happy if they would improve.

A monument on old Cleng Peerson's grave

December 3, 1886. As the Norwegian settlement in Bosque is quite big – it counts about two thousand Scandinavians, most of whom belong to the Lutheran church – it has been necessary to use a school building in addition to the older church for divine services. But now a church is being constructed in a very appropriate location, and a cemetery has already been laid out in a place close by. In addition to the church in Bosque, the Norwegians have also built churches in the town of Waco and in the settlement in Brownsboro and here at Four-Mile Prairie. Here in our settlement the first Norwegian church was built in 1854. At that time we got a pastor from Norway, and he served the congregations here and in Brownsboro for three years, and he also visited Bosque. From this it will be seen how much truth there is in the statement in the biography of Elling Eielsen that we had not had any divine service in Texas till Eielsen arrived here. In the same book are found several offensive and inaccurate statements about the Norwegians in Texas, which I would be loath to believe that old Elling Eielsen himself has made, as I know that we were all happy to see him among us, and we received him with all possible kindness.

Last summer at the expense of the Norwegians in Texas a marble monument was erected on the grave of old Cleng Peerson in the cemetery in Bosque. It will be recalled that Peerson must be regarded as the father of Norwegian emigration to America. As early as 1821 he went to America, and after three years' stay there he returned to Norway. By his descriptions of America he caused fifty-three persons from Stavanger to buy a sloop and sail to America in 1825. When some believe that it was also Cleng Peerson who induced the Norwegians to move to Texas, they are mistaken, since both I myself and several others were already living here when old Cleng came to us, which was, as far as I recall, in 1850 or perhaps a little earlier.

Besides Lutherans there are also a few Adventists in Bosque and several persons who do not belong to any particular congregation. Among the Swedes there are also some Methodists; on the train I met some Swedish Methodist preachers, one of whom lives in Bosque. I then learned that there are six Swedish Methodist ministers in Texas and that they were to have a conference in Dallas, where there are supposed to be quite a few Swedes and some Norwegians. In Austin there are a great many Swedes, and there are large Swedish settlements in the vicinity of Austin, but I know very little about them.

The most disastrous year for Texas

December 31, 1886. This has been the most disastrous year for Texas since I came to this country. Over the whole area we have suffered more or less from drought, so the crops were poor, in some counties so poor that people had to beg for help. Besides, the price of cotton was unusually low, and there was no market for livestock. Unfortunately my husband's nephew had speculated in livestock and last year purchased Ouline Reiersen's for $400, and now tomorrow he must pay $500 for his land. If he could have sold the cattle this year, there would have been no difficulty. To help him his sister-in-law called in a part of the money I had borrowed from her, because if he does not pay he may lose the farm. Niels owes me as much as I owe others, but how he could repay in such a year as this I could not imagine. Therefore, he too had to go to a town to raise a loan. It is so disagreeable to be poor; but I must thank God so long as I have food and clothing, however simple.

I have recently read *The Commodore's Daughters* and Gløersen's *Commonplace Book*, both of which interested me very much, whereas I did not at all like Bjørnson's *Beyond Human Power*. I have now subscribed to *Illustrated Weekly*, edited by a Dane, S. Rasmussen, and it is the best Norwegian-American paper I know. As you perhaps remember, I shall soon be seventy-three years old, and I am writing this without glasses, by lamplight. In the evening I read and write; during the day I sew. If I don't have anything to do for myself, I help my relatives or visit the neighbors. I have kind, pleasant neighbors, both Norwegians and Americans. I have always been fortunate enough to have good friends wherever I have been and that is a great blessing.

An old cat, a few chickens, and turkeys

December 20, 1887. Things are well with me now, yes, much better than I could expect and better than I deserve, and I cannot thank God enough, who arranges everything so well for me. From New Year's on I shall have $80 a year and free house, garden, wood, and pork, and on that I can live quite well in my old age. It was just this fall that I made this arrangement with my children. Since I have given everything over to them, I now have nothing more than an old cat, a few chickens, and turkeys. I have a living room and kitchen for myself, and the people who live in the other part of the house are kind and agreeable. Each fall I enjoy visiting Otto and my friends in Bosque as I did this year too.

What I miss most is books

December 20, 1887. I had borrowed $150 to pay a debt and have more than that due me. Then my loan was unexpectedly called in while I could not collect what was owed me. I was forced to try to get the money from a bank with good security; but it was more difficult than I had thought. The guarantor demanded not only the mortgage on my sheep and cattle but I had also to promise him to attempt to borrow the money in Norway. I wrote then to Foyn, briefly explaining my situation, and just think, he was so extremely kind that he sent me $400. There is not perhaps one man in a thousand – no, hardly one in a million – who would have done so much for a divorced wife as Foyn has done for me. I was so happy I slept very little that night.

Now I have made arrangements with my children so that I can live without worry for the future in my old house. It will be simple and frugal, as are my clothes, but you know that I have never been fond of luxury. What I miss most is that I cannot afford to buy books. Occasionally I am presented with one or two as gifts. In this way, last Christmas I received *The Sheriff's Daughters* by Camilla Collett, from a Danish cousin; and Oscar Reiersen, the oldest son of the editor, gave me Bjørnson's *The Flag Flies in the City and over the Harbor*. Kristofer Janson has sent me quite a few books too.

I gave myself a Christmas present

January 23, 1889. I received several Christmas presents and gave myself one, namely, *Norwegian Poets* by N. Rolfson. I earned the money by selling subscriptions to a good American magazine. I cannot say that I am satisfied with it, as it is so far from being complete. Authors that I think so much of, such as Gløersen and Elise Aubert, are not mentioned, while others that I feel are less important have been included. There are two books that I will try to find means to buy. They are *Lexicon of Norwegian Authors, 1814–1880*, by I. B. Halvorsen, and *Nature and Folk Life of the North* by H. G. Heggtvedt. I don't think that either one is obtainable in America.

Norwegian country dialects differ so much

May 16, 1890. A thousand thanks for the books! It was a real pleasure to read *King Midas*, which I have read about so often in the papers. I liked B. Bjørnson's *In the Paths of God* very much, far better than *The Flag Flies*. I have read a little here and there in *Nature and Folk Life of the North* and find it especially interesting but regret that there is so much Swedish. Worse yet, there is so much *landsmaal*. In spite of my being Norwegian in body and soul, this is too Norse for me, and I can really understand the Swedish better. The country dialects are so different in every district that I cannot see how it will be possible to make a language from them that can be understood by all the people. During the period when emigrants used to come to Four-Mile from Norway, we had many a good laugh over the misunderstandings that arose between the easterners and westerners as they conversed. They all came to us and stayed for a shorter or longer time.

I shall be eighty years old in February

November 15, 1894. A week ago I returned from my trip – I had been away for three months. A long trip, but it is probably the last trip I shall make, since I have decided to move to my son Otto's and settle down peacefully with him for the rest of my days. My health is still good, but I am not nearly as strong as I used to be and it is quite difficult for me to carry on my work in the house and garden as I have done up to now. I am going to have a room to myself at Otto's and take my meals with the family, so life will be easier for me; but still it will be very hard to leave my dear old home, where I have now lived forty-six years, and it is sad to think that I may never again see Niels and the dear children, my other relatives, and my kind old neighbors, for I shall be too old to take trips alone. As you know, I shall be eighty years old in February.

In Defense of the Southwest

TEXAS, as Dr. Qualey has pointed out, has "enjoyed a fame in Norwegian-American history quite out of proportion to the actual number" of Norwegians who settled in that state.* The explanation lies largely in the fact that Cleng Peerson, Johan R. Reiersen, Elise Wærenskjold, and other widely known immigrants, most of them skilled in the art of communicating their views to others, chose Texas in preference to the northern states as an area for immigrant settlement. They were not able, however persistent and eloquent their arguments, to divert large numbers of immigrants from the northern routes to the Middle West, and despite very early beginnings there were fewer than a thousand Norwegians in Texas by 1880 and only some five thousand a half-century later. Yet the Southwest is important in the immigrant story, in part because the spirited propaganda for Texas was also a defense of America and because Reiersen, Mrs. Wærenskjold, and other Texans were always ready to refute European arguments directed not only against Texas but also against the basic idea and purposes of emigration.

As early as 1841 one Johannes Nordboe, after trying his luck in Illinois and Missouri, removed to Texas and developed a large plantation near Dallas, but he seems to have had little influence on the decisions of others. On the other hand, when Reiersen chose Texas in the early 1840's, wrote vigorously about its many advantages, and led a party of emigrants to northeastern Texas in 1845, settlement by Norwegian immigrants got under way. A small colony was established near Brownsboro, but in only a few years, because of difficulties in the Brownsboro region, a move was made to Van Zandt and Kauf-

* Carlton C. Qualey, *Norwegian Settlement in the United States*, p. 198.

man counties, to the southwest of Dallas, and there a considerable colony of immigrants developed in Four-Mile Prairie, with Prairieville, a near-by village, as a center. And in the 1850's a much larger colony was created in Bosque County, not far from Waco, which was in a sense an offshoot of the earlier Illinois settlements, for its founder was a pioneer from the Fox River group in Illinois. Meanwhile, the aged and influential pathfinder, Cleng Peerson, had wandered down to Texas in 1849, visited Nordboe, and reached the conclusion that the South offered better land and a more favorable climate than the North and that he would return to settle there. This he did – and remained in Texas until his death.*

The Texas Norwegians spoke up in defense of Texas with or without provocation. In their magazine, *Norway and America*, Reiersen and Mrs. Wærenskjold argued vigorously for settlement in Texas, wrote sketches of the Southwest, and printed letters from immigrants. And when in 1851 a Norwegian newspaper translated and published a series of American travel letters by a Frenchman named Tolmer, in which Texas was portrayed in unfavorable colors, Mrs. Wærenskjold and her friends sprang to the defense of Texas. Several of the letters that follow were written in spirited reply to Tolmer, at the instigation of Mrs. Wærenskjold, and most of them came from Four-Mile Prairie. Cleng Peerson reaffirmed his devotion to Texas, which "without any reservations" he preferred to the northern states. Mrs. Wærenskjold's husband denounced Tolmer's assertions as falsehoods and fairy tales and defended the Americans for their culture and "polish." Happily ignorant of the fact that his ultimate fate was to be murdered in Texas, he contended that the Americans were not "fond of killing," though he pointed out that the worth of "white fellow human beings" was highly regarded and that offenses against that worth "might lead to a demand for bloody satisfaction." Another immigrant declared that some of the land in Texas was so rich that he did not think any better could be found on the earth. Mrs. Wærenskjold herself reminded people that no one lacking the will to work was likely to succeed in America, and the indefatigable Reiersen summed up the plans and prospects of the immigrants, proudly asserting that he felt "free and independent among a free people, who are not chained down by any old class or caste systems." The institu-

* Dr. Qualey presents a review of the Texas colonies in his *Norwegian Settlement*, pp. 198–209.

tions of America, because they are "right and correct," would ultimately "dominate the entire civilized world," he believed. After perusing these assertive letters, it is not without interest to turn to one written a decade and a half later, after the Civil War, from Galveston. This, the letter writer believed, was the "most important place for trade in the state."

I prefer Texas to the northern states

FROM CLENG PEERSON, IN AN APPENDIX TO A LETTER FROM E. WÆRENSKJOLD TO T. A. GJESTVANG *

1851

The undersigned came to the United States in August 1821, and I have lived in the states of New York, Illinois, Missouri, and Iowa and am now living in Texas, to which I came somewhat more than two years ago. Having traveled extensively otherwise in the United States, I know the conditions of the country quite well. I have read your copy of Tolmer's letters and assure you that the description he gives of the people's character, etc., is utterly false. Both in Texas and in the older states I have come to know the inhabitants as very accommodating and helpful people. I have also read Mrs. Wærenskjold's answer to your letter and find her description of conditions here correct in all details. I likewise, and *without any reservations*, prefer Texas to the northern states, both with regard to its wholesome climate and because of the advantages and pleasures it offers.

The easily aroused American sense of honor

FROM J. M. C. W. WÆRENSKJOLD, AT FOUR-MILE PRAIRIE, TEXAS, TO T. A. GJESTVANG †

March 1, 1852

In response to the desire you have expressed to my wife to know whether Captain Tolmer's report on Texas is accurate, I write the fol-

* The letter to which this was appended is dated July 9, 1851, and appeared in *Morgenbladet*, June 1852.

† This letter, which appeared in *Morgenbladet*, June 30, 1852, was originally reprinted from *Hamars Budstikke* and follows a lengthy article by Mrs. Elise Wærenskjold, replying to animadversions on Texas made by a certain Captain Tolmer.

lowing lines to give you a brief account of conditions here, hoping that this will enable you to judge the value of Tolmer's communications. I do not intend to refute his statements in detail, however, since they are too uninformed and untrue to merit such attention. Even if a refutation were called for, my wife's letter to you has, in my opinion, sufficiently proved that the man has never been to Texas and that he did not even possess a map of this country when he was writing his falsehoods. If he had possessed one, he would hardly have committed so many geographical blunders as now clutter his fairy tales.

After reading the aforementioned report I am convinced that his purpose must be to give a shocking description of demoralization in Texas. I owe it to the truth and to the country whose citizen I am to refute such gross lies vigorously, the more so as I have reason to believe that many of my countrymen in less fortunate Norway are looking longingly toward the fertile plains of the Western Hemisphere, where they may hope for a better future. It is to be regretted that there are in Norway certain influential people whose knowledge and ethics have not kept them from producing or reproducing infamous and completely unreliable writings. You need not be very sharp-sighted to discover that the purpose of such articles is to counteract emigration, the growth of which, in the interest of the common good, threatens the existence of these powerful people.

Let me turn to the lawlessness in Texas which Mr. Tolmer depicts in such gruesome colors. I think it would be easy to prove the fundamental error of his contention by this simple observation. If you examine the prisons of Norway, you will probably find that the class of people who mainly fill them are the poor who, usually because of hunger (that most dangerous enemy of morality), were in a way forced to violate the security of property and break the laws of society. This could hardly have happened if they had been free from want. Hence it follows that in a country where there are no poor in the Norwegian sense of the word, the urge to commit the kinds of crimes that Tolmer is pleased to enumerate will disappear. Besides, Americans are far too proud and know their value as human beings too well to sully themselves by acts that would mean loss of their civic rights forever and would for many years deprive them of life's highest good, liberty.

Nor do I believe that one can truthfully accuse the Americans of being fond of killing because they, spurred by their easily aroused (and perhaps excessive) sense of honor, are led to demand bloody satisfactions which would not be condoned by a strict moral judgment. In my opinion, such an excess must simply be regarded as a misconception of the way in which to maintain one's honor – a misconception that once animated the nobility and to some extent still prevails among the military in Europe. This is all I have to say about Tolmer and people like him.

In the following, therefore, I shall tell you something about conditions in general in Texas, as I assume that this will not be without interest to you.

By the latest surveys it has been found that there are still 121 million acres of open government land. By the Norwegian system of computation, this is about 480 million *maal.* This land is sufficient to feed the whole population of Scandinavia, even if you presuppose that only a twelfth of this vast area is arable. At present, our House of Representatives is examining a bill based on the advantages that would accrue to the public treasury if it were decided to give free to all settlers who arrived here before 1851 and who have not previously received any land from the government 640 acres to the head of a family and half as much to a single person. If this bill is passed, as is definitely expected, it will considerably increase the immigration here, which has been so heavy the last two years that the prices of food have risen to a surprising height, especially in the districts where the greatest influx has taken place. Wheat in Texas is now about four specie dollars for a Norwegian barrel, bacon three to four skillings, and meat two skillings for half a pound, which is about double the earlier prices here. At present, the land located between the Brazos and Colorado rivers is the object of the immigrants' attention because of its extraordinary and – according to reports from there – unique richness. It cannot be denied, however, that this land is deficient in one essential respect – the amount of forest in proportion to the vast prairies. The lack of forest products will be felt even more strongly if the already heavy immigration to this part of the country continues – unless the inventive American is able to devise a substitute for ordinary firewood, at least. Thus people would face difficulties which even the fertility of the soil could not remedy. (At many of the rivers of Texas there is said to be coal.)

As to the means of communication, it is well known that Texas has many good-sized rivers which, for longer or shorter distances, are navigable by steamboats. Nevertheless, we feel the lack of a railroad which would prevent transportation stopping when the dry season begins. The nation seems to be fully aware of this necessity, and people are now looking for a route that is suitable to the purpose and advantageous to the railroad builders. The realization of this splendid plan, which involves connecting New Orleans with the heart of Texas, would bring about incalculable advantages to our young and already flourishing state.

The quality of the soil in Texas varies considerably in both its elements and its productivity. No fixed rule can be established about its quality from its color. You have to make chemical analyses to learn this. Experience indicates, however, that black mold is not the main condition of fertile soil, since the red, clayish soil that predominates in eastern Texas is in no way inferior to mold in productivity. Besides these soils, there are many other kinds that are more or less suitable for cultivation. It is certain, however, that if there were not here such extraordinary forces in the atmosphere from which the plants can get their nourishment, as is really the case, people here, too, would have to work their land somewhat more carefully and would have to improve their fields with manure. This will probably become necessary, particularly if a more systematic method of cultivation is not adopted, with an appropriate rotation of crops to preserve the productivity of the soil. It is amazing, however, that here in Texas there are places where the soil has been abused with the most depleting crops for twenty-five years without receiving any manure or fertilizers with no noticeable decline in productivity. The holders even affirm that it seems to be more fertile than at the beginning of cultivation. From what I have said, I suppose that it will be clear that people here are not very much inclined to preserve the fertility of the soil; combined with the simple method of cultivation, this is the main reason they can pay such high daily wages. If you ask a Texan whether it will not be necessary to use manuring to preserve the productivity of the soil, he will give the answer – characteristic of the American settler in general – that there is too much land for him to introduce a burdensome method like manuring; the land is enough to provide him with all the material necessities of life for a generation.

This matter I leave, and I shall comment on the culture of the Americans. It is my personal conviction that they possess, if not more civilization, at least more polish, with a more refined and finished manner, than is found among the Norwegian middle class. It is in the nature of things that in a country where liberty and equality prevail in the widest sense of the word, every individual will seek the highest degree of development both physically and intellectually, since wealth or high birth assures no one of preferment for government positions, and competence and integrity are the only qualities on which public confidence is founded. Here you will not find that conspicuous coarseness which so clearly denotes a total lack of manners. Nor will you be annoyed by the irritating and rigid etiquette that predominates among the so-called nobility in Norway, and which often degenerates into the silly and ridiculous. Everything here is open and straightforward without neglect of mutual consideration. In the conduct of the individual there is a clear recognition of the worth of his white fellow human beings, and one is careful not to offend against this since to do so might lead to a demand for bloody satisfaction.

I shall conclude this account — already perhaps too long — by giving you my opinion about the emigration to America. From the knowledge I have gained during my five years' stay here, I have reached the conviction that Texas is the part of the United States that offers the greatest and weightiest advantages to the emigrant. I shall briefly state the main reasons for this: the extremely low price of land here enables even the poorest emigrant to become a freeholder; and the extraordinary quality of the climate not only permits the production of all the grains found in the northern states but is also excellently suited for the production of cotton, tobacco, rice, tropical fruits, sugar cane, and sweet potatoes (the latter very different in taste and appearance from those of Norway). Add to this the mild winter which frees the farmer from the very burdensome, time-consuming work connected with haying and the winter care of the animals. To my mind, these last factors are decisive, since cattle-breeding is the least difficult and most profitable source of income available to the settler.

No better land can be found on this earth

FROM J. GRIMSETH, AT FOUR-MILE PRAIRIE, TEXAS, TO T. A. GJESTVANG [*]

July 20, 1852

My dear friend, be not impatient with me because I have delayed writing you for so long; I presume that my father has informed you that I wished to look over the country somewhat before I wrote you. I supposed that by that time it would be more interesting to you to receive my humble literary endeavor – the details of which I hope you will graciously excuse, since you know quite well that I am not much good either as a stylist or as a penman. But I write sincerely and from my own experience. I shall not try, at this time, to give you detailed information about any special conditions in America, because I am, as yet, altogether too little acquainted with them.

The soil in this part of the country is of various qualities; here in Texas some of the land is so rich that I do not think any better can be found on this earth, but it is useless to look for that kind of land in the neighborhood of Four-Mile. Although the soil here is not so poor that it prevents a man from making some reasonable headway, I can tell you that I shall leave here as soon as I can obtain land somewhere else, where the yield may be ten times as much in a year. Mr. Reiersen has, so far as I am able to judge, a part of the very best land near Four-Mile, but even that is far from as good as I have seen in other districts. Mr. Reiersen himself realizes this full well; but he settled shortly after he came to this region. When I arrived here and had a talk with Mr. Reiersen he told me at once that anyone who wished to buy land should be very careful in choosing it; and he added that anyone who had not been farther into Texas than Four-Mile had not seen what may be called rich land.

After I had been here for some time, a few other Norwegians and I decided to join Mr. J. R. Reiersen in an attempt to find better farm land. Reiersen led us from here in a northwesterly direction, and we had not traveled very far beyond Cedar Creek before we realized that the land was much better and much more fertile. But I must not forget to men-

[*] This letter, and the three following, all addressed to T. A. Gjestvang, are translated and edited by Lyder L. Unstad in "The First Norwegian Migration into Texas," *Norwegian-American Studies and Records* (Northfield, Minn.) 8:39–57 (1934).

tion to you that on our journey we passed through Dallas County, where old Nordboe lives. There the land was extraordinarily good and beautiful, but lacked trees and forest. I extended greetings to Nordboe from you, and he said that he could remember you as a small boy from the time when he knew your father and that he would very much like to talk to you in person.

About 120 English miles from here, on a branch of Trinity River, which is called West Fork, at the place where it is joined with Walnut Creek, the land is located at 33° N. longitude and 79° W. latitude. Here all of us agreed we had found the most beautiful and most fertile land that any of us had ever seen; the water was crystal clear, and there was also a fair amount of useful forest. But this land is altogether unsettled. We looked over many thousands of acres of wild rye, and timothy and grass grew more luxuriantly than it would be possible to get it to grow in Norway, even though one manured the best kind of land there most extravagantly. The soil was of a black, spongy earth mixed with a great amount of limestone, and I can assure you that the surface soil was at least three yards deep. Such a soil will undoubtedly produce all possible kinds of verdure.

If you ever come to Texas, I shall consider it an honor to accompany you on an investigation journey over this country. Here would be a good market for whatever wares one could have to sell; for, on one side of this stretch of land is Fort Worth, with two hundred calvalrymen, and on the other side Fort Belknap, with five hundred men. These forts are there to keep the Indians under control. West Fork of Trinity River passes right through this tract of land, and no doubt there will be steamboats on it before so very long. This very summer a steamboat passed up Trinity River clear to a place twenty miles from here called Porter's Bluff. At Fort Worth we stopped over for a day and a night, and while we were there Reiersen and I went out on a little trip to see and talk with the Indians. These people were rather unusual creatures to see, for I had never before seen Indians. We sat in their tents a long time conversing with them; this was possible because one of them knew English quite well. They were greatly distressed at the miserable treatment they had received and because they were driven hither and thither; and they believed that in time they would die from sheer starvation.

In Texas also lives an old Norseman named Cleng Peerson; I presume that you have already heard about him. He was the first Norwegian who came to America with the purpose of founding a settlement, and he has been in this country thirty-one years.

On the Fourth of July I had the pleasure of accompanying Reiersen to the other side of Cedar Creek, where we visited a man named Captain Balhard. There the anniversary of the American constitution was celebrated. Our visit was very pleasant; no disturbances of any kind took place. The Americans do not consume strong liquors at festive occasions of this kind.

This must be sufficient until a later occasion. Please accept my most cordial thanks for the kindness and good will that you have continuously shown me, and may you live pleasantly and happily, my dear friend! Accept for yourself and your family the most genuine regards and greetings.

The Indians are not in the least dangerous

FROM J. BRUNSTAD, AT FOUR-MILE PRAIRIE, TEXAS, TO T. A. GJESTVANG

July 21, 1852

I shall take the liberty of telling you something regarding the purpose of the journey that we undertook this summer, in a westerly direction from here. The soil here at Four-Mile is poorer in quality than I had believed land of this kind could be in America, and I can assure you that it is far from being as you have been informed. In addition, we have no other water than what we can find in stagnant pools in the brook, where even the pigs wallow. Furthermore, this water has to be carried a long distance, which, of course, is an unfortunate handicap in a country with such a hot climate.

Therefore, we decided to look about the country to see if we possibly could find a tract of land of fair quality with good water and woods. In that case we then could start a new Norwegian settlement. Furthermore, I know that many people in Norway are intending to emigrate over here. At West Fork of Trinity River we found excellent land. Just the same, we have decided to undertake another journey in the coming autumn to get still better acquainted with the country. One ought not be in too much of a hurry buying land, for one might have to regret it ever afterward.

When we had passed by Fort Worth, where a force of two hundred cavalrymen are stationed, we saw many Indians. They are copper brown, very small, with slender limbs, and they go around with downcast countenances. Their apparel consisted of a pair of deerskin trousers, which reached from the ankles up on the thighs; they were almost all barefoot, but they wore garments that covered them both front and back, while their hips and their heads were bare. They have coal-black straight hair, which they comb and divide from the middle of the head to both sides and cut on a level with their shoulders, leaving sufficient hair in back to form a braid that reaches far down the spine. I am told that they are not in the least dangerous if they are not offended in any way, but that they have a tendency to steal.

On the way back we visited old Nordboe and stayed with him a whole day. He is hale and hearty, lives in a well-to-do fashion, and owns a large farm. That he is somewhat feeble from old age is not so surprising, when we remember that he is almost eighty-four years. He asked me to extend to you many cordial greetings.

I should have written you much more, but I am not as yet well from the great fever; you must, therefore, pardon me. Later on I shall send you some more detailed information about the life and conditions it may be my lot to get acquainted with; but this much I can tell you, that I do not regret that I migrated. I realize quite well that the possibilities for the future are far better here than in Norway, if only I could succeed in procuring a good piece of land in a vicinity where I could settle down among pleasant and homey neighbors.

An extraordinary form of Christian worship

FROM ELISE WÆRENSKJOLD, AT FOUR-MILE PRAIRIE, TEXAS, TO T. A. GJESTVANG

July 25, 1852

I have had the pleasure of receiving the letter that you were kind enough to send me, enclosed in the one to Grimseth, and I presently sent both letters to old Nordboe with Cleng Peerson. But the six letters mentioned have not arrived as yet. From your letter I understand that a large group of people intend to emigrate this year. I do wish that all of them would realize most thoroughly at least one thing – namely this: that the one who neither knows how nor wants to work, and who does not have enough money, will not succeed in America. For, since workers' wages are so high, one can easily surmise that it does not pay to hire people to do anything and everything. I cannot emphasize this too much, having my own countrymen in mind, for those coming over here with other expectations will necessarily be disappointed. As a good example of this we have one person among us who every day pours forth scolding phrases about America, but who has not since he arrived in this country worked enough to earn food for a single day. Obviously, this is an exception to the rule; however, there are altogether too many who, as yet, have not learned the American saying, "Time is money."

Bjerke left us at once and journeyed to Rusk, but he has also left there with his wife and mother-in-law. I presume that most of your acquaintances are writing to you, and no doubt they can tell you much better than I can how they themselves are faring and farming from day to day.

The fourth of August. On the day after I had begun writing this letter I received the package with six letters, several of which were for me.

This summer we have a good crop of all kinds of farm products. So the recently arrived immigrants will be able to procure foodstuffs at prices considerably lower than those of the last two years.

I don't know anything of interest to mention to you just now, because in my earlier letter I told you about the general conditions of this country. Well, yes, I must tell you a little about camp meetings, which are the most extraordinarily odd form of Christian worship that any person can imagine. Somewhere in the woods they build a shed – that is to say, a roof which rests on posts but has neither walls nor floor; there are a few logs to sit on, as well as a raised platform that serves as the pulpit. There are five preachers present – at times even more than that – who continue preaching day and night for a whole week. The people in the vicinity congregate around the camp and remain there – some in wagons and tents, and others in small log houses which they have constructed for their own comfort there. All of them bring from home enough food and household utensils for the length of time they intend to stay.

We arrived at the camp at noon and left the place at midnight. We were at once invited for dinner by two American families, after which we entered the church, where nothing out of the ordinary took place this time. But, later on in the evening the women folks wandered out into the forest for the so-called secret prayers; the men folks went in another direction for the same purpose. They alternately sang psalms and poured forth long prayers — which various ones present speak responsively. They become so inspired on these occasions that one after another they begin to sing and cry out as loudly as they are able, clapping their hands, "Glory! Glory!" They begin pounding on the ones nearest, throwing themselves on their knees or on their backs, laughing and crying — in short, conducting themselves like completely insane people. At the evening service the same comic behavior took place, and the preachers exerted themselves to their utmost capacities to bring the people into the highest ecstasies. At these camp meetings people are baptized, married, and tendered the Lord's Supper. On the whole, it must be said that the feelings the whole comedy aroused were something less than devotional.

Please accept for yourself and the whole family the most friendly and cordial greetings from Wilhelm, Otto, and myself.

The old, contemptible monarchic institutions

FROM J. R. REIERSEN, AT FOUR-MILE PRAIRIE, TEXAS, TO T. A. GJESTVANG

July 27, 1852

When one has postponed writing for weeks, and month after month has gone by, until the delay amounts to a number of years, then one becomes almost afraid even to try to amend the neglect, since one hardly knows even where to begin. That is the case with me. And, when, after a long delay, I then take the pen to correct an overlooked duty, I beg of you beforehand not to expect in any way a comprehensive and concise whole, but only a little fraction of what I had in mind to tell you. To begin with, I shall in all terseness merely inform you regarding myself that I live as contentedly as can be expected of a father of a family who has been bereft of his dear and faithful life partner. I have learned to love the country to which I emigrated more sincerely than my old fatherland, of which I can never think with any heartfelt longings. From my point of view I consider the old monarchic, aristocratic, and hierarchic institutions as contemptible playthings, of which the human intelligence ought to be greatly ashamed. I feel free and independent among a free people, who are not chained down by any old class or caste systems; and I am very proud of belonging to a mighty nation, whose institutions will and must in time come to dominate the entire civilized world, because they are founded on principles that sound intelligence must recognize as the only ones that are right and correct. So much with respect to myself.

Last summer when I learned that a group of immigrants were expected from Norway's most favored districts, my first thought was to try to find out if I could possibly be of any service to them in the selection of a place of settlement for the future. A long time before that I had discovered the shortcomings of the district in which I live – knowledge that can be gained only by experience. I have found the land here to be, on the whole, entirely too poor. The water is of a very inferior quality. The main defect of the land here is that the surface soil, which contains a good amount of clay, is too little mixed with sand, so that, right after the spring rains have ended, it is baked hard by the summer heat; if rainstorms do not occur frequently, the soil will bring forth a mediocre crop. I have seen good examples of this, especially during the last two years, when very limited crops were obtained and, consequently, the grain sold at very high prices.

The crop consists mostly of wheat, which, on account of its early ripening – in the latter part of May and the first part of June – is quite reliable. If the fields are not located, however, in the prairie bottoms, but at higher levels, then one cannot realize more than half a crop – from ten to twelve bushels per acre. In the western portion of this county, which borders on East Fork of Trinity River, the soil is of an entirely different nature. To a considerable depth the entire surface soil is as black as pitch, with a bluish subsoil, but it lacks the least trace of sand. It is very difficult to break – the job takes from four to five pairs of oxen; but the soil is rich and fertile and appears to be inexhaustible.

The same kind of soil is to be found in the neighboring counties of Dallas, Navarro, Elles, and Kollin – all of which are watered by branches of Trinity River, namely, East Fork, Elm Fork, and West Fork. All of these counties rest on a layer of white rock, which is rather easily pierced, and in which all the rivers and streams flow. The general characteristic of that part of the country is large, wide prairies – with a scanty supply of timber along the watercourses. My principal objections to this entire rich expanse of land – where every inch is fertile – are the lack of timber and the muddiness after a heavy rain. The wet soil cannot be compared with anything but pitch, which one cannot remove from the soles of the shoes except with the help of a knife. To be sure, this stickiness disappears after about two days of sunshine, and the plowed fields become loose and tender. The soil contains a considerable amount of elasticity; when a person steps on it it is like a sponge; however, no kind of work can be done with it during the rainy season, on account of the impossibility of plowing it then. The water is clear and clean, but very few of the watercourses have enough water for milling purposes during the entire year. For these reasons I did not believe that this district could be recommended for a Norwegian settlement.

Therefore, I turned my attention to the tract of land that is located near West Fork – between the southern and northern cross timbers. For this purpose I decided, in the month of November last year, to make a journey up through this territory; and, now, I shall inform you briefly as to the result. As soon as one arrives at cross timbers, i.e., to the actual timber belt, the black, sticky soil disappears and a loose, red, sandy soil, covered with post oak, begins. This land does not appear very fertile, but it does produce a good quality of grain and cotton, though I don't believe this quality will last so very long. The first prairies on the other side of the forest have a dark brown soil, which is sandy and somewhat porous and of an especially rich quality.

Ten miles from this forest Fort Worth is located, at the junction of Clear Fork and West Fork, on a beautiful, elevated plain, which, in turn, is surrounded by rich prairie land. This fort has existed for three years and forms the boundary line against the Indians, who are never allowed to come inside the fort. Between thirty and forty families have, during these years, settled at a distance of from five to six miles around the fort, but beyond that no settlements have been founded. Accompanied by a Captain Kartelet, who had found a good deal of land in this district, I journeyed about twenty miles up the river West Fork, which is considered navigable clear up to the fort. Here the land had an entirely different character; cliffs and valleys began to form the general outline. West Fork, the main river, and all of the branch rivers pass through valleys which are from one to two miles wide and are shut in on both sides by high, rough cliffs, of which a few reach the height of from five hundred to six hundred feet precipitously above the river. From there the cliffs in turn form the ground line for the high flatland, which continues over to the upper cross timbers. In these valleys we find land really fit for settling purposes. There the soil is deep, black, and sandy, and the wild rye and timothy indicate quite conclusively the abundantly fertile quality of the land. The brooks emerge from the pure sandstone cliffs, each brook having a foaming and audacious course with wonderful, clean, clear water, whose quantity is sufficient for milling purposes during the entire year.

On the mountain sides the woods grow all the way up to the cliffs, and the trees are of sufficient abundance and quality for all agricultural purposes; but only oak is found, not pine or cedar. A more beautiful situation, better water, and richer soil cannot possibly be found anywhere, and I dare give my head as a pledge that no man with sound sense and reasoning power can see this land without liking it.

The main river and the branch rivers have deep beds and never overflow; there are neither swamps nor stagnant water pools to infest the air with infectious diseases; and if any district can be called healthful, it must be this one. Around Fort Worth the settlers get from thirty to thirty-five bushels of wheat per acre, and from forty to sixty bushels of corn per acre. A bushel of wheat weighs seventy-one pounds – a better weight than any other known on the best wheat lands in America. After having tramped through this district for about a week, I returned quite determined to recommend, to Norwegians who were arriving, this district as the one most fit for settlements, and I, myself, was to accompany them up there. I became acquainted with Johan Grimseth; he wished me to go with him to the tract of land located near cross timbers; and when we had decided to make the journey, both Johan Brunstad, Karl Kvæstad, and several younger folks joined us. The result was of the kind that could not be doubted beforehand; all of them became so enthusiastic about the land that they determined to start a settlement there next fall, and the plan ripened into a definite decision later on.

Thus far you have, in brief, a summary of our plans and prospects here. If a larger group of emigrants from your district can be gathered, and if people with the spirit of initiative and enterprise, as well as a small amount of capital, will come to Texas, then I am positive that this district near West Fork would be best suited for a thriving settlement and would give the arriving immigrants the greatest advantages. Besides, mills and other kinds of machinery can easily be established there. I believe that the soil there is such that all kinds of farm products raised in the different sections of the country — for instance, wheat, rye, corn, cotton, tobacco, rice, sugar, sweet potatoes, and Norwegian potatoes, as well as all kinds of garden produce — will thrive there in the greatest abundance and with less work and attention than anywhere else. The district is also exceptionally well suited for cattle raising, because the wild rye grows knee-high during the winter, making the most excellent pasturage for cows and horses. The people in some of the Norwegian settlements in Iowa and Missouri intend to move to Texas next fall; and the district mentioned has been selected for their new settlement.

Last year it was my intention to write — and I had already gathered a large amount of material — a complete description of the entire older Norwegian settlement. I had it in mind to illustrate, with statistical data, the general condition of each and every family: when they arrived, their progress, and their present situation; but I was not able to secure all the necessary information. I shall therefore state briefly — and the truthfulness of my statements can be verified by the people from Hedemark who arrived from Norway last year — that all the Norwegians who came to this country in 1847 from the mountain communities in western Norway have, without exception, become well-to-do. Most of them possessed very little surplus capital when they arrived; some were without a penny, and a few were even in debt for their passage across the ocean. Now, all of them have bought land and have paid for it; they have built good houses; they have sufficient cattle, oxen, and horses for the management of their farms; and they get annual crops so large that there is a surplus to be sold to the newcomers. A few of these men, who had large families and debts of more than $100 each, can now be estimated as being worth more than $1,000 per family. They have succeeded even under unfavorable circumstances; and all of them are actually independent farmers, free from any fears of either taxes, mortgages, or foreclosures. Thus, each one of them is very well satisfied. These are the facts, which the statistical data can verify whenever that is desired; and when those immigrants who, at their arrival, were rather inferior to the Hedemarkings both as to agricultural training and culture in general have, even under conditions more unfavorable than now, succeeded so well – by sheer work and diligence – then I believe that skillful men from your district may expect to make much better progress, especially if they take favorable land.

Then a few words regarding the Hedemarkings who have come among us. Knud Olsen Ringnes was able to pay for his son's passage across the ocean and, in addition, to buy forty acres of land (he had, then, been in Texas only one year, and arrived here in debt for his own ocean ticket). He has broken up a piece of land of between four and five acres on his own farm and is at present occupied as a wheelwright. He is an efficient and true worker, and undoubtedly will make good headway in life. Mr. Grimseth and Ballishoel have moved over to my home, and in the last part of August Knud Andersen is to join me in starting a blacksmith shop on my place. Halvorsen has also stayed with me for some time. Karl Kvæstad, Jens Ringnæs, and Johan Brunstad will get fairly good crops this year. The corn crop is excellent all over the country, and corn is sold at from twenty-five to thirty cents per bushel, but the price is expected to rise to fifty cents in the winter. The wheat crop has also been good, and the sweet potato crop is promising. Thus, you see, here is an abundance of everything for the arriving immigrants. Many people from the other southern states are expected to move to Texas.

Eleven hundred new houses in Galveston

FROM A MAN LIVING IN GALVESTON, TEXAS, TO FRIENDS *

April 19, 1867

You may well believe that we are often surprised by the dispatches in *Morgenbladet* and your reports from America, colored as they all are by radical views. And we are amused to see the warnings against

* This letter appeared in *Morgenbladet*, June 23, 1867.

the many dangers that threaten those who emigrate to the southern states! Probably there can be no greater error. At present there is no place in America where capable Norwegian emigrants would be able to do so well for themselves as in Texas and some of the other southern states, now that the Negroes no longer can be depended upon. For those of your readers who might be interested I shall give a little description of Texas and its glories.

Texas is the southwesternmost of the former "Confederate States" and has a population of one million people, consisting of Americans, Germans, Irish, and Norwegians (of these perhaps twelve or fourteen hundred). Texas is generally acknowledged to be one of the most healthful and fertile states in the Union, and it only lacks people and capital, railroads, and canals to become in time one of the greatest grain- and cotton-producing areas in the world.

About two weeks ago I made a trip a couple of hundred miles up country, and I must say that in respect to picturesque waterfalls, wooded mountains, and beautiful lakes, Texas will bear comparison with any country in Europe. And of natural products there is such an abundance here that I believe it would be less difficult to list what could not grow here in Texas than to enumerate all the various kinds of tropical fruits and grains which grow and flourish here. They require only a quarter of the labor that one has to expend on them in the climate of my native country. It is said that Bosque County alone, where the largest of the Norwegian settlements is, could feed all Texas and Mexico put together. It has vast and fertile plains and fresh, clear water, but unfortunately not much forest.

Austin is the capital of the state and the seat of government. It is located approximately in the middle of the country on the Colorado River. It is an old and not very impressive city built partly in Moorish, partly in pioneer style, so that it looks a little ridiculous from a distance. It looked quite Spanish to me, but at a closer range you discover that you were mistaken. For instead of lazy Spaniards sitting or lying in the shade of the houses and black-eyed senoritas peeping out from behind jalousies, you see a kind of traffic and activity in the streets which you only find in an "American" city. But in spite of this, Austin has only two or three thousand inhabitants. The largest cities in Texas are Galveston, San Antonio, and Houston, with 25,000, 15,000, and 15,000 inhabitants respectively. San Antonio is said to be one of the most beautiful cities in America and is partly surrounded by a wall built by the Mexicans. Houston is about fifty miles from Galveston and is the junction of all railroads in Texas; it has large machine shops and cotton factories.

But Galveston is the most important place of trade in the state. It is located on a long, narrow island, Galveston Island. That is why the city is sometimes called the Island City—the inhabitants also call it the "Queen of the Gulf." The lower part of the town consists of business buildings exclusively, large four- or five-storied houses with iron fronts. More business is carried on in Galveston during a month than in Christiania during a whole year. In about eight blocks of this part are concentrated the large cotton presses where the cotton ("King Cotton") is pressed, stamped, weighed, and made ready for shipping. The upper part of the town is very beautiful and in good taste. Each house has a flower garden of matchless splendor at this time of year.

The city itself is growing day by day and is spreading out in all directions at an unparalleled speed, and I can report that since April last year ten or eleven hundred new houses have been built. The reason for this prosperity is the competence and energy of our businessmen, who during and after the war brought to Galveston much trade with the surrounding country. During the last few years especially a great change has taken place in trading conditions here, and it is predicted that in ten years Galveston will be just as large and important as New Orleans. As a small illustration, let me cite that in the business where I work we used to sell around thirty or forty dozen oxen before the war, but from March 1866 to March 1867, we sold nineteen hundred dozen from our firm alone.

There is no spring water on the island. We use only rain water, which is declared by all doctors to be a most healthful drink. And at present the general state of health is very good here. Every effort is being made to avoid contagious epidemics during the hot season.

At the south side of the island is *the beach.* Here people bathe all summer, ladies and gentlemen together in mixed crowds, as is common in southern countries (they wear bathing suits, of course). People never bathe during the daytime here. *Time is money*, and besides, it is too hot. In the evening from eight to ten o'clock you see ladies and gentlemen flock out to the beach, the gentlemen in white suits, and the ladies in skirts and blouses. On the whole, all kinds of protection are sought from the climate, which may be dangerous enough with its frequent changes. One day it may be so hot here that you could *fry an egg in the sand,* and shortly afterward a biting *norther* (north wind) may bring a complete change. It is so piercing that it will chill you through even if you wear three topcoats.

Last year from thirty to forty thousand emigrants arrived in Texas, but most of them were from the northern states. There were some Swedes and Norwegians who arrived on a ship from Hamburg and went up to a German town, New Ulm, together with a great many Germans. Earlier, too, Norwegians have immigrated to Texas and have been happy here. Thus, twelve years ago two or three hundred Norwegians immigrated to Bosque County with a fortune of $1,000 among them, and now each of them has a yearly income of $2,000 or $3,000, mainly through their vast fields of wheat.

There ought to be a consul for Norway and Sweden here in Galveston. There is one in Austin, but it is not easy to see of what use he can be up there, two hundred miles from the coast. Galveston is the only place in Texas that needs a consul. Last year ten or twelve Norwegian and Swedish ships came here. Almost all the captains complained of the lack of a consul. To telegraph to Austin would cost as much as to go to New Orleans on a steamboat.

When the group of Norwegians and Swedes that I mentioned earlier came through here, I happened to meet some of them on the street, and they told me that the landlord at their lodgings, a German, had asked $2 a day of each of them. Since I knew the landlord by reputation, I went up to the mayor and told him about the affair. He had the man summoned before court next morning, and he was fined $50 and had to give back half of the money to the emigrants. But this sort of thing happens every day both here and in other places where strangers have no one to turn to. Besides, the misfortunes of the emigrants are often caused by their own carelessness.

I advise nobody to come here from Norway unless he is forced to do so by necessity. It is true that people who can work well, especially craftsmen and farmers, are much in demand here in Texas. But I advise against people of the so-called better classes coming here if they have no capital. Craftsmen make a good living here since they can easily earn $7 or $8 a day; but a man who knows no trade, and perhaps not much English either, is just as badly off here as in the northern states.

There are hundreds of young people — Americans, Germans, and others — who have no objection to standing behind a counter, but they are not willing to get down to real work. A clerk here must not be afraid of work, and hard work at that, and it is an inescapable requirement that he should speak English and German fluently. A while ago a Swedish mate came up to me and asked me if I could get him a job in a store. "No," I answered, "but if you want to work as a dock hand here at $2.75 a day, come along." He accepted this offer and stayed with us for three months. Now he has a good job in one of the cotton presses, but he was able to speak and write English very well. I should like to write something more about conditions in the state, for instance about the Negroes (or the colored people as they are called now since "Negro" is considered a term of abuse) and their protectors "The Freedman's Bureau," but I do not have any more time.

From a Frontier Parsonage

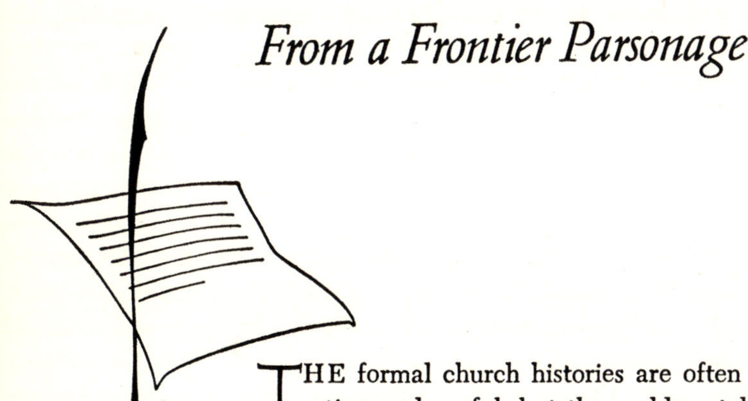

THE formal church histories are often interesting and useful, but they seldom take the reader inside a frontier parsonage for an intimate look at the home life and interests of the pioneer clergyman in the setting of his congregation and pastoral duties.

Olaus Duus was a pioneer minister on the Wisconsin frontier in the 1850's whose many letters, written from the parsonage at Waupaca to his relatives "at home" in Norway have survived the hand of time. They have been translated into English in a volume entitled *Frontier Parsonage: The Letters of Olaus Fredrik Duus, Norwegian Pastor in Wisconsin, 1855–1858,** and from this book I have selected passages that, taken as a whole, catch something of the flavor and atmosphere of the parsonage in a humble frontier immigrant community.

A master of arts from the Royal Fredrik University in Oslo and an ordained minister with five years of specialized training in theology, Duus, when he arrived on the Wisconsin frontier, had to adapt himself quickly to a mode of life for which he was scarcely prepared by his academic and religious studies. Serving immigrant farmers, he was at once a preacher, teacher, farmer, land speculator, and even an amateur doctor. He plunged into his many activities with energy and good will, and in letter after letter described the passing scenes as he saw them. "He described the husbandry of the immigrants, the transition of their speech, the consolations of their religion, the adjustment of their folkways, the passing of the seasons, the conditions of travel, the interiors of homes, the manners and customs of people."

* Translated by the Verdandi Study Club of Minneapolis and edited with a historical introduction by Theodore C. Blegen; published by the Norwegian-American Historical Association, Northfield, Minn., 1947.

Duus constantly inveighs against what he considers a crass American materialism, but he has an alert eye for land speculation, and when he earned large profits on a land deal, he apparently read into the experience the will of God, rather than an infection of materialism. The most interesting aspect of his letters lies, not in his generalizations about American life or his observations on travels that take him as far south as St. Louis, but in the intimate sketches he gives of his own home life, and particularly the place of his children in that life. His son Olaf, with "a drumstick in his hand, eating prairie chicken and drinking broth," is astonishingly real and vivid as one unpacks and translates these letters of long ago.

Ultimately Duus went back to Norway and lived out a long career in that country. His letters reveal a nostalgia that is not wholly untypical of the cultivated immigrant on the American frontier. With his wife, he accepted the physical hardships and difficulties of pioneering with good grace, but he was tormented by an incessant inner conflict. On the one hand, he sincerely wanted to serve the immigrant folk who, he believed, greatly needed the consolations of religious worship. On the other, his distaste for the rawness of the frontier West, his loneliness for the companionship of educated and cultivated people, and his awareness of the gentle culture of the circles he had left made him eager to return to Norway. His condemnation of his surroundings found expression in the disconsolate and unanswerable charge: "America is not Norway." Perhaps that very inner conflict, however, gives to his letters a value they might not otherwise have had, for his wife and children and home become the focus of his American interests. His letters "open wide the doors of the parsonage to reveal a devoted family, a tightly knit home circle within which was warmth and gaiety and love. Blizzards and bitter cold, panic and hard times, American materialism and sharp practice might beat against that circle but could not trouble its essential peace." *

* From my introduction to *Frontier Parsonage*, p. vii. I had the transcripts made from the original manuscripts of the Duus letters, which are preserved in Historiografisk Samling in Oslo.

I serve seven congregations here

October 23, 1855. This afternoon I am going down to Waupaca to get the luggage I left there last evening on my return trip from the Neenah Settlement. Since the horse was not at Waupaca and the moon was shining beautifully, I decided to use my long legs rather than spend the night there, especially as I was eager to keep the appointment I had made with my confirmands for this morning.

When I came home, I found Olaf and Mamma in the best of health. Olaf, the little rascal, because he is teething now, has become such a mamma's boy and so very cross that I really have never seen anyone worse. He is very proud of his two teeth, however, and makes use of them the livelong day. You should have seen him just now, sitting on Mamma's lap with a drumstick in his hand, eating prairie chicken and drinking broth. We no longer give him venison or fresh pork because he frightened us so the last time we had it. He almost choked to death; in fact, he turned quite blue. Now he is sitting on his chair while Mamma laces his boots. He is holding a pork bone, now nibbling at it and now striking Mamma with it, and occasionally he reaches out for my hat, which happens to be in his cradle. He is large for his age and quite a man.

Frightful news about the S.S. *Norge*! To think that Boldemann and Herm. Falchenberg should die in such a way! God comfort their families. Let us learn always to be prepared.

In one of Father's recent letters he asked me how many congregations I serve here. They are as follows: (1) Waupaca congregation, (2) Neenah congregation (all farmers), (3) congregations in the towns of Neenah and Menasha (combined into one congregation), (4) Winnecanne congregation, (5) Holden congregation in Waushara County, (6) a Swedish congregation in Waupaca County, (7) the Norwegian congregation in Stevens Point, Portage County. Numbers 2, 3, and 4 are in Winnebago County. In the course of a year I travel three or four thousand English miles.

As I sit here writing, a number of Indians are passing by—men, women, and children. All are on horseback with full packs; and, straggling alongside and among them, are a great many colts. Yesterday and today I have seen between thirty and fifty Indians, although not many have been about here recently.

A new, big mirror, hung Yankee fashion

January 8, 1856. Our parlor on Christmas Eve was so very elegant that I have not for a long time seen anything to equal it. In addition to this, when I went to Neenah on business on January 2, I purchased for $8.00 a beautiful mirror two feet nine inches long and proportionately wide, with a real gilt frame, and two small mirrors with mahogany frames edged in gold for $1.50 apiece. Now the old mirror, which cost $.31 and was used by everyone, has been demoted to the kitchen. The table stands between the windows, and above it the new, big mirror is hung in Yankee fashion by a red cord with beautiful red tassels.

From the money that is coming I have already ordered thirty apple trees at $.25 apiece, seven cherry trees at $.50 [apiece], and three pear trees at $.50 [apiece], from which we anticipate much joy in the future, if the Lord wills us to live here long enough and if He permits us to live until then.

An Indian listened during the hymn-singing *

Divine services are held round about in the largest houses of the settlement. A table covered with a white cloth serves as an altar, an ale glass as a chalice, and a saucer as a paten. It is all so pleasant, comfortable, friendly, and edifying that we all feel as uplifted as in any church. The only drawback is the lack of room, so that often a number of people must stand in the entry and even out on the lawn. They gather at the windows or wherever they can hear. As a rule, however, when we choose the largest houses, everything goes fairly well. I recall a little incident I want to recount here. On Christmas Day I preached in a rather large house that stands on a stretch of cleared land with a wooded ridge on one side and a fairly large lake surrounded by a thick forest of oak, aspen, and pine on the other. It was like a lovely April day in Norway, clear, sunny, and so warm that the melting snow lay in wide pools of water on the frozen ground. Everything was so beautiful around me that I felt exalted and grateful to God that we

* This letter has no date, but probably it was written in January 1856.

who are well and strong could rejoice in this wonderful Christmas festival and joyfully celebrate the birth of our beloved Savior, who became our brother and will save us all when we come to accept Him with childlike simplicity.

Then, just as I glanced toward the window, I noticed someone who did not understand the reason for our rejoicing. There stood a tall, powerful young Indian in his tawny deerskin garb, with a motley headdress in striking contrast to his swarthy skin and long, glistening black hair. He stood leaning his right shoulder against the window frame, his rifle at his side, holding in his left hand the ramrod which an Indian always carries with him. His coal-black glittering eyes peered curiously at us through the window. He listened intently during the singing of the hymns as though wondering what could be the reason for this gathering and this singing. For an hour he stood there, engrossed. After a long time, when my glance fell on the window, I saw him, his rifle on his shoulder, vanishing into the near-by forest.

To advise any one of you or anyone else, for that matter, to emigrate, I neither want nor dare to do. In this settlement, however, I do not know of anyone who does not live far better than in Norway. One fares better in every respect here if he is a good, diligent farmer, and everyone here is, except one – and even he has far more than he needs. Speculators, merchants, and clerks, as a rule, do not do so well, to put it mildly; but farmers, craftsmen, young laborers, and servant girls, especially the last, earn from $1 to $2 per week. As soon as the servant girls can speak some English and if they are reasonably diligent in their work, they receive wages of $2 a week. So people in these groups have no cause to wish themselves back home for lack of a living.

The river is filled with rafts of logs

March 6, 1856. Even the pastor of Waupaca felt frozen after traveling since early morning from a charge where he had served on the previous day. It was with satisfaction that he saw the smoke whirling from the kitchen and living-room chimneys of the parsonage. Had you suffered as he, you would gladly have accepted the invitation to enter the house, and I believe that you, like him, would have taken even greater pleasure in greeting the lady of the house and Olaf.

The whip, together with the thought of a meal of oats and corn awaiting him, drove the horse onward, and soon we were outside the house. The pastor's wife and Lillegut, with beaming faces, were at the window. Lillegut was all excitement. He stamped his feet on the kitchen bench and beat his hands against the window pane. He wanted to hug Kitty [the horse] and Papa at the same time. Mamma had to hold him with both hands to keep him from making too sudden an acquaintance with the floor.

I arrived here [Stevens Point] yesterday toward evening and am now sitting in a house beside the Wisconsin River, which is flowing rapidly past my windows. The river is filled with rafts of logs and other timber which are to float down from the pineries via the Wisconsin and Mississippi rivers to the southern states, where there are few pines. A poor house of planks or just a board laid crosswise over a plank serves as a shelter for the crew of the raft, who have all their possessions there. They earn from $1.50 to $4.00 a day but they are unfortunately the scum of humanity, the dregs both of Europe and America. They live a life of constant drinking, gambling, swearing and cursing, and even of occasional murder. They flee from justice, and since the language is all the same here in America they cannot be detected by their dialect. They lead a detestable existence and consider perjury as nothing.

We Norwegians speak a strange kind of English

July 8, 1856. Some time ago I was riding with a Norwegian who was asked by an American if he had hay for sale and what the price was, whereupon the Norwegian answed, "*Yes, Sir, I have; de price is $4.00 naar ye take it paa de slough.*" And he had been here sixteen years, as far as I know! Yes, we Norwegians speak a strange kind of English, and yet the Yankees say that the people of no other foreign nationality speak as well as we do. And such Norwegian as they speak here!! Our Norwegian language is so mixed with English expressions that I was quite annoyed to hear it when I first came here. One never hears the word "hvedemeel" any more, only *flour*; never "gjerde," but *fence*, never "lade," but *barn*; never "stald," but *stable*. If a horse is "garsprungen," one says in Norwegian-American "*den jomper* (jump) *fence*," and so it goes. If you have taken the wrong road and happen to meet a Norwegian along the way, he will, if he is a mountaineer, answer your question about the road like this: *Du har taekji wrong road. Du lyt tørne rundt igjen og taekji de first left hand road*, and so on.

Olaf spends most of the day outside, running here and there in a straw hat and short dress, with his legs and feet bare, flourishing Papa's riding whip in his hand and crying, "Get up, get up," as he hits at our geese that now and then come sneaking through the fence.

He laughs and shrieks when he is permitted to pull his father's nose. I stick out my tongue when he pulls hard, and then he grabs for it like lightning.

Always a sense of strangeness here

July 30, 1856. *But America is not Norway*. Here there is always a sense of strangeness, something unlike home, and I don't suppose we'll ever feel completely at home here.

Madison, with its zinc-plated cupolas

September 1, 1856. Our jaunt to Koshkonong . . . was indeed a very pleasant journey, favored by most beautiful weather. Sophie and Morten met me at Wolf River, and the same evening we reached Milwaukee, a city of about 50,000 inhabitants, of whom more than a third are Germans. The city proper, unusually well planned, is beautiful, extending along the banks of a small river which flows into Lake Michigan. Between the city proper and the lake lie rather high and extensive sand dunes dotted with charming villas and grounds, the homes of the Milwaukee elite.

Madison, a fast-growing city of some 10,000 inhabitants, is the capital of Wisconsin. Its site is so beautiful that I do not believe I exaggerate when I describe it as one of the most beautiful on earth. It lies between four lovely lakes with charming though rather rugged shore lines. The beauty of the city is further enhanced by the zinc-plated cupolas.

Feather beds are practically unknown

September 29, 1856. I have yet to see a stove in a bedroom in northern Wisconsin, and feather beds are practically unknown. A quilt on a straw mattress to lie on and a similar quilt for a covering – usually a sheet but sometimes none – are what the host offers to keep you warm. To enhance the delightful impression of such an inviting bedroom one seldom finds a chair or table. The bed is all – "*nichts weiter*" – and you are lucky when you do not have to share it with some workman, something that I have never become used to, in spite of the fact that such arrangements have been made for me several times.

The house trembles from the meat grinder

November 13, 1856. Day before yesterday we butchered a three-year-old steer and a pig that weighed about 190 pounds. The steer was small compared to what is usual here and weighed only 338 pounds. "Hack! Hack! Hack!" Now the house almost trembles while Mr. John Knudsen Brosdal from Torrisdal runs the sausage through the meat grinder.

Ragged Yankees are a common sight

December 4, 1856. On Monday, the first of December, I accepted a renewal of my present call from the congregation here. Beginning November 4, 1857, the following terms will be in force: $300 salary, $60 for wood, eight Sundays free to serve other smaller congregations not having a minister, fees for ministerial services to be optional with the giver, and free rent of the parsonage and use of the forty acres of land belonging thereto.

A town starts in this way here: first a mill is built, then comes a store or two, then a blacksmith, then a carpenter, and so on. There are few shoemakers here, since all shoes are bought ready-made in the shops and are seldom repaired because that is expensive and the material is often poor. Shoes are usually manufactured in the eastern states and always by machine. A pair of shoes that would cost about three specie dollars at home costs $4.00 to $4.25 here. Ninety-five per cent of all men's clothing is also bought ready-made in the shops, and it too is machine-made. A sewing machine in operation is an interesting sight. All these clothes have a tendency to rip in the seams, and ragged Yankees are therefore a common sight.

Shall we visit a Yankee home? Outside, a ragged man is working, chopping wood, milking cows, or doing some such chores. Notice his clothes and you will see that they are seldom mended. The coat is often full of holes and out at elbows. His hands and face are clean, and he always washes his hands before eating. With the mutual greeting *How do you do, sir*? we enter the log house. An elegant woman sits in a rocking chair, with a coiffure so perfect that you might think Lieblein had dressed it. She is sewing on a quilt or some other article for the household and sits and rocks with her feet toward the stove, which is always placed in the middle of the floor so people can sit around it. The greetings *How do you do, sir* and *How do you do, Ma'am* are exchanged. She remains seated and invites us to have chairs. We sit down and start to chat; in the midst of the conversation the elegant lady belches so loud that the room resounds.

Hunters on skis tire the deer out

January 26, 1857. I see by Father's last letter that times are still hard in Norway. Conditions here are about as bad as they can be, especially for farmers. Coffee, sugar, and staples are frightfully high, whereas grain, especially wheat, is worth only half the price it was last year, in spite of the fact that the quality is at least a third better. The result is that the trade value of grain is at least a third less than last year. Wheat sold at about this time last year for $1.50 a bushel, and this year it is difficult to get $.75 cash for a bushel. The deep snow has hindered logging, so the demand [for flour] is much less than had been expected. Just now the snow around here is two and a quarter feet deep and quite loose. As soon as I step off the path I sink down well above my knees.

The poor deer have suffered a good deal because they cannot escape the hunters on skis. The men tire a deer out, and several times they have been able to walk right up to one and plunge a hunting knife into it. Over a hundred deer have been killed by the Norwegians here.

Now we are going to build a church

February 8, 1857. I have now been a minister here – that is, in America – for over two years, and in all that time I have preached only twice in consecrated church buildings. You can understand, therefore, how I rejoice, and Sophie and all the others with me, that now we are going to build a church close to the parsonage on old Mr. Hartvig's land. The first five logs for this building have already been hauled into place. Hartvig has been kind enough to give the congregation a quarter-acre of land for this use, as the church will be more beautifully and more conveniently situated there than on the land the congregation owns. The church will be on one side of the road, and directly opposite will be the cemetery. The church was originally planned to be 60 feet long, 40 feet wide, and 20 feet high on the inside, but unfortunately there isn't enough money; so we have decided to make it 50 feet long, 35 feet wide, and 16 feet from floor to ceiling.

Religion is not taught in the public schools

February 13, 1857. Regarding sects here, you know, of course, that there are among the Americans all the usual factions, each one worse than the other. I think, though, that the largest faction here in the West consists of veritable heathens who neither have been baptized nor have learned to know Christianity. The teaching of religion is prohibited in the American public schools because people fear the Jesuits, whose instruction might make the Catholics become too powerful. The result of such complete freedom from religious education is that many people here do not know Christ except by name and consequently do not allow their children to learn about Him.

Immigrants suffer horribly on the journey

July 11, 1857. A number of newcomers have joined the Waupaca congregation this year. I have heard that all in all there are about 350, including children. Most of them are from Gusdal in Guldbrandsdalen, and have been tenant farmers; so they are wise in coming here, whereas one who owns his farm at home and who can manage does better to stay where he is. The poor immigrants suffer horribly on the journey, especially from Quebec, because the Americans in charge of them treat them worse than animals.

A few weeks ago a family arrived, one of whose children died immediately. The three children in the family all contracted measles on the journey. To find a berth to put them in was too much to ask; so the parents had to carry them in their arms day and night, exposed to wind and weather and driven from pillar to post. When I comforted the mother at the funeral, she answered: "If only the child had not suffered so much on the voyage!" She was grief-stricken. They went on to a Norwegian family they know, who live about thirteen miles from me. I held church services there last Wednesday and buried their second child, a ten-and-a-half year old boy, whose health had also given way on the trip. Their third child, a boy six or eight years old, will not live long. He is failing steadily, and they must carry him constantly.

Everything arrived in perfect condition

July 20, 1857. The lamp, the *Eau de Cologne*, and everything else arrived in perfect condition. Heartiest thanks to you all for them as well as for the stockings, shoes, spread, wooden plates, spoons, seals, sleigh bells, chocolate, Kragerø [ale], and so on.

An old wreck of a piano

August 14, 1857. A few days ago when I was in Waupaca I heard an old wreck of a piano, which I imagine is the only one in the entire county. It is the fourth I have heard since arriving in America. Sophie has heard but one!

We drank a toast in real wine

September 8, 1857. Besides the Preuses old Captain Gasmann had dinner with us on Sunday, and we drank a toast to you in real wine, a novelty in Waupaca County. I shouldn't wonder if the wine Father sent me is not the first genuine wine that has come into the county.

It is now over three years since we left you, and soon we shall have been here three years, in which time we have had "a little of this and a little of that" as one says, but still far more than we had anticipated or deserved. The progress of this local settlement is unbelievable to anyone not acquainted with American conditions.

Greetings to all of you from sweet Soph. She is just coming with wash water for the little boys, who have both been in the ashpile so that they look like Espen Askeladen in the fairy tale. Let them but get the ashes off themselves and put on the new clothes from "Nogge," as Olaf calls it, and I'll wager that the boys will be as handsome as anyone will ever see them.

Moccasins scented with wigwam smoke

October 14, 1857. During the last three weeks, I have been home scarcely more than four or five days all told. Last night I came home in the pitch dark from Stevens Point, where I had a wedding at seven o'clock in the evening, day before yesterday, and services yesterday forenoon. How good it is to get home and find all the family well and busy! Is not God wonderfully good to us? With all the traveling I have done, about four thousand English miles a year, there has never been any illness in our home while I have been gone, nor indeed have we experienced any really serious illness.

Have you received the moccasins that Elling Larsen took with him? They are really made by Indians, for I bought them from one of the handsomest Indians I have seen. They were made by an Indian maid of the Menominee tribe, and I feel quite sure that you will be able to get the scent of wigwam smoke from them.

All business is at a standstill

January 14 [1858]. Conditions here are so bad that no one living can remember times so trying. All business is at a standstill, and I am afraid that before we see the return of better times, many people will be ruined. Business houses in New York and other eastern cities are in financial difficulty, and they are now beginning to demand payment from the merchants here in the West who have purchased goods from them. For this reason, the merchants will be forced to summon their debtors to court. Where shall one get money, when it can't be borrowed at even 100 per cent, and when grain and other farm products have declined in value to one third of what they brought the three years before this? I hope that things may soon be better than they now appear.

Such wickedness that the devil rejoices

January 26, 1858. So far the merchants here in the Northwest have escaped bankruptcy. I don't see how they can avoid it long, since people have neither the money to buy from them nor the money to pay their debts. If the business houses fail, then times will be even worse than they are now. God be praised, none of the Norwegians in this settlement are in need of food, since God has given us an unusually bountiful year; but as far as money is concerned, I dare say that scarcely one out of thirty has two dollars cash in his pocket.

We Norwegian Lutherans take turns in having school in our homes just as we did in Norway; but we are, so far as I know, the only sect that follows this practice. To be sure, a few Americans use the *Sabbath schools,* but I have seen them take men for teachers of whom they know no more than you do or any one else in Norway. Often their qualifications are merely that they seem to be decent and that they can read. Concerning faith, knowledge, or baptism, the American thinks, *Never mind that.* He either knows no better, or does not wish to know better. Indeed, there is such gross wickedness and absolute ungodliness that the devil has good reason to rejoice wholeheartedly, as he undoubtedly does.

A professorship in the Norwegian language

March 8, 1858. As soon as it was rumored that I would leave Waupaca, I received an invitation to visit and choose one of six different congregations in Iowa and Wisconsin near the Mississippi River close to Pastor Stub and Pastor Koren. I preferred to go to Whitewater if such was God's will. There I would be only a day's journey from Pastor Dietrichson in Jefferson County, A. C. Preus at Koshkonong, H. A. Preus at Spring Prairie, and N. Brandt near Rock River.

Our Norwegian Synod—that is, the Norwegian Lutheran congregations which have united under a joint governing board—has decided to set up a professorship in the Norwegian language at the University of St. Louis, Missouri, in order to educate our pastors there. For some time now I have tutored an amiable, pious young man, the son of Jacob Aal's old gardener, and I hope that with God's help he will become a clergyman. The plan is to have him complete his education in Missouri.

In St. Louis you'll see traffic!

May 14, 1858. Believe me, there [in St. Louis] you'll see traffic! I myself counted fifty steamers, each with two smoke stacks, lying side by side along the levee in St. Louis. Certainly there were at least a hundred while I was there. Very often there are two hundred at one time. Though they are very large, only a few of them are attractive either inside or out; they can't be compared with those that ply the Great Lakes. Each of the lake boats costs $150,000 to $200,000, but the companies went completely bankrupt because of their magnificence. So this year these ships lie entirely unused, the large capital invested in them completely valueless. Efforts to sell them for even a quarter of their value have met with no success. Probably there are also a few attractive boats on the Mississippi, but I have seen none that could compare with those on the Lakes.

What is unpleasant for us Norwegians, who are accustomed to clear water both in lakes and rivers, is the yellow, muddy water that one sees here almost always. The water of the Mississippi is so turbid that it is impossible, I have heard, to float rafts of logs coming from the Missouri, Mississippi, or Wisconsin rivers any farther than to St. Louis because the water, constantly washing over the rafts, would deposit so much sediment that the rafts would sink. This water is used for both cooking and drinking, and I have had to drink it many times. It is considered to be perfectly healthful.

The Beautiful Land

THE first chapter in what became a migration to Iowa has already been presented in the diary-letter of Gro Svendsen, which describes in vivid phrases an Atlantic crossing of 1862. The major portion of the present chapter follows the fortunes of this pioneer woman as she makes her way to Iowa and records her life on the frontier through the 1860's and 1870's until shortly before her death in 1878. She was an exuberant woman, insatiably curious about every turn in the novel experiences in which she had a part, and not without skill in the art of telling her story to her people in Norway in the long succession of letters she wrote. These letters were cherished and preserved, in recent years found and transcribed, and in 1950 published in full in English translations as a volume entitled *Frontier Mother: The Letters of Gro Svendsen.**

The condensing of the nearly 150 pages of Gro Svendsen's letters has meant the omission of not a little interesting detail, but the reader will have no difficulty in visualizing the experience of an immigrant arrival in the New World, the travel westward by river and lake and train and buggy, the establishment of a home in Iowa, and the turbulent family life of a frontier farm woman who bore ten children from 1863 to 1878. Here, too, are contemporary chronicles of the details of rural life and frontier agriculture and of the innumerable aspects of immigrant transition across two decades, unconsciously revealed and consciously described by the letter writer.

The story told is highly personal. The storyteller is as emotional as she is observant and articulate, but as the tale unfolds it becomes clear

* Translated and edited by Pauline Farseth and Theodore C. Blegen; published by the Norwegian-American Historical Association, Northfield, Minn.

that the record is more than that of one woman and of one family. It is a social portrait of an immigrant community sketched by one of its active members. Unusual in the liveliness and range of her interests, skillful in making the everyday life of a farmer's family vivid and realistic, Gro Svendsen was still, in the main, representative of thousands of frontier immigrant women.

Her world was by no means parochial. It stretched far beyond the boundaries of her Iowa house and farm. Constantly she bridged the Atlantic to the land of her memories and traditions. She was almost painfully aware of the connections of the farming frontier with state and nation and world. She saw her husband, a newly arrived immigrant, go away to fight in the Civil War, from which he returned after marching with Sherman and parading in Washington before the President of the United States. She recorded both the financial and the natural forces that beat insistently upon the economy of the midwestern farmer. She was a devoted reader of books and a natural writer who on occasion served as a community "secretary," aiding others to write to their homes in the old country. She was interested in church and civic affairs along with her husband. And she took an unfaltering interest in education, was herself a teacher, and supervised the education of her children whose future was the inner meaning of America to her. One is not surprised to learn that a novel has been written with Mrs. Svendsen as its central character or that her memory still lingers in the Iowa community where she lived in the 1860's and 1870's.*

To the excerpts from the letters of Gro Svendsen are added portions of a few letters written by her brother Ole Nielsen,† who emigrated from Norway in 1866, four years after his sister, and went to the same community in Iowa where she lived. After a difficult Atlantic crossing, he rejoices over his safe arrival in the Promised Land. By autumn he already has taken a quarter-section of land in Iowa and is making plans to extend his property to 320 acres. He writes again in 1868 to

* I have written more fully about Gro Svendsen in the introduction to *Frontier Mother*. The novel referred to was written in Norwegian with the title (in translation) *Rose of the Valley: From the World of Reality on Both Sides of the Sea*. It was published in Minneapolis in 1928. Its chief character is "Aase Dalro," but one quickly identifies her as Gro Svendsen.

† The originals of Ole Nielsen's letters are preserved in Norway. The translations here have been made from transcripts in the possession of the Minnesota Historical Society.

describe not only his own progress but also—and in reply to questions that have been addressed to him—something of the bird, animal, and fish life of the region he has chosen. Two years later he gives another picture of the little successes he has achieved in his career. He is not afraid, it may be noted, to incur debt in acquiring the stock and possessions necessary to his frontier farming success. His letters reveal a strain of genuine piety coupled with an equally genuine streak of independence and ambition. The immigrant in America, he declares, "is completely free and independent here." No one has to "bow and scrape" either to the minister or to the sexton.

In simple terms Ole Nielsen's letters interpreted for readers in his home community in Norway both the economic opportunities and the robust democracy of the frontier world to which he had come.

FROM GRO SVENDSEN, AT ESTHERVILLE, IOWA, TO HER PARENTS

We arrived at Montreal

June 23 [1862]. We arrived at Montreal at ten o'clock, a large city and quite beautiful. Many men came aboard and offered their services as interpreters. Finally we chose one by the name of Olson. He was born in Hurrum parish and is now living in Chicago.

The vainglorious, worldly-wise city

June 24, Midsummer. We have been ordered to have our chests and boxes packed, except for hand luggage we can take with us in the steamboat. It was really fortunate that the boxes and chests were strong, for I have never witnessed such rough and careless handling of goods. Because of this slipshod handling one chest was thrown into the water, the cover flew open, and the contents floated around. It held all the possessions of a very poor family. They lost everything. They had four children – no money, no clothes but the ones they were wearing, and almost no food.

Today I went ashore and touched American soil for the first time. Just as we crossed the wharf, a group of soldiers came along, carrying a comrade. He might have been drunk, or he might have been dead. They carried him into a storehouse, and then the red-coated rascals disappeared. I have observed that there must be four or five kinds of soldiers here, since I have noticed at least that many different types of uniforms. We walked about the vainglorious, worldly-wise city with all its sham and tinsel.

Locks and dams, contraptions I have never seen

June 25. At nine o'clock we were to board the steamer. It was a sad day, leaving the kind captain and his men. He treated us to punch.

Our friendly first mate gave me a present in parting. It was a book of prayer called Gosner's *Skatkiste*. He gave it to me as a keepsake.

The steamer is a very dismal-looking, uncomfortable boat. We are going up through locks and dams, contraptions the like of which I have never seen before. The sailors often follow along on shore until we get back into open water again.

We, the humblest passengers, were crowded together on the lowest deck with freight and cordwood, so we had little space for moving about. Adding to our discomfort were the sailors, most annoying and disgusting. I more than the others had to suffer unwelcome attentions. I understood very little of what they said, but their silly behavior was clear enough.

On board I saw a Negro for the first time. He was our cook, and he gave me a special treat of steak, bread, and ale. I had previously told him with my limited supply of words that I thought he was a good cook.

Women loaded with golden trinkets

June 26. In Toronto I saw ten telegraph boats, many railroads, and many other things that my eager roving eyes discovered in these larger cities, but it would be too complicated to describe them all.

At one place where the steamer loaded timber, I saw a Catholic congregation assembled. The monks in their strange robes walked ahead of the holy nuns, who were followed by the rest of the congregation.

On our steamer [were] the vainest women I've ever seen. They were loaded down with golden trinkets. No moderation, no taste. They seemed to be interested only in themselves and their finery. Such vulgar-looking women!

Chicago, a very large city

June 29. Late in the afternoon we arrived in Chicago, a very large city. Those who had no money could go no farther. So far they had been given free passage. Almost half of them remained here.

When we entered the city we were surrounded by people who urged us to go here, there, and everywhere. When no one paid any heed to them they became angry and ceased their prattle. They left us, definitely disgusted with the apparently self-sufficient immigrant. I think they felt very cheap.

The train's speed is twenty miles an hour

June 30. We left Chicago at eleven o'clock and sped on. The speed of the train is about one English mile in three minutes. I checked the speed several times. There were about twenty or thirty cars in this train. That evening we came to a little town where we were put off. Here we spent four hours on the street. The night was bitterly cold. There were many people about, but we couldn't understand any of their noisy chatter. At last another train came along. A miserable one, with only one bench for so many people. We stayed on this train for an hour, and then we were put on another train where we remained until morning, getting off at Prairie du Chien.

We continued our tedious journey

July 2. We left McGregor and traveled northward. After a hot day we spent the night under the open skies. In the morning we continued our tedious journey up to Calmar. Here we stayed in a deserted house from the third to the fifth of July, as our driver wanted to celebrate the Fourth in Calmar.

Yet another night under the open sky

July 6, Third Sunday after Trinity. We had a scorching hot day, rode on for four hours in the broiling heat. We found no shade anywhere, either from house or tree. Finally we came to a house that offered a little shade, and we rested there for a while.

Yet another night under the open sky. There was some thunder and lightning, but strangely enough no rain.

Different from life in our mountain valley

November 20. Life here is very different from life in our mountain valley. One must readjust oneself and learn everything all over again, even to the preparation of food. We are told that the women of America have much leisure time, but I haven't yet met any woman who thought so! Here the mistress of the house must do all the work that the cook, the maid, and the housekeeper would do in an upper-class family at home. Moreover, she must do her work as well as these three together do it in Norway.

Clothes are washed in a very unusual way. First one must prepare the lye. This is poured into boiling water, and immediately the lye forms a white scum something like thick sour milk. The frothy scum must be skimmed off before one puts the clothes into the water. The lye is very strong and must be removed, so you see there is a lot of extra work in washing clothes. Without this treatment the water is much too hard.

The Indian revolt has been subdued

December. I might tell you that the Indian revolt has been somewhat subdued, so we feel much safer than we did awhile ago. It isn't enough merely to subdue them. I think that not a single one who took part in the revolt should be permitted to live. Unfortunately, I cannot make the decision in the matter. I fear that they will be let off too easily.

I long for a good alpenhorn

March 25, 1863. In America money was said to be so plentiful, and it may be. But it's hard to get any of it when it's to be used for the common good, for such as teachers' salaries, ministers' salaries, and other expenses connected with the church. The men assigned to collect this money are called trustees. They go about with a list, soliciting from the farmers and getting contributions in the same way as we collected the personal property tax and the church tax at home.

Since I've been talking about cattle, I might tell you what [Americans] say when they call animals. Whenever one calls a horse one says, "Kop, Kop, Kop." To call a cow one says, "Come Boss, come Boss"; to call a sheep one says, "Sheep, Sheep, Sheep"; a pig, "Pig, Pig, Pig"; and a dog, "Heah, Heah." If one wants to rouse a dog one calls, "Sekken, Sekken" [Sick him]. To a cat one says, "Ketty, Ketty, Kete." When one wants to stop a horse one cries a long "Haav." Horses, too, have special names, and there are always two to a wagon. Some horses' names are "Kjale" and "Beel" [Charley and Bill], "Dola" and "Fana" [Dolly and Fanny], and so forth. They are not paired according to color.

It would be wonderful to get the books. Whenever you have the opportunity, send them — but I don't want to inconvenience you too much. I got a small grammar by S. Kroble from my little brother, and I have read it through several times. I should have mastered this book when I was at home, but it is good to have it here now.

It would be fun to have a good monochord (*salmodikon*) and a good book of chorals. We do have monochords here, but they are not good and they are expensive. I also long for a good alpenhorn. We have no evergreen trees here. Only foliage trees, and the wood from these is not suited for making a good instrument.

The prairie fire is terrifying

Winter 1863. Then there is the prairie fire or, as they call it here "Faieren." This is terrifying, and the fire rages in both the spring and the fall. Whatever it leaves behind in the fall, it consumes in the spring, so there is nothing left of the long grass on the prairies, sloughs, and marshes. It is a strange and terrible sight to see all the fields a sea of fire. Quite often the scorching flames sweep everything along in their path — people, cattle, hay, fences. In dry weather with a strong wind the fire will race faster than the speediest horse. No one dares to travel without carrying matches, so that if there is a fire he can fight it by building another and in this way save his life and prevent burns, which sometimes prove fatal.

I read English just a little

July 25. I have told you that I am happy here, and I really am. If I haven't anything else to do, I take my little boy in my arms and go over to the public school. It's not very far away (as far as to Bakken).

What a remarkable change! A few months ago I was the teacher. Now I am the student and a very poor one at that. I can't boast of having learned very much. I can read just a little, but I do understand a few of the stories in the English books.

Soldiers to protect the farmers

November 8. Our land is beautiful, though there are few trees. Trees, however, can be had and planted at the cost of from five to ten dollars per acre. We have good spring water near by. Best of all, the land is good meadowland and easily plowed and cultivated.

So far as the war is concerned, I have nothing new to tell you. We are fortunate enough to have *Emigranten*, so I can keep posted on world affairs just as you do. I have read about the Indian war, too. There have been four battles this summer. The white men killed the Indian chief, took his son prisoner, killed several hundred Indians, and drove the rest of them across the Missouri River, five or six hundred miles from here. Consequently the settlers in Minnesota, as well as those in Iowa, feel quite secure. Then, too, in many places there are soldiers to protect the farmers in case of danger.

I get $12 a month for teaching school

May 24, 1864. I've taught school for one and a half months. The pupils come here three times a week, and there are five of them. They were very poor when we began, but they have improved a great deal in this short time. They are obedient, attentive, and eager to learn – quite the opposite from those I had last year. I am very much pleased with them, and they and their parents seem to be satisfied with me. I get $12.00 a month, a very good salary for one with so little education.

My little son is my great joy. He has many good traits and gives evidence of being greatly gifted. He is very apt. Whenever he has seen a thing done once, he remembers it and repeats it later. He can imitate the children at their reading. As soon as he gets hold of a book or a paper, he begins to read. He is very fond of his father. When his father is out working he calls for him constantly. He can already say many words clearly, and he is large and sturdy for his age. He gets better-looking every day, and he surpasses all the other children of the same age.

This terrible war and its aftereffects

December 5. Little Svend is growing every day. He is big and chubby. He is not yet two years old, but he can say anything he wants to. Little Niels is not so fat as Svend was at his age, but he is just as pretty, and he has eyes just like yours, Father. Almost everybody here who knows you thinks so, too. Every time I look into his eyes I think of you.

Even though one does not worry so much about making a living here, there are nevertheless countless other worries that one never had in Norway and didn't even dream of. Of late it has been particularly difficult because of this terrible war and all of the evil aftereffects. So far there has been no famine, but it's not far away. All the necessities of life have risen to prices impossible to pay. The newcomer, as well as the native, must live and consequently must pay these prices.

Vacancies for teaching positions

December 11. You ask me about teaching positions among our people. To this, I can only say that I believe that there are several good vacancies to the south of us. Some of our newspapers have carried advertisements of pastors' requests for schoolteachers prepared to direct congregational singing.

My husband is with General Sherman

April 17, 1865. I have had several letters from my husband since he went away, and I am always happy when I receive letters written in his own hand because then I know that he is still among the living. He tells me that he has been well – that he has met with no danger and he hopes with God's help to be spared – but there is no telling. I don't believe that he has been in combat unless it might have been these last days. I have not heard from him since March 25. He was then in a town called New Bern in North Carolina. His regiment is a part of General Sherman's Seventeenth Army Corps. He has been with Sherman just this last month.

He now has an honorable discharge

August 15. Yes, Ole has come home. Since last October he has journeyed more than seven thousand miles, so he has seen, heard, and felt much, far more than I could ever tell you. Through it all he was in good health, and now he has served his time and has been discharged as an honorable soldier. He was in combat but once, and that was the first of March.

An enormous quantity of watermelon

December 3. We have had a good year, a rich harvest both from the grain that we sowed and from the wild fruit and grain. We have plowed and fenced in three acres of new land. On this plot we raised 90 bushels of corn, 24 bushels of potatoes, and a plant called sugar cane or sorghum. This sugar cane is pressed and cooked into syrup or molasses. From our patch of sugar cane we got nine gallons of syrup (a gallon is equal to four *potter*). The man whose pressing and cooking machine we used also got nine gallons, so we actually got eighteen gallons all told. We also got some fruit from our garden. It would take too long to list all of it, but I must tell you something about a fruit called "watermellon" [*watermøller*]. We have an enormous quantity of them; I can't compare them to anything I ever saw in Norway. They are as big as a child's head; some are larger. They are round, and the inside is red or yellow. The melons are sweet and juicy. They are eaten just as they are taken from the field, provided they are ripe. I have cooked molasses from them, and I have also brewed juice several times.

We have only four cows. The heifer will bear her first calf this winter, and then we shall have five cows if all goes well. We have only one sheep. (The lamb died this spring when it was gelded.) I have sheared the sheep twice this year. The wool, which was of excellent quality, weighed all of seven pounds.

We butchered two pigs this week, one fully grown, the other eight or nine months old. We had fattened them since last September so they were quite large.

I also want to tell you that this fall we have sold butter for $35 – not so much, but I am satisfied for the time being.

Last fall we built a stable for twelve head of cattle.

Our house is very small and humble, but it's a shelter from the cold winter. I shall say no more about it. However, next spring, if we are all here and all is well, we hope to build a large and comfortable house. We shall build even though it costs a great deal of money to build houses in this country.

The spring of 1864 we bought twelve and a half acres of woodland for $100, or $8 an acre.

Last year at this time Ole was in a garrison in the little town of Ringgold in the state of Georgia. There they almost starved to death. They were given rations for three days at a time, but the food given them was not enough for one day. The reason for their suffering so much was that the Rebels were near by, wrecking the railroads so that it was difficult to get food shipped in. Then, too, our men had unscrupulous officers who stole the rations from the soldiers and sold the food to needy civilians, then proceeded to pocket the money for the stolen food.

These starvation rations they endured from November to the middle of February. They were then so gaunt and weak that they could hardly walk.

During the great battle at Nashville, Tennessee, between General

Thomas and the Rebel, General Hood, Ole was stationed so near that for many days he heard the distant thunder of the cannons. They were then ordered out of Georgia and were sent on through Tennessee, Illinois, Ohio, Pennsylvania, and Maryland. From Maryland they went on by sea to North Carolina and finally landed in the town of New Bern. From there they marched to the city of Kingston, where they met the enemy and fought for three days. Ole fought at the front a whole day. They were then under General Schofield's command. When they had defeated the enemy, they went back to Goldsboro, where they joined Sherman's main army. (Ole wears Sherman's picture in the photograph I sent home.) From Goldsboro they went to Raleigh, the capital of North Carolina – then ten miles beyond Raleigh, where they were once again ready for combat when Johnston capitulated. Rejoicing they went back to Raleigh, then on to Petersburg in Virginia, from Petersburg to Richmond, and on to Washington. There they were present when the troops were reviewed by the President. From Washington they were sent on to Louisville, Kentucky, where they were encamped for over a month before they were discharged, paid, and sent home.

My lads are hale and hearty. Svend can drive the young oxen in a masterly way. He can even manage the big oxen. Little Niels and he play around in their little wagon all day long when the weather permits them to be outdoors. Niels is tall for his age, very active and fleet of foot. He is not so boisterous as Svend, seems more calm and patient.

I must also tell you that I have a beautiful black dog. He is like old Faithful at home. He has curly hair. He is handsome, and his name is Prince.

Locusts like a blinding drift of snow

August 4. My little Ole, too, is very intelligent. He began to walk on Midsummer's Day, and he will be a year old the ninth of August. He is active and lusty, and he already goes in and out of the house as he pleases. He is large and chubby. Carl and Ole both resemble Niels so you almost have a picture of them when you look at the one you have of him. My baby sends you a special greeting. It is "ga," which is supposed to mean "good day." Then he bows and says "tak for sist" to all in the room. He is a charming little fellow.

The wheat had already begun to head by the first of June. Then the latter part of the month the locusts came like a blinding drift of snow. When they fly, they seem to be all white, but down on the earth they are brown. They settled down on the wheat, many — so many of them — on each straw, and then they began their devastating feast. Fortunately they stayed here only about two days, and then they left as suddenly as they had come. The damage was not too great — not to be compared to the destruction in some places where they consumed everything. The fields in three counties to the south and east of us were totally ruined.

Last year a wheat field, today a town

November 27. In September Ole took a load of wheat up to Minnesota to a town called Waseca. The new railroad runs through this town. Last year this place was a wheat field, and today it is a town with many stores and a population of one thousand!

Our herd is not large right now because we sold two yoke of small oxen, and we butchered one cow this fall, so now we have left five cows, a two-year-old heifer, and five calves, one yoke of oxen for driving, five sheep, two pigs, and two colts.

Little Svend is eager to learn

February 21, 1869. I must tell you that little Svend has been attending the English [public] school for two months, and I am happy to tell you that although he was the youngest of all the children, he was especially commended for being attentive, alert, and eager to learn. He was also praised for good conduct. He has already completed the first reader and now is going over it again for the second time. School will continue for another month.

Iowa is an Indian word

February 23. Speaking of Estherville, I might tell you that the other day some Americans came in to get warm, as it was bitterly cold outdoors. Among them was a woman named Esther, for whom the town of Estherville was named. She was the first white woman to settle here. *Ville* means city; so in Norwegian it would be Esther's town. The county is named for the first white man who settled here. His name was Emmett — hence Emmett County.

Iowa is an Indian word meaning "the beautiful land." This is the story of Iowa: When the Indians crossed the Mississippi for the first time into this region and when they saw the beauty of the land, they shouted "Iowa! Iowa!" (pronounced *Aijovai* — I is pronounced like ai, and therefore Iowa is always written with an *I* and not with a *J*. It is never pronounced like *Jova* but *Aijovai*, and it is spelled "Iowa"). The Indian chief who led this tribe across the Mississippi was called "Black Hawk," meaning the black falcon. This chief lies buried near the Des Moines River in Emmett County. This story is considered authentic.

A clock that cost nine dollars

March 4. The clock is striking the hour before midnight. This reminds me that I should tell you that this fall we bought a clock that cost nine dollars. It is a beautiful clock and keeps excellent time.

My greatest happiness is reading

August 1. I had intended to write to you just as soon as I was strong enough, but during the first two weeks after my son's birth I was not able either to read or write because my eyes were so tired. I think I must have strained them by reading too much both now and in my former confinements. As I find my greatest happiness in reading, I have used every spare moment for it, but by doing so I have strained my eyes when I was much too weak to use them.

A flock of boys who need attention

August 15. I have a flock of boys who need care and atttention. Perhaps I am too concerned about my children. If I were more indifferent, I could spare myself much work. There is no doubt of that, but I can't live that way. I would rather do my best in spite of the work.

Hardly any money in circulation

Fourth Sunday after Epiphany [February] 1870. Since I chanced to speak about my boys, I must tell you that my Albert is getting along very well. He is big for his age and he is really very intelligent.

I told you the last time I wrote that we were having a cold and rainy summer. The fall was the same. A severe winter followed very speedily. In the fall we harvested 340 bushels of wheat and 146 bushels of oats but hardly any corn, largely because of the cold summer. We expected a good crop of potatoes; but when we dug them up, we found that half of them were spoiled because of dry rot; and many of the others rotted after they were stored in the cellar.

We got about 32 bushels of turnips and later in the fall, some other vegetables.

The price of wheat is now so low that there is little buying and selling, and therefore hardly any money in circulation.

Cherished because it comes from home

July 7. Everything that you send is doubly cherished because it comes from our beloved home. Thank you, Father, for the coffee roaster. It fits our stove much better than the ones we get here. Thank you, Mother, oh so much for the kerchiefs. They are wonderful. My little boys are very much pleased with their scarves.

The harvest is small

August 16. . . . Consequently the harvest is small; there is little wheat, oats, or hay. We got 184 bushels of wheat, 250 of oats, and 38 of barley. You see it is not very much, but it is of excellent quality, what there is of it. Even so, we should be grateful to God for all His gifts to us who are so unworthy.

A name more in conformity with American

May 18, 1871. After I got well, I waited to write until my little son was christened. He was christened April 17, and I called him Steffen. As long as the original name had to be changed, I thought I'd choose one that was a little more in conformity with American so that he would not have to change it himself later in life if he should live to grow up.

Of cattle we have the following: six cows, four calves, three yokes of young oxen, and one bull. (This winter we sold a sow to Elif and a young ox to Svend Helling.) We also have fourteen sheep, four pigs, and some chickens.

The blizzard took its toll

May 11, 1873. The blizzard in January took its toll here too—an American froze to death, and a Norwegian lad was severely frozen and almost lost his life. Many cattle died from the exposure. We lost none of ours.

My little daughter was five weeks old when her picture was taken.

Far behind in their studies

December 6. My four oldest have been attending Norwegian school this fall, but I must sadly confess that they are far behind in their studies. If they were at home in Norway, I know full well that they would have learned a great deal more.

Few here who can compose letters

November 15, 1874. Torkel T. Hoff from St. Peter, Minnesota, visited us last fall, and he told me that he sent *Emigranten og Fædrelandet* home to Brother Lars. That is the paper we take. At the time that we subscribed for it, there was no other Norwegian paper in America, and we have continued to take it ever since. From time to time I have written some short articles for this paper though I don't think I have written any since you have been getting it.

You ask me if I am the only one in this neighborhood who can write. I could answer both yes and no. There are many here who can write but very few who can compose letters, so that I have to write not only for our nearest neighbors, but also for those who live far away.

Since you, Father, wished to hear something more about the children, I shall try to tell you about them. Svend will be twelve the fourth of January. He is tall and big for his age, very active but a trifle changeable and unstable so that I am often concerned about him. He is capable about the farm and is a great help to his father. In school he learns easily and quickly both Norwegian and English, but when the school term is finished, he has no further interest in books. Therefore he is not so advanced in his reading as he could be.

Niels Olaus was ten years on August 13. He is just as tall as Svend, but not so fat. Strangers think they are twins. Niels is more quiet than Svend and slower in school. He has some difficulty with his reading, but he is capable at farm work. He is especially good at caring for his younger brothers and sisters. Carl was eight years June 18. He is a very active lad, works fast, likes to jest. Niels and he are equally far advanced in their readers (both Norwegian and English). Carl learns very easily. If we only had permanently established schools!

Ole was seven years August 9. He is as chubby and firm as a freshly kneaded batch of dough. He is so vibrant with health that none of the others can measure up to him. It looks as if he were going to be very bright and alert. I started him in Norwegian last winter and in English this summer.

Albert Olai was five July 7. He is not like the others. He is frail and thin, with dark hair and dark eyes. I can't say whether his eyes are black or brown. He is so strange – seems to be thinking a great deal, and he asks questions that fill me with wonder. He often asks me strange, disturbing little questions that I am at a loss to answer, especially questions about the creation of the world. Either he is not of this world, or he will grow up to be something out of the ordinary.

Steffen is chubby and vigorous, almost as large as Albert. He is a chatterbox, talks all day, and is very amusing. He will be four years February 11, but he himself declares that he is going to be five as Albert is. The two are always together. To separate them is well-nigh impossible. We often call Steffen *Taastainsrun* because he is so strong and sturdy in every way.

Then there is my little Bergit. She will be two years January 2. She is frail and has been a sickly, whimpering baby.

All the children were ill

February 11, 1877. Quinquagesima Sunday. Last summer we had the measles, and we had a long siege because all the children were ill. The girls were quite ill. Little Sigri had been ill all summer but did not get the measles until August. She recovered from the measles, but continued to be ill until her death. She died quietly November 16.

This fall we got 124 bushels of wheat, 224 bushels of oats, and 11 bushels of barley. This is all the locusts left us. They took all the corn, all the potatoes, and all the vegetables we had planted. We did get enough for our needs this year, but we were not able to pay off any of the debt.

Next month, if God wills it, I shall have another child. This will be my ninth confinement.

Well housed, both man and beast

May 30, 1877. When I think of our sacred duties as parents and the heavy responsibilities laid upon us, I often become sad and discouraged, for I am not able to do what I would. I think it is best to do as Ole once advised. He said we should rear the children to the best of our understanding and ability, and then leave the rest to Him who said, "For of such is the Kingdom of Heaven."

The locusts have returned; they are swarming everywhere. People have planted nothing but a little corn. On the twenty-fourth of this month, all the prairie grass in this county was burned. It was agreed that we all should set fire to it everywhere, all at the same time, in order to kill the eggs. We were partly successful, but there are still many eggs left so the future looks hopelessly dark. However, He who guides the sun and the stars in their courses can also manifest Himself to us.

We are now well housed, both man and beast. This means a great deal to a pioneer because during the first years he is deprived of many comforts previously enjoyed. Nobody must doubt that we are living comfortably. We have whatever we need. As long as God gives life and strength, we shall not fear the future. We are satisfied and happy with this life, and we meet it unafraid because we have peace and unity in our home.

The boys have a three-year-old pony

November 30. Perhaps you would like to know how much stock we have this year. We have five horses. Two are ponies that we use for driving. Then the boys have a three-year-old pony which they call Greeley. They can all ride him. Finally we have a yearling and a nursing colt. (They are both mares.) The ponies will both bear colts this winter.

Then we have sixteen head of cattle. Two of them are driving oxen, six cows, three heifers that will soon calve, and two that will not. We have three calves, twenty sheep, two pigs, twenty-five chickens, one dog, and one cat – and that's all.

Here we encounter new dangers

FROM OLE NIELSEN, IN QUEBEC, CANADA,
TO HIS FAMILY

1866

Now the Almighty, who disposes everything for the best, has permitted us to see the Promised Land, America! At three o'clock in the afternoon we cast anchor in the harbor of Quebec, after a little more than six weeks' voyage from Bergen. Though we have not been spared dangers and tribulations during the passage, we must be thankful to the Lord for every day and hour he vouchsafes us out of His goodness, thankful that He lets us try the ways and hardships of the world, of which one has no understanding before he has undertaken such a voyage. During the passage we had many storms and much head wind, especially in the beginning. This caused so much delay that the ships that left Bergen eight days later, e.g., *Norden*, arrived here before we did.

Here we encounter new dangers as the Americans are arming for war. Railroads and steamboats have all they can do to transport troops and provisions to the border of the northern states. Because of this we do not know when we shall be able to leave this place, and besides the road is not safe as far as Chicago. But we hope that we shall be able to overcome this difficulty too. During the voyage two old people died, namely Knud Markegaard from Hemsedal, who was about seventy years old, and the woman Oloug Ruspergaard. Before our eyes they died quietly and peacefully. Big stones were tied to their feet, and their bodies were lowered into the water for all the monsters of the sea to feed upon. For a while I feared that I would have to bury one of mine in the same way, but the Lord spared me this trial. For two weeks

Niels was so ill that he could not eat anything. He lost several pounds and grew quite thin, so that he and I have wished more than once that we were at home with Gomme and Dagros. Now he is well again, and so is his mother, but I have a cold, which was also the cause of Niels's illness. Anne's illness was a severe attack of dysentery. The weather was terribly cold during most of the passage, and most of the passengers suffered from bad colds. We did not have any contagious diseases on board, but the ship *Martha* is said to have had cases of smallpox. About ten or twelve emigrant ships have now arrived here; most of them still have not unloaded their cargoes.

Yesterday I went ashore with the captain and had a look at the city. Today most of the passengers have gone ashore, as the captain had chartered a steamboat to take them into the city and back to the ship. This cost him eight specie dollars, which he took out of his own pocket.

I shall give you further details about the voyage when I send you my diary; but I can tell you now that Ole T. Huus and Ole Larsen Rødningen with their families had to go to the hospital for a while at the quarantine station, that is to say, the place three miles from Quebec where we were inspected by a medical officer, because each of them had a child that was ill. But more about this later. Today I shall try to write to Gro also, but I cannot fix any place where to meet her, since I do not know as yet what our itinerary will be.

In Norway a square foot of barren hill

FROM OLE NIELSEN, AT ESTHERVILLE, IOWA, TO HIS FAMILY

October 31, 1866

We should be thankful to our Lord and Creator that He lets His sun rise on us so many times, that He lets us experience both good luck and bad luck, want and tribulation, but also that He in His goodness, if only we have the wisdom to understand it, blesses our labor. As the poet has said: "All will prove fruitful to those who truly love God."

I knew only too well that you would come to miss my little Niels and myself bitterly. But the times and circumstances were such that I had to leave the country, and to this day the Lord has protected me so well that I have not yet had occasion to regret this serious step. It is true that the future is hidden to our eyes, but I still believe that if God will allow me to keep the same good health I have now, and if you, my dear parents, were here, I should be able to support you more decently than I was able to do at home. In Norway you have to quarrel with your neighbors for a square foot of barren hills with no vegetation whatsoever. All kinds of laws and regulations force pedestrians to follow certain designated roads. Yes, I would almost say that it has gone so far that the laws tell you: You must stand there, you must go in this direction, you must make your home in this place, you must not own property except in this location, and so on. And yet a man is supposed to be free, and supposed to be living in a free country! You also know my other reasons for wanting to leave, and all of this must be my excuse. Perhaps it may relieve the pain we are causing you to tell you that my little Niels has recovered his good health on this side of the ocean. Some time ago he regained all his strength, as far as I can see. His playmates are Svend, Nabne, and Karl (not Dichman as I wrote last time), a puppy (Flaai), another dog (Prince), a little pig and two chickens; so you can understand that he has enough to occupy his time. But of course he misses those who would take most care of him, those in whose company he would be most completely protected from faults and sins. Unfortunately Anne is not always quite well, but this is probably to be expected during the period of pregnancy. I am glad that she is not feeling any worse.

I see also from your letter that you have had a good year all around, and I am sure that you could use that. We have also had a good year here as far as the wheat and potato harvests are concerned, but the corn was damaged by the frost over almost the whole of America. I see by the newspapers (I myself take *Skandinaven*, Gro *Emigranten*, and the people from Sando *Fædrelandet*, so that we receive all important European news) that you have had so much rain in Norway that a good deal of the harvest was damaged before it got under roof. Ole harvested 110 bushels of wheat of the best, but not much corn. I get from him what I need, and I worked for him last fall. We are so far advanced on the building of his house that he will be able to move into it this coming winter. It is 15 feet wide and 17 feet long and 12 feet high. Thus it has a loft upstairs. I believe that I have already told you that I have taken a quarter section of railroad land and Ole Opsata has taken one beside me, but now I am planning to buy a quarter of land from a speculator. This land is located next to the lot I own already. I have written to the owner, who lives in Philadelphia, and have offered him $300 for the land, and I am now waiting for an answer from him. If I can obtain possession of these 320 acres of land, my farm will be one of the largest and best farms in this neighborhood.

Of course I need money to buy land, but Assor Grøth has promised to help me financially in any way he can. I have already borrowed $40 from him, and Lars Torsen has paid me back $50 and Iver Tostensen $10. Thus I received $100 all told from you last fall. I paid $50 for my oxen, and I want to buy forest land for the rest. I have a little lumber and kindling wood on my land now, but it is not enough, as you have to have a house, a cow barn, a fence, and boards for a sheepcote. There is enough forest here even if the whole county were settled, but unfortunately it has all been claimed and bought up by speculators, who will only sell it at exorbitant prices, up to $50 an acre. There are a few quarter-sections of unclaimed land left, but they are not located very conveniently.

The land here is so beautiful and fertile that it would be difficult to find any that is better. From the land you can get anything you need, even things like broomtwigs, spoons, and various kinds of toys for the children. Later I will send you seeds of the types we produce here. I have already sent some to Ulrik Kjerulf, who will see if he can produce American fruits in Hallingdal. I shall also send you a map of Iowa. I have borrowed two maps, one of the Union states which is as large as our big table at home, and one of Iowa, somewhat smaller, which I think can be sent through the mail.

Half an hour ago I bought five acres of land from Peder Larsen Bæra for $50. As half of this land is forest, I now have all the lumber I need. I have also bought half a pig for $7.00, a barrel of salt for $8.00, a washtub for $1.85 (this is the way that figures are always written here; that which stands before the period is dollars, and that which stands after cents), besides other things for the household. Things are expensive here, but it is easy to make money as the lowest daily pay is at present half a dollar. We sell a little butter, but we do not get more than $.20 a pound, at the most. Coffee is from $.35 to $.40 a pound, tobacco $1.00 a pound, but I still have some Norwegian tobacco left. Sugar is half the price of coffee; people here use nothing but brown sugar. All kinds of shoes and clothes can be bought in the stores, and also all sorts of medicine. Our town (the woodland I just bought is located a half Norwegian mile outside it) is still small. It has only two stores, or shops, but it has a beautiful location and will certainly grow when the railroad is put through here. On November 7 there will be a meeting of the parish council, and then it is to be decided whether I am to be schoolmaster for this winter or not. I have asked for $15 a month.

No crocodiles in the rivers

FROM OLE NIELSEN, AT ESTHERVILLE, IOWA, TO HIS PARENTS, BROTHERS, AND SISTERS

March 29, 1868

We received Father's letter of February 16 on the twenty-sixth of this month and send you our best thanks for it. It had been a long time since we had seen your handwriting, but when we did get your letter we were amply rewarded for our waiting. My own letters usually become too short because I am hard pressed for time, and besides we can never obtain good stationery here, so that the letters get too heavy if I write too much.

In consequence of this I shall not waste any time but try to answer your questions right away. First you ask where we store wheat, corn, potatoes, and root crops. The wheat is stored in the dwelling house or in a kind of storehouse which is here called a granary. Those who cannot store it in this way put together rails (the kind you use at home for making fences) to make a square container, and after they have covered the bottom and the corners with straw, the wheat is dumped into the container and covered with straw. It is kept in storage there until it is needed. This is the most common procedure in this region, and in all new regions where people cannot very well afford to put up many buildings. The corn is stored in practically the same manner, but potatoes and other root crops are kept in cellars or holes in the ground. From this you will probably conclude that there is ample opportunity for thieves to help themselves when all these products are left out all winter. But we have no fear of thieves here, and it is quite safe to leave tools out where you have used them; there is no danger of their disappearing. We do have cases of horse-stealing occasionally, but the law is now so hard on horse thieves that I believe that few persons will venture into that business from now on.

Then you ask what the houses are like in the place where I live now, and how I am getting along. The houses here are good and still new, as Ole had them constructed only last year. In the dwelling house there is only one room, but in the barn there are two so that we each have a room. Everything is very adequate in all ways, and there is enough forest on the land. The pasture is to one side of the house and the hay field to the other. A small brook flows past the house, and the road to the city is very close. My piece of land is quite similar to Ole's, but with no brook on it and less forest. I plan to finish my house this spring. It will be 25 feet long and 16 feet wide, and I have now got a section of 15 by 10 feet completed. I plan to divide the rest of the house into sections and build one section at a time. I started this project somewhat ambitiously; that is why it takes so long to finish it. As I do not have much money to hire help with, Ole Opsata and I have agreed to help each other put up our houses.

I have certainly been very busy the two years I have been here, and this will be the lot of every settler as long as he has to buy all his provisions and in addition build, till the soil, fence in the land, and procure for himself all the other necessities. Despite this heavy toil and all the privations I have felt twice as happy as before, mainly because Anne – after some experience of the ways of the big world – has now come to appreciate her husband more than she used to and is more affectionate with me, but also because a man is completely free and independent here. You do not have to bow and scrape either to the minister or the sexton or grovel before your creditors, for March 25 is just like any other day here. Poor relief taxes and beggars are also unknown. If by any chance a man happens to suffer a financial setback, everybody is ready to help him get on his feet again. Last fall, for instance, Endre Glesne and a man from Voss lost all their hay because of the extremely hot weather on the prairies, but all their neighbors helped them. Some took in their animals over the winter, others gave hay, and still others money, so that they were completely compensated for what they had lost. I gave a load of hay to each of them.

Because of the early spring this year there will be a lot of hay left over for next year. The hay is put in stacks of about twenty wagonloads in each and in the same shape of stacks as at home. We have not had real winter for much more than a month, for already in February the ground was free of snow, and in that month an American in our county sowed his wheat. Ole Engebretsen sowed his wheat on the twenty-third of this month, and I sowed mine today, the thirtieth. It is certainly exceptional that we are able to begin so early, but the weather is now almost like summer. The flies are buzzing about our ears, the frogs and toads have started their music in the ponds, the gophers and snakes have come out of their holes – almost everything that was hibernating has now come back to life. All the migratory birds, the swan, the goose, the crane (a sort of ostrich), the black thrush, the duck, and many others returned some time ago. We have almost all the kinds of birds that you have at home, except the cuckoo and the sparrow. Some of the birds here are a little different in appearance and habits from those at home, however. The grouse is found here but it does not change its color; nor does the hare, which is somewhat smaller in this country. The wolf and the fox are smaller here – we hardly ever see any wolves – and I have not seen any deer since I came here. There are very few wild animals here, and they never harm us in any way. The great horned owl and other kinds of owl are found here; one of them is as large as the horned owl and is white as snow. The raven is exactly like the Norwegian raven, and the crow and the magpie very similar, apart from the language they speak, of course. The canary is found wild here.

Since I live so close to the river I suppose that I ought to tell you a little about its inhabitants, too. There are neither crocodiles nor alligators in it, which may be a disappointment to those at home who believe that these creatures are found in all rivers here. No, the only animals in it for which I feel any revulsion are the turtles, some of which are quite large. We have several kinds of frogs, and they keep up a peculiar music during the spring and summer nights, while the blackbird entertains us every morning with his melodious notes. The river is not very rich in fish, but all the rivulets and brooks contain plenty of them. In the spring when the fish go upstream you can catch them with pitchforks and even with your bare hands, when they go right into the shoals and head toward the shore. Last spring Endre

Glesne used sacks distended by hoops instead of nets or pounds, and he got several sacks full of fish. The biggest and most common fish here is the buffalo fish, which is much like the salmon in size but not in appearance. Then there is the bullhead, which has two large feelers . . . and some other kinds that are not caught quite so often.

The beaver and the mink (the Norwegian marten) are caught in traps along the river. Here, too, the fur of the mink is regarded as highly valuable. Last winter Svend Hoff caught two minks and got a very handsome price for the furs. People also hunt the muskrat, an animal resembling both the beaver and the gopher; its furs pay from ten to twenty cents apiece. It lives both in the water and on land, though mainly in the water. It builds its houses in soft bogs or little lakes. The houses are very cleverly constructed; from the outside they look like anthills, and inside are a great many small rooms, each of which has its definite use. People catch the muskrat in these little hills, usually by placing a trap in its "bedroom," which always faces south. There are many mice here of various kinds, and that is why most farmers keep more than one cat. The stoat found here always keeps its white color. We also have squirrels, but they are much smaller than the ones in Norway. Although they are very much like the gophers in color and size, they have all the characteristics of the squirrels. The hare is very much like the Norwegian rabbit.

Frozen to death in a terrible snow storm

FROM OLE NIELSEN, AT ESTHERVILLE,
IOWA, TO HIS PARENTS

February 10, 1870

Since I wrote you last, we have all been well, except for a small ailment that I brought on myself at the beginning of this winter because I had neglected to look after my health. I was ill with a cold for some eight days, and a couple of days I had such a severe fever that some of my friends were beginning to fear that I should not recover. But I knew that my time had not come yet, for my children were too small for me to be permitted to leave them. I must also add that our two youngest children, Torjus and Tollef, have had bad attacks of whooping cough.

Whether this is due to our negligence or to an epidemic I do not know, though the latter is probably the case. At any rate it causes us a good deal of grief and worry to see these dear little ones suffer so. As I am writing these lines, I am also functioning as a nurse, looking after the members of my family, most of whom are now asleep.

Anne and Niels are in good health, as always. We now have 14 cattle, 6 sheep, and 2 pigs, to say nothing of 2 three-year-old mares. My good fortune in owning horses this soon is due to Assor Grøth, from whom I bought them. He wrote me last summer that he had two fine mares for sale, and that I should have them very cheaply if I wanted to buy them. He added that I could pay for them when it was convenient. I agreed to the price, which was $300 plus 10 per cent interest. I was tempted by these favorable conditions and by the fact that both of the mares were with colt, and so far I have not regretted the purchase, though I lost both the colts. I had been so careless as to leave the mares for a while in a stable which contained sheep manure. I also owe Assor another hundred dollars which I had to borrow in the bad year of 1867, partly in raw produce and partly in money. I plan to pay this back next spring, as I have a couple of steers that are almost worth that much now. Assor is like another Erik Nohs to me, and I wish that you, Father, would send him a few lines sometime and thank him for all his help and goodness to me and tell him what news you have of our old acquaintances. His address is: St. Ansgar P.O., Mitchell Co., Iowa.

You are probably a little alarmed to hear that I owe so much money, but you must remember that a dollar equals about a mark in your money and that it is easier for a laborer to earn a dollar a day here than it is to make a mark a day in Norway. He who can earn 2 marks a day in the old country can make $2 or $3 a day here. The same is true of the price of the several commodities. That which costs 10 marks in Norway costs $10 in this country, and so on. And if you remember that a team of three-year-old steers is worth $100 and a team of four- or five-year-olds $150, then the sum is not too large and my debt not too bad.

After I had bought these horses (with which I now do my work) I had to buy harness, which cost me $30. I also had to buy a wagon which cost me the price of six sheep, and besides I have made myself a new sleigh and harness bells which cost me $1 apiece. The old sleigh I brought from Norway is broken again, and as we do not have any Ola Bjella here to mend it, it is left with some other old scrap. A fine team of horses with new harness and wagon is more expensive here than 160 acres of land.

Close to my farm there is a quarter of a section of land (160 acres) out of which you can cultivate more than a hundred acres without encountering any rocks or swamps. I have often wished that this piece of land belonged to one of my relatives; but as this was not possible, I have done everything I could to get one of my acquaintances to buy it. Gunder G. Thune and Andreas C. Strand have written to me to ask me to buy land and forest for them, and I have answered that I would be glad to do this for them if they will only send the money. It is still doubtful whether their money will get here soon enough to buy this piece of land. Each of these men owns about $2,000 besides some other property. Tosten L. Nohs has bought land here and plans to live here in the future. I have not heard anything about Bottolf Nohs since he returned. From a letter to Ole Opsata I have seen that Knud Ellefstølen is happily arrived in Norway, and I assume that he is now very popular at home. Here he was anything but popular, though he had made a good deal of money, which he might well need when he planned to make such a long pleasure trip. He was lucky that Ragni Røesepladsen did not get hold of him, for she would probably have made his wallet a good deal lighter. I am sure that he can tell you how shingles are made in this country. I wish he would, for it would take too much space for me to describe it in this letter.

Another piece of news is that between January 15 and 16 we had a terrible snow storm which claimed a life among us Norwegians, namely the second oldest son of Tollef Medgaarden, Ole, who froze to death out on the prairie. He was as close to the nearest house as the distance from Tollef Hagene to your farm when they found him. At the burial banquet a Jew functioned as cook, and he managed very well, in the American manner, of course. Tollef is the way he has always been. He likes to have things in the grand manner, but once in a while he bites off more than he can chew. His old father is being supported by the county—he is the only Norwegian who needs relief.

As I am now almost at the end of my space, I conclude this letter with a request. If someone plans to emigrate next spring, I wish that Father or one of you would send me some black sheepskin with short wool on it for a coat. Black sheep are very rare here; most of the sheep are brown in color. I myself will pay for the shipping expenses, but perhaps one of you could put up the rest of the money for a while. If Lars Knudsen, who got my old fur coat, is still alive, then greet him from me. Also many greetings to all my other friends and relatives. But most of all my dear family is greeted from him who can never forget you and the dear memories of his youth. I wish that in all your activities you may always obey Him who sits on His heavenly throne, so that we may all meet happily in the hereafter.

The Glorious New Scandinavia

IT was Fredrika Bremer who in 1850 described Minnesota as a "glorious new Scandinavia" and prophesied for the coming North Star State a great and "beautiful" future.*

The gentle Swedish traveler and writer who journeyed up the Mississippi in pre-railroad days saw what was still nearly virgin territory, a land of primitive Sioux and Chippewa, of unfished lakes, mainly uncut woods, and unplowed prairies. A land of optimism and hope, however! Statehood was still eight years off in the future, but the Territory had been established, with St. Paul as its capital, towns were springing up, and settlers were beginning to spread out onto the fertile lands near by. With all due respect to Fredrika Bremer, no inspired prophetic vision was needed to predict a prosperous state. Every Minnesota "booster" was filling the air with glowing predictions of greatness to come.† Yet there was insight in Miss Bremer's emphasis upon a "new Scandinavia," for whereas Scandinavians had barely touched foot on Minnesota soil when she visited Minnesota, twenty-five years thereafter there would be more than eighty thousand Norwegians alone in the state. The Scandinavians, as time went on, would invest Minnesota with the most pronounced Scandinavian flavor of all the states in the Union. Minnesota became America as well as a "glorious new Scandinavia," for thousands of immigrants flocked to its lands throughout the remain-

* Fredrika Bremer, *Homes of the New World* (New York, 1853), vol. 1, p. 56. See also John T. Flanagan, "Fredrika Bremer, Traveler and Prophet," in *Minnesota History*, 20:129–139 (June 1939).

† An interesting documentary work, edited by Mary W. Berthel under the title *Horns of Thunder* (St. Paul, 1948), deals with the career and writing of James M. Goodhue, the first newspaper editor in Minnesota, and reflects faithfully the frontier spirit of boosting.

ing decades of the nineteenth century and shared in the future Miss Bremer had foretold at mid-century.

Even before Miss Bremer visited Minnesota, the aggressive minister, C. L. Clausen, had appealed to the governor of the Territory, Alexander Ramsey, for reliable information that he might draw upon in advising his countrymen to settle on Minnesota public lands; and in the following years immigrants swarmed into the area, first going to the open lands in the southeastern portions of the state, west of the Mississippi, and then, after the Civil War, striking westward until, in the later decades of the century, they flooded into the Red River Valley and beyond. The story of the advance of settlement by Norwegian pioneers has been told in a memorable chapter by Carlton C. Qualey in his book *Norwegian Settlement in the United States.**

In the present account a few first-hand narratives, in the form of letters, make vivid both the hardships and problems of the pioneers and the rich potentialities of Minnesota for settlers, particularly in the western section of the state.

An unnamed correspondent whose letter was made public in a Bergen newspaper wrote in the autumn of 1858 from Carver County describing with naive interest some of the wonders of American implements and ways. A letter of 1860 from a farmer and his wife in Nicollet County, not far from the city of St. Peter, is full of homely detail and seems quite undramatic. But two circumstances add a touch of drama to this unpretentious document. The first is that these pioneers, who had just cleared thirteen acres of land on their farm of 160 acres, were the grandparents of a man who in the twentieth century became the United States Minister to the country from which these people emigrated, Laurits S. Swenson. And the second is that this letter, from which a few excerpts are presented here, was fortunately copied in the Norwegian home where it had been preserved – and during the German occupation of Norway the house was blown up and the original destroyed.

A farmer two years later tells a tale of woe, with Civil War and Indian outrages disturbing the previous calm of "this so-called wonderful America." And yet another immigrant, writing from the heart of the region of the Sioux War, reflects the terror of the outbreak and voices sad

* See a letter from Clausen to Governor Ramsey, January 22, 1850, in the Ramsey Papers, Minnesota Historical Society. Dr. Qualey prints a facsimile of this letter in his *Norwegian Settlement*, pp. 89–90.

regret as he thinks of the peaceful home in the Old World that he had left.

The letter of Guri Endreson, written in 1866, is that of a frontier heroine over whose grave the state of Minnesota has erected a monument in her honor. Her story has been told and retold. A party of Sioux warriors swept down upon her farm in the summer of 1862, killed her husband and one son, carried off her daughters as captives, and wounded another son. Guri Endreson made her way to a near-by farm, where she found two badly wounded men, got them into an ox-drawn wagon along with her wounded boy and a small daughter, started for Forest City, thirty miles away, guarded her party through a night, and pushed doggedly on until she reached safety. She waited four years before telling her story to her relatives in Norway. The letter, here presented in an English translation, I found in Norway some years ago. It is her own firsthand story of what happened in the tumult of the Sioux Outbreak, but the heroic quality of this pioneer woman is as much revealed in her report of the resumption of her everyday duties as in its restrained tale of the disaster of 1862.

Both the Sioux and the Civil wars were over when an immigrant in the city of Faribault commented candidly and informingly on life and politics in America in a letter that appeared in a newspaper in the capital of Norway in 1866.

Possibly the most interesting of all these Minnesota letters, however, are those of Paul Hjelm-Hansen, a journalist who came to America in 1867 and who made himself a publicist for the Red River Valley, that rich farming section which in the following years became a Mecca for immigrants from Norway and for earlier settlers who, after the restless fashion of American pioneers, moved from one frontier to another. Hjelm-Hansen gloried in his western adventures. As I have written elsewhere, "He knew the tread of oxen, kept warm at night under a buffalo robe, used a sack of flour for a pillow, and, like the Vikings, 'had the blue heavens for a covering.'" * He entertained no doubts as to the coming greatness of the fertile valley that he described in glowing terms, and he correctly predicted that immigrants would stream to its lands. His reports, published both in Norwegian-American newspapers and in Norway, were read with deep interest, and immigrant action soon confirmed

* Blegen, *Norwegian Migration*, vol. 2, p. 496. See also my article "Minnesota's Campaign for Immigrants" in Swedish Historical Society of America *Yearbook*, 1926, pp. 18–20, 49.

the judgment of this pioneer of the Red River Valley. His contributions are remembered in a plaque in his honor which is displayed in the historical society of the state of his choice.*

The milk and cream are rich here

FROM A RESIDENT OF CARVER COUNTY, MINNESOTA, TO FRIENDS †

October 23, 1858

Generally our animals are larger here than they were in our home parish [Fuse clerical district] in Norway. We have now slaughtered the ox that was part of the bargain when we bought our farm, and although it was so old that it had lost several teeth, it still yielded fifty-four pounds of tallow and about five hundred pounds of meat. Our cows milk very well, and the milk and cream are richer here than they were in Norway. Our milk pails are so made that we can strain the milk as we pour it out of the pail. Churning butter is also very easy and seldom requires more than ten minutes and never more than fifteen. Our churns are made of zinc and have double walls, so that between the churn proper, in which the cream is kept, and the outer covering there is an open space which may be filled with hot or cold water, depending on the temperature desired, and on the front side of the churn there is a gauge which indicates when the cream has turned into butter.

Our washboards are also covered with zinc and designed to make the washing very easy and quick. We bake bread every day; it is put up in the morning, baked at noon, and toasted in the afternoon. In the bread we put a leaven made in the following way: to cold water are added a little salt, vinegar, sugar, and potassium. Besides we put a little hops water in the bread; the hop plant grows wild here. No bolts are used in our irons; we heat them by putting them on a stove lid, and they are much better for ironing than those we had in Norway.

The Indians (the wild ones) roam around in the forests hunting. They

* Paul Hjelm-Hansen had been appointed by the governor of Minnesota to act as an agent of the Minnesota State Board of Immigration. His letters appeared not only in the *Nordisk Folkeblad* of Minneapolis, but also in a LaCrosse, Wisconsin, newspaper, *Fædrelandet og Emigranten*. Some years after his Red River journeys he published a book entitled *Om Nordamerika* – a general account of North America.

† This letter appeared in *Bergensposten*, March 1, 1859.

live in tents that they carry along with them and have a very strange kind of dress, which consists of trousers that only reach a little above the knees, shoes made of deerskin, and a horsecloth, as I shall have to call it, around the shoulders. Their hair is arranged in long, peculiar plaits, and their faces are painted with different colors. Sometimes they stop by to sell game, ask for a cup of coffee or a bite to eat; they are very polite and do not harm us in any way. If we gave them a drink of liquor, we should be liable to a fine of $100.

People here usually dress in very distinguished fashion. In Hamilton, for instance, I saw ladies that were very nicely dressed, and in Quebec I saw ladies wearing dresses of crepe with hoop skirts underneath instead of crinolines. You could also see silken shawls and Schaefer hats, and on their legs they would wear fine stockings and shoes, or else walk around with bare legs.

January 6, 1859

On November 2 it snowed here, and since that time we have had winter. The weather has been very calm, however, except for a couple of days when it was rather cold, colder than I have ever known it to be in Norway. Yet our animals have been out in the open every single day, and we give them their hay and water in the fields though we have a barn for them. Out here in the country there are not many jobs for servant girls, since all people here are settlers that have to get along as well as they can with their own hands. But in the cities jobs are available, and the minimum pay for servant girls there is $1 a week plus free board.

Tools and implements are rather expensive

FROM SVEND SVENSSEN AND GURI SANDERS-DATTER, AT RØDNING, NEAR ST. PETER, MINNESOTA, TO FRIENDS *

February 1860

We have all been in good health up to the present, and, considering our situation, we are doing well. On October 20, 1858, I had a still-born

* This letter, only a few excerpts from which are translated here, is published in full, in the original, in Lars Reinton and Sigurd S. Reinton, *Folk og fortid i Hol*, 2:768–771. The transcript I have used for the translation was kindly sent to me by Dr. Lars Reinton, the distinguished Norwegian local historian.

baby girl. I suffered very little, and we must thank God, who governs all for the best.

We must let you know that we have taken up 160 acres of government land, including prairie and woods. It is about five English miles from Lars S. Rødningen and twelve from the town of St. Peter. Our neighbors are Ole Lofthus and our son Svend and a young man from Torp Annex. We moved onto our land last May. In the summer we built a cabin with a loft, and also a barn for the animals. We have three cows, a pair of driving oxen, two pairs of two-year-olds, three other oxen only a year old, a heifer, two pigs, and two sheep. Last fall we slaughtered six pigs. We can also tell you that we have broken thirteen acres of our land for cultivation. Five of these we planted with corn and potatoes, and we harvested 60 bushels of corn and 70 of potatoes, together with 70 bushels of cabbages. Last year we farmed seven acres belonging to Lars S. Rødningen, from which we got half and he half. Our share consisted of 30 bushels of wheat, 60 of barley, and 15 of oats. I have fenced forty acres of fields and meadow. As I see it, my land is well situated for water, fields, and hay, and is a good place to build on.

Now, to give you our honest opinion about emigration, which I know many of you want to hear about, I can say truthfully that I do not regret our coming here, especially when I think of the heavy burdens we escaped from. I feel very glad about it all, for example, when I remember the moving to the saeters, the plight of the cattle in winter, the difficulty of getting hay, and the problem of subsistence. From all this, with God's help, I regard myself as freed, not that I want anybody to think that we have escaped all worry by having come here. Still, there is a big difference, especially for women.

I must now tell you a little about conditions here. We had a very good year, but these are hard times for money, though we are hoping things will soon improve. Wages are not high. A good worker gets 50 cents a day in the winter, but the trouble is that there is not much work to be had in the winter. In the summer wages are from $.75 to $1 a day, and for girls from $4 to $6 a month, with never any lack of jobs for them. Now a little about the prices of foods: a bushel of wheat, $.70; a bushel of corn, $.35; potatoes, $.25; barley, $.40; a barrel of wheat flour, $5; a pound of butter, from $.10 to $.15; a pound of pork, from $.04 to $.04½. I will also report a little about the prices of animals: a pair of driving oxen, $60 to $70; for a team of good working horses, $200 to $300; and for a cow, $20 to $25; one-year old heifers, $5 to $6. Tools and implements are rather expensive here. A wagon costs from $50 to $100, a plow $12 to $15, a breaking plow $15 to $24, and a cook stove $15 to $35. We have bought a stove that cost us $36, and with it we can cook, roast pork, make bread, and brew coffee all at the same time.

My rifle is always loaded

FROM A FARMER IN DODGE COUNTY, MINNESOTA, TO FRIENDS *

[September 1862]

At this time life is not very pleasant in this so-called wonderful America. The country is full of danger, and at no time do we feel any security for our lives or property. A week ago in our county (Dodge County in southeastern Minnesota), the name of every citizen between eighteen and forty-five years of age was taken down, regardless of whether he, like myself, was married or not. Next month (October) there is to be a levy of soldiers for military service, and our county alone is to supply 118 men in addition to those who have already enlisted as volunteers.

Last week we therefore all had to leave our harvesting work and our weeping wives and children and appear at the place of enlistment, downcast and worried. We waited until six o'clock in the afternoon. Then finally the commissioner arrived, accompanied by a band which continued playing for a long time to encourage us and give us a foretaste of the joys of war. But we thought only of its sorrows and despite our reluctance had to give our name and age. To tempt people to enlist as volunteers, everybody who would volunteer was offered $225, out of which $125 is paid by the county and $100 by the state. Several men then enlisted, Yankees and Norwegians, and we others, who preferred to stay at home and work for our wives and children, were ordered to be ready at the next levy. Then who is to go will be decided by drawing lots. In the meantime, we were forbidden to leave the county without special permission, and we were also told that no one would get a pass-

* This letter bears no date, but appeared in *Morgenbladet*, November 22, 1862, and obviously was written in September of that year. After printing the text, *Morgenbladet* adds a strong editorial comment assailing the American consul at Bergen, O. E. Dreutzer, for agitating for emigration to America.

port to leave the country. Dejected, we went home, and now we are in a mood of uncertainty and tension, almost like prisoners of war in this formerly so free country. Our names have been taken down – perhaps I shall be a soldier next month and have to leave my home, my wife, child, and everything I have been working for over so many years.

But this is not the worst of it. We have another and far more cruel enemy near by, namely the Indians. They are raging especially in northwestern Minnesota and perpetrate cruelties which no pen can describe. As yet they have not appeared in our fairly densely populated districts, but still they are not more than ten or fifteen Norwegian miles away. Every day settlers come through here who have had to abandon everything they owned to escape a most painful death. Several Norwegians have been killed and many women have been captured. They chase the women together in groups and make them herd the cattle they have seized.

When the Indians are on horseback they rush with the speed of a whirlwind across the vast prairies. You are not safe from them anywhere, for they are as cunning as they are bold. The other evening we received the frightening message that they have been seen in our neighborhood, so we hitched our horses and made ready to leave our house and all our property and escape from the savages under the cover of darkness. But it was a false alarm, God be praised, and for this time we could rest undisturbed. How terrible it is thus, every moment, to expect that you will be attacked, robbed, and perhaps murdered! We do not go to bed any night without fear, and my rifle is always loaded. But may the will of the Lord be done. We must not grumble, for He may still save us. It is true that some cavalry have been dispatched against these hordes, but they will not avail much, for the Indians are said to be more than ten thousand strong. Besides they are so cunning that it is not easy to get the better of them. Sometimes they disguise themselves in ordinary farmers' clothes and stalk their victims noiselessly. Thus they recently attacked some Norwegians who were working at their threshing machine suspecting no danger. The men were all killed, the horses stolen, and the machine and the whole crop burned.

From this you may see how we live! On the one hand, the prospect of being carried off as cannon fodder to the South, on the other the imminent danger of falling prey to the Indians. Add to this the heavy war tax that everybody has to pay whether he is enlisted as a soldier or not. You are better off who can live at home in peaceful Norway. God grant us patience and fortitude to bear these heavy burdens.

Tomahawks and knives claim many victims

FROM E. O., AT ST. PETER, MINNESOTA, TO FRIENDS *

September 9, 1862

I take my pen to write you a few words with my warmest greetings to all your relatives and friends. Thus far we are all in good health. I must also tell you that our family has been increased by the arrival of a little American who was born on September 3. Otherwise I have no joyful or satisfactory tidings to bring to my dear home parish.

I will now describe everything to you as thoroughly as I am able, and as far as my heart, which is trembling with fear, will allow me. That which I suspected and wrote about in my last letter has come about. The Indians have begun attacking the farmers. They have already killed a great many people, and many are mutilated in the cruelest manner. Tomahawks and knives have already claimed many victims. Children, less able to defend themselves, are usually burned alive or hanged in the trees, and destruction moves from house to house. The Indians burn everything on their way – houses, hay, grains, and so on. I believe that even if I described the horror in the strongest possible language, my description would fall short of the reality. We have moved into St. Peter now to stay alive as long as possible. These troubles have now lasted for about two weeks, and every day larger numbers of settlers come into St. Peter to protect their lives from the raging Indians. They crowd themselves together in large stone houses for protection, and the misery is so great that imagination could not depict it in darker colors. A few persons arrive almost naked, others wounded by bullets or other weapons, and some with their hands and feet burned off. May I never again have to see such terrible sights! Those who have enough money to move on travel farther down in the country, but it is not safe where they go, for the whole country is in a state of turmoil and the Indians are found almost everywhere.

* This letter appeared in *Stavenger Amtstidende og Adresseavis,* October 27, 1862, reprinted from *Buskeruds Amtstidende.*

I will relate one of the most gruesome incidents in detail. The Indians had captured about thirty women whom they used to herd cattle that they had seized. Immediately a small detachment of a few soldiers we have here was dispatched to their rescue. But as soon as the Indians found out that they were being pursued, they crowded the women into a house, set it on fire and let them burn to death alive.

In these terrible times, I feel that it is my duty to write to you. It may be the last time, for our lives are in danger every moment. The nearest town, New Ulm, has already been taken. How sad it is to think of my peaceful home where I and my family might have lived quietly! Now I have thrown away so much money only to find myself in this terrible position. I certainly hope that not many people are still writing enticing letters home from America.

I shall now have to conclude my letter, for my hand is trembling constantly with fear. Do not write to me until I write to you. God knows what will become of us. Love to my old father from all of us. If you do not hear from me any more, thank you all for everything.

Atrocities still fresh in memory

FROM GURI ENDRESEN, AT HARRISON P. O., MONONGALIA COUNTY, MINNESOTA, TO HER MOTHER AND HER DAUGHTER IN NORWAY *

December 2, 1866

I have received your letter of April 14, this year, and I send you herewith my heartiest thanks for it, for it gives me great happiness to hear from you and to know that you are alive, well, and in general thriving. I must also report briefly to you how things have been going with me recently, though I must ask you to forgive me for not having told you earlier about my fate. I do not seem to have been able to do so much as to write to you, because during the time when the savages raged so fearfully here I was not able to think about anything except being murdered, with my whole

* My translation of this letter appeared in "Immigrant Women and the American Frontier," *Norwegian-American Studies and Records* (Northfield, Minn.), 5:14–29 (1930).

family, by these terrible heathen. But God be praised, I escaped with my life, unharmed by them, and my four daughters also came through the danger unscathed.

Guri and Britha were carried off by the wild Indians, but they got a chance the next day to make their escape. When the savages gave them permission to go home to get some food, these young girls made use of the opportunity to flee and thus they got away alive, and on the third day after they had been taken, some Americans came along who found them on a large plain or prairie and brought them to people. I myself wandered aimlessly around on my land with my youngest daughter, and I had to look on while they shot my precious husband dead, and in my sight my dear son Ole was shot through the shoulder. But he got well again from this wound and lived a little more than a year and then was taken sick and died. We also found my oldest son Endre shot dead, but I did not see the firing of this death shot. For two days and nights I hovered about here with my little daughter, between fear and hope and almost crazy, before I found my wounded son and a couple of other persons, unhurt, who helped us to get away to a place of greater security. To be an eyewitness to these things and to see many others wounded and killed was almost too much for a poor woman; but, God be thanked, I kept my life and my sanity, though all my movable property was torn away and stolen. But this would have been nothing if only I could have had my loved husband and children – but what shall I say? God permitted it to happen thus, and I had to accept my heavy fate and thank Him for having spared my life and those of some of my dear children.

I must also let you know that my daughter Gjærtru has land, which they received from the government under a law that has been passed, called in our language "the Homestead law," and for a quarter-section of land they have to pay $16, and after they have lived there five years they receive a deed and complete possession of the property and can sell it if they want to or keep it if they want to. She lives about twenty-four American miles from here and is doing well. My daughter Guri is away in house service for an American about a hundred miles from here; she has been there working for the same man for four years; she is in good health and is doing well; I visited her recently, but for a long time I knew nothing about her, whether she was alive or not.

My other two daughters, Britha and Anna, are at home with me, are in health, and are thriving here. I must also remark that it was four years

August 21 since I had to flee from my dear home, and since that time I have not been on my land, as it is only a sad sight because at the spot where I had a happy home, there are now only ruins left as reminders of the terrible Indians. Still I moved up here to the neighborhood again this summer. A number of families have moved back here again so that we hope after a while to make conditions pleasant once more. Yet the atrocities of the Indians are and will be fresh in memory. They have now been driven beyond the boundaries of the state, and we hope that they never will be allowed to come here again. I am now staying at the home of Sjur Anderson, two and a half miles from my home.

I must also tell you how much I had before I was ruined in this way. I had 17 head of cattle, 8 sheep, 8 pigs, and a number of chickens; now I have 6 head of cattle, 4 sheep, 1 pig. Five of my cattle stayed on my land until February 1863, and lived on some hay and stacks of wheat on the land; and I received compensation from the government for my cattle and other movable property that I lost. Of the six cattle that I now have three are milk cows, and of these I have sold butter, the summer's product, a little over 230 pounds; I sold this last month and got $66 for it. In general I may say that one or another has advised me to sell my land, but I would rather keep it for a time yet, in the hope that some of my people might come and use it. It is difficult to get such good land again, and if you, my dear daughter, would come here, you could buy it and use it, and then it would not be necessary to let it fall into the hands of strangers.

And now in closing I must send my very warm greetings to my unforgettable dear mother, my dearest daughter and her husband and children, and in general to all my relatives, acquaintances, and friends. And may the Lord by his grace bend, direct, and govern our hearts so that we sometime with gladness may assemble with God in the eternal mansions where there will be no more partings, no sorrows, no more trials, but everlasting joy and gladness, and contentment in beholding God's face. If this be the goal for all our endeavors through the sorrows and cares of this life, then through his grace we may hope for a blessed life hereafter, for Jesus sake.

Americans are practical and efficient

FROM A RESIDENT OF FARIBAULT, MINNESOTA, TO FRIENDS *

1866

After four days' stay in New York I left by railroad for the West through the states of New York, Pennsylvania, Ohio, Indiana, and Illinois, to Chicago. On my way, I went through a great many large cities and villages. In Norway I had read that the railroad tracks in America go right through the middle of the streets, and this had seemed most peculiar to me. But now I saw that it was quite true. Any possible danger is avoided by having the trains move very slowly through the cities and by the ringing of big, sonorous bells on the fronts of the locomotives.

Chicago is a large and splendid city. The degree of briskness and business activity here is not much less than in London or New York. As you know, Chicago is considered the most important grain market in the world. At the present time it has more than 200,000 inhabitants; in 1840 it had 4,470. But the location of the city is very unhealthful.

After a day's stay in Chicago I bought a ticket for La Crosse, the destination of my journey for the time being. I came through another large city, Milwaukee, which has more than 100,000 inhabitants. La Crosse, like Milwaukee, is located in the state of Wisconsin. It is on the Mississippi River and is still a small town of not over 8,000 inhabitants, of whom more than a third seem to be Norwegians. Here I met four clerks, all of whom I knew from Christiania. They had no good news for me, for they said that it would be difficult to get a job just then, as I had arrived at a very inopportune season. These clerks had not had easy going during the first period of their stay in America. For a long time they had had to earn their living by manual labor. One of them had been a painter, another a tanner, and the third had worked as a simple laborer on a raft on the Mississippi going down to St. Louis. They advised me to get a similar job until the times became more favorable, but for quite a while I did not feel much like doing this. An older clerk from Christiania, who arrived in La Crosse a couple of days after me, took service as a waiter in a boarding house, as he could not get a position in trade either in Chicago or La Crosse. After a few more days in La Crosse, I decided to go farther west.

In St. Peter I became acquainted with a Swede, L., who was head

* This letter appeared in *Aftenbladet*, September 28, 1866.

clerk in a bank there. He advised me to go to Faribault to look for a job, and he was kind enough to give me a recommendation to an important man of his acquaintance there. Consequently, I went to Faribault and got a job.

Faribault, which was founded recently, is a beautiful small town of 5,000 inhabitants six and a half Norwegian miles east of St. Peter. Like all towns here it is growing rapidly. My bosses, partners in a firm called E. A. R. and Company, are both Americans. One of them, the major as he is called because he had the rank of a major during the war, is a full-blooded Yankee from New Hampshire. The other, Daniels, is from New York. I had always wanted to work with Yankees – I never put any stock in the *Times* characterization of the Yankees, nor in its other nonsense about American conditions – and I must say that I have every reason to be satisfied. My bosses are very kind and obliging people, and working conditions with them are as good as I might wish for.

Everything is terribly expensive here, with the exception of food. Last winter the farmers offered their wheat for sale – and Minnesota wheat is the best in the world – at $.50 a bushel without getting buyers. A barrel of salt costs about $5, coffee $.35 or $.40 a pound, and nearly all other groceries are more expensive than in Norway. Almost all kinds of dry goods are twice as expensive as they are in Norway, but the Americans are not satisfied to make such a poor profit as people do in Norway. There seems almost to be a silent agreement among all kinds of businessmen here that everybody is to make a good profit on what he has to sell. It is also much more pleasant to wait on customers here than it is in Norway. All conversation and aggressive recommendation of merchandise, which was always so distasteful to me, is nonexistent here. We also have extensive barter with the farmers. They bring us wool, butter, and eggs and get in return the things they need. Butter and eggs we sell to the people of the town at a profit of 33 per cent. In New York butter costs $.60 a pound, in La Crosse $.15, and here the price is $.30. But for that matter, the prices of these goods vary considerably.

Many Norwegians trade here. In Faribault proper there are not many Norwegians, but out in the country there are a great many Norwegian and Swedish settlements. More particularly, there is a sizable settlement two Norwegian miles east of the town. Considering the short time I have been here, I have associated quite a bit with the Norwegians both here and in Wisconsin. I must say that their circumstances and way of life have surprised me highly. As you know, it was the poorest of our countrymen who, oppressed by the hardships they endured in their native country, left Norway to seek a better home in America. And they have not sought in vain.

Minnesota, which is still a young state, can undoubtedly look ahead to a great future. By the end of this century it will probably be one of the richest and mightiest states in the whole Union. Its size is about 85,000 square miles. Its fertility is unmatched by that of any other country in the world. The climate is healthful and pleasant, though the summer is terribly hot. Although the winter is short, it is said to be almost as severe as in Norway. Miles of vast prairies alternate with extensive oak forests here (the Big Woods). Nowhere in all the vast areas of land I have traveled through have I seen as great an elevation as Egebergbakken in Norway. With regard to communications, Minnesota has been backward thus far; but this is due not to lack of enterprise on the part of the inhabitants but to the huge size of the country and the newness of everything.

In the meantime construction of several important railroads is being carried forward with energy. I advise everybody in Norway who lives under unhappy and straitened circumstances to come to Minnesota. But there are many tribulations and privations to be faced in the beginning. This is not the fault of the country; it must simply be attributed to a deficient knowledge of the language and conditions here. I have talked to many who were dissatisfied in the beginning, but this dissatisfaction soon changed into a feeling of content.

As to the general character of the Americans, I must say that they are a very strong, enterprising, and energetic people with a practical approach to all kinds of problems. Even if it is only a matter of making an insignificant thing like a lamp chimney or a shoebrush, you note that they are more efficient than people in the old country. All kinds of machines have been developed to a high degree of perfection. They use machines for the harvesting of grain and the mowing of hay. They have machines for taking up potatoes; these are designed in such a way that the potatoes are seized and thrown up into the barrel. They also have machines for milking and churning, for washing clothes and wringing them dry. Horses are used in the sawing of wood.

I like American customs and habits, opinions, and views very much — especially the fact that there is no class distinction here. The principle of equality has been universally accepted and adopted. The artisan, the farmer, and the laborer enjoy the same degree of respect as the merchant and the official. There is one class, however, which the Americans look askance at, that is the saloonkeepers – those who sell beer and liquor.

In this small town there are seven churches belonging to seven different congregations. Indeed, religious sects and nationalities are blended here in the most variegated manner: deep and sincere religious feeling is found side by side with the most uncompromising kind of rationalism. With regard to political opinion, the parties are very sharply divided. The deep split between the President and the Congress which was recently adjourned you probably know about just as well as I do. Presumably you are also familiar with the murders in Memphis and New Orleans, with Wilkes Booth, John-copper-son, Arm in Arm or the Bread-and-Butter Convention in Philadelphia, as the Republican newspapers call it.

I now consider President Johnson a big ———, though I defended him when I was in Christiania. He has surrendered completely to "the copperheads" and the rebels in the South allied with them, and is furiously opposing the party that elevated him to power. Because of this, the rebels have begun to stir once more. It has almost got to be so that a loyal man cannot travel, let alone stay in most of the southern states. During the absence of Sheridan – he has received military charge of Texas and Louisiana – the military in New Orleans was placed under the command of a former rebel general by telegraphed order from the President. It is hard to imagine a greater insult either to the Army or the country. But President Johnson is hardly furthering the cause of the South by behaving in this manner, as time will show very soon. The Republican press is breathing smoke and fire. Hundreds of newspapers which supported the President six months ago have changed their attitude completely. But the Republican party is so strong that for a while yet it will have a majority both in the Senate and in Congress, and the South will not be allowed to send representatives until the North has received complete guarantees that the money and the blood expended on the defense of the Union were not sacrificed in vain.

The thunder and lightning here are quite dreadful. There is really something terrifying about the electric storms in this country. When they get really severe it is as if the sky and everything you see were in flames, and the peals of thunder are so loud that they sound as if a thousand of the biggest Armstrong guns were being fired at the same time. I have never been afraid at sea even during the most furious storms, and I believe that I am not chicken-hearted; but I must confess that when the thunderstorms really break loose here, I do get scared.

Of immigration we have seen only the beginning

FROM PAUL HJELM-HANSEN, TO THE PUBLIC *

1868

The United States still has vast stretches of land waiting for capable hands to till them, and there is enough land for agriculture here for many, many years, even if the number of immigrants should become twice as large as it has been thus far.

Nor can there be any doubt that hitherto we have seen only the beginning of the European immigration to America. When the thousands of miles of railroad that have been planned across the western states to the Pacific have been built – as far as one line is concerned this probably will have come about within three years – many new sources of income will be opened up by the addition of the immense natural resources which are at present unexploited. The land now thousands of miles away from markets and consequently regarded as little better than a desert will be incorporated and become valuable. Not till then, I imagine, shall we see an immigration of real proportions.

Doctors and apothecaries seem to be doing well here, but as this business, too, is absolutely unregulated, the competition with charlatans is terrible. To be sure, it is still possible for theologians from Norway to get employment here; but I suppose that more and more Norwegian farmers' sons will study at American universities, especially theology, so that I hope that the time will not be remote when we shall be able to avoid having to get clerical assistance from Norway.

America is an excellent country for capable and moral servant girls, because usually young American women show a decided unwillingness to submit to the kind of restraint connected with the position of a servant, though God knows that this restraint is not very great in this country People are constantly looking for Norwegian and Swedish servant girls;

*This letter appeared in *Nordisk Folkeblad,* April 16, 1868.

and as they are treated very well, especially in Yankee families, there is no one whom I can so safely advise to emigrate as diligent, moral, and well-mannered young girls. But they should learn a little English before they leave home.

A journey through the Red River Valley

FROM PAUL HJELM-HANSEN, AT ALEXANDRIA, MINNESOTA, TO THE PUBLIC *

July 31, 1869

Having returned from the Red River, I hasten to send you a few lines in order that you may know that I have not fallen into the hands of Indians, half-breeds, buffaloes, bears, or other such uncivilized beings, but that, on the contrary, I find myself in the best of health.

I have made a journey, a real American pioneer trip, into the wilderness, with oxen and a farm wagon. I have spent the nights in the open wagon with a buffalo hide as mattress, a hundred-pound flour sack as a pillow, and, like Frithjof's Vikings, the "blue sky" as a tent. In storms, lightning, thunder, and rain I have lain thus under the open sky. On bad roads I have been thrown from one side of the wagon to the other. Occasionally, when going over sticks and stones, I have been thrown up in the air to fall down again on the hard wagon planks. I have been so tortured and tormented by mosquitoes that I have had to sit upright in the wagon throughout the night unceasingly beating the air with my handkerchief to guard myself against these little creatures which are so greedy for human blood.

Nevertheless, on the whole trip, I have enjoyed good health as never before. In twelve days spent under the open sky on Minnesota's high plains, about halfway between the Atlantic and Pacific oceans, I have become free of my rheumatism, and in place of it I have gained physical strength and a cheerful disposition. In that respect alone I benefited greatly from this trip. In truth, the air here is just as wondrously invigorating as the land is beautiful and fruitful. As I have drawn deep breaths of this clean air, I have often thought of the pitiable creatures who resort

* This letter, the translation of which is by Carlton C. Qualey, appeared in *Nordisk Folkeblad,* August 11, 1869.

to Ayer's Pills or Sweet's Blood Renewer, and occasionally I have caught myself in sorrowful consideration of that lovely half of humanity, whom young men love so much, and who, in order to please us, get their rosy cheeks at the apothecary's. Oh, if only these fine, lovable human beings could come up here and move about in this clean air! Then the prettiest natural roses and lilies would come of themselves, and to doctors and druggists one could justifiably say, "Good-by."

On the afternoon of July 12 I started on my journey, accompanied by Messrs. Brown and Torgerson. As we left, our friends sent a salvo of laughter after us. We could expect nothing else, for our position, sitting in the midst of all our boxes of provisions and all the rattling cooking and baking utensils in the long farm wagon drawn by two powerful oxen that walked with the slowest possible gait through the town, was indeed comical. Our friends, as we learned later, had estimated that on that afternoon we would get only ten miles from town, and so it happened. Just as we were about to pitch camp near Darling House, we noticed some riders pursuing us. They were Messrs. Lewiston, Rasch, my host, Johnson, and the chief clerk, Rasmussen, who formed a "surprise party." We spent the greater part of the night together very enjoyably, and when at length we became tired we lay down on the floor of Darling's cabin to get a little rest.

At five o'clock in the morning we had breakfast together, and at six o'clock our friends said farewell to the "Red River men," as they were pleased to call us. We started immediately on the way, and that day we reached the Pomme de Terre River in the northeastern corner of Grant County, about thirty-four miles from Alexandria. We passed Chippewa station and Evansville, where the stage changes horses and where there are some stores. At the last-named place, which is surrounded by new Norwegian and Swedish settlements, Mr. Lewiston has established himself as trader. Dr. Rasch also intends to settle there. From the hill on which Evansville lies there is a fine view of fertile prairie, woodland scenery, and small lakes. All the land hereabouts is either taken up by the men who cleared the land or is in the hands of speculators.

About four miles north of Evansville, the road goes past the northern end of Pelican Lake, the most beautiful spot I saw on this journey. The lake is quite large, about eight miles in length and six miles in breadth. It is connected by a narrow strait with Lake Christina, which is about the same size. Out from the lake the land rises like an amphitheater. The fine farming land is dotted with groves of trees, and in the lake is a small island, closely overgrown with trees. This charming landscape lay open for homesteaders until two years ago. Now it has been taken by Norwegians and Swedes, among whom are a great many bachelors, of whom some may perhaps be willing to sell their homestead right or their labor when a favorable opportunity presents itself.

At the northern end of Pelican Lake, the great unsettled prairie, which stretches to Fort Garry in the English possessions, begins. About halfway between Pelican Lake and Pomme de Terre station, there is a pretty little lake surrounded by woods. Here two Scandinavians have this year taken homesteads. From Pomme de Terre to Fort Abercrombie the prairie is a green sea, with waves of tall grass. To the eastward, land elevations are visible here and there in the large Otter Tail County, but to the westward one sees nothing but the green sea. Ten miles from Pomme de Terre and close to the road is a small lake fringed with woods. A full-blooded Frenchman lives there with an Indian woman. He has begun to raise some potatoes but lives chiefly by hunting and fishing.

The evening of the third day, we camped near the station, Old Crossing, which is a ferry. From this place one has a fine view. Toward the east one can see the Leaf Mountains rise up out of the green sea. About fourteen miles from Old Crossing, near Ottertail River in Wilkins County (previously called Andy Johnson's County), there is a little woodland. The place is called Breckenridge, and it is to this place that the new railroad, running from Minneapolis through Hennepin, Wright, Meeker, Kandiyohi, Chippewa, Lac Qui Parle, Stevens, and Traverse counties, is to come, if possible, this fall. The town has a very fine location in the middle of the fertile prairie. There is no doubt that a fine town will develop here when the railroad comes in and the country becomes settled.

In the evening of the fourth day we reached Fort Abercrombie, which has a garrison of a hundred men. This is very beautiful country with plenty of woods. The Red River forms the boundary between Dakota Territory and Minnesota, and the fort lies on the Dakota side. Opposite, on the Minnesota side, there is a fairly large steam sawmill. Here by the fort, the breadth of the prairie between the Red River on the west and the Buffalo River on the east is only eighteen or twenty miles. This breadth gradually decreases as one approaches Georgetown, where the rivers unite and flow together in their course toward the British possessions. From Alexandria to Fort Abercrombie is ninety-five miles. About twenty miles north of the fort, the prairie is only from six to eight miles in breadth. Along the rivers on both sides of the prairie there is a great deal of woods as far as Georgetown. The rivers, by their curves and bends, cut the land into areas of larger or smaller size. The pieces of land within these curves are surrounded on three sides by woods while the fourth side lies open toward the prairie, and are places of exceptional beauty in the lee of the woods. The whole prairie, which does not have the slightest bulge or rise, is the most fertile land one could wish. It consists of rich black soil with a slight intermixture of sand on a substratum of clay. On this prairie there is room for several thousand farmers. The woods are largely composed of elm, ash, and oak trees.

Twenty-five miles north of Fort Abercrombie, a French Catholic missionary has a station, for there are in these parts a large number of so-called half-breeds, that is, half French and half Indian, who as a rule speak only French. In the neighborhood of this station, two Norwegian settlers have taken up homestead land.

We camped, the fifth evening, about three miles north of the station near four or five half-breeds' huts. The evening of the sixth day we reached Georgetown, which lies fifty miles from Fort Abercrombie at the point where the Buffalo River and the Red River unite. Here they have begun to lay out a town. There are supposed to have been quite a number of settlers here before the Indians began their horrible outrages. During the Indian War the settlers fled and have not returned. At the present time there are only two families here, a German settler and a clerk of the Hudson's Bay Company, which has quite a large warehouse for all kinds of goods here.

The location of Georgetown makes it certain that in the near future it will be an active and pleasant town. It is the central point in a very large tract of land onto which settlers will flow in large numbers as soon as the railroads are built. Even now it is the docking place for the Hudson's Bay Company's steamboats, which, in the spring when the water is high, come up here to call for the goods that are brought from St. Cloud. In the summer, when the river is low, they have to stop at Frog Point, forty miles farther down. (From Frog Point the river could, some think, at very slight cost, be cleared of those obstacles which now stop the steamboats during the summer months.) This is also the central point for four or five forts which now must fetch all their necessities by wagon from

St. Cloud. Georgetown is in the best locality for trading with the Indians and half-breeds, who now must bring the results of their hunting to St. Paul. Enormous water power for manufacturing purposes is available. It is surrounded by a considerable amount of forest and can, at least for quite a while, count the whole Red River Valley up to Fort Garry as its upland, for the people who live there now have to fetch all their necessities from St. Paul or St. Cloud. As an active and well-stocked town, Georgetown would naturally draw to itself a good deal of the trade and would hardly lose it again, except if, when more land becomes cultivated, more towns are founded farther north.

On our journey we met daily several hundred wagonloads of goods, part of which went to the forts and part to Hudson Bay. We spoke with quite a few of the drivers who told us that they had five hundred miles to go from St. Cloud to their homes, and that they usually covered twenty or twenty-five miles per day. The round trip takes about fifty days. The goods which they transport come from New York through St. Paul to St. Cloud and are brought from there by horses and oxen to the Red River. For a barrel of flour the freight charge is ten dollars, and a wagonload consists usually of nine barrels. From Georgetown to Fort Garry, which lies seventy miles from the Minnesota boundary, is about two hundred miles. The drivers said that the land in that whole stretch is of the same character as the prairie here but that it is for the most part more plentifully supplied with woods. Farmers from Canada are beginning to settle on the land in the British possessions. We met many wagonloads of farm implements and also met five Canadians who were emigrating to Hudson Bay. They described conditions in Canada as pitiable.

Inasmuch as it was the consensus among all persons we met, either on the way or in Georgetown, that the land north of Georgetown was at least as good as that south of there, we decided not to go any farther north. We had already seen excellent land for several thousand farmers, and for the present that should be sufficient in these parts. It was our plan to make the return trip along the Buffalo River so that we might see the land there, but we were told in Georgetown that since the time of the Indian troubles the road had not been used, and that it was now so overgrown with grass that people who were not acquainted in that region would not be likely to find it. We therefore decided to return by the same road we had come, that is, on the Red River side. The land along the Buffalo River, according to reports, is very beautiful and fertile and has a good deal of woods.

Concerning the problem of settlement, it is not only my opinion but that of all who have seen this part of the country, that it presents so many advantages for Scandinavian farmers that immigrants are likely to stream in here within the next year, that this tract of land will in ten years be built up and under cultivation, and that it then will become one of the richest and most beautiful regions in America. The soil is fertile to the highest degree and is exceptionally easy to cultivate, for there is not as much as a stone or a stump in the way of the plow. Woods are to be found in great quantities along the rivers. Railroads are to run through the middle of the whole long valley. Steamships already come up from the British possessions to Georgetown and will in a few years probably come much farther. The sale of farm products to the forts and Hudson Bay will become extraordinarily profitable. The water power in the rivers on both sides of the prairie is more than sufficient for all kinds of factories. And the climate is exceptionally healthful. In the summer months, May, June, July, and August, the heat may at times be great, but the atmosphere is always fresh. In September and October, the weather is usually very pleasant. Winter sets in in November with about the same degree of cold as in western Norway, and it continues, as a rule, into March. In the wintertime, the snow is usually two or three feet deep and lies in a solid mass over the whole prairie so that roads may be made wherever one may wish. Spring work commences the latter part of March or the first part of April, and harvesting begins the latter part of July or the first part of August.

From my impression of the country, I have the hope that a good many of my countrymen, the Scandinavians, will come up here to settle on the tract of land which lies between Fort Abercrombie and Georgetown, especially along the rivers on both sides of the prairie. A man can take 160 acres of homestead land, and, if he has the opportunity to do so, he can in addition buy 160 acres for $200. With an area of 320 acres of this land, every family that does not care to live too pretentiously can make a comfortable livelihood. Provided, as I hope, that a settlement can be established here this fall of at least fifty neighbors such as I desire to have and who would be immediately willing to build a church and school, I shall settle here myself. Messrs. Brown and Torgerson and several other able men will do the same. North of Georgetown will be found land and opportunity for those who primarily want to keep stock or go into cattle raising.

In connection with the problem of settlement, it should not be overlooked that a part of this land at times of overflow is subject to floods. In the last twenty years, however, I am told that there has been only one flood, and that was two years ago when there were floods in many other parts of Minnesota as well as here. If people were to refrain from settling on places subject to such catastrophes in nature, which surrounds us all, the largest and most fertile parts of the earth would lie desolate.

Another thing is that many are afraid of new attacks by the Indians. I admit that there may be some ground for such a fear, for Indians, like all other cowardly barbarians, are vindictive, cruel, improvident, and unreliable. If they had the opportunity, they would undoubtedly clear out all white men west of the Mississippi. Meanwhile, it is to be remarked that the Chippewa Indians, who live here in Minnesota, did not take part in the massacre of 1862. That was carried on by the Sioux and a few allied minor tribes. These are now roaming about in Dakota and do not dare come into Minnesota. Between the Chippewas and the Sioux there is unquenchable hatred, for which reason the Sioux do not dare to approach the stronghold of the Chippewas, especially because the Sioux know that in case of war the Chippewas would have the support of all white men. Although I, personally, do not attribute much significance to that reason for fearing the Indians, I do grant that one can never be entirely secure, and that is partly why I am hoping that the Scandinavians will begin the cultivation of the land with a big and well-planned settlement strong and watchful enough to overawe the Indians.

I have grounds for expecting that a society of honorable men will be formed here in Alexandria to guide those Scandinavian families that might wish to settle in the Red River Valley. To this society such families could go to obtain the more detailed information they might want.

On the return trip, I had the pleasure of meeting Governor Marshall at Fort Abercrombie. He was accompanied by a large number of men who, in the interests of railroads, were going to Georgetown and from there on through the Dakota Territory to the Missouri River. I exchanged a few words with His Excellency, who expressed his pleasure in meeting me so far out in the wilderness, to which I replied that I regarded it as the most important part of my mission to investigate those tracts of land which as yet lie open to immigration.

Upon my return to Alexandria I was very pleasantly surprised to meet Pastor Brandt of Decorah. He uses his vacations to travel about amongst the Norwegian settlements in this region and conduct divine services for the people. He baptizes, confirms, conducts communion services, and preaches. He conducted divine services immediately after his arrival here in the small but beautiful local Methodist church, to the great joy and edification of the Scandinavian people here. He left the next day for the vicinity of Pelican Lake. Today, Saturday, he is attending a large meeting of Norwegian farmers in the neighborhood of Holmes City. These farmers intend to pledge themselves to purchase a parsonage and hire a minister. There are many sober Christians among the farmers here who feel deeply the lack of the regular preaching of God's Word and who would gladly pledge themselves to remedy this want as soon as possible.

Fifteen lakes only a few hundred yards apart

FROM PAUL HJELM-HANSEN, AT ALEXANDRIA, MINNESOTA, TO THE PUBLIC *

August 19, 1869

We left Evansville on August 4 – this time with a horse-drawn wagon – and traveled via Pomme de Terre to Dayton, the ferrying place in Otter Tail. About halfway between these two places lies a pretty and good-sized lake called Ten Mile Lake. The country around this lake consists partly of woodland and partly of excellent agricultural land. It has been settled solely by Norsemen, numbering about fifty, most of whom are old farmers from Illinois, Wisconsin, and Iowa. But the whole country to the north of the lake is as yet unsettled. To the south of the lake, the whole country as far as Evansville is settled.

We passed the night with . . . Americans, who receive and treat travelers kindly, and the next day we continued our journey northward to Prairie Lake. About twelve miles from Dayton and two miles from the Otter Tail River, a large group of Norwegians (about forty) from

* This letter appeared in *Nordisk Folkeblad*, September 1, 1869. The translation, a carbon copy of which is in the Minnesota Historical Society, is by Sigurd Melby. A Mr. Lewiston was the companion of Hjelm-Hansen on the trip described.

Fillmore and other southern counties have settled this summer. They are located among a group of about fifteen small lakes, some of which are only a few hundred yards apart. These pioneers possess horses, oxen, and milch cows, and are in full swing cultivating the soil and building. They possess the best agricultural land and have plenty of woodland. Among these well-satisfied farmers are many from Hedemark. . . . We had our dinner with these kindly people, who expressed their entire satisfaction with the land they had homesteaded.

Inhabited only by bears

FROM PAUL HJELM-HANSEN, IN OTTER TAIL COUNTY, TO THE PUBLIC *

1869

Through a stretch of forest two or three miles wide we arrived at a fairly large prairie in Otter Tail. On this prairie, which is surrounded by woods and full of small lakes, live two Danes and nine Americans, but otherwise it is completely settled by Norwegians, most of them old farmers from Wisconsin, Illinois, and Missouri. None of these farmers has less than 160 acres of land, while several have 320 acres and more, besides woodland in sufficient quantity. The oldest settlers have only lived here for two years, but they have already cultivated from ten to forty acres of land. They have good, to some extent even beautiful houses, many milch cows, sheep, oxen, and horses, and on the whole their economic condition is very satisfactory.

From Fergus Falls we set out the next morning toward the south to the Pomme de Terre station in Grant County. A stretch of about ten miles along this road is completely desolate, though the land is very good and well supplied with forest and small lakes. A considerable part of this area bears a striking resemblance to Norwegian landscapes, especially to Røken and Asker. Among the hills, the woods, and the water we felt very much at home; but at the present time this fine country is only inhabited by bears, which seem to be thriving.

Leaving this hilly country, you arrive at a large and attractive prairie which immediately presents to view two small lakes surrounded by

* This letter appeared in *Nordisk Folkeblad,* September 8, 1869.

forest. This is the beginning of the fine, large Norwegian settlement known as the Ten Mile Lake Settlement, which toward the southwest extends to and around Ten Mile Lake, toward the south almost as far as Pomme de Terre station, and toward the east to Eleonora and Christina Lake. The number of Norwegian farmers in these parts is estimated to be at least 170 – I dare not vouch for the correctness of the figure – and they are said to be in very good circumstances. This settlement is likewise no more than two years old.

These settlements and the new Norwegian settlement near Pelican River, which was mentioned in my previous correspondence, are at the present time the most important Scandinavian colonies in Otter Tail. It is true that there are also Scandinavians in other places, especially at Battle Lake and Otter Lake City, but their number is said to be very small and the land in those parts barren and sandy.

Scandinavians must become assimilated

FROM A FAREWELL SPEECH OF PAUL HJELM-HANSEN,
AT ALEXANDRIA, MINNESOTA *

September 4, 1869

Since now most of the men I have met in these parts are old farmers who in the southern part of the state have suffered many hardships and from nothing have worked themselves up to such a degree of prosperity that here they were able to take large farms and work them with energy and insight for the benefit of themselves and their children, I draw the conclusion that their emigration from the native country has not only been useful to them economically, but also, and this is more important, morally. And this, ladies and gentlemen, is the great thing to note about emigration. If one could not here attain economic prosperity without deteriorating morally, it would be better to live at home in the old country in the most miserable hovel. For what does it avail a man that he win all the gold in the world, if he lose his soul?

Therefore I say to you: Be agreed among yourselves, you Swedish, Norwegian, and Danish men and women, help and support one another. As the bearers of peace and harmony you must love one another, and he

* This speech was published in *Nordisk Folkeblad*, September 22, 1869.

who loves goes with God, for God is love. But do not misunderstand me: I do not wish to say that the Scandinavians should form a power all to themselves or be a state within the state. No, that is by no means my desire. My reading in history has been sufficient to convince me that attempts of that nature are doomed to failure. On the contrary, I believe that it is the sacred duty of the emigrants who wish to make this country their future home and who have taken the oath of allegiance to this society, to become united and assimilated with the native population of the country, the Americans, to learn the English language and to familiarize themselves with and uphold the spirit and institutions of the Republic. The sooner this comes about, the better.

INDEX

Index

Index

Index

Index

Index

Index

Index